THOMAS WRIGHT, freelance writer and researcher. His book *Table Talk Oscar Wilde* was published in 2000. He carried out the research for Peter Ackroyd's *London: The Biography*.

PETER ACKROYD, CBE, novelist, critic and biographer, formerly literary editor of *The Spectator* and chief non-fiction reviewer for *The Times*, has won numerous literary awards. His *London: The Biography* took the South Bank Show Annual Award for Literature.

A TRAVELLER'S COMPANION TO
LONDON

INTRODUCED BY

Peter Ackroyd

EDITED BY

Thomas Wright

ROBINSON
London

The author has made every attempt to trace existing copyright holders, but in a small number of cases this has not been possible.

Constable & Robinson Ltd
3 The Lanchesters
162 Fulham Palace Road
London W6 9ER
www.constablerobinson.com

First published in the UK by Robinson,
an imprint of Constable & Robinson Ltd 2004

A copy of the British Library Cataloguing in
Publication Data is available from the British Library

ISBN 1-84119-789-0

Printed and bound in the EU

2 4 6 8 10 9 7 5 3 1

For Clare Wright

Contents

THE EARLY HISTORY OF THE CITY

OUTSIDE THE WALLS

BEDLAM

THE CHARTERHOUSE

AROUND FLEET STREET

THE THAMES

THE WEST END

BUCKINGHAM PALACE

THE BRITISH MUSEUM

COVENT GARDEN

HYDE PARK

WESTMINSTER AND WHITEHALL

WESTMINSTER ABBEY AND HALL

LONDON LIFE, CUSTOMS, MORALS

LONDON CHARACTERS

Illustrations

Plates

Map of the city locating the places described

1 Newgate and the Old Bailey
2 The Royal Exchange
3 St Paul's Cathedral
4 Soho
5 The Tower of London
6 Bedlam (Bethlem
  Psychiatric Hospital)
7 The Charterhouse (moved
  out of London in June 1872)
8 Fleet Street
9 Temple
10 Blackfriars
11 London Bridge
12 Southwark
13 St James's Park
14 Globe Theatre
15 Smithfield
16 St Bartholomew's
17 The Thames
18 The West End
19 Buckingham Palace
20 The British Museum
21 Covent Garden
22 Drury Lane Theatre
23 Piazza
24 Opera House
25 Brooks's

26 Speakers' Corner
27 Trafalgar Square
28 Tyburn
29 The East End
30 Aldgate
31 Whitechapel
32 Sidney Street
33 Cable Street
34 Canary Wharf
35 Westminster and Whitehall
36 Westminster Abbey
37 Westminster Bridge
38 The Houses of Parliament
39 Parliament Square
40 The Garrick Club
41 Lords

Map of London from Tudor times

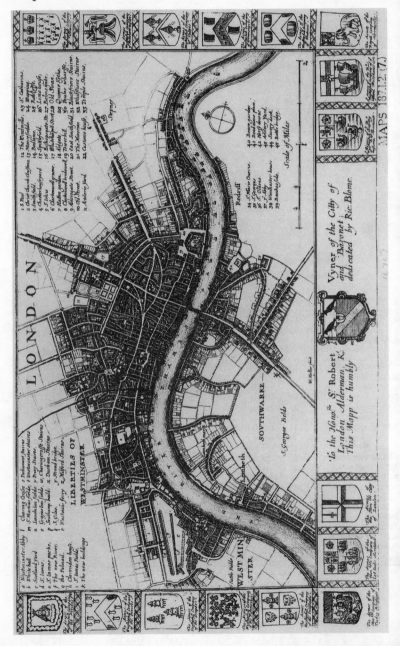

LONDON

LIBERTIES OF WESTMINSTER

WESTMINSTER

SOVTHWARKE

S: Georges Fields

Lambeth

Redruff

Scale of Miles

Vyner of the Citty of
and Baronet;
dedicated by Ric: Blome.

To the Hono.ble S.r Robert
London Alderman K.t
This Mapp is humbly

1 S. Paul
2 Christ Church Orphans.
3 Black fryers
4 Charterhowseyard
5 S: Iohns
6 Clarkenwelgreene
7 Hatton garden
8 Ely house
9 Clarkenwelinclosed
10 Old Bread.
11 Anthony Iard

12 The Windmills.
13 Moorefields
14 Bedlam
15 Spittlefield
16 Bishopsgate Str.
17 Whitechapell Str.
18 Aldgate
19 Tower
20 East Smithfeild
21 The Mauree
22 Custome house.

23 S. Katherines.
24 Wappin
25 Ratcliff
26 Lime house
27 Redcross gate
28 Old Swan
29 Queene Hyke
30 Bridwel wharffe
31 Blackfriers Stairer
32 Whitefriers Stairer
33 Temple Stairer

34 S. Marie Overie.
35 S: Georges
36 S: Oliues
37 S: Iohn
38 Winchester house
39 Bankeyside

40 Beare garden
41 Bead house place.
42 Hope howse
43 Dirty Lane
44 Sauory Iard
45 Bath bridge

a Westminster Abby
b Whitehall
c Scotland yard
d S: Iames.
e S: Iames parke,
f The new Riuer
g The Pellmell.
h S: Giles
i Clarendon house.
k S: Iames Feild
l The new buildings

m S: Martins Feilds
n Lincolns feilds
o Greys Inne
p Soultony hall
q S. Iohn.
r Westminster ferry

1 Charing Crosse
2 Westminster Staires
3 Privy Staires
4 Charinngrosse Staires
5 Durham Staires
6 Broad bridge
7 Milford Staires

2

Scale of Miles

MAPS 187.2.(7)

Acknowledgements

I would like to thank the staff of the following libraries
for their assistance during the preparation of this book:
The British Library, The London Library, The Guildhall Library, The Bishopsgate Library and The Bodleian
Library.

I would also like to express my gratitude to the following people: Ben Glazebrook and Laurence Kelly, for making excellent suggestions concerning the contents; Peter
Ackroyd, for his ideas and for kindly agreeing to write the
introduction; Nicola Chalton of Constable & Robinson
for her generosity and patience, and for the competence
with which she oversaw the editing and publication of this
book; and the late Giles Gordon, for his encouragement
and advice. In addition, I would like to thank the following
people for their help along the way: Jamie Glazebrook,
Terrence Henry, Martin Mavellen, Chiara Nicolini, Bob
Pyres and Clay Wright, exemplary Londoner, and proud
wearer of the magic hat.

Finally, I would like register my debt to the London
anthologist Xavier Barron, and to the great London ency-

clopaedists W. Thornbury and E. Walford, whose works have been of great help to me.

The editors have made every effort to locate all persons having any rights in the selections appearing in this anthology and to secure permission from the holders of such rights. The editors apologize in advance for any errors or omissions inadvertently made. Queries regarding the use of material should be addressed to the editor c/o the publishers.

The publishers and I also wish to make acknowledgement to the following for extracts used from their editions, translations or where copyright permission was needed: extract from *The Day the War Ended: VE Day 1945 in Europe and around the world* by M. Gilbert, reprinted by permission of HarperCollins Publishers Ltd © M. Gilbert 1995; extract from *William Caxton* by G.D. Painter, published by Chatto & Windus, used by permission of The Random House Group Limited; extract from *Diana in Private* by Lady Colin Campbell, reprinted by permission of Time Warner Books UK; extract from *Sweeney Todd* by Peter Haining, reprinted by permission of The Chrysalis Books Group; extract from *Geata Henri Quinti* (The Deeds of Henry V), 1975, edited by Taylor, F. & Roskell, J.S., by permission of Oxford University Press; extract from *The Oxford Dictionary of Nursery Rhymes*, 1951, edited by Opie, I. & P., by permission of Oxford University Press; extract from *London: The Biography* by Peter Ackroyd, published by Chatto & Windus, used by permission of The Random House Group Limited; St Paul's in wartime, *History of Saint Paul's*, by W.R. Matthews and W.M. Atkins, published by Phoenix House; Inspector Dew at the scene of the Ripper's last crime, W. Dew, *I Caught Crippen*, published by Blackie & Son, 1938; Churchill's funeral, *The Crossman Diaries* ed. Howard, published by Magnum Books, 1979; 'The Suffragettes in Parliament Square', Pankhurst 'The Suffragette', published by Sturgis & Walton Co, 1912; Dan Leno, Max Beerbohm, *Around Theatres*, published by Rupert Hart-Davis, 1953; London Conversations, F. Maddox Ford *The Soul of London*, published by Alston Rivers, 1905.

Introduction

The earliest accounts of London are the stuff of legend and exotic travellers' tales. The first and most important account is that of Geoffrey of Monmouth in which it is narrated that Brutus, the son of Aeneas, establishes London and calls it by the name of 'New Troy'. This is significant as a pedigree, because in the ancient and medieval worlds Troy was considered to be the first of all cities and the very pattern of city life. It was the original, the pristine form, of the city. London therefore acquired a distinctive inheritance from the beginning. But there is often truth in old legends, which is perhaps the reason why John Milton adopted this story of London's origin in his history of England. The relation of Troy and London may not in fact be as speculative or as nebulous as it seems. A black two-handled cup of 900 BC from Asia Minor, the terrain of Troy, was found in the waters of the Thames and it is believed that traders carried tin from the shores of the British Isles to the markets of Troy itself.

The story is also appropriate because the early history of London is striated with legend and with myth. There is evidence of Druidism around some of the London mounds, among them Tothill in Westminster and Pentonville in north London. There are legends around the origin of London Stone, that strange fragment that still exists in the centre of London and that has been variously explained as a marker of distance and a Druidic altar. There are mythical stories about the construction of London Bridge, popularly believed to have been hallowed by the blood of infants at the time of its first erection.

In fact throughout this anthology it is difficult, if not impossible, to distinguish between 'true history' and legend. The foundation of many of the city's buildings, for example, is hidden within accretions of stories and fables. The establishment of St Paul's Cathedral upon a temple to Diana, the legendary history of Westminster Abbey, and the miraculous prophecy concerning St Bartholomew's in Smithfield are only some of the mystery tales that have surrounded the sacred places of the capital. And why should it not be so? From its foundation London has been the object of mystery and enchantment. That is why it is fitting and appropriate that there are extracts here from poets such as Chaucer and novelists such as Dickens as well as from the more 'authentic' works of Tacitus or of Stow. London is a city of visionaries, and visionary history emerges from it as naturally and inevitably as great buildings rise from its soil. It is the home of a thousand different stories, some of them grandiloquent and some of them bitter, some of them filled with comedy and some of them filled with pathos. Why should its own origins not also take the form of a story?

The early history of the capital, however, reaches slightly firmer ground during the time of the Roman occupation and conquest. It is possible that there was already on the banks of the Thames a city in embryo, a British city, but in Tacitus's account of the revolt of Boudicca and in Hume's account of Roman London a recognizable and identifiable city does seem to emerge. In fact the Romans have left an enduring legacy within the very streets of the capital. It was they who first planned

London on a grid or network system, and the remnants of that grid are still to be found in the streets north and south of Cheapside. The Romans built the bridge, and they also erected the first walls for the city's defence. So after a period of two thousand years the marks and traces of the Roman presence can still be identified.

There are more evanescent, but equally enduring, marks of the original occupation. The Romans first stamped the neighbourhood of London with the true image of mercantilism. London has always been a market place, a place of trade, but the Romans turned it also into a place of bankers and businessman. They were known as *negotiatores*, or negotiators, and can be compared with the present occupation of stock-broking that takes place on exactly the same small patch of ground where the Romans worked. Ever since the earliest occupation London has been a city built upon money and upon the power of finance. It became a centre of world commerce in the 18th century, and has remained in that eminent position until the 21st century. But the first inklings of this destiny are to be discovered in the activities of the Roman merchants who traded by the banks of the Thames.

The Romans also left the traces of military endeavour in the very stones of London. It was once popularly believed that the Tower of London was first constructed by Julius Caesar, during one of his forays into this island fastness, so distant from the centre of Roman imperium. We may dismiss this story out of hand, but there is no doubt that the Tower did for many centuries spread a minatory and military aura over that part of the city. It was the stronghold of the kings as opposed to the civic authorities, and can be described quite legitimately as an alien presence within the capital. The wall of London was of course always associated with military matters, and it remained in use until the 18th century when the demands of faster and easier access decreed its demise. But Londoners have never been averse to this military context. They have always been pugnacious, and ready to fight. The London mobs were dangerous and difficult. In the medieval period London even had its own army, that used to expedite its manoeuvres at Mile End. The wards had their regiments, and the London army marched beneath its own banner. The city often had to defend itself against invaders, whether Saxon or Danish. It armed and defended itself against the royalist armies of Charles during the Civil War, and built great earthworks around its perimeter.

After the Roman occupation the chronological sequence of travellers' tales is momentarily lost since, of all periods in London's history, that concerning the arrival of the Anglo-Saxons is the least known. It is sometimes surmised that, during this period, the city was in fact deserted. But this seems most unlikely. A great city, with its streets and its harbour, would not willingly be left to die. In the mythical and legendary narratives of this period, for example, it remains the leading city or capital city of the country. It was the seat of the British kings, whose palace was supposed to be very near the site of the present Guildhall. It was the place where the citizens were called together in assembly. It was a place of defence, well fortified with its walls. It was reported that King Arthur was crowned by the 'archbishop of London'. Merlin made many prophecies concerning the city. There is also indirect evidence of continuity. Roman law was still being practised in medieval London, so there is no reason to suppose any gap or breach in its history. The last contribution in the section of this volume devoted to early history is concerned with the Danes who, of all races, might seem to have the least to do with the growth and development of London. But the church of St Clement Danes at the mouth of the Strand is evidence that this is far from the case. It marks the spot where the tribal community of the Danes lived and worked for several generations. A runic monument in their home country declares that three great Danish leaders 'lie in Luntunum'.

And there, so far as matters of chronology are concerned, the anthology ends. This is in itself appropriate and significant since any account of the last thousand years of London's history is still much more familiar to the contemporary reader. The city before that time still seems an alien place, unfurnished with any familiar signs and tokens. A chronological account, from this time forward, is not in fact the best way of dealing with the capital's life. That is because time, in London, moves in a variety of different directions. It is not a swiftly running stream. It is more like a lava flow from some unknown source of fire. Some parts of time move slowly, some parts of time move quickly, and some parts seem to have stopped moving altogether.

There is a force in London which I have chosen to call the territorial imperative, by means of which the inhabitants of a certain street or neighbourhood seem actively to be influenced by the territory upon which they live. Clerkenwell, for example, has been the home of radical activity ever since Wat Tyler encamped upon Clerkenwell Green in the 14th century. The area of St Giles has been a refuge for the homeless and vagrant ever since a leper hospital was built there in the early medieval period. Bloomsbury has always been the home of occult sects or groups. The list is a long one, testifying to the innate power of the London earth to harbour certain activities and certain tendencies.

There is evidence for it in this anthology itself. In the discussion of Fleet Street, for example, it is revealed that Wynkyn de Worde and then Pynson brought printing to that famous street in the early 1500s; and of course the centre of the printing industry remained there until the 1980s. If the reader glances at the entries for Trafalgar Square, he or she may be surprised by the number of riots that have occurred in that place. The accounts of St Paul's begin with the report that the cathedral was built upon the site of a Roman temple to Diana, and end with a record of the marriage of Charles and Diana. It seems unlikely that the late princess knew of the temple to her illustrious ancestor, and so the connection is doubly suggestive.

So it is possible that the topographical or geological approach adopted in this anthology is more faithful to the city's secret history than any conventional or orthodox chronology. It also offers the reader the opportunity to explore small areas of the city's life in diverse and unexpected manner. It helps to reveal, for example, how one neighbourhood or patch of ground can be a microcosm of the whole. If we look again at the history of St Paul's Cathedral, as gathered together here, we find accounts of the building of the church in the Anglo-Saxon period succeeded by Henry the Fifth's triumphant return after the battle of Agincourt; these are followed by various chapters in the sorrowful history of the English reformation, a reformation that was in fact more successful in London than in most other areas of the country. That is because the life of the city is instinctively more democratic and more egalitarian than elsewhere. The London crowd tends to be anti-authoritarian, led by principles of trade and commerce rather than by the rites and precepts of faith. There are accounts here of St Paul's at the time of the Great Fire and of the Blitz, suggesting the parallels and contrasts between those two great historical events. The funerals of Nelson, Wellington and Churchill, pass in sequence as if the great men of the city could be seen in dumb-show parading before us.

Yet the city's history can be seen in small, as well as great, places. The history of Saint Giles, as I have suggested, is a rosary of sorrowful mysteries in which can be traced the permanent presence of the dispossessed at the heart of London. It is sometimes said that you can see the shape of London most clearly by the shadow that it casts, and the lives of the derelict and the desperate are indeed the shadow of London. From the earliest times to the day before yesterday the streets of St Giles have been a repository of suffering and need. The long history of Fetter Lane, in the heart of London, can also be seen as a simulacrum of the larger whole. Did not William Morris once remark that a single street in Whitechapel contained the history of the world? There were so many people, so many meetings and partings, so many spectacles, so many stray words and conversations, so many emotions crowding one upon another, that the entire history of human feeling could be composed on one of these forlorn streets.

There is an extract in this anthology from John Earle's *Microcosmographie* in which he states that 'Paul's Walk is the land's epitome, as you may call it; the lesser isle of Great Britain. It is more than this; the whole world's map, which you may here discern in its perfected motion, jostling and turning'. He is referring here to the evident truth that the world did indeed come to London, to see and to be seen. As this anthology demonstrates in remarkable detail, it was the lodestone or the magnet of the traveller through the ages. But, perhaps more importantly, it was constituted of foreigners – or rather London was a city of every race and every creed. It was known as the 'city of nations', a place of refuge and work. In the 19th century there were more Irish living in London than in Dublin, and more Roman Catholics than in Rome. London needed people in order to replenish itself. If it is a human organism, then it is a cannibalistic one. It lives off people. It devours people. Until recent times the death rate was far higher than the birth rate, so the city had to attract immigrants simply to keep up its numbers.

There is another suggestive way of examining London's history and character. By examining the metaphors that have been applied to it we learn a great deal about its mythical and symbolic life. So this book is an anthology of metaphors as well as buildings and people. Dostoyevsky evoked both the horror and the grandeur of London, for example, by comparing it to Babylon. He wrote that 'it is a biblical sight, something to do with Babylon, some prophecy out of the Apocalypse being fulfilled before your very eyes'. Such was the immensity of the city that it needed to be described by sacred and apocalyptic association. It was too large for ordinary human response. Its reality was too pressing, and powerful, a force for secular comparisons. It was truly a city of heathens and pagans, many of them bowing down to the great god Baal. Its only true worship was of money and of power. The citizens themselves were the slaves of its mighty and gloomy spirit.

London was also compared to a labyrinth, and to the maze where the voracious Minotaur found his victims.

This is indeed an ancient concept of London. In the medieval chronicles of Richard of Devizes, for example, we read that 'whatever of evil or perversity there is in all parts of the world, you will find in that city alone'. London was the epitome of city life itself. It was all that cities ever were or ever would be. It was the pinnacle of the city. It represented all that was unnatural and unhealthy about urban living. It was the source and origin of all the urban vices that moralists had for centuries excoriated. It was the agent of egalitarianism. It was the source of social change. It encouraged the mingling of classes and of sexes. It was dangerous. It was always in motion.

When Marx and Engels came to London they knew that they were viewing a whole new phase in human existence itself. London was the first megalopolis, and in that condition it became the laboratory or breeding ground for the world of the future. There is a case for saying that communism itself was born in the streets of East London. The great communist leaders stayed in the East End. Lenin edited an underground newspaper from Clerkenwell Green. The condition of the oppressed in the streets of London was a material influence upon the ideology that was later to rule half the world. For Engels itself the reality was too large and too various properly to be comprehended. He speaks of streets as being beyond counting, beyond number. The ships beside the docks of the Thames are too numerous to be calculated. Everything had grown too large.

Yet in the 19th century, too, there was an older sense of London that was still being sustained. It is what Charles Lamb understood to be the city as theatre. In a world where spectacle and appearance matter, then the whole of city life can be seen as a form of drama. The street sellers dressed in characteristic uniform, as did the shopkeepers and the tradesmen. Everyone had his or her part in the great play, and dressed up accordingly. 'London,' Lamb once wrote to Wordsworth in a letter quoted in this anthology, 'is itself a pantomime and a masquerade.' It is a pantomime because here are all the 'types' of human society that were mocked in the commedia dell'arte that was so popular in the London playhouses. Here is the zany and here is the buffoon, here is the loving couple and here is the braggart. All forms of human personality are to be found on the streets of London, proclaiming their existence with vociferousness and energy. Lamb wrote in the same letter that 'I often shed tears in the motley Strand from fullness of joy at so much Life'. That is the word for the sensations he experienced – 'fullness'. The life all around was extraordinarily rich and strange. It is full because it cannot be impeded nor diverted. It streams on in a continual procession, truly a masquerade in which rich and poor, young and old, healthy and diseased, all take their part.

That is why it has always been a city of theatrical 'types', of eccentrics and dandies, of poseurs and posturers. Certain Londoners seem deliberately to have turned themselves into examples of living theatre. The strange career of Jack Sheppard, for example, is included in this anthology. He was the toast of the London crowd for escaping so often and with such ease from Newgate and other London prisons. His escapes were always so spectacular, and his reappearance so dramatic, that he satisfied all the tastes of Londoners. There are other famous Londoners, among them Sir Thomas More and Quentin Crisp, who reacted to the artificiality of their surroundings by becoming artificial. In a city of spectacle they deliberately played a part. They dressed up for the delectation of their respective audiences, and they spoke their lines accordingly.

There was another metaphor for London, that of the fair, which was most memorably used by William Wordsworth in his memories of London contained in *The Prelude*. Wordsworth was a man of the country who did not readily or easily take to London. In some respects he failed to understand it but in his account of Bartholomew Fair he comes close to one of the enduring realities of the city.

It is a site of 'anarchy and din' because there is no power on earth that can control it. That is why all attempts at limiting its size have signally failed. There have been numerous attempts to subdue the capital to order, but nonetheless it has continued to grow and to expand in apparently unplanned and unanticipated ways.

The metaphors of London as a theatre and a fair also suggest another obvious characteristic of London. It is a place of variety. It is variety itself. Rich and poor may live side by side. The rich people pass the vagrants on the roadside. The beggar woman stands before a goldsmith's shop. There are contraries and opposition at every turn of the road. It is a city of extremes where every possible variety of the human condition can be found. That variety is reflected in a number of different ways. Addison's celebration of the heterogeneity of the Stock Exchange is one summary of the fervour with which an observer can watch the unlimited spectacle of life and business in the middle of the city. It is what Samuel Johnson, in a conversation extracted in this anthology, called 'the wonderful immensity of London' and 'the multiplicity of human habitations'. It is what Pierce Egan, in another extract here, suggests when he states that 'the Metropolis is a complete CYCLOPAEDIA', a summary of all human wants and needs, a record of all desires, a source book of all human behaviour, a picture book of all human appearance.

London is also a 'phantasma', as Wordsworth suggests in his poem of recollection, because it is in part a vision and in part a dream. It defies rationality and common sense. It provides bizarre sights. Its atmosphere of perpetual movement and perpetual noise is itself dream-like, a continuing vortex of activity that has no beginning and no ending. 'It was a troubled dream?' Richard Carstone asks on his death-bed at the end of Dickens's novel, *Bleak House*, in which the forces of London are seen to join together with terrible consequences, when the east wind of wretchedness and disease sweeps over the richer portions of the city, when fog and mud and dust are all compounded in a vision of London's darkness. Yes, it was a troubled dream. It was the dream of London.

In a later section of his poem Wordsworth also adverts to the condition of London as being 'of one identity', by which he means that the condition of urban living renders everyone and everything alike. The individual is simply part of the crowd, and human existence itself becomes one monotonous round with 'no law, no meaning and no end'. That is indeed one of the characteristics of London. It can emphasize the sense of helplessness and hopelessness. The mean streets, the endless and continuous development of area after area, can induce feelings of despair in the inhabitants. There are proportionately more suicides and more cases of mental illness in the city than in any other part of the country. That is one of the aspects of the city.

But it can also induce a sense of freedom and well-being. There are many people who feel liberated by the anonymity of London, for example, and who see the city as an arena for adventure and chance encounter. It is characteristic that novels set in the capital, for example, depend to a large extent upon the forces of accident and coincidence to shape their plots – as if the endless and adventitious array of people can spark off incident and action.

There are other metaphors. Throughout the recorded history of the city London has often been compared to a prison. It is in a literal sense the prison city of Europe. There are more prisons in London than in any other capital city. But in a larger sense it has also been seen as a prison house of the spirit. In the writings of Blake and of Dickens – to take two examples of Cockney visionaries – the materialism and constriction of the city turn into one vast gaol or prison yard in which the citizens are all inmates.

The city has also been deemed to be a vast market place. Of individual markets there is no end – Covent Garden, Smithfield, Leather Lane, Billingsgate, Borough Market, Chapel Market. The list is endless. London is the home of commerce and of trade, but it is also an arena where profit and loss are the only imperatives and where everything is put out for sale. One of the earliest poems about the city, 'London Lickpenny', is devoted to the travails of the medieval market places where all the goods of the world are to be found. But this is a city in which only money counts, where the rich can dine and the poor can starve. That is the essential meaning of the market. The Stocks Market of the medieval period was one in which fish and flesh, vegetables and fruit, were readily available. The term has since been adopted by the Stock Market, just a few hundred yards away from the original site of the Stocks Market. The same greed and appetite prevail. It is the condition of London itself.

This anthology also helps to illuminate specific aspects of the experience of London. It has, for example, always been a violent and belligerent city. One of the possible derivations of the word itself may be *londos*, the Celtic word for cruel. Ever since its inception it has been the arena for street conflict and for individual assault. The records of medieval London are filled with killing and battering. The citizens of London themselves were compared to a swarm of bees which, when angry, cluster together and sting. The streets of the city have been filled with violent crowds. The word mob, from *mobile vulgus*, was coined in London. There is an account here of William Pitt being set upon by an angry crowd in the late 18th century, but that is only example of the many occasions when violence has arisen suddenly and casually in the heart of the city.

Whenever Samuel Johnson took a stroll, he always carried a stout cudgel with him. It was sensible to have some protection from the depredations of the drunken, the angry or the desperate. Until recent times it was not considered safe to walk the streets after dark. When travellers wished to make the journey down St John Street, towards Smithfield, they would wait together until a large assembly of them had collected. Only then did they feel safe enough to walk down the thoroughfare. There were many 'no go' areas in the heart of London, where there was no civic authority of any kind. Areas such as St Giles and Seven Dials were often compared to the jungles in the heart of Africa, so fearsome they had become.

There are also accounts in this anthology of the pride and pleasure that ordinary Londoners took in street fights, and of the aptitude with which they would form rings around the contestants. There are accounts, too, of the insolence of the mob when confronted with its so-called 'betters'. Londoners were also excessively jingoistic, and a foreign traveller walked through the streets at his or her peril. The French and the Spanish were particularly unpopular, while the Dutch and Germans passed almost unnoticed. It was not the 'lower' members of society only who were engaged in brutal behaviour. There is a description here of gang of young gallants, known as the Mohawks, who terrorized the inhabitants of the West End with their brutal antics. They were in fact only one of a number of gangs in the 18th century who paraded through the streets and wreaked havoc wherever they ventured. There is general agreement among foreign writers, however, that London was a more ferocious city than any of its counterparts in Europe – and that Londoners, as a race, were rude and pugnacious.

That is why the crueller forms of blood sport have been very popular with the London crowd. For many centuries the sports of bull-baiting and bear-baiting were the most successful entertainment along the south bank of the river. To foreigners it was a matter of wonder, and indeed of horror, that such barbarous sports should draw such large crowds.

The history of London has also been the history of riot. There are accounts in this volume of the theatrical riots of the 18th century, when the crowds demanded the reinstatement of the 'old prices'. But there were riots over plays and players, to such an extent that it became an act of bravery to enter a theatre. There were riots by coalheavers and car-men, by apprentices and by vagrants. There were election riots and food riots. In the Gordon Riots of 1780 the capital was seized with paralysis when it seemed likely that the mob would take total command of the entire city. In a city as large and as constricting as London these riots represent some kind of hectic fever. You cannot contain so many people within such narrow streets and alleys without some kind of explosion. Or the riots may be seen as an attempt to tear down the bars of the prison world that is London.

Another aspect of London life to which foreign observers often adverted was the general voraciousness of Londoners. In a sense the citizens had simply acquired the characteristics of their city. London itself has always been voracious, drawing in people from all over the kingdom and indeed people from all over the world. But Londoners, too, were great devourers. They consumed endless quantities of food and drink. The taverns and eating houses of the city were replete with beef. The streets were filled with drunks of every class and age. There are accounts here of Charles Lamb, that quintessential Londoner, becoming very drunk indeed at an 'immortal dinner' in Hampstead in the company of Wordsworth and Keats. Keats himself, being a Londoner, was also a very great drinker. It is possible that the first stanza of his 'Ode To a Nightingale' was inspired by a hangover. There is an account here by William Hickey of returning home drunk from a party which is almost too vivid, and too painful, to be read.

With excessive drink, of course, comes the desire for sex. London has always been a promiscuous place, filled with strange vices. In a city of finance, the poor have nothing to sell but their bodies. So throughout the centuries the prostitutes have congregated here, advertising themselves in the 21st century as in the 18th century as 'new in town'.

There are other characteristics of the city and its inhabitants evinced in these pages. The loneliness of Londoners must always be taken into account. The impersonality and anonymity of the city have often been noticed, and the surprising ease with which an individual can be swallowed up by the crowd is only one indication of the vast solitariness which can be experienced in the midst of millions of fellow creatures. That is why London has often been compared to a desert or to a jungle. Londoners have generally been described as gruff or taciturn, bland or laconic, as if the conditions of their existence did not call for profound or elaborate utterance. It was simply a case of getting on with a hard task. That also accounts for the well-known Cockney stoicism in the case of dangers or emergencies.

Churchill captures this in his accounts of the Blitz, included here, when he remarks that 'London was like some huge prehistoric animal, capable of enduring terrible injuries, mangled and bleeding from many wounds, and yet preserving its life and movement'. The phrase at the time of the German Blitz was 'London can take it'. Indeed it did. It has taken a great many other disasters, before and since, without losing its identity or continuity. It dances on its own ashes. It is revived after every assault, and is reborn in every generation. It cannot cease growing. When Christopher Wren looked for a large stone to mark the exact centre for the new dome of St Paul's, he was given part of a gravestone with the single word 'Resurgam'. I will rise again. It became the symbol of his own resurrection of the cathedral, and indeed it can be seen as the true legend of London. As this anthology demonstrates, it is the infinite and inexhaustible city.

A TRAVELLER'S COMPANION TO

LONDON

THE EARLY
HISTORY OF
THE CITY

[1] The foundation of the city of London (c. 1100 BC); from *The History of the Kings of Britain* by Geoffrey of Monmouth.

After the Trojan war, Æneas, flying with Ascanius from the destruction of their city, sailed to Italy. There he was honourably received by King Latinus, which raised against him the envy of Turnus, King of the Rutuli, who thereupon made war against him. Upon their engaging in battle, Æneas got the victory and, having killed Turnus, obtained the kingdom of Italy, and with it Lavinia the daughter of Latinus . . . the woman brought forth a son, and died of his birth; but the child was delivered to a nurse and called Brutus.

At length, after fifteen years were expired, the youth accompanied his father in hunting, and killed him undesignedly by the shot of an arrow . . . Upon his death, he was expelled from Italy, his kinsmen being enraged at him for so heinous a deed. Thus banished he went into Greece . . . at length he arrived at a certain island called Leogecia, which had been formerly wasted by the incursions of pirates, and was then uninhabited. Brutus, not knowing this, sent three hundred armed men ashore to see who inhabited it; but they finding nobody, killed several kinds of wild beasts which they met with in the groves and woods, and came to a desolate city, in which they found a temple of Diana, and in it a statue of that goddess which gave answers to those that came to consult her. At last, loading themselves with the prey which they had taken in hunting, they returned to their ships, and gave their companions an account of this country and city. Then they advised their leader to go to the city, and after offering sacrifices, to inquire of the deity of the place, what country was allotted them for their place of settlement. To this proposal all assented; so that Brutus, attended with Gerion, the augur, and twelve of the oldest men, set forward to the temple, with all things necessary for the sacrifice. Being arrived at the place, and presenting themselves before the shrine with garlands about their temples, as the ancient rites required, they made three fires to the three deities, Jupiter, Mercury, and Diana, and offered sacrifices to each of them. Brutus himself, holding before the altar of the goddess a consecrated vessel filled with wine, and the blood of a white hart, with his face looking up to the image, broke silence in these words:

'Diva potens nemorum, terror sylvestribus apris;
     Cui licet amfractus ire per æthereos,
Infernasque domos; terrestria jura resolve,
     Et dic quas terras nos habitare velis?
Dic certam sedem qua te venerabor in ævum,
     Qua tibi virgineis templa dicabo choris?'

Goddess of woods, tremendous in the chase
To mountain boars, and all the savage race!
Wide o'er the ethereal walks extends thy sway,
And o'er the infernal mansions void of day!
Look upon us on earth! unfold our fate,
And say what region is our destined seat?
Where shall we next thy lasting temples raise?
And choirs of virgins celebrate thy praise?

These words he repeated nine times, after which he took four turns round the altar, poured the wine into the fire, and then laid himself down upon the hart's skin, which he had spread before the altar, where he fell asleep. About the third hour of the night, the usual time for deep sleep, the goddess seemed to present herself before him, and foretell his future success as follows:

'Brute! sub occasum solis trans Gallica regna
     Insula in oceano est undique clausa mari:
Insula in oceano est habitata gigantibus olim,
     Nunc deserta quidem, gentibus apta tuis.
Hanc pete, namque tibi sedes erit illa perennis:
     Sic fiet natis altera Troja tuis.
Sic de prole tua reges nascentur: et ipsis
     Totius terræ subditus orbis erit.'

Brutus! there lies beyond the Gallic bounds
An island which the western sea surrounds,
By giants once possessed; now few remain
To bar thy entrance, or obstruct thy reign.
To reach that happy shore thy sails employ;
There fate decrees to raise a second Troy,
And found an empire in thy royal line,
Which time shall ne'er destroy, nor bounds confine.

Awakened by the vision, he was for some time in doubt
with himself, whether what he had seen was a dream or a
real appearance of the goddess herself, foretelling to what
land he should go. At last he called to his companions,
and related to them in order the vision he had in his sleep,
at which they very much rejoiced, and were urgent to
return to their ships, and while the wind favoured them,
to hasten their voyage towards the west, in pursuit of
what the goddess had promised ... He repaired to the
fleet, and loading it with the riches and spoils he had
taken, set sail with a fair wind towards the promised
island, and arrived on the coast of Totness ...

The island was then called Albion, and was inhabited
by none but a few giants. Notwithstanding this, the pleasant situation of the places, the plenty of rivers abounding
with fish, and the engaging prospect of its woods, made
Brutus and his company very desirous to fix their habitation in it. They therefore passed through all the prov-
inces, forced the giants to fly into the caves of the
mountains, and divided the country among them according to the directions of their commander. After this they
began to till the ground and build houses, so that in a
little time the country looked like a place that had been
long inhabited. At last Brutus called the island after his
own name Britain, and his companions Britons; for by
these means he desired so perpetuate the memory of his
name. From whence afterwards the language of the nation,
which at first bore the name of Trojan, or rough Greek,
was called British ...

Brutus ... formed a design of building a city and, with

this view, travelled through the land to find out a convenient situation; and, coming to the river Thames, he
walked along the shore, and at last pitched upon a place
very fit for his purpose. Here, therefore, he built a city,
which he called New Troy; under which name it continued
a long time after, till [the reign of] his grandson Lud
became famous for the building of cities, and for rebuilding the walls of Trinovantum, which he also surrounded
with innumerable towers. He likewise commanded the
citizens to build houses, and all other kinds of structures
in it, so that no city in all foreign countries to a great
distance round could show more beautiful palaces. He was
withal a warlike man, and very magnificent in his feasts
and public entertainments. And though he had many other
cities, yet he loved this above them all, and resided in it
the greater part of the year; for which reason it was
afterwards called Kaerlud, and by the corruption of the
word, Caerlondon; and again by change of languages, in
process of time, London; as also by foreigners who arrived
here, and reduced this country under their subjection, it
was called Londres. At last, when he was dead, his body
was buried by the gate which to this time is called in the
British tongue after his name . . .

[2] The revolt of Boudicca, AD 61; from *The Life of
Agricola* by Tacitus.

The Britons, relieved from present dread by the absence of
the governor, began to hold conferences, in which they
painted the miseries of servitude, compared their several
injuries, and inflamed each other with such representations
as these: 'That the only effects of their patience were more
grievous impositions upon a people who submitted with
such facility. Formerly they had one king respectively; now
two were set over them, the lieutenant and the procurator,
the former of whom vented his rage upon their life's blood,
the latter upon their properties; the union or discord of
these governors was equally fatal to those who they ruled,

while the officers of the one, and the centurions of the other, joined in oppressing them by all kinds of violence and contumely; so that nothing was exempted from their avarice, nothing from their lust. In battle it was the bravest who took spoils; but those whom *they* suffered to seize their houses, force away their children, and exact levies, were, for the most part, the cowardly and effeminate; as if the only lesson of suffering of which they were ignorant was how to die for their country. Yet how inconsiderable would the number of invaders appear did the Britons but compute their own forces! From considerations like these, Germany had thrown off the yoke, though a river and not the ocean was its barrier. The welfare of their country, their wives, and their parents called *them* to arms, while avarice and luxury alone incited their enemies; who would withdraw as even the deified Julius had done, if the present race of Britons would emulate the valour of their ancestors, and not be dismayed at the event of the first or second engagement. Superior spirit and perseverance were always the share of the wretched; and the gods themselves now seemed to compassionate the Britons, by ordaining the absence of the general, and the detention of his army in another island. The most difficult point, assembling for the purpose of deliberation, was already accomplished; and there was always more danger from the discovery of designs like these, than from their execution.'

Instigated by such suggestions, they unanimously rose in arms, led by Boadicea, a woman of royal descent (for they make no distinction between the sexes in succession to the throne) and, attacking the soldiers dispersed through the garrisons, stormed the fortified posts, and invaded the colony itself, as the seat of slavery. They omitted no species of cruelty with which rage and victory could inspire barbarians; and had not Paullinus, on being acquainted with the commotion of the province, marched speedily to its relief, Britain would have been lost. The fortune of a single battle, however, reduced it to its former subjection; though many still remained in arms, whom the consciousness of revolt, and particular dread of the governor, had driven to despair. Paullinus, although otherwise exemplary in his administration, having treated those who surrendered with severity, and having pursued too rigorous measures, as one who was revenging his own personal injury also, Petronius Turpilianus was sent in his stead, as a person more inclined to lenity, and one who, being unacquainted with the enemy's delinquency, could more easily accept their penitence. After having restored things to their former quiet state, he delivered the command to Trebellius Maximus.

[3] Description of Roman London, c. 4th century; from *Roman London* by G. Home.

Londinium can be pictured as a city containing a fair proportion of stone and brick structures, with public buildings of stone relieved with bands of brick-coursing rising massively above them. But this does not complete the scene, for interspersed along the quaysides and in all the less important streets there would be timber-built houses of all sizes and condition, thatched and with wattle and daub walls.

In planning the essential features of the new city, one of the first considerations would have been the provision of a forum and the necessary public buildings. There is now ample archaeological evidence for placing the basilica on the site of Leadenhall Market, where its extensive foundations have gradually been discovered. This building has been found to be one of very large dimensions, but whether it was the first built or a later reconstruction is not yet known. The chief forum would have normally occupied a considerable space on the south side of the basilica; it is there that one looks for a parallelogram without foundations. Excavations on both sides of Gracechurch Street in 1934 have, however, confirmed previous reports of buildings in this area. The lengths of wall exposed were very massive and must have been associated with imposing structures of approximately the same age as the basilica itself. They occupied a central position in the western half of the presumed forum space and it may be that they are all that survives of the substructures of more than one temple that stood there.

That a Capitoline temple arose within the area of the city during this period of growing prosperity is very probable, but no temple sites have yet been identified. It is possible that the pagan fanes were demolished for the purpose of building Christian churches in later ages. There is some reason for thinking that a Mithraeum stood near the Walbrook and five or six other temples have been inferred. Public baths, an invariable adjunct to Roman cities, must have existed, and after the Great Fire of London what appeared to be the remains of one of these came to light. Places of amusement have left no trace, and yet there is no doubt at all that they existed in the city – to cite one piece of evidence, the memorial to a gladiator is sufficient to point to the prevalence in Londinium of the sanguinary displays that made a Roman holiday . . .

The chief streets leading into the heart of the city may have averaged 30 feet in width. A section discovered near Pewterers' Hall has more than that in width, while lesser ones were, as found in Eastcheap, not broader than 16 feet. Solid stone paving would have been the rule in all the main streets and in the lesser ways the surface may have consisted of rammed flint and gravel. Flanking the chief streets there were most probably more or less continuous frontages separated fairly frequently by narrow passages from 3 to 4 feet in width. Much of the building material then as now was brick, but there was widespread use of stone and rubble covered externally with stucco that was frequently painted dark red. The ground floors possessed wide arched openings in which were the shops, banks and offices, and the effect as a whole may have resembled in essentials what is found today in many provincial towns in Italy. There was great regularity in the windows of the first and other floors, if one may judge by the examples standing today in Rome and at Ostia. The height to which buildings were carried in Londinium can only be estimated by the great thickness of lower walls. On this basis there would have been houses here and there that rose high above those surrounding them. It is not uncommon to find walls 3 feet in thickness – witness the house beneath the Coal Exchange in Lower Thames Street – and such structures would, according to modern standards, have been capable of carrying four or five floors at least. From the foundations brought to light in the heart of the city, it is evident that buildings were laid out with almost fantastic irregularity in spite of the fact that some of them possessed walls with foundations about 8 feet in thickness. Therefore, if regularity of frontages be accepted for the streets of certain quarters, the conclusion cannot be avoided that the central area, or ancient nucleus of the city, doubtless for very good reasons, presented in some areas an appearance greatly lacking in uniformity.

[4] The Danes, c. 9th century; from *The London Life of Yesterday* by Arthur Compton Rickett.

Wild, imaginative, brave, and brutal, the new settlers were to make a permanent impression upon the life of the City. The thing that they esteemed above all others was physical courage, and their kings had perforce to abdicate when too old to do their proper share of fighting.

Meat, bread, and ale in large quantities satisfied their physical needs at the close of the day. And for relaxation there were various rough games, which sufficiently indicate the primitive tastes of the revellers. For instance, a game which delighted these mighty men above others seems to have consisted in the 'chucking' of large beef bones at one another – a perilous pastime, which put a speedy end to the career of one unhappy Archbishop – Alphege of Canterbury. Being sent for on a certain festive occasion by a troop of Danish soldiers, the ecclesiastic interrupted their bone-throwing merriment, and, being less skilful in 'ducking' than the Danes presumably were, he was struck on the head and killed.

THE CITY

London Stone

[5] Origin of London stone 1598; from *Survey of London* by J. Stow.

On the south side of Candlewick Street, near unto the channel, is pitched upright a great stone called London stone, fixed in the ground very deep, fastened with bars of iron, and otherwise so strongly set, that if carts do run against it through negligence, the wheels be broken, and the stone itself unshaken.

The cause why this stone was set there, the time when, or other memory hereof, is none, but that the same hath long continued there is manifest, namely, since (or rather before) the Conquest; for in the end of a fair written Gospel book given to Christ's church in Canterburie, by Ethelstane, King of the West Saxons, I find noted of lands or rents in London belonging to the said church, whereof one parcel is described to lie near unto London stone. Of later time we read, that in the year of Christ 1135, the 1st of King Stephen, a fire, which began in the house of one Ailward, near unto London stone, consumed all east to

Aldgate, in the which fire the priory of the Holy Trinitie was burnt, and west to St Erkenwald's shrine in Paule's church. And these be the eldest notes that I read thereof.

Some have said this stone to be set as a mark in the middle of the city within the walls; but in truth it standeth far nearer unto the river of Thames than to the wall of the city; some others have said the same to be set for the tendering and making of payment by debtors to their creditors at their appointed days and times, till of later time payments were more usually made at the font in Poules church, and now most commonly at the Royal Exchange; some again have imagined the same to be set up by one John or Thomas Londonstone dwelling there against; but more likely it is, that such men have taken name of the stone than the stone of them, as did John at Noke, Thomas at Stile, William at Wall, or at Well, etc.

London Wall

[6] Construction (AD 306) and maintenance of the wall (medieval); from *Survey of London* by J. Stow.

Helen, the mother of Constantine the Great, was the first that inwalled this city, about the year of Christ 306 ... William Fitzstephen, in the reign of King Henry II, writing of the walls of this city, hath these words: 'The wall is high and great, well towered on the north side, with due distances between the towers. On the south side also the city was walled and towered, but the fishful river of Thames, with his ebbing and flowing, hath long since subverted them.' ...

And now touching the maintenance and repairing the said wall. I read, that in the year 1215, the 16th of King John, the barons, entering the city by Aldgate, first took assurance of the citizens, then brake into the Jews' houses, searched their coffers to fill their own purses, and after with great diligence repaired the walls and gates of the city with stone taken from the Jews' broken houses ... also in the year 1282, King Edward I, having granted to

Robert Kilwarby, archbishop of Canterbury, license for the enlarging of the Blackfriars' church, to break and take down a part of the wall of the city, from Ludgate to the river of Thames; he also granted to Henry Walleis, mayor, and the citizens of London, the favour to take, toward the making of the wall and enclosure of the city, certain customs or toll, as appeareth by his grant. This wall was then to be made from Ludgate west to Fleet bridge along behind the houses, and along by the water of the Fleet unto the river of Thames. Moreover, in the year 1310, Edward II commanded the citizens to make up the wall already begun, and the tower at the end of the same wall, within the water of Thames near unto the Blackfriars, etc ... In the 17th of Edward IV Ralph Joceline, mayor, caused part of the wall about the city of London to be repaired; to wit, betwixt Aldgate and Aldersgate. He also caused Moorfield to be searched for clay, and brick thereof to be made and burnt; he likewise caused chalk to be brought out of Kent, and to be burnt into lime in the same Moorfield, for more furtherance of the work. Then the Skinners to begin in the east made that part of the wall betwixt Aldgate and Bevis Marks, towards Bishopsgate, as may appear by their arms in three places fixed there: the mayor, with his company of the Drapers, made all that part betwixt Bishopsgate and Allhallows church, and from Allhallows towards the postern called Moorgate. A great part of the same wall was repaired by the executors of Sir John Crosby, late alderman, as may appear by his arms in two places there fixed: and other companies repaired the rest of the wall to the postern of Cripplegate. The Goldsmiths repaired from Cripplegate towards Aldersgate, and there the work ceased. The circuit of the wall of London on the land side, to wit, from the Tower of London in the east unto Aldgate, is 82 perches; from Aldgate to Bishopsgate, 86 perches; from Bishopsgate in the north to the postern of Cripplegate, 162 perches; from Cripplegate to Aldersgate, 75 perches; from Aldersgate to Newgate, 66 perches; from Newgate in the west to Ludgate, 42 perches; in all, 513 perches of assize. From Ludgate to the Fleet-dike west, about 60 perches; from Fleetbridge south to the river Thames, about 70 perches; and so the total of these perches amounteth to 643, every perch consisting of five yards and a half, which do yield 3,536 yards and a half, containing 10,608 feet, which make up two English miles and more by 608 feet.

Newgate and the Old Bailey

[7] Defoe in the pillory (1703); from *Memoirs of the Life and Times of Daniel Defoe, Vol. II.*

His wit having been construed into a libel by the grand jury, he was indicted at the Old Bailey sessions, 24 February 1703, and proceeded to trial in the following July . . . The jury found him guilty of composing and publishing a seditious libel; his sentence was: that he pay a fine of 200 marks to the queen; stand three times in the pillory; be imprisoned during the queen's pleasure; and find sureties for his good behaviour for seven years.

It has been justly remarked, that 'This very infamous sentence reflected much more dishonour upon the Court by which it was pronounced, than upon De Foe upon whom it was inflicted.' And so it was considered by many persons at the time; for he was guarded to the pillory by the populace, as if he was about to be enthroned in a chair of state, and descended from it with the triumphant acclamations of the surrounding multitude. In allusion to this, one of his adversaries has the following couplet:

> The shouting crowds their advocate proclaim,
> And varnish over infamy with fame.

De Foe has himself told us, 'That the people, who were expected to treat him very ill, on the contrary pitied him, and wished those who set him there were placed in his room, and expressed their affections by loud shouts and acclamations when he was taken down.' ... The mob, instead of pelting him, resorted to the unmannerly act of drinking his health ...

Tradition reports, that the machine, which was graced with one of the keenest wits of the day; was adorned with garlands, it being in the midst of summer. The same authority states, that refreshments were provided for him after his exhibition.

[8] Jack Sheppard escapes from Newgate (1724); from *The Newgate Calendar*, edited by A. Knapp & W. Baldwin.

On Monday 30 August 1724, a warrant was sent to Newgate for the execution of Sheppard, with other convicts under sentence of death.

We must here observe, that in the old gaol of Newgate there was within the lodge, a hatch, with large iron spikes, which opened into a dark passage, whence there were a few steps into the condemned hold. The prisoners being permitted to come down to the hatch to speak with their friends, Sheppard, having been supplied with instruments, took an opportunity of cutting one of the spikes in such a manner that it might easily be broken off.

On the evening of the above-mentioned 30 August, two women of Sheppard's acquaintance going to visit him, he broke off the spike, and thrusting his head and shoulders through the space, the women pulled him down, and he effected his escape, notwithstanding some of the keepers were at that time drinking at the other end of the lodge.

On the day after his escape he went to a public-house in Spital-fields, whence he sent for an old acquaintance, one Page, a butcher in Clare-market ... some of Sheppard's old acquaintance informing him that strict search was making after him, he and Page retired to Finchley, in hope of laying there concealed, till the diligence of the gaol-keepers should relax; but the keepers of Newgate having intelligence of their retreat, took Sheppard into custody, and conveyed him to his old lodgings.

Such steps were now taken as were expected to be effectual in preventing his future escape. He was put into a strong room called the Castle, hand-cuffed, loaded with a heavy pair of irons, and chained to a staple fixed in the floor.

The curiosity of the public being greatly excited by his former escape, he was visited by great numbers of people of all ranks, and scarce any one left him without making him a present in money; though he would have more gladly received a file, a hammer, or a chissel; but the utmost care was taken, that none of his visitors should furnish him with such implements.

Sheppard, nevertheless, was continually employing his thoughts on the means of another escape. On 14 October the sessions began at the Old Bailey, and the keepers being much engaged in attending the court, he thought they would have little time to visit him; and therefore the present juncture would be the most favourable to carry his plan into execution.

About two o'clock in the afternoon of the following day, one of the keepers carried him his dinner, and having carefully examined his irons, and finding them fast, he left him for the day.

Some days before this Jack had found a small nail in the room, with which he could, at pleasure, unlock the padlock that went from the chain to the staple in the floor; and in his own account of this transaction, he says, 'that he was frequently about the room, and had several times slept on the barracks, when the keepers imagined he had not been out of his chair.'

The keeper had not left him more than an hour when he began his operations. He first took off his hand-cuffs, and then opened the padlock that fastened the chain to the staple. He next, by mere strength, twisted asunder a small link of the chain between his legs, and then drawing up his fetters as high as he could, he made them fast with his garters.

He then attempted to get up the chimney; but had not advanced far before he was stopped by an iron bar that went across it; on which he descended, and with a piece of his broken chain picked out the mortar, and moving a small stone or two, about six feet from the floor, he got out the iron bar, which was three feet long, and an inch square, and proved very serviceable to him in his future proceedings.

He in a short time made such a breach, as to enable him to get into the red-room over the castle; and here he found a large nail, which he made use of in his farther operations. It was seven years since the door of this red-room had been opened; but Sheppard wrenched off the lock in less than seven minutes, and got into the passage leading to the chapel. In this place he found a door which was bolted on the opposite side; but making a hole through the wall, he pushed the bolt back, and opened it.

Arriving at the door of the chapel, he broke off one of the iron spikes, which keeping for his farther use, he got into an entry between the chapel and the lower leads. The door of this entry was remarkably strong, and fastened with a large lock; and night now coming on, Sheppard was obliged to work in the dark. Notwithstanding this disadvantage, he, in half an hour, forced open the box of the lock, and opened the door; but this led him to another room still more difficult, for it was barred and bolted as well as locked; however, he wrenched the fillet from the main post of the door, and the box and staples came off with it.

It was now eight o'clock, and Sheppard found no farther obstruction to his proceedings; for he had only one other door to open, which being bolted on the inside, was opened without difficulty, and he got over a wall to the upper leads.

His next consideration was, how he should descend with the greatest safety; accordingly he found that the most convenient place for him to alight on, would be the turner's house adjoining to Newgate; but as it would have been very dangerous to have jumped to such a depth, he went back for the blanket with which he used to cover himself when he slept in the castle, and endeavoured to fasten his stocking to the blanket to ease his descent; but not being able to do so, he was compelled to use the blanket alone: wherefore he made it fast to the wall of Newgate with the spike that he took out of the chapel; and sliding down, dropped on the turner's leads just as the clock was striking nine. It happened that the door of the garret next the turner's leads was open, on which he stole softly down two pair of stairs, and heard some company talking in a room. His irons clinking, a woman cried, 'What noise is that?' and a man answered, 'Perhaps the dog or cat.'

Sheppard, who was exceedingly fatigued, returned to the garret, and laid down for more than two hours; after which he crept down once more, as far as the room where the company were, when he heard a gentleman taking leave of the family, and saw the maid light him down stairs. As soon as the maid returned, he resolved to venture all hazards; but in stealing down the stairs, he stumbled against a chamber door; but instantly recovering himself, he got into the street.

By this time it was after twelve o'clock, and passing by the watch-house of St Sepulchre, he bid the watchman good morrow, and going up Holborn, he turned down Gray's-Inn-lane, and about two in the morning got into the fields near Tottenham-court, where he took shelter in a place that had been a cow-house, and slept soundly about three hours. His fetters being still on, his legs were greatly bruised and swelled, and he dreaded the approach of day-light, lest he should be discovered. He had now above forty shillings in his possession, but was afraid to send to any person for assistance.

At seven in the morning it began to rain hard, and

continued to do so all day, so that no person appeared in the fields: and during this melancholy day he would, to use his own expression, have given his right hand for 'a hammer, a chissel, and a punch'. Night coming on, and being pressed by hunger, he ventured to a little chandler's shop in Tottenham-court-road, where he got a supply of bread and cheese, small beer, and some other necessaries, hiding his irons with a long great coat. He asked the woman of the house for a hammer; but she had no such utensil; on which he retired to the cow-house, where he slept that night, and remained all the next day.

At night he went again to the chandler's shop, supplied himself with provisions, and returned to his hiding-place. At six the next morning, which was Sunday, he began to beat the basils of his fetters with a stone, in order to bring them to an oval form, to slip his heels through. In the afternoon the master of the cow-house, coming thither and seeing his irons, said, 'For God's sake who are you?' Sheppard said he was an unfortunate young fellow, who having had a bastard-child sworn to him, and not being able to give security to the parish for its support, he had been sent to Bridewell, from whence he had made his escape. The man said that if that was all it did not much signify; but he did not care how soon he was gone, for he did not like his looks.

Soon after he was gone Sheppard saw a journeyman shoemaker, to whom he told the same story of the bastard-child, and offered him twenty shillings if he would procure a smith's hammer and a punch. The poor man, tempted by the reward, procured them accordingly, and assisted him in getting rid of his irons, which work was completed by five o'clock in the evening.

When night came on, our adventurer tied a handker-chief about his head, tore his woollen cap in several places, and likewise tore his coat and stockings, so as to have the appearance of a beggar; and in this condition he went to a cellar near Charing-cross, where he supped on roasted veal, and listened to the conversation of the company, all of whom were talking of the escape of Sheppard.

On the Monday he sheltered himself at a public-house of little trade, in Rupert-street, and conversing with the landlady about Sheppard, he told her it was impossible for him to get out of the kingdom; and the keepers would certainly have him again in a few days; on which the woman wished that a curse might fall on those who should betray him. Remaining in this place till evening, he went into the Haymarket, where a crowd of people were surrounding two ballad singers, and listening to a song made on his adventure and escape.

On the next day he hired a garret in Newport-market, and soon afterwards, dressing himself like a porter, he went to Black-friars, to the house of Mr Applebee, printer of the dying speeches, and delivered a letter, in which he ridiculed the printer, and the Ordinary of Newgate, and enclosed a letter for one of the keepers of Newgate.

Some nights after this he broke open the shop of Mr Rawlins, a pawnbroker in Drury-lane, where he stole a sword, a suit of wearing apparel, some snuff-boxes, rings, watches, and other effects to a considerable amount. Determining to make the appearance of a gentleman among his old acquaintance in Drury-lane and Clare-market, he dressed himself in a suit of black and a tie-wig, wore a ruffled shirt, a silver hilted sword, a diamond ring, and a gold watch, though he knew that diligent search was making after him at that very time.

On 31 October he dined with two women at a public-house in Newgate-street, and about four in the afternoon they all passed under Newgate in a hackney-coach, having first drawn up the blinds. Going in the evening to a public-house in Maypole-alley, Clare-market, Sheppard sent for his mother, and treated her with brandy, when the poor woman dropped on her knees, and begged he would immediately quit the kingdom, which he promised to do, but had no intention of keeping his word.

Being now grown valiant through an excess of liquor, he wandered from ale-houses to gin-shops in the neighbourhood till near twelve o'clock at night, when he was apprehended in consequence of the information of an alehouse-boy who knew him. When taken into custody he was quite senseless, from the quantity and variety of liquors he had drank, and was conveyed to Newgate in a coach, without being capable of making the least resistance, though he had then two pistols in his possession . . .

He regularly attended the prayers in the chapel; but though he behaved with decency there, he affected mirth before he went thither, and endeavoured to prevent any degree of seriousness among the other prisoners on their return.

Even when the day of execution arrived, Sheppard did not appear to have given over all expectations of eluding justice; for having been furnished with a penknife, he put it in his pocket, with a view, when the melancholy procession came opposite Little Turnstile, to have cut the cord that bound his arms, and throwing himself out of the cart among the crowd, to have run through the narrow passage where the sheriff's officers could not follow on horseback; and he had no doubt but he should make his escape by the assistance of the mob.

It is not impossible but this scheme might have succeeded; but before Sheppard left the press-yard, one Watson, an officer, searching his pockets, found the knife, and was cut with it so as to occasion a great effusion of blood.

Sheppard had yet a farther view to his preservation, even after execution; for he desired his acquaintance to put him into a warm bed as soon as he should be cut down, and try to open a vein, which he had been told would restore him to life.

He behaved with great decency at the place of execution, and confessed to having committed two robberies, for which he had been tried and acquitted. He suffered in the 23rd year of his age. He died with difficulty, and was much pitied by the surrounding multitude. When he was cut down, his body was delivered to his friends, who carried him to a public house in Long-acre, whence he was removed in the evening, and buried in the churchyard of St Martin in the Fields.

[9] Storming of the prison during the Gordon riots (1780); from *Barnaby Rudge* by Charles Dickens.

Breaking the silence they had hitherto preserved, they raised a great cry as soon as they were ranged before the jail, and demanded to speak with the governor. Their visit was not wholly unexpected, for his house, which fronted the street, was strongly barricaded, the wicket-gate of the prison was closed up, and at no loophole or grating was any person to be seen. Before they had repeated their summons many times, a man appeared upon the roof of the governor's house, and asked what it was they wanted.

Some said one thing, some another, and some only groaned and hissed. It being now nearly dark, and the house high, many persons in the throng were not aware that any one had come to answer them, and continued their clamour until the intelligence was gradually diffused through the whole concourse. Ten minutes or more elapsed before any one voice could be heard with tolerable distinctness: during which interval the figure remained perched alone, against the summer-evening sky, looking down into the troubled street.

'Are you,' said Hugh at length, 'Mr Akerman, the head jailer here?'

'Of course he is, brother,' whispered Dennis. But Hugh, without minding him, took his answer from the man himself.

'Yes,' he said. 'I am.'

'You have got some friends of ours in your custody, master.'

'I have a good many people in my custody.' He glanced downward, as he spoke, into the jail: and the feeling that he could see into the different yards, and that he over-looked everything which was hidden from their view by the rugged walls, so lashed and goaded the mob, that they howled like wolves.

'Deliver up our friends,' said Hugh, 'and you may keep the rest.'

'It's my duty to keep them all. I shall do my duty.'

'If you don't throw the doors open, we shall break 'em down,' said Hugh: 'for we will have the rioters out.'

'All I can do, good people,' Akerman replied, 'is to exhort you to disperse; and to remind you that the consequences of any disturbance in this place, will be very severe, and bitterly repented by most of you, when it is too late.' ... There was no more parley. A shower of stones and other missiles compelled the keeper of the jail to retire ... hammers began to rattle on the walls; and every man strove to reach the prison, and be among the foremost rank.

And now the strokes began to fall like hail upon the gate, and on the strong building; for those who could not reach the door, spent their fierce rage on anything – even on the great blocks of stone, which shivered their weapons into fragments, and made their hands and arms to tingle as if the walls were active in their stout resistance, and dealt them back their blows. The clash of iron ringing upon iron, mingled with the deafening tumult and sounded high above it, as the great sledge-hammers rattled on the nailed and plated door: the sparks flew off in showers; men worked in gangs, and at short intervals relieved each other, that all their strength might be devoted to the work; but there stood the portal still, as grim and dark and strong as ever, and, saving for the dints upon its battered surface, quite unchanged.

While some brought all their energies to bear upon this toilsome task; and some, rearing ladders against the prison tried to clamber to the summit of the walls they were too short to scale; and some again engaged a body of police a hundred strong, and beat them back and trod them under foot by force of numbers; others besieged the house on which the jailer had appeared and, driving in the door, brought out his furniture, and piled it up against the prison-gate, to make a bonfire which should burn it down. As soon as this device was understood, all those who had laboured hitherto, cast down their tools and helped to swell the heap; which reached half-way across the street, and was so high, that those who threw more fuel on the top, got up by ladders. When all the keeper's goods were flung upon this costly pile, to the last fragment, they smeared it with the pitch, and tar, and rosin they had brought, and sprinkled it with turpentine. To all the woodwork round the prison-doors they did the like, leaving not a joist or beam untouched. This infernal christening performed, they fired the pile with lighted matches and with blazing tow, and then stood by, awaiting the result.

The furniture being very dry, and rendered more combustible by wax and oil, besides the arts they had used, took fire at once. The flames roared high and fiercely, blackening the prison-wall, and twining up its lofty front like burning serpents. At first they crowded round the blaze, and vented their exultation only in their looks: but when it grew hotter and fiercer – when it crackled, leaped, and roared, like a great furnace – when it shone upon the opposite houses, and lighted up not only the pale and wondering faces at the windows, but the inmost corners of each habitation – when through the deep red heat and glow, the fire was seen sporting and toying with the door, now clinging to its obdurate surface, now gliding off with fierce inconstancy and soaring high into the sky, anon returning to fold it in its burning grasp and lure it to its ruin – when it shone and gleamed so brightly that the church clock of St Sepulchre's, so often pointing to the hour of death, was legible as in broad day, and the vane upon its steeple-top glittered in the unwonted light like something richly jewelled – when blackened stone and sombre brick grew ruddy in the deep reflection, and windows shone like burnished gold, dotting the longest distance in the fiery vista with their specks of brightness – when wall and tower, and roof and chimney-stack, seemed drunk, and in the flickering glare appeared to reel and stagger – when scores of objects, never seen before, burst out upon the view, and things the most familiar put on some new aspect – then the mob began to join the whirl, and with loud yells, and shouts, and clamour, such as happily is seldom heard, bestirred themselves to feed the fire, and keep it at its height . . .

A shout! Another! Another yet, though few knew why, or what it meant. But those around the gate had seen it slowly yield, and drop from its topmost hinge. It hung on that side by but one, but it was upright still, because of the bar, and its having sunk, of its own weight, into the heap of ashes at its foot. There was now a gap at the top of the doorway, through which could be described a gloomy passage, cavernous and dark. Pile up the fire!

It burnt fiercely. The door was red-hot, and the gap wider. They vainly tried to shield their faces, with their hands, and standing as if in readiness for a spring, watched the place. Dark figures, some crawling on their hands and knees, some carried in the arms of others, were seen to pass along the roof. It was plain the jail could hold out no longer. The keeper, and his officers, and their wives and children, were escaping. Pile up the fire!

The door sank down again: it settled deeper in the cinders – tottered – yielded – was down!

As they shouted again, they fell back, for a moment, and left a clear space about the fire that lay between them and the jail entry. Hugh leapt upon the blazing heap, and scattering a train of sparks into the air, and making the dark lobby glitter with those that hung upon his dress, dashed into the jail.

The hangman followed. And then so many rushed upon their track, that the fire got trodden down and thinly strewn about the street; but there was no need of it now, for, inside and out, the prison was in flames . . .

When darkness broke away and morning began to dawn, the town wore a strange aspect indeed.

Sleep had scarcely been thought of all night. The general alarm was so apparent in the faces of the inhabitants, and its expression was so aggravated by want of rest (few persons with any property to lose, having dared go to bed since Monday), that a stranger coming into the streets would have supposed some mortal pest or plague was raging. In place of the usual cheerfulness and animation of morning, everything was dead and silent. The shops remained closed, offices and warehouses were shut, the coach and chair stands were deserted, no carts or waggons rumbled through the slowly waking streets, the early cries were all hushed; a universal gloom prevailed. Great numbers of people were out even at daybreak, but they flitted to and fro as though they shrank from the sound of their own footsteps; the public ways were haunted rather than frequented; and round the smoking ruins . . .

As the day crept on, still stranger things were witnessed in the streets. The gates of the King's Bench and Fleet Prisons being opened at the usual hour, were found to have notices affixed to them, announcing that the rioters would come that night to burn them down. The wardens, too well knowing the likelihood there was of this promise being fulfilled, were fain to set their prisoners at liberty, and give them leave to move their goods; so, all day, such of them as had any furniture were occupied in conveying it, some to this place, some to that, and not a few to the brokers' shops, where they gladly sold it, for any wretched price those gentry chose to give. There were some broken men among these debtors who had been in jail so long, and were so miserable and destitute of friends, so dead to the world, and utterly forgotten and uncared for, that they implored their jailers not to set them free, and to send them, if need were, to some other place of custody. But they, refusing to comply, lest they should incur the anger of the mob, turned them into the streets, where they wandered up and down, hardly remembering the ways untrodden by their feet so long, and crying – such abject things those rotten-hearted jails had made them – as they slunk off in their rags, and dragged their slipshod feet along the pavement.

Even of the three hundred prisoners who had escaped from Newgate, there were some – a few, but there were some – who sought their jailers out and delivered themselves up: preferring imprisonment and punishment to the horrors of such another night as the last. Many of the convicts, drawn back to their old place of captivity by some indescribable attraction, or by a desire to exult over it in its downfall and glut their revenge by seeing it in ashes, actually went back in broad noon, and loitered about the cells.

[10] Death of a hundred spectators at an execution in 1807; from *The Newgate Calendar*, edited by A. Knapp & W. Baldwin.

During the whole of Sunday night, the convicts were engaged in prayer, never slept, but broke the awful stillness of midnight by frequent protestations of reciprocal innocence. At five they were called, dressed and shaved, and about seven were brought into the press-yard: There was some difficulty in knocking off the irons of Haggerty; he voluntarily assisted, though he seemed much dejected, but by no means pusillanimous . . .

Owen Haggerty then ascended the scaffold. His arms were pinioned, and the halter round his neck: he wore a white cap, and a light olive shag great coat; he looked downwards, and was silent. He was attended by a Roman Catholic clergyman, who read to him, and to whom the unfortunate culprit seemed to pay great attention: he made no public acknowledgment of either guilt or innocence. After the executioner tied the fatal noose, he brought up John Holloway, who wore a smock frock and jacket, as it had been stated by the approver that he did at the time of the murder: he had also a white cap on; was pinioned, and had a halter round his neck: he had his hat in his hand; and, mounting the scaffold, he jumped and made an awkward bow, and said, 'I am innocent, innocent, by God!' He then turned round, and, bowing, made use of the same expressions. 'Innocent, innocent, innocent! Gentlemen! – No verdict! No verdict! No verdict! Gentlemen – Innocent! innocent!' At this moment, and while in the act of saying something more, the executioner proceeded to do his office by placing the cap over the face of Holloway; to which he, with apparent reluctance, complied; at the same time uttering some words. As soon as the rope was fixed round his neck, he continued quiet. He was attended in his devotions by an assistant at the Rev. Rowland Hill's Chapel.

The last that mounted the scaffold was Elizabeth Godfrey. She had been a woman of the town, aged 34, who had been capitally convicted of the wilful murder of Richard Prince, in Mary-le-bone parish, on 25 December 1806, by giving him a mortal wound with a pocket-knife in the left eye, of which wound he languished and died. Immediately on receiving sentence, this woman's firmness and recollection seemed to fail her, and she appeared bordering upon a state of frenzy. At the place of execution she was dressed in white, with a close cap, and long sleeves, and was attended by the Rev. Mr Ford, the Ordinary of Newgate; but her feelings appeared to be so much overpowered, that notwithstanding she bore the appearance of resignation in her countenance, her whole frame was so shaken by the terror of her situation, that she was incapable of any actual devotion.

They were all launched off together, at about a quarter after eight. It was a long time before the body of the poor female seemed to have gone through its last suffering.

The crowd which assembled to witness this execution was unparalleled, being, according to the best calculation, near 40,000; and the fatal catastrophe, which happened in consequence, will cause the day long to be remembered. By eight o'clock not an inch of ground was unoccupied in view of the platform. The pressure of the crowd was such, that, before the malefactors appeared, numbers of persons were crying out in vain to escape from it: the attempt only tended to increase the confusion. Several females of low stature, who had been so imprudent as to venture amongst the mob, were in a dismal situation: their cries were dreadful. Some, who could be no longer supported by the men, were suffered to fall, and were trampled to death. This also was the case with several men and boys. In all parts there were continued cries of Murder! Murder! particularly from the female part of the spectators and children, some of whom were expiring without the possibility of obtaining the least assistance, every one being employed in endeavours to preserve his own life. The most affecting scene of distress was seen at Green-Arbour-Lane, nearly opposite the Debtors' door. The terrible occurrence which took place near this spot was attributed to the circumstance of two piemen attending there to dispose of their pies; and one of them having his basket overthrown, which stood upon a sort of stool with four legs, some of the mob, not being aware of what had happened, and at the same time severely pressed, fell over the basket and the man at the moment he was picking it up, together with its contents. Those who once fell were never more suffered to rise, such was the violence of the mob. At this fatal place a man of the name of Herrington was thrown down, and had in his hand his youngest son, a fine boy about twelve years of age. The youth was soon trampled to death: the father recovered, though much bruised, and was amongst the wounded in St Bartholomew's Hospital. A woman who was so imprudent as to bring with her a child at the breast was one of the number killed: whilst in the act of falling, she forced the child into the arms of the man nearest to her, requesting him, for God's sake, to save its life: the man, finding it required all his exertion to preserve himself, threw the infant from him, but it was fortunately caught at a distance by another man, who, finding it difficult to ensure its safety or his own, got rid of it in a similar way. The child was again caught by a person who contrived to struggle with it to a cart, under which he deposited it until the danger was over, and the mob had dispersed. In other parts the pressure was so great, that a horrible scene of confusion ensued, and seven persons lost their lives by suffocation alone. It was shocking to behold a large body of the crowd, as one convulsive struggle for life, fight with the most savage fury with each other; the consequence was that the weakest, particularly the women, fell a sacrifice. A cart which was overloaded with spectators broke down, and some of the persons falling from the vehicle were trampled under foot, and never recovered. During the hour the malefactors hung, little assistance could be afforded to the unhappy sufferers;

but after the bodies were cut down, and the gallows removed to the Old Bailey Yard, the marshals and constables cleared the street where the catastrophe occurred, and, shocking to relate, there lay nearly 100 persons dead, or in a state of insensibility, strewed round the street! Twenty-seven dead bodies were taken to St Bartholomew's Hospital; four to St Sepulchre's church; one to the Swan on Snow-hill; one to a public-house opposite St Andrew's church, Holborn; one, an apprentice, to his master's; Mr Broadwood, piano-forte maker, to Golden-Square; a mother was seen carrying away the body of her dead boy; Mr Harrison, a respectable gentleman, was taken to his house at Holloway. There was a sailor-boy killed opposite Newgate, by suffocation: he carried a small bag, in which he had some bread and cheese, as it is supposed he came some distance to behold the execution. After the dead, dying, and wounded, were carried away, there was a cartload of shoes, hats, petticoats, and other articles of wearing apparel, picked up. Until four o'clock in the afternoon, most of the surrounding houses had some person in a wounded state: they were afterwards taken away by their friends on shutters, or in hackney-coaches. The doors of St Bartholomew's Hospital were closed against the populace. After the bodies of the dead were stripped and washed, they were ranged round a ward on the first floor, on the women's side: they were placed on the floor with sheets over them, and their clothes put as pillows under their heads: their faces were uncovered: there was a rail along the centre of the room: the persons who were admitted to see the shocking spectacle went up on one side, and returned out on the other. Until two o'clock, the entrances to the Hospital were beset with mothers weeping for sons! wives for their husbands! and sisters for their brothers! various individuals for their relatives and friends!

Seldom has such a scene of distress and misery presented itself in this metropolis. When the gates were opened a great concourse was admitted; and when the yard was full, the gates were again closed, until the first

visitors retired from this scene of woe: as soon as any of
the deceased were recognized, the body was either put into
a shell, or the face covered over, with the name of the
party written on a paper, and pinned over the body.

[11] Elizabeth Fry visits Newgate in 1814; from *An
Inquiry whether Crime and Misery are produced or
prevented by our present System of Prison Discipline*
by Thomas Fowell Buxton.

About four years ago, Mrs Fry was induced to visit
Newgate, by the representations of its state made by some
persons of the Society of Friends.

She found the female side in a situation which no
language can describe. Nearly *three hundred women*, sent
there for every gradation of crime, some untried, and some
under sentence of death, were crowded together in the two
wards and two cells, which are now quite appropriated to
the untried, and which are found quite inadequate to
contain even this diminished number with any tolerable
convenience. Here they saw their friends, and kept their
multitudes of children; and they had no other place for
cooking, washing, eating and sleeping.

They all slept on the floor; at times one hundred and
twenty in one ward, without so much as a mat for
bedding; and many of them were very nearly naked. She
saw them openly drinking spirits; and her ears were
offended by the most dreadful imprecations. Every thing
was filthy to excess, and the smell was quite disgusting.
Every one, even the Governor, was reluctant to go
amongst them. He persuaded her to leave her watch in the
office, telling her that his presence would not prevent its
being torn from her! She saw enough to convince her that
every thing bad was going on. In short, in giving me this
account, she repeatedly said, 'All I tell thee, is a faint
picture of the reality; the filth, the closeness of the rooms,
the ferocious manners and expressions of the women

towards each other, and the abandoned wickedness which everything bespoke, are quite indescribable!'

(ii) The next day she commenced the school, in company with a young lady, who then visited a prison for the first time, and who since gave me a very interesting description of her feelings upon that occasion. The railing was crowded with half-naked women, struggling together for the front situations with the most boisterous violence, and begging with the utmost vociferation. She felt as if she was going into a den of wild beasts; and she well recollects quite shuddering when the door closed upon her, and she was locked in, with such a herd of novel and desperate companions. This day, however, the school surpassed their utmost expectations: their only pain arose from the numerous and pressing applications made by young women, who longed to be taught and employed. The narrowness of the room rendered it then impossible to yield to their requests: but they tempted these ladies to project a school for the employment of the tried women, for teaching them to read and to work.

When this intention was mentioned to the friends of these ladies, it appeared at first so visionary and unpromising, that it met with very slender encouragement . . . But the noble zeal of these unassuming women was not to be repressed; and feeling that their design was intended for the good and the happiness of others, they trusted that it would receive the guidance and protection of Him, who often is pleased to accomplish the highest purposes by the most feeble instruments.

[12] Oscar Wilde sentenced at the Old Bailey (1895); from *The Trials of Oscar Wilde* by H. Montgomery Hyde.

The judge then turned to the two prisoners in the dock and continued: 'Oscar Wilde and Alfred Taylor, the crime of which you have been convicted is so bad that one has to put stern restraint upon oneself to prevent oneself from describing, in language which I would rather not use, the sentiments which must rise to the breast of every man of honour who has heard the details of these two terrible trials. That the jury have arrived at a correct verdict in this case, I cannot persuade myself to entertain the shadow of a doubt; and I hope, at all events, that those who sometimes imagine that a judge is half-hearted in the cause of decency and morality, because he takes care no prejudice shall enter into the case, may see that that is consistent at least with the utmost sense of indignation at the horrible charges brought home to both of you.

'It is no use for me to address you. People who can do these things must be dead to all sense of shame, and one cannot hope to produce any effect upon them. It is the worst case I have ever tried. That you, Taylor, kept a kind of male brothel it is impossible to doubt. And that you, Wilde, have been the centre of a circle of extensive corruption of the most hideous kind among young men, it is equally impossible to doubt.

'I shall, under such circumstances, be expected to pass the severest sentence that the law allows. In my judgement it is totally inadequate for such a case as this. The sentence of the Court is that each of you be imprisoned and kept to hard labour for two years.'

There were a few murmurs of 'Oh!' and 'Shame!', since the harsh words employed by the judge in passing the maximum sentence had contrasted strongly with the comparatively moderate language of his summing-up. But the protests were quickly drowned in a hum of approval from the majority of the spectators in the gallery. Meanwhile all eyes were focused on the dock. There Taylor heard his sentence with seeming indifference, but the other frock-coated figure swayed slightly, his face suffused with horror, and tried to utter a few words. 'And I?' he began. 'May I say nothing, my lord?' But Mr Justice Wills made no reply beyond a wave of the hand to the warders in attendance, who touched the prisoners on the shoulder and hurried them out of sight to the cells below, there to await the 'Black Maria' to take them to Pentonville Prison . . .

Meanwhile, in the streets outside the Old Bailey the verdict was received with sundry marks of popular approval. A few people literally danced with joy, and some prostitutes were seen to kick up their skirts with glee at the news. ''E'll 'ave 'is 'air cut reglar *now*,' shouted one of them. This sally provoked a loud chorus of laughter from others on the pavement. Further up the social scale feelings were more decently disguised, except perhaps by Lord Queensberry and his friends.

The Royal Exchange

[13] The royal exchange opened by Elizabeth I (1570); from *Survey of London* by J. Stow.

Next is the Royal Exchange, erected in the year 1566, after this order, namely, certain houses upon Cornehill, and the like upon the back thereof, in the ward of Brode street, with three alleys, the first called Swan alley, opening into Cornehill, the second New alley, passing throughout of Cornehill into Brode street ward, over against St Bartholomew lane, the third St Christopher's alley, opening into Brode street ward, and into St Christopher's parish, containing in all fourscore households, were first purchased by the citizens of London, for more than three thousand five hundred and thirty-two pounds, and were sold for four hundred and seventy-eight pounds, to such persons as should take them down and carry them thence; also the ground or plot was made plain at the charges of the city; and then possession thereof was by certain aldermen, in the name of the whole citizens, given to Sir Thomas Gresham, knight, agent to the queen's highness, thereupon to build a burse, or place for merchants to assemble, at his own proper charges. And he, on 7 June, laying the first stone of the foundation, being brick, accompanied with some aldermen, every of them laid a piece of gold, which the workmen took up, and forthwith followed upon the same with such diligence, that by the month of November, in the year 1567, the same was covered with slate, and shortly after fully finished.

In the year 1570, on 23 January, the queen's majesty, attended with her nobility, came from her house at the Strand, called Somerset house, and entered the city by Temple Bar, through Fleet street, Cheape, and so by the north side of the burse, through Threeneedle street, to Sir Thomas Gresham's in Bishopsgate street, where she dined. After dinner her majesty returning through Cornehill, entered the burse on the south side; and after that she had viewed every part thereof above the ground, especially the pawn, which was richly furnished with all sorts of the finest wares in the city, she caused the same burse by an herald and trumpet to be proclaimed the Royal Exchange, and so to be called from thenceforth, and not otherwise.

[14] Addison visits the exchange (1711); from *The Spectator* by J. Addison.

There is no place in the town which I so much love to frequent as the Royal Exchange. It gives me a secret satisfaction, and, in some measure, gratifies my vanity, as I am an Englishman, to see so rich an assembly of country-men and foreigners consulting together upon the private business of mankind, and making this metropolis a kind of emporium for the whole earth. I must confess I look upon High 'Change to be a great council, in which all considerable nations have their representatives. Factors in the trading world are what ambassadors are in the politic world; they negotiate affairs, conclude treaties, and main-tain a good correspondence between those wealthy so-cieties of men that are divided from one another by seas and oceans, or live on the different extremities of a continent. I have often been pleased to hear disputes adjusted between an inhabitant of Japan and an alderman of London, or to see a subject of the Great Mogul entering into a league with one of the Czar of Muscovy. I am infinitely delighted in mixing with these several ministers of commerce, as they are distinguished by their different walks and different languages: sometimes I am jostled among a body of Armenians; sometimes I am lost in a crowd of Jews; and sometimes make one in a group of Dutchmen. I am a Dane, Swede, or Frenchman at different times, or rather fancy myself like the old philosopher, who, upon being asked what countryman he was, replied that he was a citizen of the world.

Though I very frequently visit this busy multitude of people, I am known to nobody there but my friend Sir Andrew, who often smiles upon me as he sees me bustling in the crowd, but at the same time connives at my presence without taking any further notice of me. There is indeed a merchant of Egypt who just knows me by sight, having formerly remitted me some money to Grand Cairo; but as I am not versed in the modern Coptic, our conferences go no further than a bow and a grimace.

This grand scene of business gives me an infinite variety of solid and substantial entertainments. As I am a great lover of mankind, my heart naturally overflows with pleasure at the sight of a prosperous and happy multitude, insomuch that at many public solemnities I cannot forbear expressing my joy with tears that have stolen down my cheeks. For this reason I am wonderfully delighted to see such a body of men thriving in their own private fortunes, and at the same time promoting the public stock; or in other words, raising estates for their own families, by bringing into their country whatever is wanting, and carrying out of it whatever is superfluous.

Nature seems to have taken a particular care to disseminate her blessings among the different regions of the world, with an eye to this mutual intercourse and traffic among mankind, that the natives of the several parts of the globe might have a kind of dependence upon one another, and be united together by their common interest. Almost every degree produces something peculiar to it. The food often grows in one country, and the sauce in another. The fruits of Portugal are corrected by the products of Barbados; the infusion of a China plant sweetened with the pith of an Indian cane; the Philippic Islands give a flavour to our European bowls. The single dress of a woman of quality is often the product of an hundred climates. The muff and the fan come together from the different ends of the earth. The scarf is sent from the torrid zone, and the tippet from beneath the pole. The brocade petticoat rises out of the mines of Peru, and the diamond necklace out of the bowels of Indostan.

If we consider our own country in its natural prospect, without any of the benefits and advantages of commerce, what a barren uncomfortable spot of earth falls to our share! Natural historians tell us, that no fruit grows originally among us, besides hips and haws, acorns and pig-nuts, with other delicacies of the like nature; that our climate of itself, and without the assistances of art, can make no further advances towards a plum than to a sloe, and carries an apple to no greater a perfection than a crab; that our melons, our peaches, our figs, our apricots, and cherries, are strangers among us, imported in different ages, and naturalized in our English gardens; and that they would all degenerate and fall away into the trash of our own country, if they were wholly neglected by the planter, and left to the mercy of our sun and soil. Nor has traffic more enriched our vegetable world, than it has improved the whole face of nature among us. Our ships are laden with the harvest of every climate; our tables are stored with spices, and oils, and wines; our rooms are filled with pyramids of China, and adorned with the workmanship of Japan. Our morning's draught comes to us from the remotest corners of the earth. We repair our bodies by the drugs of America, and repose ourselves under Indian canopies. My friend Sir Andrew calls the vineyards of France our gardens, the Spice Islands our hotbeds, the

Persians our silk-weavers, and the Chinese our potters. Nature indeed furnishes us with the bare necessaries of life, but traffic gives us a great variety of what is useful, and at the same time supplies us with everything that is convenient and ornamental. Nor is it the least part of this our happiness, that whilst we enjoy the remotest products of the North and South, we are free from those extremities of weather which give them birth; that our eyes are refreshed with the green fields of Britain, at the same time that our palates are feasted with fruits that rise between the tropics.

For these reasons there are not more useful members in a commonwealth than merchants. They knit mankind together in a mutual intercourse of good offices, distribute the gifts of nature, find work for the poor, add wealth to the rich, and magnificence to the great. Our English merchant converts the tin of his own country into gold, and exchanges his wool for rubies. The Mahomedans are clothed in our British manufacture, and the inhabitants of the frozen zone warmed with the fleeces of our sheep.

When I have been upon the 'Change, I have often fancied one of our old kings standing in person, where he is represented in effigy, and looking down upon the wealthy concourse of people with which that place is every day filled. In this case, how would he be surprised to hear all the languages of Europe spoken in this little spot of his former dominions, and to see so many private men, who in his time would have been the vassals of some powerful baron, negotiating like princes for greater sums of money than were formerly to be met with in the royal treasury! Trade, without enlarging the British territories, has given us a kind of additional empire. It has multiplied the number of the rich, made our landed estates infinitely more valuable than they were formerly, and added to them an accession of other estates as valuable as the lands themselves.

[15] The South Sea Bubble affair (1720); from *Extraordinary Popular Delusions* by Charles Mackay.

It seemed at that time as if the whole nation had turned stock-jobbers. Exchange Alley was every day blocked up by crowds, and Cornhill was impassable for the number of carriages. Every body came to purchase stock. 'Every fool aspired to be a knave.' In the words of a ballad published at the time, and sung about the streets,

> 'Then stars and garters did appear
>   Among the meaner rabble;
> To buy and sell, to see and hear
>   The Jews and Gentiles squabble.
>
> The greatest ladies thither came,
>   And plied in chariots daily,
> Or pawned their jewels for a sum
>   To venture in the Alley.'

The inordinate thirst of gain that had afflicted all ranks of society was not to be slaked even in the South Sea. Other schemes, of the most extravagant kind, were started. The share-lists were speedily filled up, and an enormous traffic carried on in shares, while, of course, every means were resorted to raise them to an artificial value in the market.

Contrary to all expectations, South-Sea stock fell when the bill received the royal assent. On 7 April the shares were quoted at three hundred and ten, and on the following day at two hundred and ninety. Already the directors had tasted the profits of their scheme, and it was not likely that they should quietly allow the stock to find its natural level without an effort to raise it. Immediately their busy emissaries were set to work. Every person interested in the success of the project endeavoured to draw a knot of listeners around him, to whom he expatiated on the treasures of the South American seas. Exchange Alley was crowded with attentive groups. One rumour alone, asserted with the utmost confidence, had an immediate effect upon the stock.

On 12 April, five days after the bill had become law, the directors opened their books for a subscription of a million, at the rate of 300*l.* for every 100*l.* capital. Such was the concourse of persons of all ranks, that this first subscription was found to amount to above two millions of original stock. It was to be paid at five payments, of 60*l.* each for every 100*l.* In a few days the stock advanced to three hundred and forty, and the subscriptions were sold for double the price of the first payment.

In the meantime, innumerable joint-stock companies started up everywhere. They soon received the name of Bubbles, the most appropriate that imagination could devise. The populace are often most happy in the nicknames they employ. None could be more apt than that of Bubbles. Some of them lasted for a week or a fortnight, and were no more heard of, while others could not even live out that short span of existence. Every evening produced new schemes, and every morning new projects. The highest of the aristocracy were as eager in this hot pursuit of gain as the most plodding jobber in Cornhill. The Prince of Wales became governor of one company, and is said to have cleared 40,000*l.* by his speculations. The Duke of Bridgewater started a scheme for the improvement of London and Westminster, and the Duke of Chandos another. There were nearly a hundred different projects, each more extravagant and deceptive than the other. To use the words of the *Political State*, they were 'set on foot and promoted by crafty knaves, then pursued by multitudes of covetous fools, and at last appeared to be, in effect, what their vulgar appellation denoted them to be – bubbles and mere cheats.' It was computed that near one million and a half sterling was won and lost by these unwarrantable practices, to the impoverishment of many a fool, and the enriching of many a rogue.

Some of these schemes were plausible enough, and, had they been undertaken at a time when the public mind was unexcited, might have been pursued with advantage to all concerned. But they were established merely with the view of raising the shares in the market. The projectors took the first opportunity of a rise to sell out, and next morning the scheme was at an end. Maitland, in his *History of London*, gravely informs us, that one of the projects which received great encouragement, was for the establishment of a company 'to make deal boards out of saw-dust.' This is no doubt intended as a joke; but there is abundance of evidence to shew that dozens of schemes, hardly a whit more reasonable, lived their little day, ruining hundreds ere they fell. One of them was for a wheel for perpetual motion – capital one million; another was 'for encouraging the breed of horses in England, and improving of glebe and church lands, and repairing and rebuilding parsonage and vicarage houses.' Why the clergy, who were so mainly interested in the latter clause, should have taken so much interest in the first, is only to be explained on the supposition that the scheme was projected by a knot of the fox-hunting parsons, once so common in England. The shares of this company were rapidly subscribed for. But the most absurd and preposterous of all, and which shewed, more completely than any other, the utter madness of the people, was one started by an unknown adventurer, entitled, '*A company for carrying on an undertaking of great advantage, but nobody to know what it is.*' Were not the fact stated by scores of credible witnesses, it would be impossible to believe that any person could have been duped by such a project. The man of genius who essayed this bold and successful in-road upon public credulity, merely stated in his prospectus that the required capital was half a million, in five thousand shares of 100*l.* each, deposit 2*l.* per share. Each subscriber, paying his deposit, would be entitled to 100*l.* per annum per share. How this immense profit was to be obtained, he did not condescend to inform them at that time, but promised that in a month full particulars should be duly announced, and a call made for the remaining 98*l.* of the subscription. Next morning, at nine o'clock, this great man opened an office in Cornhill. Crowds of people beset his door, and when he shut up at three o'clock, he found that no less than one thousand shares had been subscribed for, and the deposits paid. He was thus, in five hours, the winner of 2000*l.* He was philosopher enough to be contented with his venture, and set off the same evening for the Continent. He was never heard of again.

. . . Persons of distinction, of both sexes, were deeply engaged in all these bubbles; those of the male sex going to taverns and coffee-houses to meet their brokers, and the ladies resorting for the same purpose to the shops of milliners and haberdashers. But it did not follow that all these people believed in the feasibility of the schemes to which they subscribed; it was enough for their purpose that their shares would, by stock-jobbing arts, be soon raised to a premium, when they got rid of them with all expedition to the really credulous. So great was the confusion of the crowd in the alley, that shares in the same bubble were known to have been sold at the same instant ten per cent higher at one end of the alley than at the other. Sensible men beheld the extraordinary infatuation of the people with sorrow and alarm. There were some both in and out of parliament who foresaw clearly the ruin that was impending. Mr Walpole did not cease his gloomy forebodings. His fears were shared by all the thinking few, and impressed most forcibly upon the government. On 11 June, the day the parliament rose, the king published a proclamation, declaring that all these unlawful projects should be deemed public nuisances, and prosecuted accordingly, and forbidding any broker, under a penalty of five hundred pounds, from buying or selling any shares in them.

It is time, however, to return to the great South-Sea gulf, that swallowed the fortunes of so many thousands of the avaricious and the credulous. On 29 May, the stock had risen as high as five hundred, and about two-thirds of the government annuitants had exchanged the securities of the state for those of the South-Sea company. During the whole of the month of May the stock continued to rise, and on the 28th it was quoted at five hundred and fifty. In four days after this it took a prodigious leap, rising suddenly from five hundred and fifty to eight hundred and ninety. It was now the general opinion that the stock could rise no higher, and many persons took that opportunity of selling out, with a view of realizing their profits. Many noblemen and persons in the train of the king, and about to accompany him to Hanover, were also anxious to sell out. So many sellers, and so few buyers, appeared in the Alley on 3 June, that the stock fell at once from eight hundred and ninety to six hundred and forty. The directors were alarmed, and gave their agents orders to buy. Their efforts succeeded. Towards evening, confidence was restored, and the stock advanced to seven hundred and fifty. It continued at this price, with some slight fluctuation, until the company closed their books on 22 June.

It would be needless and uninteresting to detail the various arts employed by the directors to keep up the price of stock. It will be sufficient to state that it finally rose to one thousand per cent. It was quoted at this price in the commencement of August. The bubble was then full-blown, and began to quiver and shake preparatory to its bursting.

Many of the government annuitants expressed dissatisfaction against the directors. They accused them of partiality in making out the lists for shares in each subscription. Further uneasiness was occasioned by its being generally known that Sir John Blunt the chairman, and some others, had sold out. During the whole of the month of August the stock fell, and on 2 September it was quoted at seven hundred only.

The state of things now became alarming. To prevent, if possible, the utter extinction of public confidence in their proceedings, the directors summoned a general court of the whole corporation, to meet in Merchant Tailors' Hall on 8 September . . .

Several resolutions were passed at this meeting, but they had no effect upon the public. Upon the very same evening the stock fell to six hundred and forty, and on the morrow to five hundred and forty. Day after day it continued to fall, until it was as low as four hundred . . .

The day succeeding was a holiday (the 29th of September), and the Bank had a little breathing time. They bore up against the storm; but their former rivals, the South-Sea company, were wrecked upon it. Their stock fell to one hundred and fifty, and gradually, after various fluctuations, to one hundred and thirty-five . . .

In the hey-day of its blood, during the progress of this dangerous delusion, the manners of the nation became sensibly corrupted. The parliamentary inquiry, set on foot to discover the delinquents, disclosed scenes of infamy, disgraceful alike to the morals of the offenders and the intellects of the people among whom they had arisen. It is a deeply interesting study to investigate all the evils that were the result. Nations, like individuals, cannot become desperate gamblers with impunity. Punishment is sure to overtake them sooner or later.

During the progress of this famous bubble, England presented a singular spectacle. The public mind was in a state of unwholesome fermentation. Men were no longer satisfied with the slow but sure profits of cautious industry. The hope of boundless wealth for the morrow made them heedless and extravagant for today. A luxury, till then unheard of, was introduced, bringing in its train a corresponding laxity of morals. The overbearing insolence of ignorant men, who had arisen to sudden wealth by successful gambling, made men of true gentility of mind and manners blush that gold should have power to raise the unworthy in the scale of society. The haughtiness of some of these 'cyphering cits,' as they were termed by Sir Richard Steele, was remembered against them in the day of their adversity. In the parliamentary inquiry, many of the directors suffered more for their insolence than for their speculation. One of them, who, in the full-blown pride of an ignorant rich man, had said that he would feed his horse upon gold, was reduced almost to bread and water for himself; every haughty look, every over-bearing speech, was set down, and repaid them a hundredfold in poverty and humiliation.

The state of matters all over the country was so

alarming that George I shortened his intended stay in Hanover, and returned in all haste to England. He arrived on 11 November, and parliament was summoned to meet on 8 December. In the meantime, public meetings were held in every considerable town of the empire, at which petitions were adopted, praying the vengeance of the legislature upon the South-Sea directors, who, by their fraudulent practices, had brought the nation to the brink of ruin. Nobody seemed to imagine that the nation itself was as culpable as the South-Sea company. Nobody blamed the credulity and avarice of the people—the degrading lust of gain, which had swallowed up every nobler quality in the national character, or the infatuation which had made the multitude run their heads with such frantic eagerness into the net held out for them by scheming projectors. These things were never mentioned. The people were a simple, honest, hard-working people, ruined by a gang of robbers, who were to be hanged, drawn, and quartered without mercy.

Saint Paul's Cathedral

[16] Legends surrounding the Roman temple on the site of Saint Paul's (4th century); from *Old & New London* by W. Thornbury.

Camden, the Elizabethan historian, revived an old tradition that a Roman temple to Diana once stood where St Paul's was afterwards built; and he asserts that in the reign of Edward III an incredible quantity of ox-skulls, staghorns, and boars' tusks, together with some sacrificial vessels, were exhumed on this site. Selden . . . derived the name of London from two Welsh words, 'Llan-den' – church of Diana. Dugdale, to confirm these traditions, drags a legend . . . to the effect that during the Diocletian persecution, in which St Alban, a centurion, was martyred, the Romans demolished a church standing on the site of St Paul's, and raised a temple to Diana on its ruins, while in Thorny Island, Westminster, St Peter, in the like manner, gave way to Apollo.

[17] The building of Saint Paul's (604); from *The Ecclesiastical History of the English people* by Bede.

In the year of our Lord 604, Augustine, Archbishop of Britain, consecrated two Bishops, namely, Mellitus and Justus; Mellitus to preach to the province of the East Saxons, who are divided from Kent by the River Thames, and border on the eastern sea. Their metropolis is the City of London, situated on the bank of the aforesaid river, and is the mart of many nations resorting to it by sea and land. At that time Sebert, nephew to Ethelbert (the King of Kent whom Augustine converted) by his sister Ricula, reigned over the nation, though under subjection to Ethelbert, who had command over all the nations of the English as far as the River Humber. But when this province (the East Saxons) also received the word of truth by the preaching of Mellitus, King Ethelbert built the church of St Paul in the City of London, where he and his successors should have their Episcopal seat.

[18] Miracles at the tomb of Saint Erkenwald (c. 8th century); from *The Saint of London. The Life and Miracles of Saint Erkenwald*, edited and translated by E. Gordon Whatley.

Miracle 14 *Concerning the foiling of an attempt by some thieves to steal his body, and concerning the translation, and the supernatural enlargement of the sarcophagus, with the concurrent miracles*

It was imputed to several English monasteries at that time that, astonished at the fame of Erkenwald's miracles, they wanted to steal the body of the saint by night. So it happened that in the dead of night, a goodly number of men broke down the doors of the crypt where the saint was buried and coming to the altar gates dared, with shameless audacity, to begin to break their way in.

But the noise they were making awoke a youth, just barely out of boyhood, who habitually spent the night alone in the church and who had the job, along with two boys from the cathedral school, of guarding the place. His shouting and yelling frightened the crowd of thieves out of their wits, so much so that, disheartened by this divine judgement, at the sound of the mighty little fellow's voice they ran off at top speed back through the door by which they had entered.

Although the custodians of the upper church added their own shouts to this uproar and called for help by ringing the bell, they were unable to catch the thieves. But they made great joy over the watchmen for their opportune vigilance, until the following morning.

When morning came, however, we appointed eight priests to be watchmen to guard the precious and holy treasure until, after three days, we could enclose the saint's relics in a safer place which was to be got ready for them in the meantime.

And so when all things were prepared for the rite, and the priests with crucifixes and candles were present in readiness for this holy ceremony, we came in procession, singing litanies, to the tomb of Bishop Erkenwald, and having raised the lid of the wooden shrine, we found the most sacred body still protected by the same seals with which it had long before been secured.

Certainly we had not announced any of this to any one in the city, but divine providence brought it about that a crowd of people assembled and those who were outside the doors, their way being blocked by the great press inside, tore the very doors off the hinges and posts, refusing to be cheated of their desire, which was to see with us the inexpressibly holy rite.

What more? Since we could not withstand the onrush of the multitude any longer, we picked up the lead coffin in which the most holy body was resting, and tearfully we bore it to the new home that had been prepared for it. And lo, all our preparation appeared to be in vain, for the coffin was clearly too large both in length and breadth, for the structure we had built to house it. But then a marvellous thing happened. For the sake of him who was being denied burial by the craftman's ignorance, the opening in the stone was made larger by the right hand of him who extends the heavens. When the saint was being placed inside it, the hardness of the slabs became soft, the stone forgot its natural condition and submitted to the gaze of its creator.

Truly I myself who write these things found our stone housing fitted the measurements of the lead coffin as well as if it had been constructed by rule and plumb-line to the exact size of the coffin. For I frequently checked it myself with my own hands, and, God be my witness, I could not fit my finger between coffin and stone at any point.

Those present affirmed that the same thing had happened once to the most holy Ethelburga, his sister. Nor is there any doubt that the wiser men present also called to mind what the venerable Bede, jewel among Englishmen, wrote concerning the holy king, Sebbe. Filled with boundless joy, therefore, writing the *Te Deum* with such fervour that the faces of clergy and people alike streamed with pious tears.

And thus was the body of the most holy Erkenwald translated, in the year eleven hundred and forty after the incarnation of the Lord, in the month of February, on the sixteenth day of the month.

Two miracles in particular shone forth in this translation, besides those we have told already and many others we will pass over so as not to be tedious. One of them, which happened in front of everyone, involved one of our canons, who by chance at that time was sick with a fever; the other befell a boy who was not present but who for half a year and more had been sickening even unto death. The one was healed for the benefit of those present at the translation, the other for the benefit of those not present. As for the former, it was the saint's close presence that relieved him, while the latter was healed by a sprinkling of the dust from the wooden shrine in which he had lain.

The master of this boy, Theoldus our colleague, canon of the church of the blessed Martin situated in the city of London, reported that as soon as he gave the dust he had collected, in water, to the sick boy, he came out of the illness completely. He added also that he filled the nostrils of the sick boy with the slight odour of the incense which he had found in the same wooden shrine and, as if the incense were driving it forth, banished every trace of the disease . . .

[19] Henry V returns to London after the battle of Agincourt (1415); from *Gesta Henri Quinti* (The Deeds of Henry V), edited by F. Taylor and J. S. Roskell.

When the tower at the entrance to the bridge was reached, there was seen placed high on top of it, and representing as it were the entrance into the city's jurisdiction, an image of a giant of astonishing size who, looking down upon the king's face, held, like a champion, a great axe in his right hand and, like a warder, the keys of the city hanging from a baton in his left. At his right side stood a figure of a woman, not much smaller in size, wearing a scarlet mantle and adornments appropriate to her sex; and they were like a man and his wife who, in their richest attire, were bent upon seeing the eagerly awaited face of their lord and welcoming him with abundant praise. And, all around them, projecting from the ramparts, staffs bearing the royal arms and trumpets, clarions, horns ringing out in multiple harmony embellished the tower, and the face of it bore this choice and appropriate legend inscribed on the wall: *Civitas Regis Iusticie* . . . And from the very top of the castle to the bottom, on the towers, ramparts, arches, and pillars, were innumerable boys, like a host of archangels and angels, beautiful in heavenly splendour, in pure white raiment, with gleaming wings, their youthful locks entwined with jewels and other resplendent and exquisite ornaments; and they let fall upon the king's head as he passed beneath golden coins and leaves of laurel, singing together in perfect time and in sweetly sounding chant accompanied by organs, to the honour of Almighty God and as a token of victory, this angelic hymn, following their texts: *Te deum laudamus, te dominum confitemur*, etc.

And when, further on, they had come to the tower of the conduit in the way out from Cheapside towards St Paul's, they saw encircling that tower, about half-way up, many canopied niches skilfully contrived, and in each one was a most exquisite young maiden, like a statue, decked out with emblems of chastity, richly fashioned; all of them, crowned with laurels and girt about with golden belts, held in their hands chalices of gold from which, with gentlest breath scarcely perceptible, they puffed out round leaves of gold upon the king's head as he passed by. And, higher up, the tower was covered by a canopy, sky-blue in colour, with clouds inwoven, massed with great artistry. There adorned the very top of it the figure of an archangel seemingly made of the brightest gold, and with other vivid colours resplendently intermingled, and the four poles on which the canopy was borne were themselves upheld by four angels of a design no less artistic. And underneath the canopy was, enthroned, a figure of majesty in the form of a sun and, emitting dazzling rays, it shone more brightly than all else. Around it, in heavenly splendour, archangels moved rhythmically together, psalming sweetly and accompanied by every kind of musical instrument, following their texts . . .

And apart from the dense crowd of men standing still or hurrying along the streets, and the great number of those, men and women together, gazing from windows and openings, however small, along the route from the bridge, so great was the throng of people in Cheapside, from one end to the other, that the horsemen were only just able, although not without difficulty, to ride through. And the upper rooms and windows on both sides were packed with some of the noblest ladies and womenfolk of the kingdom and men of honour and renown, who had assembled for this pleasing spectacle, and who were so very becoming and elegantly decked out in cloth of gold, fine linen, and scarlet, and other rich apparel of various kinds, that no one could recall there ever having previously been in London a greater assemblage or a more noble array.

Amid these public expressions of praise and the display made by the citizens, however, the king himself, wearing a gown of purple, proceeded, not in exalted pride and with an imposing escort or impressively large retinue, but with an impassive countenance and at a dignified pace, and with only a few of the most trusted members of his household in attendance, there following him, under a guard of knights, the dukes, counts, and marshal, his prisoners. Indeed, from his quiet demeanour, gentle pace, and sober progress, it might have been gathered that the king, silently pondering the matter in his heart, was rendering thanks and glory to God alone, not to man. And then, after he had visited the thresholds of the Apostles Peter and Paul, he departed to his palace of Westminster, the citizens escorting him.

[20] The Pope's sentence against Luther is published at Paul's Cross (1521); from *Chronicles of London*, edited by C. L. Kingsford.

The Lord Thomas Wolsey, by the grace of God Legate de Latere, Cardinal of St Cecilia and Archbishop of York, came unto St Paul's Church, with the most part of the Bishops of the realm, where he was received with procession, and censed by Mr Richard Pace, the Dean of that Church. He was conducted to the high altar by four Doctors holding a canopy over him, and there made his oblation. He proceeded under his cloth of state, and took his seat on a scaffold near Paul's Cross, with his two crosses; on either side, the Pope's Ambassador, the Archbishop of Canterbury, and the Imperial Ambassador; the Bishop of Durham sat below, with other prelates. Fisher, Bishop of Rochester, preached by the Pope's command against one Martinus Eleutherius and his works, because 'he erred sore and spake against the holy faith,' and denounced them accursed which kept any of his books; and there 'were many burned in the said churchyard of the said books during the sermon'. After that the Lord Cardinal went home to dinner with all the other prelates.

[21] The Pope's authority is denied at Paul's Cross (1536); from *A Chronicle of England by Charles Wriothesley*, edited by W. D. Hamilton.

The Soundaie of Quinquegesima, being the 27th daie of Februarie and Leepe yeare, A.D. 1535[–6], preached at Paules Crosse the Bushoppe of Durhame, named Dr Dunstall, sometime Bishopp of London, and afore that, being Mr of the Rolls; and their were present at his sermon the Archbishopp of Canterberie with eight other bishopps, sitting at the crosse before the preacher; and the Lord Chauncellor of Englande, the Duke of Norfolke, the Duke of Suffolke, with six Erles and divers other lordes, stoode behinde the preacher within the pulpit, and also fower monkes of the Charterhouse of London were brought to the said sermon, which denied the King to be supreame heade of the Church of Englande. And their the said preacher declared the profession of the Bishopp of Rome when he is elected Pope, according to the confirmation of eight universall general counsels, which were congregate for the faith of all Christendome; and everie Pope taketh an othe on the articles, promising to observe, keepe, and hould all that the said counsels confirmed, and to dampen all that they dampned; and how he, contrarie to his oth, hath usurped his power and aucthoritie over all Christendome; and also how uncharitably he had handled our Prince, King Henrie the Eight, in marying [him to] his brother's wife, contrarie to Godes lawes and also against his owne promise and decrees, which he opened by scriptures and by the cannons of the Appostles; and also how everie Kinge hath the highe power under God, and ought to be the supreame head over all spirituall prelates, which was a goodlie and gracious hearing to all the audience being their present at the same sermon. And in his prayers he said, after this manner, ye shall pray for the universall church of all Christendome, and especiall for the prosperous estate of our Soveraigne and Emperour King Henrie the Eight, being the onelie supreame head of this realme of Englande; and he declared also in his said sermon how that the Cardinalls of Rome bee but curattes and decons of the cittie and province of Rome, and how that everie curate of any parrish have as much power as they have, according to scripture, save onelie that the Pope of Rome hath made them so high aucthorities onelie for to exhalt his name and power in Christen realms for covetousness, as by his owne decrees he evidentlie their approved.

[22] Catholic icons are destroyed at Paul's (1538–1559); from *A Chronicle of England by Charles Wriothesley*, edited by W. D. Hamilton.

The xxviith daie of November [AD 1547], being the first Soundaie of Aduent, preched at Poules Crosse Doctor Barlowe, Bishopp of Sainct Davides, where he shewed a picture of the resurrection of our Lord made with vices, which putt out his legges of sepulchree and blessed with his hand, and turned his heade; and their stoode afore the pilpitt the imag of our Ladie which they of Poules had lapped in seerecloth, which was hid in a corner of Poules Church, and found by the visitors in their visitation. And in his sermon he declared the great abhomination of idolatrie in images, with other fayned ceremonies contrarie to scripture, to the extolling of Godes glorie, and to the great compfort of the awdience. After the sermon the boyes brooke the idols in peaces . . .

Saterdaye 12 August [1559] the aulter in Paules, with the roode, and Marye and John in the rood-loft, were taken downe, and the Prebendaries and Pettie Canons commaunded to leave of the grey amises of furre, and to use onelye a surplesse in the service tyme, by the commaundement of Dr Grindall, Bishop of London elect, and

Dr Mey, the new deane of Paules, and other of the commissioners.

This moneth allso, on the Eeven of St Bartlemewe, the daye and the morrowe after, were burned in Paules Church-yarde, Cheape, and divers other places of London, all the roodes and images that stoode in the parishe churches. In some places the coapes, vestments, aulter clothes, bookes, banners, sepulchres, and other ornaments of the churches were burned; which cost above 2,000*l*. renuinge agayne in Queen Maries tyme.

[23] A Pageant at Saint Paul's for the coronation of Queen Mary (1553); from *The Chronicle of Queen Jane and of two years of Queen Mary*, edited by J. G. Nichols.

Note, the last daie of September 1553, the quene came thoroughe London towardes hir coronation, sytting in a charret of tyssue, drawne with vj. horses, all betrapped with redd velvett. She sat in a gown of blew velvet, furred with powdered armyen, hanging on hir heade a call of clothe of tynsell besett with perle and ston, and about the same apon her hed a rond circlet of gold, moche like a hooped garlande, besett so richely with many precyouse stones that the value therof was inestymable; the said call and circle being so massy and ponderous that she was fayn to beare uppe hir hedd with hir handes; and a canopy was borne over the char. Before hir rydd a number of gentlemen and knightes, and then dyverse judges, then diverse doctours of dyvynity; then followed certeyn bush-opes; after theym came certayn lordes; then followed most part of hir counsaille; after whom followed xiij. knights of the bathe, every one in thir order, the names wherof were theis, the erle of Devonshire, the lorde of Cardyf, son to the erle of Pembroke, the erle of Arundell's son, being lorde Mountryvers. Then followed the lorde of Winchester, being lorde chauncellor, the merques of Winchester, lorde highe treasurer, having the seale and mace before them; next came the duke of Norfolk, and after him the erle of Oxforde, who bare the sworde before hir; sir Edward Hastinges led hir horse in his hande. After the quenes chariott cam another chariott having canapie all of one covereng, with cloth of sillver all whitt, and vj. horses betrapped with the same, bearing the said charyat; and therin sat at the ende, with hir face forwarde, the lady Elizabeth; and at the other ende, with her backe forwarde, the lady Anne of Cleves. Then cam theyre sondry gentyll-women rydyng on horses traped with redd vellvet, after that charyet, and their gownes and kertelles of red vellvet likewise. Then rid sir Thomas Stradlyng after theym; then followed ij. other charyots covered with redd sattyn, and the horses betraped with the same; and certayne gentell-women betwen every of the saide charyots rydyng in chrymesyn satteyn, their horses betraped with the same. The nomber of the gentill- women that rydd were xlvj. in noumber, besides theym that wer in the charyots.

At Phanchurche was one pageaunt made by the Gene-ways, and ther a childe dressed in a girles apparell was borne uppe by ij. men siting in a chaire, and gave the quene a salutation. At Gracechurche corner ther was another pageant made by the Esterlings, and theron was made a mount on hie, and a littell condyt which ran wyn. Upon the saide mount stoode iiij. childeren, which with certayn salutacions did likewise gratefye the quene. Over that ther was a device that maister *(blank)* flyed downe from the tope of the pageant as she ryd by. At the ende of Gracechurche ther was another pageant made by the Florentyns, very highe, on the toppe wherof ther stode iiij. pictures, and on the syde of them, on the highest toppe, ther stoode an angell clothed in grene, with a trompete in his hande, and he was made with suche a device that when the trompeter, who stoode secretly in the pageant, ded blow his trompet, the angell dyd put his trompet to his mowth, as though it should be he that blewe the same, to the marvaling of many ignorant persons. The pageant was made with iij. thorough-fares like gates, and on either syde of the great gat ther dyd hang ij. tables of clothe of sillver, wherin was wrytten certayn verses; the one table in Latten, and the other in Inglyshe myter, gratefyeng. And in the myds of the saide pageant ther stoode vj. persons clothed in longe colord gownes with coputances hats, who gave hir a salutacion of goode lucke. At the condyt in Cornehill, ther was a very prity pageant made very gorgosly, wheron ther set iij. childeren clothed in womens apparell; the myddlemost of theym, having a crowne on hir hedd, and a septer in hir hande, was called Grace; the other on her right hand, called Vertue, a cupp; and the other on her left hande, called Nature, a branch of olyf. And when the quene cam by, they in order kneled down, and every one of them sung certayn verses of gratefyeng the quene. Ther sonded also trompets on high.

At the great conduit ther was also another pageant made by the cyty. At the lytell condyt ther was another pageant, wheron stoode certayn children in women's apparell, and after a certayn oracion and salutacion ther was geven the quene, by one of the children, for the cyty, in a goodly purse a thousande li. which she most thankfully receyved.

At the scholehouse in Palles church ther was certayn children and men sung dyverse staves in gratefying the quene; ther she stayed a good while and gave diligent ere to their song.

At this tyme a fellow who had made ij. scaffoldes apon the tope of Polles steeple, the one upon the ball therof, and the other upon the tope therof above that, and had set out viij. streamers vean grat apon the same scaffolde, having the red crosse and the sworde as the arms of the cyty of London doth geve; and he himself standing apon the veary toppe or backe of the wether cocke, dy(d) shake a lytel flag with his hande, after standing on one foot dy(d) shak his other legg, and then knelled on his knees apon the saide wether cock, to the great mervayle and wondering of all the people which behelde him, because yt was thought a mattyer impossyble.

Over agaynst the deanes house in Polles churche yarde ther was another pageant, wher on ether syde stoode sondery persons singing dyverse salutacions as the quene cam by, and certayn lytell children stoode apon the pageant on highe, with tapers light and burning, which tapers wer made of most swete perfumes.

[24] Elizabeth I interrupts a Sermon at Saint Paul's (1565); from *A History of Saint Paul's*, edited by W. R. Matthews and W. M. Atkins.

The day was Ash Wednesday, 1565, and the Queen had come in person to Paul's Cross accompanied by the Spanish ambassador. She was doubtless anxious not to embarrass her companion and was consequently not pleased when the dean, in the course of his sermon, condemned the use of images, handling his subject 'very roughly'.

'Leave that alone', Elizabeth shouted from her seat. The zealous preacher did not hear and continued his tirade. 'To your text, Mr Dean,' she cried, her voice growing more angry, 'To your text! Leave that; we have heard enough of that! To your subject!'

The unfortunate Dr Nowell completely lost his nerve. He managed to stammer out a few inaudible words, but was then quite unable to continue. Elizabeth stamped off in a rage with the ambassador. The congregation, at least so we are told, were in tears. Archbishop Parker, seeing the dean 'utterly dismayed', took him 'for pity home to Lambeth to dinner and wrote Cecil a respectful but firm remonstrance'.

[25] John Donne preaches his last sermon at Saint Paul's (1631); from *Life of John Donne* by I. Walton.

He was appointed to preach upon his old constant day, the first Friday in Lent; he had notice of it, and had in his sickness so prepared for that employment, that as he had long thirsted for it, so he resolved his weakness should not hinder his journey; he came therefore to London some few days before his appointed day of preaching. At his coming thither, many of his friends – who with sorrow saw his sickness had left him but so much flesh as did only cover his bones – doubted his strength to perform that task, and did therefore dissuade him from undertaking it, assuring him, however, it was like to shorten his life; but he passionately denied their requests, saying he would not doubt that that God, who in so many weaknesses had assisted him with an unexpected strength, would now withdraw it in his last employment; professing an holy ambition to perform that sacred work. And when, to the amazement of some beholders, he appeared in the pulpit, many of them thought he presented himself not to preach mortification by a living voice, but mortality by a decayed body and a dying face. And doubtless many did secretly ask that question in Ezekiel: 'Do these bones live? or, can that soul organize that tongue, to speak so long as the sand in that glass will move towards its centre, and measure out an hour of this dying man's unspent life? Doubtless it cannot.' And yet, after some faint pauses in his zealous prayer, his strong desires enabled his weak body to discharge his memory of his preconceived meditations, which were of dying; the text being, 'To God the Lord belong the issues from death.' Many that then saw his tears, and heard his faint and hollow voice, professing they thought the text prophetically chosen, and that Dr Donne had preached his own funeral sermon.

Being full of joy that God had enabled him to perform this desired duty, he hastened to his house; out of which he never moved, till, like St Stephen, 'he was carried by devout men to his grave.' . . .

[26] Saint Paul's is occupied by soldiers during the Republic (1649–1660); from *The History of the Rebellion* by E. H. Clarendon.

The Cathedral was left to chance, exposed at least to neglect, too often to wanton or inevitable mischief. As it was, the only part secure was the east end, set apart for the congregation of Burgess. From Inigo Jones's noble portico the statues of the two kings (James I and Charles I) were tumbled ignominiously down, and dashed to pieces. The portico was let out for mean shops, to sempstresses and hucksters, with chambers above and staircases leading to them. The body of the Church, Dugdale, who saw it, declares, with sorrow and bitterness of heart, became a cavalry barrack and stable. The pavement was trampled by horses, the tombs left to the idle amusement of the rude soldiers, who, even if religious, were not much disposed to reverence the remains of a Popish edifice . . .

[27] Paul's Cross is demolished (1650s); from *Annals of Saint Paul's Cathedral* by Henry H. Milman.

The famous adjunct to the Cathedral was not left to slow decay. It might have been supposed that Paul's Cross, from which so many sermons had been preached in the course of years, some, as has appeared, as fiercely condemnatory of Popish superstition as the most devout Puritan could have wished; that the famous pulpit, which we might have expected Presbyterian and Independent divines, the most powerful and popular, would have aspired to fill, and from thence hoped to sway to their own purposes, and to guide to assured salvation, the devout citizens of London, would have been preserved as a tower of strength to the good cause. But it was (called) a cross, and a cross was obstinately, irreclaimably Popish. (It had quite lost its original appearance and shape, and had in the course of time become a kind of octagonal garden-house or booth, with open sides, and steps leading up to it, and a bulging roof, all of decadent architecture.) Down it went . . . Its place knew it no more; tradition alone pointed to where it had stood; it never rose again . . .

[28] Saint Paul's is destroyed in the Great Fire (1666); from *Diaries* by John Evelyn.

3 September:

I went on foot to (Bankside) and saw the whole south parts of the City burning from Cheapside to the Thames, and all along Cornhill (for it likewise kindled back against the wind as well as forward), Tower Street, Fenchurch Street, Gracechurch Street, and so along to Baynard's Castle, and was now taking hold of St Paul's Church, to which the scaffolds (for repairs) contributed exceedingly . . .

4 September.

The burning still rages, and it was now gotten as far as the Inner Temple; all that street, the Old Bailey, Ludgate Hill, Warwick Lane, Newgate, Paul's Chain, Watling Street now flaming, and most of it reduced to ashes; the stones of Paul's flew like grenades, the melting lead running down the streets in a stream, and the very pavements glowing with fiery redness, so as no horse nor man was able to tread on them, and the demolition had stopped all the passages, so that no help could be applied. The Eastern wind still more impetuously driving the flames forward, nothing but the Almighty power of God was able to stop them, for vain was the help of man . . .

7 September.

I went this morning on foot from Whitehall as far as London Bridge, through the late Fleet Street, Ludgate Hill, by St Paul's, Cheapside, Exchange, Bishopsgate, Aldersgate, and out to Moorfields, thence through Cornhill, etc; with extraordinary difficulty, clambering over heaps of yet smoking rubbish, and frequently mistaking where I was; the ground under my feet so hot that it even burnt the soles of my shoes. In the meantime His Majesty got to the

Tower by water, to demolish the houses about the graff, which being entirely built about it, had they taken fire and attacked the White Tower where the magazine of powder lay, would undoubtedly not only have beaten down and destroyed all the bridge, but sunk and torn the vessels in the river, and rendered the demolition beyond all expression for several miles about the country.

At my return I was infinitely concerned to find that goodly Church St Paul's now a said ruin, and that beautiful portico (for structure comparable to any in Europe, as not long before repaired by the late King), now rent in pieces, flakes of vast stone split asunder, and nothing remaining entire but the inscription in the architrave, showing by whom it was built, which had not one letter of it defaced. It was astonishing to see what immense stones the heat had in manner calcined, so that all the ornaments, columns, friezes, capitals and projectures of massy Portland stone flew off, even to the very roof, where a sheet of lead covering a great space (no less than six acres by measure) was totally melted; the ruins of the vaulted roof falling broke into St Faith's, which being filled with the magazines (stores) of books belonging to the Stationers, and carried thither for safety, they were all consumed, burning for a week following. It is also observable that the lead over the altar at the east end was untouched, and among the divers monuments the body of one Bishop remained entire. Thus lay in ashes that most venerable Church, one of the most antient pieces of early piety in the Christian world, besides near 100 more.

[29] The foundation stone is laid at Wren's Saint Paul's (1675); from *The Life and work of Sir Christopher Wren from Parentalia or Memoirs of his son Christopher Wren.*

In the beginning of the new Works of St Paul's, an Incident was taken notice of by some People as a memorable Omen, when the Surveyor in Person had set out upon the Place, the Dimensions of the great Dome, and fixed upon the Centre; a common Labourer was ordered to bring a flat Stone from the Heaps of Rubbish (such as should first come to Hand) to be laid for a Mark and Directions to the Masons; the Stone which was immediately brought & laid down for that Purpose, happened to be a piece of a Gravestone, with nothing remaining of the Inscription but this single Word in large Capitals, RESURGAM [I will arise].

[30] Saint Paul's Walk (18th century); from *Microcosmographie* by J. Earle.

Paul's Walk is the land's epitome, as you may call it; the lesser isle of Great Britain. It is more than this; the whole world's map, which you may here discern in its perfected motion, justling and turning. It is a heap of stones and men, with a vast confusion of languages; and were the steeple not sanctified, nothing liker Babel. The noise in it is like that of bees, a strange hum, mixed of walking tongues and feet; it is a kind of still roar or loud whisper. It is the great exchange of all discourse, and no business whatsoever but is here striving and afoot. It is the synod of all parties politic, jointed and laid together, in most serious position, and they are not half so busy at the Parliament . . . It is the market of young lecturers, who you may cheapen here at all rates and sizes. It is the general mint of all famous lies, which are here, like the legends of Popery, first coined and stamped in the Church. All inventions are emptied here and not few pockets. The best sign of a temple in it is that it is the thieves' sanctuary, which rob more safely in a crowd than in a wilderness, whilst every searcher is a bush to hide them. . . . The visitants are all men without exceptions, but the principal inhabitants and possessors are stale knights and captains out of service; men of long rapiers and breeches, which after all turn merchants here and traffic for news. Some make it a preface to their dinner, and travel for a stomach; but thriftier men make it their ordinary, and board here very cheap.

[31] Lord Nelson's funeral (1805); from *Annals of Saint Paul's Cathedral* by Henry H. Milman.

The Cathedral opened wide her doors to receive the remains of the great admiral, followed, it might almost be said, by the whole nation as mourners. The death of Nelson, whose victories of Aboukir and Copenhagen had raised his name above any other in our naval history, had stirred the English heart to its depths of pride and sorrow. The manifest result of that splendid victory at Trafalgar was the annihilation of the fleets of France and Spain, and it might seem the absolute conquest of the ocean, held for many years as a subject province of Great Britain. The procession, first by water, then by land, was, of course, magnificent, as far as generous cost could command magnificence.

The body was preceded to St Paul's by all that was noble and distinguished in the land; more immediately by all the Princes of the Blood, headed by the Prince of Wales (afterwards George IV). The chief mourner was Admiral of the Fleet, Sir Peter Parker.

The place of interment was under the centre of the dome. As a youth I was present, and remember the solemn effect of the sinking of the coffin. I heard, or fancied that I heard, the low wail of the sailors who bore and encircled the remains of their admiral.

By a singular chance, the body of Nelson is deposited (beneath) a sarcophagus in which Cardinal Wolsey expected to repose.

[32] The Duke of Wellington's funeral (1868); from *Annals of Saint Paul's Cathedral* by Henry H. Milman.

The scene under the dome was in the highest degree imposing. The two Houses of Parliament assembled in full numbers: on the north side of the area the House of Commons, behind these the civic authorities, the City companies and the members of the Corporation: on the south side of the area the peers, behind them the clergy of the Cathedral and their friends. The foreign ambassadors sat on seats extending (from the entrance of the choir) to the organ gallery (across the chancel). Every arcade, every available space, was crowded; from 12,000 to 15,000 persons (it was difficult closely to calculate) were present. The body was received by the Bishop, and the Dean, and the clergy, with the choir, at the west door, and conducted to the central area under the dome, on which shone down the graceful coronal of light which enriched it under the Whispering Gallery. The pall was borne by eight of the most distinguished general officers who had survived the wars of their great commander, or other glorious wars in which their country had been engaged.

The service was the simple burial office of the Church of England, with the fine music of Croft and Purcell wedded to that office, and other music, including an anthem of a very high order, composed by the organist, Mr Goss.

The prayers and lesson were read by the Dean ... Nothing could be imagined more solemn than the responses of all the thousands present, who repeated, as had been suggested, the words of the Lord's Prayer. It fulfilled the sublime Biblical phrase, 'Like the roar of many waters'; only that it was clear and distinct: the sad combined prayer, as it were, of the whole nation.

The gradual disappearance of the coffin, as it slowly sank into the vault below, was a sight which will hardly pass from the memory of those who witnessed it.

The sarcophagus which, after some time, was prepared to receive the remains of Wellington, was in perfect character with that great man. A mass of Cornish porphyry (weighing 17 tons) wrought in the severest and simplest style, unadorned, and because unadorned more grand and impressive; in its grave splendour, and, it might seem, time-defying solidity; it is emblematic of him who, unlike most great men, the more he is revealed to posterity, shows more substantial, unboastful, unquestionable greatness.

[33] Saint Paul's in wartime (1939–45) by W. R. Matthews; from *A History of Saint Paul's*, edited by W. R. Matthews and W. M. Atkins.

The last three months of 1940 and the first three of 1941 were the time of the most unrelaxing strain on the Cathedral Watch. No night was peaceful and sleep was hard to get. 29 December 1940 was a night when catastrophe seemed imminent and for a time the dome was on fire. The great fire raid on the City began with a shower of incendiary bombs which caused fires if not immediately extinguished. A large section of the buildings near St Paul's, including the chapter house, were gutted by fire and the flaming timbers, which were whirled by the wind on to the Cathedral roof, added to its danger. All the incendiaries which fell on St Paul's were dealt with effectively, except one, which lodged in the dome and set the timbers of which it is constructed on fire. The hoses provided for such an emergency were of no use, because the water mains failed during the first few minutes of the raid and the arrangements made by the authorities to pump water from the Thames proved of no avail – the tide was low, we were told. A great spurt of flame rose from the dome, causing the representatives of American newspapers to cable that St Paul's was in flames. At this juncture Mr Winston Churchill sent a message to the City that St Paul's must be saved at all costs. It was saved – though one does not know precisely how. Was it by the efforts of the watch who climbed up into the dome at great peril with stirrup pumps and buckets of water, or was it by what men call 'chance' that the bomb fell down into the stone gallery where it could be extinguished before it had started a conflagration beyond control? However that may be, there was no major damage to the Cathedral at the end of this night of terror, but we suffered the loss of Wren's chapter house and, with it, some archives in the shape of chapter minutes together with a beautiful table of the Wren period which we had neglected to move. In this raid two of the Cathedral houses in Amen Court were destroyed and others damaged, none of them of Wren's building.

On the night of 16–17 April 1940, St Paul's received its most serious wound which might well have proved mortal. At 2.50 a.m., a bomb pierced the roof of the north transept and exploded in the Cathedral, bringing down much masonry which crashed through the floor and destroyed most of the organ pipes which had been stored there for safety. No one was killed or seriously injured, which is surprising because the watch was fully deployed on the roof. The damage to the building was extensive and alarming. Only after careful examination could its full extent be determined and it was found that, in addition to the gaping holes in the roof and the floor, the walls had been pushed outwards by the blast. The entrance to the transept, which bore Wren's famous epitaph, *Si monumentum requiris, circumspice*, was wrecked and all that remained of the glass throughout the Cathedral was shattered. But the worst had not happened. All those who were in St Paul's when the bomb exploded described the effect as 'like an earthquake' and it seemed incredible that the dome should not be shaken or displaced, but so it was, and we were spared the almost impossible task of shoring it up. Once again, however, immediate steps had to be taken to prevent the destruction in the north transept from spreading, and once again Mr Allen and Mr Linge, with the Cathedral works staff, were equal to the occasion. On that same night, the Cathedral had a narrow escape from a mine which came down by parachute and landed near the site of St Paul's Cross without exploding. It was rendered harmless, though the mechanism was ticking over, by a gallant squad of the Royal Navy.

From that time until the end of the war no damage of any consequence was suffered by St Paul's. Though the dreaded flying bombs, V1 and V2, which made their appearance in January 1944, passed over and around us in large numbers, the Cathedral was not hit. One of the last of the V2s which came near us went off just as we were starting the Watch Night Service on New Year's Eve,

1945, breaking one of the few surviving windows in the crypt where the congregation was assembled. I shall always remember the reaction of the crowded worshippers, most of them in uniform. After a moment of complete silence, they burst into spontaneous laughter! The last V2 of all, so far as the City was concerned, was that of the morning of Saturday, 8 March 1945, which exploded in Smithfield causing terrible casualties. It left us unscathed though the blast shook the building and almost blew men who were working on the damaged deanery off the roof . . .

During the years of which I have been writing, the reader must remember that the Cathedral services continued unbroken, but of course not unaffected. For several long periods they were held in the crypt and when they were in the main body of the Cathedral it will be understood that the whole chancel was in a dangerous condition so that a temporary altar had to be erected under the dome. Not a few, including myself, felt regret when the intimacy of services in which we gathered round the altar changed back to a more impersonal atmosphere when the altar was again removed into the choir . . .

8 May 1945 is a day which lives in the memory of all who were in the City. VE day, the day of the German surrender, came almost suddenly and there was no time to prepare for it. The people spontaneously came to St Paul's, as the place where they could best express their feelings of thankfulness, relief, patriotic pride and aspiration for the future. Nine very simple services were provided, each of which was attended by a vast concourse. It is estimated that more than 30,000 joined in these services and many more came in the intervals to pray. In its own way, VE day was even more moving than the most impressive state Victory Thanksgiving Service on 13 May, at which the King and Queen were present—on this occasion the choir school finally returned from exile to its home, which had, almost miraculously, survived bombs and fire.

[34] Churchill's funeral (1965); from *The Crossman Diaries 1964–1970*, edited by A. Howard.

Winston's funeral. All through the week London had been working itself up for the great day. The lying-in-state in Westminster Hall had taken place on Wednesday, Thursday and Friday. I went on all three evenings, taking Molly and our doorman, Arthur, on one night, and Anne and Tommy Balogh the second night, and then on the third night Mr Large who cuts my hair. Each time one saw, even at one o'clock in the morning, the stream of people pouring down the steps of Westminster Hall towards the catafalque. Outside the column wound through the garden at Millbank, then stretched over Lambeth Bridge, right round the corner to St Thomas's Hospital. As one walked through the streets one felt the hush and one noticed the cars stopping suddenly and the people stepping out into the quietness and walking across to Westminster Hall. We as Members of Parliament could just step into the Hall through our side door.

I really hadn't wanted to go to the funeral. But it was obvious that I couldn't be known to have stayed away and I was a bit surprised, but also relieved, when Anne finally rang up and said she would like to go too and would come up on Friday. My chief memory is of the pall-bearers, in particular poor Anthony Eden, literally ashen grey, looking as old as Clement Attlee. And then of the coffin being carried up the steps by those poor perspiring privates of the Guards, sweat streaming down their faces, each clutching the next in order to sustain the sheer weight. As they came past us they staggered and they weren't properly recovered when they had to bring the coffin down the steps again to put it on the gun carriage to be taken to Tower Bridge. My other chief memory was the superb way the trumpets sounded the Last Post and the Reveille. The trumpeters were right up in the Whispering Gallery, round the inside of the dome, and for the first time a trumpet had room to sound in a dimension, a hemisphere of its own. But, oh, what a faded, declining establishment surrounded me. Aged marshals, grey, dreary ladies, decadent Marlboroughs and Churchills. It was a dying congregation gathered there and I am afraid the Labour Cabinet didn't look too distinguished either. It felt like the end of an epoch, possibly even the end of a nation.

[35] Wedding of Prince Charles and Lady Diana (1981); from *Diana in Private* by Lady Colin Campbell.

All over the land and the world, people gravitated towards their television sets, irrespective of the time. No one, it seemed, wanted to miss the early morning preparations or the arrival of the many distinguished guests at St Paul's Cathedral. Everyone of consequence to the Royal Family, or of national interest to the government, trooped in at some point. From Nancy Reagan and Princess Grace of Monaco, to the deposed monarchs of Eastern Europe and the Household staff at Buckingham Palace, they all took their seats in Wren's historic edifice, to be joined, later on, by the immediate members of Diana's family. Her mother and grandmother, I was intrigued to notice, sat as far apart as it was possible to be, and remained so throughout the rest of the day. Nor was the Lord Chamberlain, whose responsibility the arrangements were, daunted by the anomalies of an extended family. Blood proved to be thicker than a marriage certificate, resulting in Raine Spencer's and Peter Shand Kydd's banishment to the general congregation. There was room too for only one formidable granny, so Queen Elizabeth The Queen Mother took her seat in the royal pews, facing those of the bride's family, without the distracting and detracting presence of the other *grande dame* with a penchant for pearls, hats and fussy costumes: Barbara Cartland . . .

The celebrations began the evening before. In Hyde Park, Prince Charles lit the first in a chain of 102 bonfires, following which there was a vast fireworks display illuminating London's skyline for nearly an hour. There were half a million onlookers in Hyde Park alone, and traffic came to a standstill, but no one minded. The air rang with good-natured celebration, presaging the mood of all. I was but one of the many residents of Belgravia, which flanks both Hyde Park and Buckingham Palace, who commented on how everyone seemed to become involved, treating the fireworks display, and, the next morning, the wedding, as if they were one gigantic party, and everyone, invited or otherwise, was a guest.

One person who remained out of view during that last evening was Diana herself. She was safely tucked up in bed, at Clarence House, to which she had moved for her last night as a commoner . . .

Diana went to her solitary bed early, to rest up for her big day, which had a 6.30 am start. After an enormous breakfast, 'to stop my tummy rumbling in St Paul's,' she received Kevin Shanley, the hairdresser from Headlines, to whom she would faithfully cling until he later baulked at giving her a new hairstyle for the State Opening of Parliament.

. . .When Diana's glass coach, pulled by Kestrel and Lady Penelope, two bays from the Royal Mews, pulled out from Clarence House into the Mall, she looked beautiful. Smiling radiantly, waving as she had been taught by Lady Susan Hussey, she was a veritable picture of loveliness beside her father. From that moment until the coach pulled up at the steps of St Paul's Cathedral, Diana presented a perfect façade . . .

The Prince of Wales presented a complementary picture of romance in his admiral's uniform, and as Diana began the three-and-a-half minute walk down the aisle on her father's arm, a treat was in store for the world. A great idealist and a perfectionist, Charles had taken pains over the service. A lover of music as well as architecture, he had chosen St Paul's as the setting because it could house a full orchestra and also had a world-famous boys' choir. In consultation with Sir David Willcocks, Director of the Royal College of Music, he selected a programme that was both joyous and moving, and included works by Purcell,

Handel and Jeremiah Clarke. These were performed by three orchestras, the Bach Choir, and the soprano Kiri Te Kanawa, who was made a Dame shortly afterwards by The Queen, upon the recommendation of her native New Zealand government.

Charles was greatly moved by the whole event. He told a cousin, 'There were several times when I was perilously close to crying from the sheer joy of it all. It was tremendous to learn that one was so appreciated, to feel that everyone cared so much, that people were there with one. It was magical.'

Diana mirrored Charles's feelings. She told a friend, 'It was heaven, amazing, wonderful, though I was so nervous when I was walking up the aisle that I swore my knees would knock and make a noise.'

The crowd outside played their part. Princess Katarina of Yugoslavia told me, 'When Diana said "I do" – or was it "I will"? – the crowd let out a huge roar which washed over us like a great wave. It felt as if there were no walls separating us from them. It really was the most extraordinary thing, and very affecting. Everyone was moved by the wonderful feeling of oneness which we all felt.'

The Tower of London

[36] Richard II resigns the crown in the tower, dies and is buried (1399); from *Chronicles* by Froissart.

Then the Duke of Lancaster and his council took advice what should be done with King Richard, being in the Tower of London ... then it was thought that King Richard should be put from all his royalty and joy that he hath lived in; for they said the news of his taking should spread abroad into all realms christened ... then they regarded what case the realm stood in and did put all his deeds in articles to the number of twenty-eight. Then the Duke of Lancaster and his council went to the Tower of London and entered into the chamber where King Richard was, and without any reverence making to him there was openly read all the said articles; to the which the king made none answer, for he saw well all was true that was laid to his charge, saving he said: 'All that I have done passed by my council.' Then he was demanded what they were that had given counsel and by whom he was most ruled. He named them, in trust thereby to have been delivered himself in accusing of them, as he had done beforetime, trusting thereby to scape and to bring them in the danger and pain; but that was not the mind of them that loved him not. So as at that time they spake no more, but departed; and the Duke of Lancaster went to his lodging and suffered the mayor and the men of law to proceed. They went to the Guildhall, whereas all the matters of the city were determined, and then much people assembled there. When they saw the governours of the city go thither, they thought some justice should be done, as there was indeed: I shall shew you how.

First, the articles that were made against the king, the which had been read before him in the Tower, were read again there openly: and it was shewed by him that read them, how the king himself denied none of them, but confessed that he did them by the counsel of four knights of his chamber, and how by their counsel he had put to death the Duke of Gloucester and the Earl of Arundel, Sir Thomas Corbet and others, and how they had long incited the king to do those deeds; which deeds, they said, were not to be forgiven, but demanded punition, for by them and their counsel the justice of right was closed up through all the courts of England, Westminster and other, whereby many evil deeds followed, and companies and routs of thieves and murderers rose and assembled together in divers parts of the realm, and robbed merchants by the ways and poor men in their houses; by which means the realm was in great peril to have been lost without recovery: and it is to be imagined that finally they would have rendered Calais or Guines or both into the Frenchmen's hands. These words thus shewed to the people made many to be abashed, and many began to murmur and said: 'These causes demand punition, that all other may take ensample thereby, and Richard of Bordeaux to be deposed: for he is not worthy to bear a crown, but ought to be deprived from all honour and to be kept all his life in prison with bread and water.' Though some of the villains murmured, others said on high: 'Sir mayor of London and ye other that have justice in your hands to minister, execute justice: for we will ye spare no man, for ye see well the case that ye have shewed us demandeth justice incontinent; for they are judges upon their own deeds.' Then the mayor and other of the governours of the law went together into the chamber of judgment. Then these four knights were judged to die, and were judged to be had to the foot of the Tower, whereas King Richard was, that he might see them drawn along by the dike with horses each after other through the city into Cheapside, and then their heads stricken off there and set upon London bridge, and their bodies drawn to the gibbet and there hanged.

This judgment given, they were delivered to execution; for the mayor of London and such as were deputed to the matter went from the Guildhall to the Tower and took out the four knights of the King's, whose names were called Sir Bernard Brocas, Sir Magelars, Master John Derby, receiver of Lincoln, and Master Sely, the king's steward. Each of them were tied to two horses in the presence of them that were in the Tower, and the king might well see it out at the windows; wherewith he was sore discomforted, for all other that were there with the king looked to be in the same case, they knew them of London so cruel. Thus these four knights were drawn one after another along through the city till they came into Cheap, and there on a fisher's stall their heads were stricken off and set upon London bridge, and their bodies drawn by the shoulders to the gibbet and there hanged up.

This justice thus done, every man went to their lodgings. King Richard, knowing himself taken and in the danger of the Londoners, was in great sorrow in his heart and reckoned his puissance nothing; for he saw how every man was against him, and if there were any that ought him any favour, it lay not in their powers to do him any aid, nor they durst not shew it. Such as were with the King said: 'Sir, we have but small trust in our lives, as it may well appear; for when your cousin of Lancaster came to the castle of Flint and with your own good will ye yielded you to him, and he promised that you and twelve of yours should be his prisoners and have no hurt, and now of those twelve four be executed shamefully, [and] we are like to pass the same way. The cause is, these Londoners, who hath caused the duke of Lancaster your cousin to do this deed, had him so sore bound to them, that he must do as they will have him. God doth much for us if he suffer that we might die here our natural death and not a shameful death: it is great pity to think on this.' With those words King Richard began tenderly to weep and wring his hands, and cursed the hour that ever he was born, rather than to have such an end. Such as were about him had great pity and re-comforted him as well as they might. One of his knights said: 'Sir, it behoveth you to take comfort. We see well, and so do you, that this world is nothing: the fortunes thereof are marvellous and sometime turn as well upon kings and princes as upon poor men. The French king, whose daughter ye have married, cannot now aid you; he is too far off. If ye might scape this mischief by dissimulation and save your life and ours, it were a good enterprise: peradventure within a year or two there would be had some recovery.'

'Why,' quoth the king, 'what would ye that I should do? There is nothing but I would be glad to do it to save us thereby.'

'Sir,' quoth the knight, 'we see for truth that these Londoners will crown your cousin of Lancaster as king, and for that intent they sent for him, and so have aided him and do. It is not possible for you to live without ye consent that he be crowned king: wherefore, sir, we will counsel you, to the intent to save your life and ours, that when your cousin of Lancaster cometh to you to demand anything, then with sweet and treatable words say to him, how that ye will resign to him the crown of England and all the right that ye have in the realm clearly and purely into his hands, and how that ye will that he be king: thereby ye shall greatly appease him and the Londoners also. And desire him affectuously to suffer you to live and us also with you, or else every man apart, as it shall please him, or else to banish us out of the realm for ever; for he that looseth his life, looseth all.'

King Richard heard those words well and fixed them surely in his heart, and said he would do as they counselled him, as he that saw himself in great danger. And then he said to them that kept him, how he would gladly speak with his cousin of Lancaster . . .

It was shewed the Duke of Lancaster how Richard of Bordeaux desired to speak with him. The Duke in an evening took a barge and went to the Tower by water, and went to the King, who received him courteously and humbled himself greatly, as he that saw himself in great danger, and said: 'Cousin of Lancaster, I regard and consider mine estate, which is as now but small, I thank God thereof. As any more to reign or to govern people or to bear a crown, I think it not; and as God help me, I would I were dead by a natural death, and that the French king had again his daughter. We have had as yet no great joy together; nor sith I brought her into England, I could never have the love of my people, as I had before. Cousin, all things considered, I know well I have greatly trespassed against you and against other noblemen of my blood; by divers things I perceive I shall never have pardon nor come to peace. Wherefore with mine own free and liberal will I will resign to you the heritage of the crown of England, and I require you take the gift thereof with the resignation.' . . .

It was not long after that true tidings ran through London, how Richard of Bordeaux was dead; but how he died and by what means, I could not tell when I wrote this chronicle. But this King Richard dead was laid in a litter and set in a chare covered with black baudkin, and four horses all black in the chare, and two men in black leading the chare, and four knights all in black following. Thus the chare departed from the Tower of London and was brought along through London fair and softly, till they came into Cheapside, whereas the chief assembly of London was, and there the chare rested the space of two hours. Thither came in and out more than twenty thousand persons men and women, to see him whereas he lay, his head on a black cushion and his visage open. Some had on him pity and some none, but said he had long deserved death. Now consider well, ye great lords, kings, dukes, earls, barons and prelates, and all men of great lineage and puissance: see and behold how the fortunes of this world are marvellous and turn diversely. This King Richard reigned King of England twenty-two year in great prosperity, holding great estate and seignory. There was never before any king of England that spent so much in his house as he did, by a hundred thousand florins every year; for I, Sir John Froissart, canon and treasurer of Chimay, knew it well, for I was in his court more than a quarter of a year together, and he made me good cheer, because that in my youth I was clerk and servant to the noble King Edward the third, his grandfather, and with my lady Philippa of Hainault, Queen of England, his grandam; and when I departed from him, it was at Windsor, and at my departing the king sent me by a knight of his called Sir John Golofre a goblet of silver and gilt weighing two mark of silver, and within it a hundred nobles, by which I am as yet the better, and shall be as long as I live: wherefore I am bound to pray to God for his soul, and with much sorrow I write of his death; but because I have continued this history, therefore I write thereof to follow it . . .

Thus when King Richard had lain two hours in the chare in Cheapside, then they drave the chare forward: and when the four knights that followed the chare afoot were without London, they leapt then on their horses, which were there ready for them, and so they rode till they came to a village called Langley, a thirty mile from London, and there this King Richard was buried. God have mercy on his soul!

[37] The Lollard Sir John Oldcastle escapes from the tower but is caught and executed (1417); from *Chronicles of London*, edited by C. L. Kingsford.

In this same yeer the Lorde Cobham, callyd Syr John Oldecastell, was y-dampned ffor a Lollard and an heretyk by alle hooly chirche, and komytted to the Toure off London; and there he brak oute with Inne a ffewe dayes.

And anoon after he and his affynytes, that weren off his secte coniecten and conspirden nat only the deeth off the kyng and off his brethren, but also the destruccion off all hooly chirche; ffor they purposeden hem to haue y-sembled togedris by nyht in Seint Gyles ffelde, a myle oute off the citee, and there to haue gadred the strenht to haue ffulfilled here Cursed purposes.

But, blessed be god, the kyng and his lordes weren y-warned off her purposes; and toke the ffelde rather thanne they, and awaytynge after her komyng; and so they tooke many off her preestes and clerkes and other lowe men, that weren off her sectes, komyng thedir, wenyng to haue y-ffounde ther Syr John Oldecastell, but they ffeyled off her purpos.

And anoon after ther weren y-drawe and hanged xxxvj vpon oon day, vpon newe galowes y-made ffor hem vpon the hyh way ffaste bysyde the same ffelde, wher they touht to haue assembled togedris. Off which company vij off the grettest Lollardes weren y-brent both they and the galowes, at they henge vpon. And so they made an ende off this worlde. And anoon after was Syr Roger Acton, knyht, y-take and drawe and hanged vpon the same galowes, ffor the same cause.

[38] The murder of the Princes in the Tower (1483); from *The History of King Richard III* by Thomas More.

I shall rehearse you the dolorous end of those babes, not after euery way that I haue heard, but after that way y I haue so hard by suche men & by such meanes, as me thinketh it wer hard but it should be true. King Richarde after his coronacion, takyng his way to Gloucester to visit in his newe honor, the towne of which he bare the name of his old, deuised as he roode, to fulfil y thing which he before had intended. And forasmuch as his minde gaue him, y his nephewes liuing, men woulde not recken that hee could haue right to y realm, he thought therfore without delay to rid them, as though the killing of his

kinsmen, could amend his cause, and make him a kindly
king. Whereuppon he sent one Iohn Grene whom he
specially trusted, vnto Sir Robert Brakenbery constable of
the Tower, with a letter and credence also, that the same
Sir Robert shoulde in any wise put the two children to
death. This Iohn Grene did his errande vnto Brakenbery
kneling before our Lady in the Tower, who plainely
answered that he would neuer putte them to death to dye
therfore, with which answer Ihon Grene returning
recounted the same to Kynge Richarde at Warwick yet in
his way. Wherwith he toke such displeasure and thought,
that the same night, he said vnto a secrete page of his: Ah
whome shall a man trust? those that I haue broughte vp
my selfe, those that I had went would most surely serue
me, euen those fayle me, and at my commaundemente
wyll do nothyng for me. Sir quod his page there lyeth one
on your paylet without, y I dare well say to do your grace
pleasure, the thyng were right harde that he wold refuse,
meaning this by Sir Iames Tyrell, which was a man of
right goodlye parsonage, and for natures gyftes, woorthy
to haue serued a muche better prince, if he had well serued
god, and by grace obtayned asmuche trouthe & good wil
as he had strength and witte. The man had an high heart,
and sore longed vpward, not rising yet so fast as he had
hoped, being hindered and kept vnder by the meanes of
Sir Richard Ratclife and Sir William Catesby, which long-
ing for no moo parteners of the princes fauour, and
namely not for hym, whose pride thei wist would beare
no pere, kept him by secrete driftes oute of all secrete
trust. Whiche thyng this page wel had marked and
knowen. Wherefore thys occasion offered, of very speciall
frendship he toke his time to put him forward, & by such
wise doe him good, that al the enemies he had except the
deuil, could neuer haue done him so muche hurte. For
vpon this pages wordes King Richard arose. (For this
communicacion had he sitting at the draught, a conuenient
carpet for such a counsaile) and came out in to the pailet
chamber, on which he found in bed Sir Iames and Sir
Thomas Tyrels, of parson like and brethren of blood, but

nothing of kin in condicions. Then said the king merely to
them: What sirs be ye in bed so soone, and calling vp Syr
Iames, brake to him secretely his mind in this mischieuous
matter. In whiche he founde him nothing strange. Wherfore on the morow he sente him to Brakenbury with a
letter, by which he was commaunded to deliuer Sir Iames
all y kayes of the Tower for one nyght, to y ende he might
there accomplish the kinges pleasure, in such thing as he
had geuen him commaundement. After which letter deliuered and the kayes receiued, Sir Iames appointed the
night nexte ensuing to destroy them, deuysing before and
preparing the meanes. The prince as soone as the protector
left that name and toke himself as king, had it shewed
vnto him, that he should not reigne, but his vncle should
haue the crowne. At which worde the prince sore abashed,
began to sigh and said: Alas I woulde my vncle woulde
lette me haue my lyfe yet, though I lese my kingdome.
Then he y tolde him the tale, vsed him with good wordes,
and put him in the best comfort he could. But forthwith
was the prince and his brother bothe shet vp, and all other
remoued from them, onely one called Black Wil or William Slaughter except, set to serue them and see them sure.
After whiche time the prince neuer tyed his pointes, nor
ought rought of hymselfe, but with that young babe hys
brother, lingered in thought and heauines til this tratorous
death, deliuered them of that wretchednes. For Sir Iames
Tirel deusied that thei shold be murthered in their beddes.
To the execucion wherof, he appointed Miles Forest one
of the foure that kept them, a felowe fleshed in murther
before time. To him he ioyned one Iohn Dighton his own
horsekeper, a big brode square strong knaue. Then al y
other beeing remoued from them, thys Miles Forest and
Iohn Dighton, about midnight (the sely children lying in
their beddes) came into the chamber, and sodainly lapped
them vp among y clothes so be wrapped them and entan-
gled them keping down by force the fetherbed and pil-
lowes hard vnto their mouthes, that within a while smored
and stifled, theyr breath failing, thei gaue vp to god their
innocent soules into the ioyes of heauen, leauing to the

tormentors their bodyes dead in the bed. Whiche after that
the wretches parceiued, first by y strugling with the paines
of death, and after long lying styll, to be throughly dead:
they laide their bodies naked out vppon the bed, and
fetched Sir Iames to see them. Which vpon the sight of
them, caused those murtherers to burye them at the stayre
foote, metely depe in the grounde vnder a great heape of
stones. Than rode Sir Iames in great hast to King Richarde,
and shewed him al the maner of the murther, who gaue
hym gret thanks, and as som say there made him knight.
But he allowed not as I haue heard, y burying in so vile a
corner, saying that he woulde haue them buried in a better
place, because thei wer a kinges sonnes. Loe the honourable corage of a kynge. Wherupon thei say that a prieste
of Syr Robert Brakenbury toke vp the bodyes again, and
secretely entered them in such place, as by the occasion of
his deathe, whiche onely knew it could neuer synce come
to light. Very trouthe is it & well knowen, that at such
time as Syr Iames Tirell was in the Tower, for Treason
committed agaynste the moste famous prince King Henry
the seuenth, bothe Dighton and he were examined, &
confessed the murther in maner aboue writen, but whither
the bodies were remoued thei could nothing tel. And thus
as I haue learned of them that much knew and litle cause
had to lye, wer these two noble princes, these innocent
tender children, borne of moste royall bloode, brought vp
in great wealth, likely long to liue to reigne and rule in the
realme, by traytorous tiranny taken, depryued of their
estate, shortly shutte vp in prison, and priuily slaine and
murthered, theyr bodies cast god wote where by the cruel
ambicion of their vnnaturall vncle and his dispiteous tormentors. Which thinges on euery part wel pondered: god
neuer gaue this world a more notable example, neither in
what vnsuretie standeth this worldly wel, or what mischief
worketh the prowde enterprise of an hyghe heart, or
finally what wretched end ensueth such dispiteous crueltie.
For first to beginne with the ministers, Miles Forest at
sainct Martens pecemele rotted away. Dighton in dede yet
walketh on a liue in good possibilitie to bee hanged ere he

dye. But Sir Iames Tirel dyed at Tower Hill, beheaded for treason. King Richarde himselfe as ye shal herafter here, slain in the fielde, hacked and hewed of his enemies handes, haryed on horsebacke dead, his here in despite torn and togged lyke a cur dogge. And the mischief that he tooke, within lesse then thre yeares of the mischiefe that he dyd. And yet all the meane time spente in much pain and trouble outward, much feare anguish and sorow within. For I haue heard by credible report of such as wer secrete w his chamberers, that after this abhominable deede done, he neuer hadde quiet in his minde, hee neuer thought himself sure. Where he went abrode, his eyen whirled about, his body priuily fenced, his hand euer on his dager, his countenance and maner like one alway ready to strike againe, he toke ill rest a nightes, lay long wakyng and musing, sore weried with care & watch, rather slumbred then slept, troubled wyth feareful dreames, sodainly sommetyme sterte vp, leape out of his bed & runne about the chamber, so was his restles herte continually tossed & tumbled w the tedious impression & stormy remembrance of his abominable dede.

[39] Thomas More is executed on Tower Hill (1535); from *The Life of Thomas More* by William Roper.

And so upon the next morrow, being Tuesday, St Thomas's eve, and the utas of St Peter, in the Year of Our Lord, one thousand five hundred thirty and five (according as he in his letter the day before had wished) early in the morning came to him Sir Thomas Pope, his singular friend, on message from the King and his Council, that he should before nine of the clock the same morning suffer death, and that therefore forthwith he should prepare himself thereto.

'Master Pope,' quoth he, 'for your good tidings I most heartily thank you. I have been always much bounden to the King's Highness for the benefits and honours that he hath still from time to time most bountifully heaped upon me, and yet more bound am I to His Grace for putting me into this place, where I have had convenient time and space to have remembrance of my end. And so help me, God, most of all, Master Pope, am I bound to His Highness that it pleaseth him so shortly to rid me out of the miseries of this wretched world. And therefore will I not fail earnestly to pray for His Grace, both here and also in another world.'

'The King's pleasure is further,' quoth Master Pope, 'that at your execution you shall not use many words.'

'Master Pope,' quoth he, 'you do well to give me warning of His Grace's pleasure, for otherwise I had purposed at that time somewhat to have spoken, but of no matter wherewith His Grace, or any other, should have had cause to be offended. Nevertheless, whatsoever I intended I am ready obediently to conform myself to His Grace's commandments. And I beseech you, good Master Pope, to be a mean unto His Highness that my daughter Margaret may be at my burial.'

'The King is content already', quoth Master Pope, 'that your wife, children and other your friends shall have liberty to be present thereat.'

'O how much beholden then,' said Sir Thomas More, 'am I to His Grace that unto my poor burial vouchsafeth to have so gracious consideration.'

Wherewithal Master Pope, taking his leave of him, could not refrain from weeping. Which Sir Thomas More perceiving, comforted him in this wise, 'Quiet yourself, good Master Pope, and be not discomforted, for I trust that we shall, once in heaven, see each other full merrily, where we shall be sure to live and love together, in joyful bliss eternally.'

Upon whose departure, Sir Thomas More, as one that had been invited to some solemn feast, changed himself into his best apparel, which Master Lieutenant espying, advised him to put it off, saying that he that should have it was but a javel.

'What, Master Lieutenant,' quoth he, 'shall I account him a javel that shall do me this day so singular a benefit?

Nay, I assure you, were it cloth of gold, I would account it well bestowed on him, as St Cyprian did, who gave his executioner thirty pieces of gold.' And albeit at length, through Master Lieutenant's importunate persuasion, he altered his apparel, yet after the example of St Cyprian, did he, of that little money that was left him, send one angel of gold to his executioner.

And so was he by Master Lieutenant brought out of the Tower, and from thence led towards the place of execution. Where, going up the scaffold, which was so weak that it was ready to fall, he said merrily to Master Lieutenant, 'I pray you, Master Lieutenant, see me safe up, and for my coming down let me shift for myself.'

Then desired he all the people thereabout to pray for him, and to bear witness with him that he should now suffer death in and for the faith of the Holy Catholic Church. Which done, he knelt down, and after his prayers said, turned to the executioner and with a cheerful countenance spake thus to him: 'Pluck up thy spirits, man, and be not afraid to do thine office; my neck is very short; take heed therefore thou strike not awry, for saving of thine honesty.'

So passed Sir Thomas More out of this world to God, upon the very same day in which himself had most desired.

[40] Anne Boleyn is executed (1536); from *A Chronicle of England by Charles Wriothesley*, edited by W. D. Hamilton.

Item, on Munday, the 15th of May, 1536, there was arreigned within the Tower of London Queene Anne, for treason againste the Kinges owne person, and there was a great scaffold made in the Kinges Hall within the Tower of London, and there were made benches and seates for the lordes, my Lord of Northfolke sittinge under the clothe of estate, representinge there the Kinges person as Highe Steward of Englande and uncle to the Queene, he holdinge a longe white staffe in his hande, and the Earle of Surrey, his sonne and heire, sittinge at his feete before him hold-

Tessellated pavement discovered on the SE corner of the Excise Office

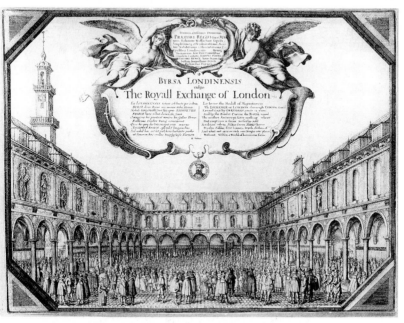

The Royal Exchange, interior facing west

St Paul's Cathedral standing above the surrounding burning
buildings during the London Blitz, 31 December 1940

London Bridge and
the Tower of London from
a MS of the Poems of
Charles Duke of Orleans

St Paul's Cross. A sermon
being preached by the Bishop
of London in the presence of
James I, his Queen, Charles
Prince of Wales, the Archbishop
of Canterbury and others

Treatment of the insane, from Hogarth's engraving 'Scene in Bedlam', (from *The Rake's Progress*)

The Fire of London from an engraving by Hollar

Traffic on London Bridge, 1892

Visscher's Long View (Western half)

Visscher's Long View (Eastern half)

The old Globe Theatre

The order and manner of the burning of *Anne Askew*, *Iohn Lacels, Iohn Adams, Nicolas Belenian*, with certaine of the Counsell sitting in Smithfield.

Burning of Anne Askew, John Lacels, John Adams, Nicolas Belenian, with certane of the Councell sitting in Smithfield

inge the golden staffe for the Earle Marshall of Englande, which sayde office the saide duke had in his handes; the Lord Awdley, Chauncellour of England, sittinge on his right hande, and the Duke of Suffolke on his left hande, with other marqueses, earles, and lordes, everie one after their degrees.

And first the Kinges commission was redd, and then the Constable of the Tower and the Lieutenant brought forthe the Queene to the barre, where was made a chaire for her to sitt downe in, and then her indictment was redd afore her, whereunto she made so wise and discreet aunsweres to all thinges layde against her, excusinge herselfe with her wordes so clearlie, as thoughe she had never bene faultie to the same, and at length putt her to the triall of the Peeres of the Realme, and then were 26 of the greatest peeres there present chosen to passe on her, the Duke of Suffolke beinge highest, and, after thei had communed together, the yongest lorde of the saide inquest was called first to give verdict, who sayde guiltie, and so everie lorde and earle after their degrees sayde guiltie to the last and so condemned her. And then the Duke of Northfolke gave this sentence on her, sayinge: Because thou haste offended our Sovereigne the Kinges grace, in committinge treason against his person, and here attaynted of the same, the lawe of the realme is this, that thou haste deserved death, and thy judgment is this: That thow shalt be brent here within the Tower of London on the Greene, els to have thy head smitten of as the Kinges pleasure shal be further knowne of the same; and so she was brought to warde agayne, and two ladies wayted on her, which came in with her at the first, and wayted still on her, whose names were the Ladie Kingstone and the Ladie Boleyn, her aunte . . . of the lawe, the King was divorsed from his wife Queene Anne, and there at the same cowrte was a privie contract approved that she had made to the Earle of Northumberlande afore the Kings tyme; and so she was discharged, and was never lawfull Queene of England, and there it was approved the same.

The Fridaye followinge, being the 19th day of May,

1536, and the 28th yeare of King Henry the VIIIth, at eight of the clocke in the morninge, Anne Bulleyn, Queene, was brought to execution on the greene within the Tower of London, by the great White Tower; the Lord Chauncelloure of England, the Duke of Richmond, Duke of Suffolke, with the moste of the Kings Councell, as erles, lordes, and nobles of this realme, beinge present at the same; allso the Major of London, with the Alldermen and Sheriffs, and certayne of the best craftes of London, beinge there present allso. On a scaffolde made there for the sayde execution the sayde Queen Ann sayde thus: Maisters, I here humblye submitt me to the lawe as the lawe hath judged me, and as for myne offences, I here accuse no man, God knoweth them; I remitt them to God, beseechinge him to have mercye on my sowle, and I besche Jesu save my sovereigne and maister the Kinge, the moste godlye, noble, and gentle Prince that is, and longe to reigne over yow; which wordes were spoken with a goodlye smilinge countenance; and this done, she kneeled downe on her knees and sayde: To Jesu Christe I commend my sowle; and suddenlye the hangman smote of her heade at a stroke with a sworde; her bodye with the head was buried in the Chappell within the Tower of London, in the queere there, the same daye at afternoone, when she had reygned as Queene three yeares, lackinge 14 dayes, from her coronation to her death.

[41] Lady Jane Grey is executed (1554); from *The Chronicle of Queen Jane and of two years of Queen Mary*, edited by J. G. Nichols.

The Monday, being the xijth of Februarie, about ten of the clocke, ther went out of the Tower to the scaffolde on Tower hill, the lorde Guilforde Dudley, sone to the late duke of Northumberland, husbande to the lady Jane Grey, daughter to the duke of Suffolke, who at his going out tooke by the hande sir Anthony Browne, maister John Throgmorton, and many other gentyllmen, praying them to praie for him; and without the bullwarke Offeley the sheryve receyved him and brought him to the scaffolde, where, after a small declaration, having no gostlye father with him, he kneeled downe and said his praiers; then holding upp his eyes and handes to God many tymes; and at last, after he had desyred the people to pray for him, he laide himselfe along, and his hedd upon the block, which was at one stroke of the axe taken from him.

Note, the lorde marques stode upon the Devyl's towre, and sawe the executyon. His carcas throwne into a carre, and his hed in a cloth, he was brought into the chappell within the Tower, wher the ladye Jane, whose lodging was in Partrige's house, dyd see his ded carcase taken out of the cart, aswell as she dyd see him before on lyve going to his deathe – a sight to hir no lesse then death.

By this tyme ther a scaffolde made upon the grene over agaynst the White tower, for the saide lady Jane to die apon. Who with hir husband was appoynted to have ben put to deathe the fryday before, but was staied tyll then, for what cause is not knowen, unlesse yt were because hir father was not then come into the Tower. The saide lady, being nothing at all abashed, neither with feare of her owne deathe, which then approached, neither with the sight of the ded carcase of hir husbande, when he was brought in to the chappell, came fourthe, the levetenaunt leding hir, in the same gown wherin she was arrayned, hir countenance nothing abashed, neither her eyes enything moysted with teares, although her ij. gentylwomen, mistress Elizabeth Tylney and mistress Eleyn, wonderfully wept, with a boke in hir hande, wheron she praied all the way till she cam to the saide scaffolde, wheron when she was mounted, &c ... the Ende of the lady Jane Dudley, daughter of the duke of Suffolk, upon the scaffolde, at the houre of her death.

First, when she mounted upon the scaffolde, she sayd to the people standing thereabout: 'Good people, I am come hether to die, and by a lawe I am condemned to the same. The facte, in dede, against the quenes highnesse was unlawfull, and the consenting thereunto by me: but touching the procurement and desyre therof by me or on my halfe, I doo wash my handes thereof in innocencie, before God, and the face of you, good Christian people, this day,' and therewith she wrong her handes, in which she had hir booke. Then she sayd, 'I pray you all, good Christian people, to beare me witnesse that I dye a true Christian woman, and that I looke to be saved by none other meane, but only by the mercy of God in the merites of the blood of his only sonne Jesus Christ: and I confesse, when I dyd know the word of God I neglected the same, loved my selfe and the world, and therefore this plague or punyshment is happely and worthely happened unto me for my sins; and yet I thank God of his goodnesse that he hath thus geven me a tyme and respet to repent. And now, good people, while I am alyve, I pray you to assyst me with your prayers.' And then, knelyng downe, she turned to Fecknam, saying, 'Shall I say this psalme?' And he said, 'Yea.' Then she said the psalme of *Miserere mei Deus* in English, in most devout maner, to the end. Then she stode up, and gave her maiden mistris Tilney her gloves and handkercher, and her book to maister Bruges, the lyvetenantes brother; forthwith she untyed her gown. The hangman went to her to help her of therewith; then she desyred him to let her alone, turning towardes her two gentlewomen, who helped her off therwith, and also with her frose paast and neckercher, geving to her a fayre handkercher to knytte about her eyes.

Then the hangman kneeled downe, and asked her forgevenesse, whome she forgave most willingly. Then he willed her to stand upon the strawe: which doing, she sawe the block. Then she sayd, 'I pray you dispatch me quickly.' Then she kneeled down, saying, 'Wil you take it of before I lay me downe?' and the hangman answered her, 'No, madame.' She tyed the kercher about her eys; then feeling for the blocke, saide, 'What shall I do? Where is it?' One of the standers-by guyding her therunto, she layde her heade down upon the block, and stretched forth her body and said: 'Lorde, into thy hands I commende my spirite!' And so she ended.

[42] A Catholic priest is tortured in the tower (1597); from *The Autobiography of an Elizabethan* by John Gerard.

On the third day the warder came to my room straight from his dinner. Looking sorry for himself, he said the Lords Commissioners had arrived with the Queen's Attorney-General and that I had to go down to them at once.

'I am ready,' I said, 'but just let me say an *Our Father* and *Hail Mary* downstairs.'

He let me go, and then we went off together to the Lieutenant's lodgings inside the walls of the Tower. Five men were there waiting for me, none of whom, except Wade, had examined me before. He was there to direct the charges against me . . .

'You say,' said the Attorney-General, 'you have no wish to obstruct the Government. Tell us, then, where Father Garnet is. He is an enemy of the state, and you are bound to report on all such men.'

'He isn't an enemy of the state,' I said . . . 'But I don't know where he lives, and if I did, I would not tell you.'

'Then we'll see to it that you tell us before we leave this place.'

'Please God you won't,' I answered.

Then they produced a warrant for putting me to torture. They had it ready by them and handed it to me to read. (In this prison a special warrant is required for torture.)

I saw the warrant was properly made out and signed, and then I answered: 'With God's help I shall never do anything which is unjust or act against my conscience or the Catholic faith. You have me in your power. You can do with me what God allows you to do – more you cannot do.'

Then they began to implore me not to force them to take steps they were loath to take. They said they would have to put me to torture every day, as long as my life lasted, until I gave them the information they wanted.

'I trust in God's goodness,' I answered, 'that He will prevent me from ever committing a sin such as this – the sin of accusing innocent people. We are all in God's hands and therefore I have no fear of anything you can do to me.'

This was the sense of my answers, as far as I can recall them now.

We went to the torture-room in a kind of solemn procession, the attendants walking ahead with lighted candles.

The chamber was underground and dark, particularly near the entrance. It was a vast place and every device and instrument of human torture was there. They pointed out some of them to me and said I would try them all. Then they asked me again whether I would confess.

'I cannot,' I said.

I fell on my knees for a moment's prayer. Then they took me to a big upright pillar, one of the wooden posts which held the roof of this huge underground chamber. Driven into the top of it were iron staples for supporting heavy weights. Then they put my wrists into iron gauntlets and ordered me to climb two or three wicker steps. My arms were then lifted up and an iron bar was passed through the rings of one gauntlet, then through the staple and rings of the second gauntlet. This done, they fastened the bar with a pin to prevent it slipping, and then, removing the wicker steps one by one from under my feet, they left me hanging by my hands and arms fastened above my head. The tips of my toes, however, still touched the ground, and they had to dig away the earth from under them. They had hung me up from the highest staple in the pillar and could not raise me any higher, without driving in another staple.

Hanging like this I began to pray. The gentlemen standing around asked me whether I was willing to confess now.

'I cannot and I will not,' I answered.

But I could hardly utter the words, such a gripping pain came over me. It was worst in my chest and belly, my hands and arms. All the blood in my body seemed to rush up into my arms and hands and I thought that blood was oozing from the ends of my fingers and the pores of my skin. But it was only a sensation caused by my flesh swelling above the irons holding them. The pain was so intense that I thought I could not possibly endure it, and added to it, I had an interior temptation. Yet I did not feel any inclination or wish to give them the information they wanted. The Lord saw my weakness with the eyes of His mercy, and did not permit me to be tempted beyond my strength. With the temptation He sent me relief. Seeing my agony and the struggle going on in my mind, He gave me this most merciful thought: the utmost and worst they can do is to kill you, and you have often wanted to give your life for your Lord God. The Lord God sees all you are enduring – He can do all things. You are in God's keeping. With these thoughts, God in His infinite goodness and mercy gave me the grace of resignation, and with a desire to die and a hope (I admit) that I would, I offered Him myself to do with me as He wished. From that moment the conflict in my soul ceased, and even the physical pain seemed much more bearable than before, though it must, in fact, I am sure, have been greater with the growing strain and weariness of my body . . .

Sometime after one o'clock, I think, I fell into a faint. How long I was unconscious I don't know, but I think it was long, for the men held my body up or put the wicker steps under my feet until I came to. Then they heard me pray and immediately let me down again. And they did this every time I fainted – eight or nine times that day – before it struck five . . .

A little later they took me down. My legs and feet were not damaged, but it was a great effort to stand upright . . .

[43] Colonel Blood attempts to steal the Crown Jewels (1671); from *The Tower of London* by Lord R. S. Gower.

The most sensational event that occurred in the Tower during the reign of Charles II was the attempt made by a ruffian who called himself 'Colonel' Blood to steal the

Crown and Regalia. Blood, half sailor, half highwayman, and a complete scoundrel, was about fifty years old when, in the month of May 1671, he made what was literally a dash for the Crown. Blood appears to have served under Cromwell, and consequently styled himself 'Colonel'; after the war he became a spy of the Government, and a short time before his performance at the Tower he had almost succeeded in having the old Duke of Ormond hanged on the gallows at Tyburn.

At this time Sir Gilbert Talbot held the appointment of 'Master of the Jewel House'. The allowance for this charge had been reduced, and, as a kind of compensation, the Master had permission to allow the public to inspect the Regalia, then kept in the Martin Tower, or Jewel Tower, as it was then called, a fee being charged which became the Master's perquisite. Three weeks before Blood made his attempt, he had called at the Martin Tower disguised as a clergyman, 'with a long cloak, cassock, and canonical girdle'. He was accompanied by a woman whom he represented as his wife. The lady requested permission to see the Regalia, but soon after being admitted to the Tower complained of 'a qualm upon her stomach', and old Talbot Edwards, who had been an old servant of Sir Gilbert's, and had been placed by him in charge of the Regalia, called to his wife to look after the *soi-disant* Mrs Blood. That lady having been given something to remove her 'qualms' was, together with her husband, most profuse in the expression of her gratitude to the old keeper and his wife, and promised to return upon an early occasion.

The next time Blood came to the Tower he was alone, bringing some gloves for Edwards's wife as a token of gratitude for the kindness shown to 'Mrs Blood'. On this occasion he informed Edwards that he had a young nephew who was well off, and in search of a wife, and suggested that a match might be arranged between him and their daughter. Blood was invited to bring his nephew to make acquaintance of the young lady, and it was arranged that the old couple should give a dinner at which the meeting should take place. At the dinner Blood took it upon himself, being still in his clerical disguise, to say grace, which he did with great unction, concluding with a long-winded oration, and a prayer for the Royal family. After the meal he visited the rooms in the Tower, and seeing a fine pair of pistols hanging on the wall, asked if he might buy them to give to a friend. He then said that he would return with a couple of friends who were about to leave London, and who were anxious to see the Regalia before leaving, it being decided that he should bring them the next morning. That day was 9 May, and at seven in the morning old Talbot Edwards was ready to receive his reverend friend and his companions, who soon put in an appearance. Blood and his confederates had arms concealed about them, each carrying daggers, pocket pistols, and a rapier blades in their canes.

They were taken up the stairs into the room where the Regalia was kept, but immediately they had entered, the ruffians threw a cloak over Edwards's head and gagged him with a wooden plug, which had a small hole in it so that the person gagged could breathe; this they fastened with a piece of waxed leather which encircled his neck, and placed an iron hook on his nose so as to prevent him from crying out. They swore they would murder him if he attempted to give an alarm – which the poor old fellow could scarcely have done under the circumstances. But the plucky old keeper struggled hard, whereupon they beat him upon the head with a wooden mallet, and stabbed him until he fainted. The villains, thinking they had killed him, then turned their attention to rifling the treasures in the room. One of them, Parrot, put the orb in his breeches pocket, Blood placed the Crown under his cloak, and the third began to file the sceptre in two pieces, it being too long to carry away without being seen. At this moment steps were heard; Edwards's young son having just returned from Flanders in the very nick of time. The thieves dashed down the stairs past the young man who was coming up, carrying with them the orb and crown, the sceptre being left behind in the hurry of their flight. The pursuit was immediate; young Edwards had brought

with him his brother-in-law, a Captain Beckman, and the
latter hearing cries of 'Treason! Murder!' from the terrified
women in the Tower, and the cry 'The Crown is stolen!'
rushed after Blood and the two other men. These had
meanwhile crossed the drawbridge between the Main
Guard at the White Tower and the Wharf; at the bridge a
warder had tried to stop them, but Blood fired his pistol,
and the man, although not wounded, fell to the ground,
and they dashed past him. At St Katharine's Gate, near
which horses were in waiting for the thieves, Beckman
overtook them; Blood again discharged his pistol but
missed his pursuer who, ducking his head, promptly seized
the sham clergyman, from under whose cloak the Crown
fell to the ground, rolling in the gutter. Then followed
what the *London Gazette* of the day called a 'robustious
struggle', Blood ultimately being secured, remarking that
'It was a gallant attempt, for it was for a Crown!'

When the Crown fell to the ground, some of the gems
came loose from their settings, and a large ruby, which
had belonged to the sceptre, was found in Parrot's pocket.
Little harm, however, was done, except to the poor old
keeper, who was nearly eighty years of age and had been
terribly injured; he was soon past all suffering, and was
buried in the Chapel of St Peter's, where his gravestone
can still be seen.

After his capture Blood occupied a prison in the White
Tower for a short time, but the King soon sent for him.
And although it is not, and cannot be known, whether
Charles was an accessory or not in the attempted theft, or
whether Blood knew too much of the King's affairs, yet,
whatever the reason, Blood was not only pardoned but
rewarded, the King giving him a pension of £500 a year,
and bestowing upon him landed estates in Ireland, the
'Colonel' becoming one of the most assiduous of the
Whitehall courtiers. Whether Charles also rewarded
Blood's accomplices is not recorded, but none of them
were ever punished for the attempted robbery. John Evelyn
recounts meeting Blood at court on 10 May 1671. 'How
he came to be pardoned,' he writes, 'and ever received

into favour, not only after this but several other exploits almost as daring, both in Ireland and here, I never could come to understand. This man had not only a daring, but a villainous unmerciful look, a false countenance, but very well-spoken, and dangerously insinuating.'

Charles the Second, always in want of money, might very possibly have commissioned Blood, after he had stolen the Crown, to pawn or sell its gems in Holland or elsewhere, and the thieves could then have divided the spoil. There can be little doubt that had not young Edwards and his brother-in-law arrived at the Tower when they did, Blood and the two, or others, would have got safely away with the jewels. The plot had been admirably planned, and only the accident of the return of the keeper's son, which Blood could not possibly have foreseen, prevented its successful accomplishment.

In later years Blood is said to have become a Quaker – not a desirable recruit for that most respectable body, one would imagine. He died in 1680, and has had the honour of having had his bold, bad face placed in the National Portrait Gallery; it fully bears out Evelyn's description of the 'villainous unmerciful' look of the man.

OUTSIDE
THE WALLS

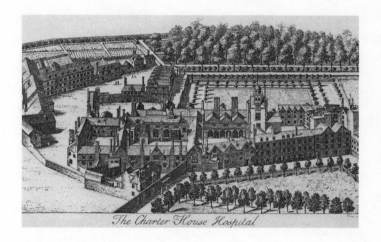

The Charter House Hospital

Bedlam

---

[44] Ned Ward describes Bedlam (1720); from *The London Spy* by Ned Ward.

We prattled away our time till we came in sight of a noble pile of building, which diverted us from our former discourse, and gave my friend the occasion of asking me my thoughts on this magnificent edifice. I told him, I conceived it to be the Lord Mayor's Palace, for I could not imagine so stately a structure could be designed for any quality inferior. He smiled at my innocent conjecture, and informed me this was Bedlam, an hospital for mad folks.

'In truth,' said I, 'I think they were mad that built so costly a College for such a crackbrain society,' adding, it was a pity so fine a building should not be possessed by such as had a sense of their happiness. It was a mad age when this was raised, and no doubt the chief of the City were in a great danger of losing their senses, so contrived it the more noble for their own reception, or they would never have flung away so much money to so foolish a purpose . . .

Accordingly we were admitted through an iron gate, within which sat a brawny Cerberus of an indigo colour, leaning upon a money-box. We turned in through another iron barricade, where we heard such a rattling of chains, drumming of doors, ranting, holloaing, singing and rattling, that I could think of nothing but Don Quevado's vision, where the damned broke loose, and put Hell in an uproar.

The first whimsy-headed wretch of this lunatic family that we observed, was a merry fellow in a straw cap, who was saying to himself that he had an army of eagles at his command. Then clapping his hand upon his head he swore by his crown of moonshine that he would battle all the stars in the skies but he would have some claret. In this interim came a gentleman with a red face to stare at him. 'No wonder,' said his Aerial Majesty, 'that claret is so scarce, look there's a rogue carries more in his nose than I, that am Prince of the Air, have had in my belly for a twelvemonth.'

'If you are the Prince of the Air,' said I, 'why don't you command the Man in the Moon to give you some?' To which he replied, 'The Man in the Moon's a sorry rascal; I sent to him for a dozen bottles but t'other day, and he swore by his bush, his cellar had been dry this six months. But I'll be even with the rogue. I expect a cloud laden with claret to be sent me by the Sun every day, and if a spoonful of lees would save him from choking, the old drunkard should not have a drop.'

We then moved on till we found another remarkable figure worth our observing, who was peeping through his wicket, eating bread and cheese, and talking all the while like a carrier at his supper, chewing his words with his victuals. All that he spoke was in praise of bread and cheese. Bread was good with cheese, and cheese was good with bread, and bread and cheese was good together, and abundance of such stuff, to which my friend and others stood listening.

The next unhappy object amongst this scatter-brained fraternity was a scholar of St John's College, in Cambridge, who was possessed with melancholy, but was very inoffensive, and had the liberty of the gallery. He was a very musical man, which is thought to be one great occasion of his distemper. My friend walked up to him, and introduced some talk, to divert himself with a few of his frenzical extravagancies.

Another lunatic who had liberty of ranging the house caught hold of my school-fellow's arm, and expressed himself after this manner: 'Dost thou know, friend, what thou art doing? Why, thou art talking to a madman, a fiddling fellow, who has so many crotchets in his head that he cracked his brains about his bass and trebles.' 'Prithee,' says my companion, 'what was the occasion of thy distemper?' To which he answered, I am under the confinement for the noble sin of drinking; and if thou hast not a care it will bring thee into the same condition.'

We peeped into another room where a fellow was as hard at work as if he'd been treading mortar.

'What is it, friend,' said I, 'thou art taking all this pains about?'

He answered me thus, still continuing in action: 'I am trampling down conscience under my feet, lest he should rise up and fly in my face. Have a care he does not fright thee, for he looks like the devil and is as fierce as a lion, but that I keep him muzzled. Therefore get thee gone, or I will set him upon thee.' Then he fell a-clapping his hands, and cried, 'Halloo, halloo, halloo, halloo, halloo,' and thus we left him raving.

Another was holding forth with as much vehemence against Kingly government, as a brother of Commonwealth doctrine rails against plurality of livings. I told him he deserved to be hanged for talking treason. 'Now,' says he, 'you're a fool; we madmen have as much privilege of speaking our minds, within these walls, as an ignorant dictator, when he spews out his nonsense to a whole parish. Prithee come and live here, and you may talk what you will, and nobody will call you in question for it. Truth is persecuted everywhere abroad, and flies hither for sanctuary. I can use her as I please and that's more than you dare do. I can tell great men such bold truths as they don't love to hear, without the danger of a whipping post, and that you can't do. For if ever you see a madman hanged for speaking of truth, or a lawyer whipped for lying, I'll be bound to prove my wig a wheel-barrow.'

We then walked into the women's apartment to see what whimsical vagaries their wandering fancies would move them to entertain us withal.

One poor object that happened under our observation was a meagre, old, grey-headed wretch, who looked as wild as an angry cat, and all her tone was, 'The wind is – blow, devil, blow; the wind is – blow, devil blow.' A seaman who was staring at her, and listening to what she said, must needs be inquisitive how the wind sat, and asking her, 'Where is the wind, mother?' She hastily replied, 'The wind is at my stern. Blow, fool, blow.' She was so pleased she had sold him a bargain, that she fell into an extravagant fit of laughter in which he left her.

Having well tired ourselves with the frantic humours and rambling ejaculations of the mad folks, we took a turn to make some few remarks upon the looseness of the spectators, amongst whom we observed abundance of intriguing. Mistresses, we found, were to be had of all ranks, qualities, colours, prices and sizes, from the velvet scarf to the Scotch plaid petticoat. Commodities of all sorts went off, for there wanted not a suitable Jack to every Jill. Every fresh comer was soon engaged in an amour; though they came in single they went out by pairs; 'tis a new Whetstone's Park now the old one's ploughed up, where a sportsman at any hour in the day may meet with game for his purpose; 'tis as great a conveniency to London, as the Long Cellar to Amsterdam, where any stranger may purchase a purge at a small expense. All that I can say of Bedlam, is this, 'tis an almshouse for madmen, a showing room for harlots, a sure market for lechers, a dry walk for loiterers.

The Charterhouse

[45] The foundation of the Charterhouse (1349); from *The History of the London Charterhouse* by W. St J. Hope.

In the year of Our Lord 1349, a violent pestilence breaking out beyond measure in the whole of the kingdom of England, and especially in the city of London where people superabounded, so great a multitude eventually died there that all the cemeteries of the aforesaid city were insufficient for the burial of the dead. For which reason very many were compelled to bury their dead in places unseemly and not hallowed or blessed; for some, it was said, cast the corpses into the river ... most noble knight Sir Walter Mawny heard of this, and moved by Christian piety, was greatly distressed. He therefore summoned his servants and enquired whether anyone of them knew any place apart and enclosed near the city which could be acquired and dedicated for the seemly burial of Christians. One of his servants answered him, 'Behold, my lord, the master of the hospital of St Bartholomew in Smithfield and his brethren have a place enclosed outside Smithfield aforesaid which is called Spitell Crofte where you might very well be able to obtain the accomplishment of your devotion.' He therefore with all diligence and haste sent to the said master and brethren with a view to acquiring the said close . . .

An agreement having been made between Lord de Mawny and the said brethren for having the said farm, the same lord went with the deepest and most earnest devotion to the Lord Ralph then bishop of London, humbly beseeching him to bless the cemetery within the said enclosure. The bishop approving of his devotion, assembled a great multitude, and with a solemn procession came to the said place, and at the instance of Lord Mawny, hallowed it in honour of the Holy and Undivided Trinity and the Annunciation of Our Lady, because that feast is the first Joy of the glorious Virgin Mary, mother of God, and the beginning of all our salvation. But so greatly did the aforesaid mortality increase in the city of London, that in the same new cemetery, as appears by the papal bull, there were buried more than sixty thousand bodies of the dead. And it came to pass, when the very glorious day of the Annunciation of Our Lady arrived, the aforesaid prelate, with the mayor of the City and the sheriffs, as well as the more eminent citizens who are called aldermen, and many others, nearly all barefooted and with a most devout procession, went to the said cemetery, and there the bishop celebrated and preached a solemn sermon to the people, and he took for his text that word 'Hail'.

On the same day the said Lord Mawny founded a chapel, which is now the conventual church, and the bishop of London, Lord Mawny, and the mayor of the same City laid the foundations, namely in the year of Our Lord 1349.

And afterwards the said Lord Mawny purposed to institute there a college of twelve priests, but later on, the Lord so disposing it, as we believe, he changed his purpose. For when that very venerable prelate had gone the way of all flesh, there arose another of pious and most holy memory, master Michael of Northburgh, who, on a certain occasion when, crossing over from the Roman Court, he came through France to Paris and was there making some little stay, visited for the sake of devotion, on various occasions, a house of the Carthusian Order, near the same city. This house, with the austerity of the Order, having carefully considered, he began to be very sad, because there was no house of that Order near the city of London. Moreover from that day he determined of set purpose to take order for and establish there, as far as he could, a house in which he himself intended with all devotion to obtain with the habit of a monk a place both for the honour of God and the safety of his own soul. Further, coming into England, he approached the afore-said Lord Mawny, advising him to found without loss of time in the said cemetery of new sepulture a house of the Carthusian Order, heartily beseeching him that he would agree to have him as an associate and helper for the same work. At length they arranged that the bishop should give Lord Mawny one thousand marks, so that he might become his associate, and after the same lord, the first founder of the house and his successors, the bishops of London, perpetual patrons of the same house.

[46] Sutton establishes a school at the Charterhouse in 1610; from *The Charterhouse of London* by W. F. Taylor.

Of the business before the Governors there was first the definition as to what manner of persons should partake of Sutton's charity. There were to be fourscore of these, and 'They shall not be holden qualified and capable of the Place, unless they can bring good Testimony and Certificate of their good Behaviour, and soundness in Religion, and such as have been Servants to the King's Majesty, either Decrepit or Old, Captains either at Sea or Land, Soldiers maimed or impotent, decayed Merchants, Men fallen into decay thro' Shipwreck, Casuality of Fire, or such evil Accident, those that have been Captives under the Turks, and such like.'

The maimed may be admitted at forty years, and the whole at fifty.

As to the boys for the school only those shall be admitted whose parents have no estates to leave them, or want means to bring them up.

The constitution and rules of Charterhouse were drawn up with remarkable fullness and care, and are largely due to the original Governors. They were a body of men among the best of their period, and they included, in Lancelot Andrewes and John Coke, two men, in particular, of great power and character.

The constitution which was thus elaborated may be here briefly described. The Governors were to be in number sixteen, of which the Master was to be one. The three high offices were those of Master, Preacher, and School-master, and the spheres of these three formed the 'triple good', as Bacon termed it, of Sutton's foundation. The master is the most important of the three, and he shall have 'the œconomical Government of the House and Household during the Governors' pleasure.'

The Preacher must be at least thirty, but twenty-seven years would qualify the Schoolmaster. By the original foundation the boys were to number forty, and to this number the foundation scholars, or 'gown boys', were restricted till the nineteenth century. Each boy was to bring with him to school a change of outer apparel, two new shirts, three new pairs of stockings, three new pairs of shoes, and books for the form he is in, or money to buy them. Boys of the highest form shall every Sunday 'set up in the Great Hall four Greek and four Latin verses apiece, upon any Part of the second Lesson appointed for that Day, for the Master of the Hospital or any Stranger to view and examine; as also two shall be weekly appointed for reading the Chapters and saying Grace at every meal in both Halls.'

The Schoolmaster 'shall be careful and discreet to observe the Nature and Genius of the Scholars, and accordingly instruct and correct them. In correction they shall be moderate, in instruction diligent, correcting according to the quality of the fault in Matters of manners, and according to the Capacity of the fault in matters of learning.'

Each Pensioner shall bring two pair of new sheets with him on entry. All Pensioners shall give dutiful reverence to the Master, they shall stand before him with their heads uncovered, not presuming while they are in his 'Presence to put on their hats (except it be at the Table at Dinner or Supper), and none shall give or use any evil reviling or railing Speeches of him before his Face, or behind his back.'

'No pensioner, nor inferior Officer, shall wear any Weapon or unseemly Apparel in the Hospital, but only such as it becometh Hospital men to wear.'

They must wear their gowns whilst within the Hospital, but never in a tavern or ale house 'upon Pain of such Punishment as the Master in his discretion shall inflict.' They are allowed two months' leave of absence a year, with allowance then of two-thirds of commons.

It was established that 'There shall be an Anniversary Commemoration of the Founder kept every 12th Day of December with solemn Service, a Sermon, and such Increase of Commons, as is allowed on great Festivals.'

[47] Life at the school in the 1840s, Mr Locker and Mr Howard Staunton; from *Old & New London* by W. Thornbury.

'I was,' says Mr Locker, 'at the Charterhouse from 1842 to 1847. At that time Dr A. P. . . . while I was there the numbers of the school varied from about 150 to 180. Of these 44 (and, at one time, by a special privilege, 45) were foundationers, or gown-boys, who were fed, educated, and partially clothed, by the institution. Each governor (the governors were the leading men of the country, cabinet ministers, archbishops, &c.) selected a boy in turn, as a vacancy occurred, and the eligible age was from ten till fourteen. Most of the gown-boys were either aristocratically connected, or possessed interest with the higher class. The remainder of the boys, whose parents paid for their education, lived respectively in the three boarding-houses of Messrs Saunders, Walford, and Dicken, and were called Sanderites, Verrites, and Dickenites. There were also about twenty day-scholars. The upper school consisted of the sixth and fifth forms, which had the privilege of fagging; then came the fourth form, a sort of neutral class, neither allowed to fag or be fagged, and very often, in consequence, great bullies. The lower school (all subject to fagging) were the shell, the third, second, first forms, and the petties. In our house we had four monitors, who exercised some of the duties of masters. They could cane boys for breach of rules, and could put their names down in the black book (three insertions during one week in that volume involved a flogging; and the floggings, administered with long apple-twigs, were very severe). These monitors, and some others of the big boys, had little slips of rooms for their own use, called "studies", and each proprietor of a study had a study-fag, who, besides keeping his books free from dust and in good order, made his coffee, toasted his roll, washed his hair-brushes, &c. Boys rather liked this special service, as it saved them from the indiscriminate fagging inflicted by strangers. The cricket-fagging was the worst. I have been kept stopping balls behind a wicket for a fellow practising for five hours at a stretch, and beaten on the back with a bat if I missed a ball. Fagging produced laziness and tyranny among the big boys, and lying and deception among the little ones. The monitors, by the way, had a special set of fags called "basinites," whose business it was to take care that the basins were filled, towels dried, and soap ready in the monitors' bedroom, for they washed up-stairs. We washed in a public room, fitted up with basins. The dietary arrangements at Charterhouse were under the management of a jolly old red-faced gentleman named Tucker, who had formerly been in the army. He was called the

"Manciple". The food was very good; and on Fridays (perhaps as a protest against Roman Catholicism) we fared especially well. Friday was styled "Consolation Day", and we had roast lamb and currant tart, or roast pork and apple tart, according to the season of the year . . .'

'In former times,' says Mr Howard Staunton, 'there was a curious custom in this school, termed "pulling-in", by which the lower boys manifested their opinion of the seniors in a rough but very intelligible fashion. One day in the year the fags, like the slaves in Rome, had freedom, and held a kind of saturnalia. On this privileged occasion they used to seize the upper boys, one by one, and drag them from the playground into the schoolroom, and, accordingly as the victim was popular or the reverse, he was either cheered and mildly treated, or was hooted, groaned at, and sometimes soundly cuffed. The day selected was Good Friday, and, although the practice was nominally forbidden, the officials, for many years, took no measures to prevent it. One ill-omened day, however, when the sport was at the best, the doctor was espied approaching the scene of battle. A general *sauve qui peut* ensued, and, in the hurry of flight, a meek and quiet lad (the Hon. Mr Howard), who happened to be seated on some steps, was crushed so dreadfully that, to the grief of the whole school, he shortly after died. "Pulling-in" was thenceforth sternly interdicted.'

Charterhouse School left London in June 1872.

Around Fleet Street

[48] The foundation and early history of the Temple (1240); from *Survey of London* by J. Stow.

This house was founded by the Knights Templars in England, in the reign of Henry II, and the same was dedicated to God and our blessed Lady, by Heraclius, Patriarch of the church called the Holy Resurrection, in Jerusalem, in the year of Christ, 1185.

These Knights Templars took their beginning about the year 1118, in manner following. Certain noblemen, horsemen, religiously bent, bound by vow themselves in the hands of the Patriarch of Jerusalem, to serve Christ after the manner of regular canons in chastity and obedience, and to renounce their own proper wills for ever; the first of which order were Hugh Paganus, and Geffrey de S. Andromare. And whereas at the first they had no certain habitation, Baldwin, King of Jerusalem, granted unto them a dwelling place in his palace by the Temple, and the canons of the same Temple gave them the street thereby to build therein their houses of office, and the patriarch, the king, the nobles, and prelates gave unto them certain revenues out of their lordships.

Their first profession was for safeguard of the pilgrims coming to visit the sepulchre, and to keep the highways against the lying in wait of thieves, etc . . .

Many noble men in all parts of Christendom became brethren of this order, and built for themselves temples in every city or great town in England, but this at London was their chief house, which they built after the form of the temple near to the sepulchre of our Lord at Jerusalem . . .

This Temple was again dedicated 1240, belike also newly re-edified then . . .

King Edward I in the year 1283, taking with him Robert Waleran, and others, came to the Temple, where calling for the keeper of the treasure house, as if he meant to see his mother's jewels, that were laid up there to be safely kept, he entered into the house, breaking the coffers of certain persons that had likewise brought their money thither, and he took away from thence to the value of a thousand pounds.

Many parliaments and great councils have been there kept, as may appear by our histories. In the year 1308, all the Templars in England, as also in other parts of Christendom, were apprehended and committed to divers prisons. In 1310, a provincial council was holden at London, against the Templars in England, upon heresy and other articles whereof they were accused, but denied all except one or two of them, notwithstanding they all did confess that they could not purge themselves fully as faultless, and so they were condemned to perpetual penance in several monasteries, where they behaved themselves modestly.

[49] Printing comes to Fleet Street (1476); from *Fleet Street in Seven Centuries* by W. G. Bell.

Wynkyn de Worde . . . was brought to England by Caxton, when the father of English printing in the year 1476

set up his press within the Almonry at Westminster, under
the heraldic sign of the Red Pale . . .

Late in the year 1500, or early in 1501, Wynkyn de
Worde moved into Fleet Street: his reason, one may
assume, partly because the Red Pale had become too small
for a growing business, and partly to be near the centre of
the book-selling trade, which at that time was settled
about St Paul's Churchyard. The site occupied by his press
is known within a small compass. He rented two houses,
one of which, no doubt, was his printing office, and the
other a dwelling-house, paying the high rental of 66s. 8d.
a year. Over the narrow street in front of his printing
house swung the sign of the Sun. It was in St Bride's
parish, over against (or opposite) the conduit in Fleet
Street. It was on the south side, and near the church.

In the years from his establishment in Fleet Street until
his death in 1535, Wynkyn de Worde printed upwards of
500 books, known either by complete volumes or by
fragments, and probably many others that are lost – a
production that marks him as by far the busiest of the
early English printers . . .

Wynkyn de Worde is justly credited with having introduced the art of printing into Fleet Street, by reason of the
importance of his press and its large output, as well as by
date . . .

In 1503 Richard Pynson followed de Worde into Fleet
Street. His sign was the George (St George) next St Dunstan's Churchyard, by the Chancery Lane corner. He, too,
was a law printer, but something more – his books, by
their unrivalled merit, proclaim him the foremost artist-
craftsman that had been known in this country till his day.
Indeed, the Continent had nothing to show in typographi-
cal art excelling his Boccacio of 1494, his Morton Missal
of 1500 – a really splendid work – and the *Intrationum
excellentissimus liber* of 1510.

Pynson's output was scarcely one-half that of Wynkyn
de Worde, but the quality is uniformly higher. From his
press came editions of the works of Chaucer, Skelton,
Lydgate, and Froisart, and Æsop's Fables. The Princess

Margaret, mother of King Henry the Seventh, was his early patron, and her support encouraged him in printing rich books. He was the first English printer to abandon the sole use of black letter, and introduce the Roman type now in universal use.

[50] Catherine of Aragon tried at Blackfriars (1527); from *The Life of Cardinal Wolsey* by Thomas Cavendish.

There was a court placed with tables, benches, and bars, like a consistory, a place judicial for the judges to sit on. There was also a cloth of estate under the which sat the king; and the queen sat some distance beneath the king: under the judges' feet sat the officers of the court. The chief scribe there was Dr Stephens (which was after Bishop of Winchester); the apparitor was one Cooke, most commonly called Cooke of Winchester. Then sat there within the said court, directly before the king and judges, the Archbishop of Canterbury, Doctor Warham, and all the other bishops. Then at both the ends, with a bar made for them, the counsels on both sides. The doctors for the king was Doctor Sampson, which was after Bishop of Chichester, and Doctor Bell, which after was Bishop of Worcester, with divers other. The proctors on the king's part were Doctor Peter, which was after made the king's chief secretary, and Doctor Tregonell, and divers others.

Now on the other side stood the counsel for the queen, Doctor Fisher, Bishop of Rochester, and Doctor Standish, some time a Grey Friar, and then Bishop of St Asaph in Wales, two notable clerks in divinity, and in especial the Bishop of Rochester, a very godly man and a devout person, who after suffered death at Tower Hill; the which was greatly lamented through all the foreign Universities of Christendom. There was also another ancient doctor, called, as I do remember, Doctor Ridley, a very small person in stature, but surely a great and an excellent clerk in divinity.

The court being thus furnished and ordered, the judges commanded the crier to command silence; then was the judges' commission, which they had of the pope, published and read openly before all the audience there assembled. That done, the crier called the king, by the name of 'King Harry of England come into the court, etc.' With that the king answered and said, 'Here, my lords!' Then he called the queen, by the name of 'Katherine Queen of England, come into the court, etc.;' who made no answer to the same, but rose up incontinent out of her chair, where as she sat, and because she could not come directly to the king for the distance which severed them, she took pain to go about unto the king, kneeling down at his feet in the sight of all the court and assembly, to whom she said in effect, in broken English, as followeth:

'Sir,' quoth she, 'I beseech you for all the loves that hath been between us, and for the love of God, let me have justice and right, take of me some pity and compassion, for I am a poor woman and a stranger born out of your dominion, I have here no assured friend, and much less indifferent counsel; I flee to you as to the head of justice within this realm. Alas! Sir, wherein have I offended you, or what occasion of displeasure have I designed against your will and pleasure? Intending (as I perceive) to put me from you, I take God and all the world to witness, that I have been to you a true humble and obedient wife, ever conformable to your will and pleasure, that never said or did anything to the contrary thereof, being always well pleased and contented with all things wherein ye had any delight or dalliance, whether it were in little or much, I never grudged in word or countenance, or showed a visage or spark of discontentation. I loved all those who ye loved only for your sake, whether I had cause or no; and whether they were my friends or my enemies. This twenty years I have been your true wife or more, and by me ye have had divers children, although it hath pleased God to call them out of this world, which hath been no default in me.

'And when ye had me at the first, I take God to be my

judge, I was a true maid without touch of man; and whether it be true or no, I put it to your conscience. If there be any just cause by the law that ye can allege against me, either of dishonesty or any other impediment to banish and put me from you, I am well content to depart, to my great shame and dishonour; and if there be none, then here I most lowly beseech you let me remain in my former estate, and receive justice at your princely hands. The king your father was in the time of his reign of such estimation thorough the world for his excellent wisdom, that he was accounted and called of all men the second Solomon; and my father Ferdinand, King of Spain, who was esteemed to be one of the wittiest princes that reigned in Spain many years before, were both wise and excellent kings in wisdom and princely behaviour. It is not therefore to be doubted, but that they elected and gathered as wise counsellors about them as to their high discretions was thought meet. Also, as me see-meth there was in those days as wise, as well-learned men, and men of as good judgment as be at this present in both realms, who thought then the marriage between you and me good and lawful. Therefore is it a wonder to me what new inventions are now invented against me, that never intended but honesty. And cause me to stand to the order and judgment of this new court, wherein ye may do me much wrong, if ye intend any cruelty; for ye may condemn me for lack of sufficient answer, having no indifferent counsel, but such as be assigned me, with whose wisdom and learning I am not acquainted. Ye must consider that they cannot be indifferent counsellors for my part which be your subjects, and taken out of your own council before, wherein they be made privy, and dare not, for your displeasure, disobey your will and intent, being once made privy thereto. Therefore I most humbly require you, in the way of charity, and for the love of God, who is the just judge, to spare the extremity of this new court, until I may be advertised what way and order my friends in Spain will advise me to take. And if ye will not extend to me so much indifferent favour, your pleasure then be fulfilled, and to God I commit my case!'

And even with that she rose up, making low courtesy to the king, and so departed from thence. Many supposed that she would have resorted again to her former place; but she took her direct way out of the house, leaning (as she was wont always to do) upon the arm of her General Receiver, called Master Griffith. And the king being advertised of her departure, commanded the crier to call her again, who called her by the name of 'Katherine Queen of England, come into the court, etc.' With that quoth Master Griffith, *'Madam, ye be called again.'* 'On, on,' quoth she, 'it maketh no matter, for it is no indifferent court for me, therefore I will not tarry: go on your ways.' And thus she departed out of that court, without any farther answer at that time, or at any other, nor would never appear at any other court after.

[51] Sir Thomas Wyatt is defeated in Fleet Street (1553); from *The Chronicle of Queen Jane and of two years of Queen Mary*, edited by J. G. Nichols.

Some saide [Wyat's] entent was to have been in London, yf he had coulde, before daye; but hering that the erle of Pembroke was come into the feldes, he stayed at Knightesbridge untyll daye, wher his men being very wery with travel of that night and the daye before, and also partely feble and faynte, having receyved small sustenance since ther comyng out of Southwarke, rested.

The quenes scout, apon his retourne to the court, declared their coming to Brainforde, which subden newes was so fearefull that therwith the quene and all the court was wonderfully affryghted. Dromes went thoroughe London at iiij. of the clocke, warninge all soldears to arme themselves and to repaire to Charing crosse. The quene was once determyned to come to the Tower furthwith, but shortelie after she sende worde she would tarry ther to se the uttermost. Mayny thought she wolde have ben in the felde in person.

Here was no small a-dowe in London, and likewise the Tower made great preparation of defence. By x. of the clocke, or somewhat more, the erle of Penbroke had set his troopp of horsemen on the hill in the higheway above the new brige over against saynct James; his footemen was sett in ij. battailles somewhat lower, and nerer Charing crosse. At the lane turning downe by the brike wall from Islington-warde he had sett also certayn other horsemen, and he had planted his ordenance apon the hill side. In the meane season Wyat and his company planted his ordenance apon the hill beyonde sainct James, almost over agaynst the park corner; and himself, after a fewe words spoken to his soldears, came downe the olde lane on foote, hard by the courte gate at saincte James's, with iiij. or v. auncyentes; his men marching in goode array. Cutbart Vaughan, and about ij. auncyentes, turned downe towards Westminster. The erle of Pembroke's horsemen hoveryd all this while without moving, untyll all was passed by, saving the tayle, upon which they dyd sett and cut of. The other marched forwarde, and never stayed or retourned to the ayde of their tayle. The greate ordenaunce shott of fresly on bothe sydes. Wyat's ordenance overshott the troope of horsemen. The quenes ordenance one pece struck iiij. of Wyat's companye in a ranck, apon ther hedes, and, sleying them, strake through the wall into the parke. More harme was not done by the great shott of neither partie. The quenes hole battayle of footemen standing stille, Wyat passed along by the wall towardes Charing crosse, wher the saide horsemen that wer ther sett upon parte of them, but were soone forced backe.

At Charinge crosse ther stoode the lorde chamberlayne, with the garde and a nomber of other, almost a thousande persons, the whiche, upon Wyat's coming, shott at his company, and at last fledd to the court gates, which certayn pursued, and forced them with shott to shyt the court gates against them. In this repulse the said lord chamberlayn and others were so amased that men cryed Treason! treason! in the court, and had thought that the erle of Penbroke, who was assayling the tayle of his enemeys, had gon to Wyat, taking his part agaynst the quene. There should ye have seene runninge and cryenge of ladyes and gentyll women, shyting of dores, and such a scryking and noyse as yt was wonderfull to here.

The said Wyat, with his men, marched still forwarde, all along to Temple barre, also thoroghe Fleete street, along tyll he cam to Ludgate, his men going not in eny goode order or array. It is saide that in Fleet street certayn of the lorde treasurer's band, to the nomber of CCC. men, mett theym, and so going on the one syde passyd by theym coming on the other syde without eny whit saying to theym. Also this is more strandge: the saide Wyat and his company passyd along by a great company of harnessyd men, which stoode on bothe sydes, without eny withstandinge them, and as he marched forwarde through Fleet street, moste with theire swords drawne, some cryed 'Queene Mary hath graunted our request, and geven us pardon.' Others said, 'The quene hathe pardoned us.' Thus Wyat cam even to Ludgate, and knockyd calling to come in, saying, there was Wyat, whome the quene had graunted their requestes; but the lorde William Howard standing at the gate, saide, 'Avaunt, traytour! thou shalt not come in here.' And then Wyat awhill stayed, and, as some say, rested him apon a seate (at) the Bellsavage gate; at last, seing he coulde not come in, and belike being deceaved of the ayde which he hoped out of the cetye, retourned backe agayne in arraye towards Charing crosse, and was never stopped tyll he cam to Temple barre, wher certayn horsemen which cam from the felde met them in the face; and then begann the fight agayne to waxe hote, tyll an heralde saide to maister Wyat, 'Sir, ye were best by my counsell to yelde. You see this day is gon agaynst you, and in resysting ye can get no goode, but be the death of all theis your souldears, to your greate perill of soule. Perchaunce ye may fynde the quene mercyfull, and the rather yf ye stint so greate a bloudshed as ys like here to be.' Wyat herewith being somewhat astonished (although he sawe his men bent to fyght it out to the death), said, 'Well, yf I shall needs yelde, I will yelde me to a gentyll-man;' to whom Sir Morice Barkeley cam straight up, and bayd him lepe up behinde him; and another toke Thomas Cobham and William Knevet; and so caryed them behind theym upon their horses to the courte. Then was taking of men on all sydes. It is saide that in this conflyct one pikeman, setting his backe to the wall at sainct James, kept xvij. horsemen of him a great tyme, and at last was slayne. At this battell was slayne in the felde, by estymacion, on both sydes, not past xl^{ty} persons, as far as could be lerned by certayne that viewed the same; but ther was many sore hurt; and some thincke ther was many slayne in houses. The noys of women and children, when the conflyct was at Charing crosse, was so great and shirle, that yt was harde to the toppe of the White tower; and also the great shot was well deserned ther out of sainct James felde. Ther stood apon the leddes there the lorde marques, Sir Nicholas Poyns, Sir Thomas Pope, Master John Seamer, and others. From the battayle when one cam and brought worde that the quene was like to have the victory, and that the horsemen had dyscomfyted the tayle of his enemyes, the lorde marques for joye gave the messenger x^{s} in golde, and fell in great rejoysing.

[52] 1710, First Catalogue of the Royal Society & description of a Society meeting held in Crane Court, Fleet Street; from *Old and New London* by W. Thornbury.

The quills of a porcupine, which on certain occasions the creature can shoot at the pursuing enemy and erect at pleasure.

The flying squirrel, which for a good nut-tree will pass a river on the bark of a tree, erecting his tail for a sail.

The leg-bone of an elephant, brought out of Syria for the thigh-bone of a giant. In winter, when it begins to rain, elephants are mad, and so continue from April to September, chained to some tree, and then become tame again.

Tortoises, when turned on their backs, will sometimes fetch deep sighs and shed abundance of tears.

A humming-bird and nest, said to weigh but twelve grains; his feathers are set in gold, and sell at a great rate.

A bone, said to be taken out of a mermaid's head.

The largest whale – liker an island than an animal.

The white shark, which sometimes swallows men whole.

A siphalter, said with its sucker to fasten on a ship and stop it under sail.

A stag-beetle, whose horns, worn in a ring, are good against the cramp.

A mountain cabbage – one reported 300 feet high. . . .

The Royal Society . . . combines within itself the purposes of the Parisian Academy of Sciences and that of Inscriptions; it cultivates, in fact, not only the higher branches of science, but literature also. Every one, whatever his position, and whether English or foreign, who has made observations which appear to the society worthy of its attention, is allowed to submit them to it either by word of mouth or in writing. I once saw a joiner, in his working clothes, announce to the society a means he had discovered of explaining the causes of tides. He spoke a long time, evidently not knowing what he was talking about; but he was listened to with the greatest attention, thanked for his confidence in the value of the society's opinion, requested to put his ideas into writing, and conducted to the door by one of the principal members.

The place in which the society holds its meetings is neither large nor handsome. It is a long, low, narrow room, only furnished with a table (covered with green cloth), some morocco chairs, and some wooden benches, which rise above each other along the room. The table, placed in front of the fire-place at the bottom of the room, is occupied by the president (who sits with his back to the fire) and the secretaries. On this table is placed a large silver-gilt mace, similar to the one in use in the House of Commons, and which, as is the case with the latter, is laid at the foot of the table when the society is in committee.

The president is preceded on his entrance and departure by the beadle of the society, bearing this mace. He has beside him, on his table, a little wooden mallet for the purpose of imposing silence when occasion arises, but this is very seldom the case. With the exception of the secretaries and the president, everyone takes his place haphazard, at the same time taking great pains to avoid causing any confusion or noise. The society may be said to consist, as a body corporate, of a committee of about twenty persons, chosen from those of its associates who have the fuller opportunities of devoting themselves to their favourite studies. The president and the secretaries are *ex-officio* members of the committee, which is renewed every year – an arrangement which is so much the more necessary that, in 1765, the society numbered 400 British members, of whom more than forty were peers of the realm, five of the latter being most assiduous members of the committee.

[53] Jacobite riots (1716); from *Old and New London* by W. Thornbury.

The Papists and Jacobites, in pursuance of their rebellious designs, assembled a mob on Friday night last, and threatened to attack Mr Read's mug-house in Salisbury Court, in Fleet Street; but, seeing the loyal gentlemen that were there were resolved to defend themselves, the cowardly Papists and Jacobites desisted for that time. But on Monday night the villains meeting together again in a most rebellious manner, they began first to attack Mr Goslin's house, at the sign of the 'Blew Boar's Head', near Water Lane, in Fleet Street, breaking the windows thereof, for no other reason but because he is well-affected to his Majesty King George and the present Government. Afterwards they went to the above-said mug-house in Salisbury Court; but the cowardly Jacks not being able to accomplish their hellish designs that night, they assembled next day in great numbers from all parts of the town, breaking the windows with brick-bats, broke open the cellar, got into the lower rooms, which they robb'd, and pull'd down the sign, which was carried in triumph before the mob by one Thomas Bean, servant to Mr Carnegie and Mr Cassey, two rebels under sentence of death, and for which he is committed to Newgate, as well as several others, particularly one Hook, a joyner, in Blackfriars, who is charged with acting a part in gutting the mug-house. Some of the rioters were desperately wounded, and one Vaughan, a seditious weaver, formerly an apprentice in Bridewell, and since employed there, who was a notorious ringleader of mobs, was kill'd at the aforesaid mug-house. Many notorious Papists were seen to abet and assist in this villanous rabble, as were others, who call themselves Churchmen, and are like to meet with a suitable reward in due time for their assaulting gentlemen who meet at these mug-houses only to drink prosperity to the Church of England as by law established, the King's health, the Prince of Wales's, and the rest of the Royal Family, and those of his faithful and loyal Ministers. But it is farther to be observed that women of mean, scandalous lives, do frequently point, hiss, and cry out 'Whigs' upon his Majesty's good and loyal subjects, by which, raising a mob, they are often insulted by them. But 'tis hoped the magistrates will take such methods which may prevent the like insults for the future.

Thursday last the coroner's inquest sat on the body of the person killed in Salisbury Court, who were for bringing in their verdict, wilful murder against Mr Read, the man of the mug-house; but some of the jury stick out, and will not agree with that verdict; so that the matter is deferr'd till Monday next.

[54] Johnson compiles the first English dictionary (1755); from *The Life of Samuel Johnson* by James Boswell.

For the mechanical part he employed, as he told me, six amanuenses; and let it be remembered by the natives of

North-Britain, to whom he is supposed to have been so hostile, that five of them were of that country.

. . . While the Dictionary was going forward, Johnson lived part of the time in Holborn, part in Gough-square, Fleet-street; and he had an upper room fitted up like a counting-house for the purpose, in which he gave to the copyists their several task. The words, partly taken from other dictionaries, and partly supplied by himself, having been first written down with spaces left between them, he delivered in writing their etymologies, definitions, and various significations. The authorities were copied from the books themselves, in which he had marked the passages with a black-lead pencil, the traces of which could easily be effaced. I have seen several of them, in which that trouble had not been taken; so that they were just as when used by the copyists. It is remarkable, that he was so attentive in the choice of the passages in which words were authorized, that one may read page after page of his Dictionary with improvement and pleasure; and it should not pass unobserved, that he has quoted no author whose writings had a tendency to hurt sound religion and morality . . .

Dr Adams found him one day busy at his Dictionary, when the following dialogue ensued: 'ADAMS. This is a great work, Sir. How are you to get all the etymologies? JOHNSON. Why, Sir, here is a shelf with Junius, and Skinner, and others; and there is a Welch gentleman who has published a collection of Welch proverbs, who will help me with the Welch. ADAMS. But, Sir, how can you do this in three years? JOHNSON. Sir, I have no doubt that I can do it in three years. ADAMS. But the French Academy, which consists of forty members, took forty years to compile their Dictionary. JOHNSON. Sir, thus it is. This is the proportion. Let me see; forty times forty is sixteen hundred. As three to sixteen hundred, so is the proportion of an Englishman to a Frenchman.' With so much ease and pleasantry could he talk of that prodigious labour which he had undertaken to execute.

[55] Thomas Chatterton commits suicide (1770); from *The Life of Chatterton* by G. Gregory.

There can be little doubt that his death was preceded by extreme indigence. Mr Cross, an apothecary in Brook-street, informed Mr Warton, that while Chatterton lived in the neighbourhood, he frequently called at the shop, and was repeatedly pressed by Mr Cross to dine or sup with him in vain. One evening, however, human frailty so far prevailed over his dignity, as to tempt him to partake of the regale of a barrel of oysters, when he was observed to eat most voraciously. Mrs Wolfe, a barber's wife, within a few doors of the house where Mrs Angel lived, has also afforded ample testimony, both to his poverty and his pride. She says, 'that Mrs Angel told her, after his death, that on 24 August, as she knew he had not eaten any thing for two or three days, she begged he would take some dinner with her; but he was offended at her expressions, which seemed to hint he was in want, and assured her he was not hungry.' In these desperate circumstances . . . Chatterton, as appears by the Coroner's Inquest, swallowed arsenic in water, on 24 August 1770, and died in consequence thereof the next day. He was buried in a shell, in the burying ground of Shoe-lane workhouse.' Whatever unfinished pieces he might have, he cautiously destroyed them before his death; and his room, when broken open, was found covered with little scraps of paper.

[56] A Sweeney Todd murder (1798); from *Sweeney Todd* by P. Haining.

It was a dark, rainy afternoon in late autumn as Thomas Shadwell made his way along Fleet Street to his job as a Beadle at St Bartholomew's Hospital. He lived in Covent Garden and normally walked the mile from his home by way of Temple Bar, down Fleet Street and Farringdon Street, and then up Snow Hill to the hospital. Normally he worked during the day; but the rising tide of crime in

the city of late had made the hospital authorities concerned for security and they had instructed Shadwell to be
doubly vigilant. He had therefore decided to work the
occasional night shift.

Shadwell was a comfortably-off man, and took pride in
his job and his appearance. He wore with pride the three-
cornered hat and cloak of his office which was provided
by St Bartholomew's and he was always well turned out
and clean shaven. In his pockets he always kept some
change for a drink on his way home.

This day, however, his beard was feeling decidedly
rough and he decided to have a shave before starting
work. He had passed the shop with 'Sweeney Todd,
Barber' over the door many times, but never ventured
inside. Previously he had always gone to a barber he knew
in Drury Lane, but today he felt like a change. It was to
prove a fatal mistake.

As he neared Temple Bar, Shadwell became aware of
how few people were about. Those like him who had to
brave the elements were pressing as close to the buildings
as they could to escape the worst of the weather. Although
it was not yet quite five o'clock, the general gloom made
it seem like evening already. It was going to be a long, wet
night, Thomas Shadwell thought.

Lights were visible in the windows of most of the
taverns and shops he passed, but it was only when a door
was hastily opened by someone going in or out that any
flash of colour and warmth illuminated the road outside.

In the downpour, the outlines of the buildings all
around seemed indistinct, and the few people about huddled shapelessly into their clothes as they hurried by. There
was not much traffic, either, and even the usual street
sellers who peddled their wares had disappeared into the
alleyways or taverns.

Shadwell paused just as he reached St Dunstan's
Church. A whirring sound had caught his ear, and as his
eyes glanced upwards at the big clock projecting from the
side of the church, he saw the hour was just about to
strike. For a moment there was stillness and then two

small doors opened beside the clock face. A pair of gold-painted figures emerged, their heads moving from side to side. With mechanical efficiency they struck five blows on the bells suspended between them. Shadwell allowed the rain to drizzle onto his face as he watched. The sight of the clock in operation never failed to impress him, though he must have seen it a thousand times.

It was the flash of something from the nearby window of a shop which disturbed his thoughts. A flash of something silver illuminated by an oil lamp. It had come from the window of 'Sweeney Todd, Barber'.

The shop was pretty dark and evil-looking, Shadwell had decided on past occasions as he walked by; and on a day like this with the overhanging gables throwing everything beneath into even deeper shadows, it looked, if anything, more sinister still.

The Beadle ran his hand over his chin. It was definitely heavy with stubble: he couldn't turn up for work like this. He shrugged. What shop in this grimy city didn't look the worse for wear after some of the bad winters there had been recently? he thought.

Shadwell made up his mind. He pushed open the door and walked into the barber's shop.

The man he saw standing inside in the feeble glow of a pair of oil lamps seemed very much what one would expect from the outside of his premises. He was heavily built, had small, glinting eyes and a mouth with a rather unpleasant droop to it. His hair grew thickly on his head, and behind both ears he had a pair of combs. His hands were large, and his finger nails rather dirty. When the man smiled his ingratiating smile it became something akin to a squint.

For a moment, Thomas Shadwell stood rooted to the spot. The barber put down the razor he had been stropping and crossed the room to his side. Todd indicated the big wooden chair standing in the centre of the shop.

'Is it a shave you require, sir? he said. 'Sit down. I'll soon polish you off.'

Shadwell then became aware of another, smaller, figure

standing in the gloom. He made out the features of a young boy wearing an apron similar to that of the barber. He was obviously the man's 'soap boy'.

As if suddenly becoming aware of the boy, too, the barber spoke to him. 'Now, lad, I've just realized the time. I want you to hurry off and fetch me some fish for my tea while I attend to this gentleman. Here is the money. Now be off with you.'

The boy seemed to hesitate momentarily before taking the two coins from his master's outstretched hand. But once he had taken them, he hurried out of the front door without a backward glance.

Shadwell felt just the smallest twinge of unease as he allowed himself to be led to the chair: it was made of very sturdy wood, he thought, and he wondered why it was set in the centre of the room so far away from the table on which the barber kept his soap bowls and razors.

As he took off his cloak and hat and handed them to the barber whom he assumed must be the curiously named Sweeney Todd, Shadwell was conscious of the rain beating with increasing force against the window and the sound of some rusty hinges swinging to and fro outside.

'What a day it is, Mr Todd,' he said. 'I hope you have a steady hand.'

'Oh, don't be afraid of that, my dear sir,' the barber replied with something close to a smirk on his face. 'My hand is as steady as it was twenty years ago when I was a boy. The elements have no effect upon me, I assure you!'

At this he gave a sinister, rather mirthless laugh which made the hairs on the back of Thomas Shadwell's neck stand up.

'Do seat yourself comfortably, sir,' Sweeney Todd continued, taking down one of his Magnum Bonum razors and strapping it carefully on the belt hanging beside the fireplace.

As he settled back in the chair, Shadwell was conscious of a smell – a rather unpleasant smell. He was just about to sniff again, when the barber spoke.

'I have not seen you before, sir,' the tradesman said,

finishing his stropping and now poised above his customer. 'I can see you are a man of distinction. A Beadle, too,'

'Indeed,' Shadwell replied. 'I am employed by St Bartholomew's Hospital. A fine hospital. Do you know it?'

'I have not had the need of its services,' the barber grinned his evil grin again, 'but I have heard good reports. You have an important position there?'

Shadwell could not resist preening himself.

'I am the most senior of the Beadles,' he said. 'Thirty years service. This fine timepiece was given to me only last year.'

The Beadle put his hand into his pocket and withdrew a gold watch on a chain that glinted in the light of the oil lamp. Some coins also jingled in his pocket as he moved.

'A fine piece. A fine piece, *indeed*,' the barber said, the gleam in his eyes hidden as he moved around to the back of the chair. Then:

'Oh, pardon me, sir. What am I thinking of. About to shave you without hot water! Do excuse me a moment while I go to my back room for a bowl and some more clean towels.'

Sweeney Todd instantly left the room. Shadwell allowed his eyes to roam around the place. It did not look as if it had been properly cleaned for years. Should he take this moment to get up and leave before this unsavoury man got to work on him? Polish him off, hadn't he said. After all, why should he pay to be frightened half to death?

The Beadle's thoughts were suddenly interrupted by a sound from the back room where the barber had disappeared. It sounded like the noise of a heavy bolt being drawn, followed by a noise of creaking that seemed to come from beneath his feet.

Before the startled man could even move, however, he felt the chair beneath him begin to tip backwards. The floorboards in front of his feet also started to rise up in front of his startled eyes, and an involuntary cry sprang from the lips. Then the ceiling seemed to spin before the Beadle's eyes and the last thing Thomas Shadwell ever felt was falling backwards out of his chair and plunging down, down into a stygian darkness . . .

Scarcely had the victim of Sweeney Todd's chair struck the floor of the cellar below with a sickening crunch and lapsed into instant unconsciousness, than another chair had revolved noiselessly to take the place of the original.

From behind the door, the Demon Barber peered into the room to assure himself that everything was as it should be. The shaving chair was once more empty awaiting the next customer.

Sweeney Todd selected another Magnum Bonum from the rack on the wall and began to descend the stairs to his cellar.

'Another rich one for the picking,' he smirked to himself. 'See how I polish 'em off!'

[57] The newspapers leave Fleet Street in the 1980s; from *Goodbye Fleet Street* by R. Edwards.

The great exodus in fact began when Maxwell succeeded in transferring the production of the *Sporting Life* after tumultuous rows with the printing chapels as early as 1985. It was followed by Rupert Murdoch's stunning overnight flit to Fortress Wapping, at which the newest production techniques replaced the oldest, without restrictive practices, and with no more than a couple of issues wholly lost. The other papers had to follow or face ruin. The *Daily Mail* and the *Mail on Sunday* planned to move their editorial teams to Barker's in Kensington High Street, which would have been unthinkable three years ago, and their printing to dockland. The *Daily* and *Sunday Telegraphs*, already printing on the Isle of Dogs, decided to shift their journalists and management to South Plaza Quay, also in dockland. The *Observer* headed for Battersea, with regional printing, and the *Financial Times* to its new print works near the Blackwall Tunnel. Only the Express papers seemed to linger. They followed Maxwell's example and shed many staff at great cost, unassisted by the pension fund. The manager responsible was later fired.

London Bridge

[58] The foundation of the bridge; from *Survey of London* by J. Stow.

The original foundation of London bridge, by report of Bartholomew Linsted, alias Fowle, last prior of St Mary Overies church in Southwark, was this: A ferry being kept in place where now the bridge is built, at length the ferryman and his wife deceasing, left the same ferry to their only daughter, a maiden named Mary, which with the goods left by her parents, and also with the profits arising of the said ferry, built a house of Sisters, in place where now standeth the east part of St Mary Overies church, above the choir, where she was buried, unto which house she gave the oversight and profits of the ferry; but afterwards the said house of Sisters being converted into a college of priests, the priests built the bridge (of timber) as all the other great bridges of this land were, and from time to time kept the same in good reparations, till at length, considering the great charges of repairing the same, there was, by aid of the citizens of London, and others, a bridge built with arches of stone, as shall be shown.

[59] The Norwegian King Olaf and King Aethelred attack the Bridge (1014); from *The Olaf Sagas* by Snorri Sturluson, with poems by Ottar Svarte, translated by S. Laing.

They steered first to London, and sailed into the Thames with their fleet; but the Danes had a castle within [on the site of the Tower of London]. On the other side of the river is a great trading place, which is called *Suthvirki* [Southwark]. There the Danes had raised a great work, dug large ditches, and within had built a bulwark of stone, timber and turf, where they had stationed a strong army. King Aethelred ordered a great assault; but the Danes defended themselves bravely, and King Aethelred could make nothing of it. Between the castle and *Suthvirki* there was a bridge so broad that two waggons could pass each other upon it. On the bridge were raised barricades, both towers and wooden parapets in the direction of the river, which were nearly breast high; and under the bridge were piles driven into the bottom of the river. Now when the attack was made the troops stood on the bridge everywhere, and defended themselves. King Aethelred was very anxious to get possession of the bridge, and he called together all the chiefs to consult how they should get the bridge broken down. Then said King Olaf he would attempt to lay his fleet alongside of it, if the other ships would do the same. It was then determined in this council that they should lay their war forces under the bridge; and each made himself ready with ships and men. King Olaf ordered great platforms of floating wood to be tied together with hazel bands, and for this he took down old houses; and with these, as a roof, he covered over his ships' sides. Under this screen he set pillars so high and stout, that there was both room for swinging their swords, and the roofs were strong enough to withstand the stones cast down upon them. Now when the fleet and men were ready, they rowed up along the river; but when they came near the bridge, there were cast down upon them so many stones and missile weapons, such as arrows and spears, that neither helmet nor shield could hold against it; and the ships themselves were so greatly damaged that many retreated out of it. But King Olaf, and the Northmen's fleet with him, rowed quite up under the bridge, laid their cables around the piles which supported it, and then rowed off with all the ships as hard as they could down the stream. The piles were thus shaken in the bottom, and were loosened under the bridge. Now as the armed troops stood thick upon the bridge, and there were likewise many heaps of stones and other weapons upon it being loosened and broken, the bridge gave way; and a great part of the men upon it fell into the river, and all the others fled, some into the castle, some into Southwark . . .

> London Bridge is broken down,
> Gold is won, and bright renown.
> Shields resounding,
> War-horns sounding,
> Hildur shouting in the din!
> Arrows singing,
> Mailcoats ringing –
> Odin makes our Olaf win!
>
> King Aethelred has found a friend
> Brave Olaf will his throne defend –
> In bloody fight
> Maintain his right
> Win back his land
> With blood-red hand,
> And Edmund's son upon his throne replace –
> Edmund, the star of every royal race!

[60] Foundation of the Stone Bridge (1176); from *Survey of London* by J. Stow.

Now touching the foundation of the stone bridge, it followeth: About the year 1176, the stone bridge over the river of Thames, at London, was begun to be founded by the aforesaid Peter of Cole church, near unto the bridge of timber, but somewhat more towards the west, for I read, that Buttolfe wharf was, in the Conqueror's time, at the head of London bridge. The king assisted this work: a cardinal then being legate here; and Richard, archbishop of Canterbury, gave one thousand marks towards the foundation; the course of the river, for the time, was turned another way about, by a trench cast for that purpose, beginning, as is supposed, east about Radriffe, and ending in the west about Patricksey, now termed Batersey. This work; to wit, the arches, chapel and stone bridge, over the river of Thames at London, having been thirty-three years in building, was in the year 1209 finished by the worthy merchants of London, Serle Mercer, William Almaine, and Benedict Botewrite, principal masters of that work, for Peter of Cole church deceased four years before, and was buried in the chapel on the bridge, in the year 1205.

[61] Jack Cade attacks the bridge (1450); from *Chronicles of London*, edited by C. L. Kingsford.

Item, this yere was a grete assemble of the commones in Kent, which came downe to blak heth in June, and ther made their feld, abidyng there vij daies. Wherof when the kyng herde, beyng at Leiceter, he assemblid his lordes; and cam in all haste agayne the Kentisshemen, and at his comyng sent dyuers lordes to theym to knowe their Entent. And when these lordes came to their Capeteyn namyd Jak Cade, otherwyse Mortymer, cosyn to the Duke of York as the saide Capitayne named hym self, he seid he and his people were commen to redresse many poyntes wherby the kynges subgettes and comons were grevously wrongid; but his fynall purpoos was to robbe, as after it shall appere. Wherfore the kyng and his counsaill, seyng the dowblenesse of this Capitayn, the xviijth day of the said moneth addressid his people toward theym; but whan the kynges people cam to the blak heth the Capitayne was goon ... and the first day of July he w^t his people cam into Sothewerke, and becawse he myght not entre the Cite he lay there that nyght ... and the day at v at after none the Capteyne came in to the Cite per force; and in his entre at the Brigge he hewe the Ropys of the drawe brigge asonder; and whan he came to Saynt Magnus he made a proclamacion vpon payne of deth, that no man of his Ost shuld Robbe ne dispoile no man w^t in the Cite. And in like wise at ledynhall and so thurgh the Cite w^t grete pride. And at London Stone he strak vpon it like a Conquerour . . . then the vth day of July he smote of a mannys hed in Suthwerk, and the same nyght folowyng the Mair, the Aldermen, w^t the thrifty comoners of the Cite concluded to dryve away the Capiten and his Oste. Wherfor they sent vnto the lord Scalis and to one Mathew Gowgh, a Capitayne of Normandy, that they wold that nyght assaile the Capitayne and his people; so they did, and at the Brigge was a sore and a long fyght, wher sometyme the Cite had the better and sometyme the Kentishemen. And thus they faught all the nyght till nyne of the Clok on the morne. And at the last they brent the drawe brigge, by means wherof many men of the Cite wer drowned; and in that fight an Alderman namyd Sutton was slayn, Roger Heysant, and Mathew Gowgh, and many other. And after this the Chaunceler of Englond, vpon the morne after, graunted to all the Kentisshemen w^t their Capiteyne a generall pardon. And so they departed euery man to his awne. And when all were departed and goon there were made proclamacions, that what man cowde take the Capeteyn, Quyk or Deed, shuld haue a M marks for his labour; after whiche proclamations made One Alexander Idon, Gentilman of Kent, toke hym in a garden in Sowsex; but in the takyng the said Capiteyn was slayne. And so brought into Southwerk that all men myght see hym, and that nyght left in the kynges bench, and from thens he was drawyn to newgate, and then hedid and quarterid; and his hede set vpon London Brigge. And his iiij quarters were sent in to dyuers Townes in Kent. And anone after the kyng Rode into Kent and commaundid his Justices to sit at Caunterbury, to Enquere who wer accessariis and cawsers of this Insurreccion; and there were viij men Jugged to deth in oon day, and in other places moo. And from thens the kyng Rode into Sowthsex, and from thens in to the West Cuntre, where a litell before was slayn the Bisshop of Salisbury. And this yere wer so many juggid to deth that xxiij hedis stode vpon London Bryge. Vpon whos soules Jhesu haue mercy.

[62] The miracle associated with Bishop Fisher's head, which was set on the bridge in 1535; from *Chronicles* by E. Hall.

The next day after his burial, the head being somewhat parboiled in hot water, was pricked upon a pole and set on high upon London Bridge among the rest of the holy Carthusians' heads that suffered death lately before him. And here I cannot omit to declare unto you the miraculous sight of this head, which, after it had stand up the space of fourteen days upon the bridge, could not be perceived to waste nor consume, neither for the weather, which then was very hot, neither for the parboiling in hot water, but grew daily fresher and fresher, so that in his lifetime he never looked so well. For his cheeks being beautified with a comely red, the face looked as if it had beholden the people passing by and would have spoke.

[63] Sir Thomas Wyatt attacks the bridge in 1553; from *The Chronicle of Queen Jane and of two years of Queen Mary*, edited by J. G. Nichols.

This day, about iij. of the clocke, sir Thomas Wyat and the Kentyshemen marched forwarde from Debtford towardes London with v. auncientes, being by estimation about ij. thousand men; which their comyng, so soone as it was perceyved, ther was shot off out of the White tower a vj. or viij. shott; but myssed them, somtymes shoting over, and somtymes shoting short. After the knowledge therof once had in London, forthwith the draybridge was cutt downe and the bridge gates shut. The mayre and the sheryves harnessyd theymselves, and commanded eche man to shutt in their shoppes and wyndowes, and being redy in harnes to stande every one at his dore, what chance soever myght hapen. Then should ye have seen taking in wares of the stalles in most hasty manner; ther was renning upp and downe in every place to wepons and harnes; aged men were astoyned, many women wept for feare; children and maydes ran into their howses, shytting the dores for feare; moche noyse and tumult was every where; so terryble and fearfull at the fyrst was Wyat and his armyes comyng to the most part of the cytezens, who wer seldom or nere wont before to here or have eny suche invasions to their cyty.

At this time was Wyat entered into Kent street, and so by sainct George's church into Southwarke. Himselfe and parte of his compaynye cam in goode array downe Barmesey strete. Note, they wer sufferyd peceably to enter into Southwarke without repulse or eny stroke stryken either by the inhabitours or by eny other; yit was ther many men of the contry in the innes, raysed and brought thether by the lord William, and other, to have gone agaynst the saide Wyat and Kentyshmen, but they all joyned themselves to the said Kentyshe rebelles, taking their partes; and the said inhabitantes most willinglye with their best entertayned them. Imediatly upon the said Wyates comynge, he made a proclamation that no souldear should take eny thing, but that he should pay for it, and that his coming was to resyst the comyng in of the Spanyshe kynge, &c.

At his comyng to the bridge foote, he ladd forthwith ij. peces of ordenance, and began a great trenche between the bridge and him; he laid another pece at sainct George's, another going into Barmesey strett, and another towardes the bushopes house.

[64] Charles II greeted at the bridge on his return to England (1660); from *England's Joy*, Anon.

In this order proceeding towards London, there were placed in Deptford, on his right hand (as he passed through the town) above an hundred proper maids, clad all alike, in white garments, with scarfs about them; who, having prepared many flaskets covered with fine linnen, and adorned with rich scarfs and ribbands, which flaskets were full of flowers and sweet herbs, strowed the way before him as he rode.

From thence passing on, he came to St George's Fields in Southwark, where the lord mayor and aldermen of London, in their scarlet, with the recorder, and other city council, waited for him in a large tent, hung with tapestry; in which they had placed a chair of state, with a rich canopy over it. When he came thither, the lord mayor presented him with the city sword, and the recorder made a speech to him; which being done, he alighted, and went into the tent, where a noble banquet was prepared for him . . .   In . . . magnificent fashion his majesty entered the borough of Southwark, about half an hour past three of the clock in the afternoon; and, within an hour after, the city of London at the Bridge; where he found the windows and streets exceedingly thronged with people to behold him; and the walls adorned with hangings and carpets of tapestry and other costly stuff; and in many places sets of loud musick; all the conduits, as he passed, running claret wine; and several companies in their liveries, with the ensigns belonging to them; as also the trained bands of the city standing along the streets as he passed, welcoming him with joyful acclamations.

[65] Pepys witnesses the beginning of the Great Fire at the Bridge (1666); from *Diaries* by S. Pepys.

2d. (Lord's day.) Some of our maids sitting up late last night to get things ready against our feast today, Jane called us up about three in the morning, to tell us of a great fire they saw in the City. So I rose, and slipped on my night-gown and went to her window, and thought it to be on the back side of Mark Lane at the farthest; but, being unused to such fires as followed, I thought it far enough off, and so went to bed again, and to sleep. About seven rose again to dress myself, and there looked out at the window, and saw the fire not so much as it was, and further off. So to my closet to set things to rights after yesterday's cleaning. By and by Jane comes and tells me that she hears that above 300 houses have been burned down tonight by the fire we saw, and that it is now burning down all Fish Street, by London Bridge. So I made myself ready presently, and walked to the Tower; and there got up upon one of the high places, Sir J. Robinson's little son going up with me; and there I did see the houses at that end of the bridge all on fire, and an infinite great fire on this and the other side the end of the bridge; which, among other people, did trouble me for poor little Michell and our Sarah on the bridge.

So down, with my heart full of trouble, to the Lieutenant of the Tower, who tells me that it begun this morning in the King's baker's house in Pudding Lane, and that it hath burned St Magnus's Church and most part of Fish Street already. So I down to the water-side, and there got a boat, and through bridge, and there saw a lamentable fire. Poor Michell's house, as far as the Old Swan, already burned that way, and the fire running further, that, in a very little time, it got as far as the Steelyard, while I was there. Everybody endeavouring to remove their goods, and flinging into the river or bringing them into lighters that lay off; poor people staying in their houses as long as till the very fire touched them, and then running into boats, or clambering from one pair of stairs by the waterside to another. And, among other things, the poor pigeons, I perceive, were loth to leave their houses, but hovered about the windows and balconies, till they, some of them, burned their wings, and fell down.

Having stayed, and in an hour's time seen the fire rage every way, and nobody, to my sight, endeavouring to quench it, but to remove their goods, and leave all to the fire; and, having seen it get as far as the Steelyard, and the wind mighty high, and driving it into the City; and everything, after so long a drought, proving combustible, even the very stones of churches; and, among other things, the poor steeple by which pretty Mrs—lives, and whereof my old schoolfellow Elborough is parson, taken fire in the very top, and there burned till it fell down . . .

[66] Eighteenth-century nursery rhyme 'London Bridge is broken down'; from *The Oxford Dictionary of Nursery Rhymes*, I. & P. Opie.

'London Bridge is broken down' is mentioned again in *The Fashionable Lady, or, Harlequin's Opera* (1730); and in *Tommy Thumb's Pretty Song Book* (c. 1744) appears the earliest text:

> London Bridge
> Is Broken down,
> Dance over my Lady Lee.
> London Bridge
> Is Broken down
> With a gay Lady.
>
> How shall we build
> It up again,
> Dance over my Lady Lee, &c.
>
> Build it up with
> Gravel, and Stone,
> Dance over my Lady Lee, &c.
>
> Gravel, and Stone,
> Will wash away,
> Dance over my Lady Lee, &c.
>
> Build it up with
> Iron, and Steel,
> Dance over my Lady Lee, &c.
>
> Iron and Steel,
> Will bend, and Bow,
> Dance over my Lady Lee, &c.
>
> Build it up with
> Silver, and Gold,
> Dance over my Lady Lee, &c.

Silver, and Gold
Will be stolen away,
Dance over my Lady Lee, &c.

Then we'l set
A man to Watch,
Dance over my Lady Lee.
Then we'l set
A Man to Watch
With a gay Lady.

Tommy Thumb's 200-year-old version stops significantly when it has been decided to set a man to watch. The builders have had to meet what has every appearance of being supernatural opposition. The bridge cannot be made to stand by ordinary means. Even stone will be washed away. So a 'watchman' is required. Somehow, it is felt, this watchman can protect the bridge even against the malicious forces of nature. (Only when it is proposed that the edifice be made of 'silver and gold', possibly a later interpolation, is there a suggestion of human sabotage.) Clearly the watchman himself has special powers. It is on record that in 1872 when the Hooghly Bridge was being built across the Ganges the native population feared that to placate the river each structure would have to be founded on a layer of children's skulls. Fraser in *The Golden Bough* quotes examples of living people being built into the foundations of walls and gates to serve as guardian spirits; and all over the world stories of human sacrifice are associated with bridges, to the erection of which the rivers are supposed to have an especial antipathy. In Germany as recently as 1843, when a new bridge was to be built at Halle, the notion was abroad among the people that a child was wanted to be built into the foundation. When the Bridge Gate at Bremen was demolished in the last century the skeleton of a child was found embedded in the foundations. The bridge of Aryte in Greece is said to have kept falling down until they walled in the wife of the master-mason. The building of the bridge of Rosporden in Brittany is another case where legend has it that all attempts were unsuccessful until a four-year-old boy was immured at the foot of it. Further, the legend goes, the little boy was buried with a candle in one hand and a piece of bread in the other. Food and light was given so that the guardian might keep alive and watchful, which immediately recalls the words of the old Stuart lady:

> Suppose the man should fall asleep?
> Then we must put a pipe in his mouth.

In similar verses, handed down in oral tradition, the man is given a bag of nuts to crack, a dog which will bark all night, and a horse on which he can gallop around. At Stoneleigh Park, the seat of the Leigh family in Warwickshire, the story is maintained that one or more human victims lie buried under the foundations, and attempts have been made to connect the name of Leigh with the refrain 'Dance over my Lady Lea'. Another suggestion is that 'my Lady Lea' is the river Lea, which loses its identity in the river Thames. And London Bridge itself is not without a tainted reputation, for there is in the capital a tradition that the stones of this great bridge, too, were once bespattered with the blood of little children.

Southwark

[67] Chaucer's pilgrims meet at Southwark (14th century); from *The Canterbury Tales* by G. Chaucer.

> Whan that Aprill with his shoures soote
> The droghte of March hath perced to the roote,
> And bathed every veyne in swich licour
> Of which vertu engendred is the flour;
> Whan Zephirus eek with his sweete breeth
> Inspired hath in every holt and heeth
> The tendre croppes, and the yonge sonne
> Hath in the Ram his half cours yronne,
> And smale foweles maken melodye,
> That slepen al the nyght with open ye
> (So priketh hem nature in hir corages),
> Thanne longen folk to goon on pilgrimages,
> And palmeres for to seken straunge strondes,
> To ferne halwes, kowthe in sondry londes;
> And specially from every shires ende
> Of Engelond to Caunterbury they wende,
> The hooly blisful martir for to seke,
> That hem hath holpen whan that they were seeke.

Bifil that in that seson on a day,
In Southwerk at the Tabard as I lay
Redy to wenden on my pilgrymage
To Caunterbury with ful devout corage,
At nyght was come into that hostelrye
Wel nyne and twenty in a compaignye
Of sondry folk, by aventure yfalle
In felaweshipe, and pilgrimes were they alle,
That toward Caunterbury wolden ryde.
The chambres and the stables weren wyde,
And wel we weren esed atte beste.
And shortly, whan the sonne was to reste,
So hadde I spoken with hem everichon
That I was of hir felaweshipe anon,
And made forward erly for to ryse,
To take oure wey ther as I yow devyse.
Why that assembled was this compaignye
In Southwerk at this gentil hostelrye
That highte the Tabard, faste by the Belle.
But now is tyme to yow for to telle
How that we baren us that ilke nyght,
Whan we were in that hostelrie alyght;
And after wol I telle of our viage
And al the remenaunt of oure pilgrimage . . .

Greet chiere made oure Hoost us everichon,
And to the soper sette he us anon.
He served us with vitaille at the beste;
Strong was the wyn, and wel to drynke us leste.
A semely man OURE HOOSTE was withalle
For to been a marchal in an halle.
A large man he was with eyen stepe –
A fairer burgeys was ther noon in Chepe –
Boold of his speche, and wys, and wel ytaught,
And of manhod hym lakkede right naught.
Eek therto he was right a myrie man;
And after soper pleyen he bigan,
And spak of myrthe amonges othere thynges,
Whan that we hadde maad oure rekenynges,
And seyde thus: 'Now, lordynges, trewely,

Ye been to me right welcome, hertely;
For by my trouthe, if that I shal nat lye,
I saugh nat this yeer so myrie a compaignye
Atones in this herberwe as is now.
Fayn wolde I doon yow myrthe, wiste I how.
And of a myrthe, I am right now bythoght,
To doon yow ese, and it shal coste noght.
    'Ye goon to Caunterbury – God yow speede,
The blisful martir quite yow youre meede!
And wel I woot, asye goon by the weye,
Ye shapen yow to talen and to pleye;
For trewely, confort ne myrthe is noon
To ride by the weye doumb as a stoon;
And therfore wol I maken yow disport,
As I seyde erst, and doon yow som confort.
And if yow liketh alle by oon assent
For to stonden at my juggement,
And for to werken as I shal yow seye,
Tomorwe, whan ye riden by the weye,
Now, by my fader soule that is deed,
But ye be myrie, I wol yeve yow myn heed!
Hoold up youre hondes, withouten moore speche.'

    Oure conseil was nat longe for to seche.
Us thoughte it was noght worth to make it wys,
And graunted hym withouten moore avys,
And bad him seye his voirdit as hym leste.
'Lordynges,' quod he, 'now herkneth for the beste;
But taak it nought, I prey yow, in desdeyn.
This is the poynt, to speken short and pleyn,
That ech of yow, to shorte with oure weye,
In this viage shal telle tales tweye
To Caunterbury-ward, I mene it so,
And homward he shal tellen othere two,
Of aventures that whilom han bifalle.
And which of yow that bereth hym best of alle –
That is to seyn, that telleth in this caas
Tales of best sentence and moost solaas –
Shal have a soper at oure aller cost
Heere in this place, sittynge by this post,

Whan that we come agayn fro Caunterbury.
And for to make yow the moore mury,
I wol myselven goodly with yow ryde,
Right at myn owene cost, and be youre gyde;
And whoso wole my juggement withseye
Shal paye al that we spenden by the weye.
And if ye vouche sauf that it be so,
Tel me anon, withouten wordes mo,
And I wol erly shape me therfore.'

    This thyng was graunted, and oure othes swore
With ful glad herte, and preyden hym also
That he wolde vouche sauf for to do so,
And that he wolde been oure governour,
And of oure tales juge and reportour,
And sette a soper at a certeyn pris,
And we wol reuled been at his devys
In heigh and lough; and thus by oon assent
We been acorded to his juggement.
And therupon the wyn was fet anon;
We dronken, and to reste wente echon,
Withouten any lenger taryynge.

[68] The burning of the Globe theatre in 1613; from *Reliquiae Wottoniae*.

Now to let matters of state sleep, I will entertain you at the present with what hath happened this week at the Bankside. The King's Players had a new play, called *All is true*, representing some principal pieces of the reign of Henry VIII, which was set forth with many extraordinary circumstances of pomp and majesty, even to the matting of the stage; the Knights of the Order, with their Georges and Garter, the Guards with their embroidered coats, and the like: sufficient in true within a while to make greatness very familiar, if not ridiculous. Now, King Henry making a masque at the Cardinal Wolsey's house, and certain cannons being shot off at his entry, some of the paper, or other stuff, wherewith one of them was stopped, did light on the thatch, where being thought at first but an idle smoke, and their eyes more attentive to the show, it kindled inwardly, and ran round like a train, consuming within less than an hour the whole house to the very ground.

This was the fatal period of that virtuous fabric; wherein yet nothing did perish, but wood and straw, and a few forsaken cloaks; only one man had his breeches set on fire, that would perhaps have broiled him, if he had not by the benefit of a provident wit put it out with bottle-ale.

[69] John Wilkes is committed to the King's-Bench prison in 1768; from *The Correspondence of the late John Wilkes.*

On 7 May, the outlawry was argued again; but judgment was postponed until next term.

Mr Wilkes gave full credit to some information he had received, that lord Mansfield had made up his mind, to establish the outlawry. What happened between 7 May and 8 June, when the outlawry was reversed, to alter lord Mansfield's opinion, cannot now be explained. The outlawry was reversed by the unanimous judgment of the court; and, on 18 June, Mr Wilkes was again brought before the court to receive sentence. After the usual exordium, the senior judge pronounced the sentence as follows: 'For the re-publication of the North Briton, N° 45, he should pay a fine of 500l., and be imprisoned ten calendar months. And for publishing the Essay on Woman he should pay a fine of 500l. and be imprisoned twelve calendar months; to be computed from the expiration of the term of the former imprisonment. And that he afterwards should find security for good behaviour for seven years; himself in the sum of 1000l. and two sureties in 500l. each.' – He had already been imprisoned two months; so that the whole imprisonment made exactly two years. The severity of the sentence was universally condemned. Upon a candid review and consideration of the several circumstances of the case, all impartial people thought it cruel, malignant, and indefensible.

From the time of Mr Wilkes's commitment, a number of people daily assembled round the prison, to indulge the simple curiosity of seeing him at the windows. They always behaved very quietly, and were very orderly. But the ministry apprehending, or affecting to apprehend, that a contrary conduct might happen; they sent a guard of soldiers every day to protect the prison . . .

On Tuesday, 10 May, the new parliament met, *pro formâ*. A number of the lower order of people entertained an opinion that Mr Wilkes would go to the house of commons on that day to take his seat; and they assembled round the prison in greater numbers than usual, in order to see him go. When the soldiers came, who consisted of a detachment from the third regiment of foot guards, commonly called the Scots regiment, they pushed the people away from the places where they were standing very quietly, in the most rude and brutal manner, and with the most vulgar language. The editor of this work was with Mr Wilkes at the time. Some of the people, who had been thus driven and insulted, in a few minutes afterwards began to throw stones and gravel at the soldiers. Messrs Ponton and Gillam, two magistrates, instantly appeared, and ordered the proclamation in the riot-act to be read. The people still hissed and hooted, and some of them threw stones; particularly a young man in a red waistcoat. His violent conduct provoked three of the soldiers, under the command of ensign Alexander Murray, to quit the rank in which they were stationed, in order to take him, or shoot him. The man fled, and the soldiers pursued. He took refuge in a cow-house belonging to a Mr Allen, a stable-keeper in Blackman-street in the Borough; and from thence he escaped. The soldiers entered the cow-house, and seeing a young man in a red waistcoat, they immediately shot him. This was an unfortunate circumstance; for the person whom they shot was not the right object. This sacrifice to revenge was no party in the riot.

When it was known that Allen was killed, the people

assembled in greater numbers, and became more riotous and violent. The magistrates and military officers became no less intemperate on their part. Much firing followed; several persons were killed, and many were wounded. Mr Wilkes wrote a pamphlet on the transactions of this disgraceful day, which he entitled 'The Inhuman Massacre in St George's Fields on the 10th of May, 1768.'

[70] Dickens visits his father at the Marshalsea (1822); from *The Life of Charles Dickens, Vol. I* by J. Forster.

'My father was waiting for me in the lodge, and we went up to his room (on the top storey but one), and cried very much. And he told me, I remember, to take warning by the Marshalsea, and to observe that if a man had twenty pounds a year, and spent nineteen pounds nineteen shillings and sixpence, he would be happy but that a shilling spent the other way would make him wretched. I see the fire we sat before, now; with two bricks inside the rusted grate, one on each side, to prevent its burning too many coals. Some other debtor shared the room with him, who came in by-and-by; and as the dinner was a joint-stock repast, I was sent up to "Captain Porter" in the room overhead, with Mr Dickens's compliments, and I was his son, and could he lend me a knife and fork?

'Captain Porter lent the knife and fork, with his compliments in return. There was a very dirty lady in his little room; and two wan girls, his daughters, with shock heads of hair. I thought I should not have liked to borrow Captain Porter's comb. The Captain himself was in the last extremity of shabbiness; and if I could draw at all, I would draw an accurate portrait of the old, old brown great-coat he wore, with no other coat below it. His whiskers were large. I saw his bed rolled up in a corner; and what plates, and dishes, and pots he had, on a shelf; and I knew (God knows how) that the two girls with the shock heads were Captain Porter's natural children, and that the dirty lady was not married to Captain P. My timid, wondering station on his threshold, was not occupied more than a couple of minutes, I dare say; but I came down again to the room below with all this as surely in my knowledge, as the knife and fork were in my hand.'

[71] The new Globe theatre opens in 1996; from *Daily Telegraph* article by N. Reynolds.

Up in heaven Sam Wanamaker and William Shakespeare would have smiled, probably in that order.

The Globe Theatre – or rather the replica of the Bard's 'Wooden O', closed by the Puritans in 1642 – re-opened last night to a popular triumph 200 yards away from the original in Southwark by the Thames.

There was not a single hitch. It was a hot night and the audience in the open-roofed playhouse was spared a drenching.

The aeroplanes on their run-in to Heathrow were irritating but did not drown out Shakespeare and the cast was hastily rearranged successfully after an actor broke his leg at a public rehearsal which had to be abandoned the previous night.

However, if Shakespeare and Wanamaker, who spent almost 25 years on his cherished project only to die in 1993 before seeing it realized, were happy, mere mortals may have been puzzled.

The 25 million pounds theatre with thatch and galleries was built with authentic materials as close to the original as Wanamaker could make it. It was perverse then that last night's production, of *The Two Gentlemen of Verona*, was done in modern costume.

Shakespeare's thoughts on late 20th-century designer suits, wrap-around sunglasses and a kinky PVC mini-skirt can only be wondered at.

As a modern playwright he may have approved. But if this approach is to be continued, the coachloads of tourists searching for 'an authentic Shakespeare experience', who will be the theatre's financial mainstay, may be flabbergasted.

Mark Rylance, the Globe's director, announced that he wanted the audience of 1,500 – 500 of them stand in 'the groundings', an open courtyard in front of the stage – to behave as they might have done in Shakespeare's day.

The cast delivers *Two Gentlemen*, an odd choice for the re-opening as it is such an inconsequential play, as if it were vaudeville. It was in its way a 'theatre experience' such as London has not seen since music hall.

No rotten tomatoes, no ale, no groats were thrown, but the audience, whipped up ferociously by Rylance himself playing Proteus, hissed, booed, cheered and groaned as if this was an end of the pier show.

If this was Shakespeare-as-she-was-watched, it was not entirely comfortable. In the galleries the bench seats were uncompromisingly hard and a four-hour Hamlet would be an insufferable experience.

Standing for two and a half hours was bearable but future audiences would be advised to take a shooting stick. Drinking (tip – take your own as the Globe has no licence) is allowed as are picnics. But there was no chewing or spitting baccy and no smoking allowed within 100 yards of the thatch – a wise precaution.

Smithfield

[72] Foundation of St Bartholomew the Great in 1123; from *London: The Biography* by P. Ackroyd.

The founder of the church, Rahere, was on a journey in Italy when in a dream he was taken up by a beast with four feet and two wings to a 'high place' where St Bartholomew appeared to him and addressed him: 'I, by the will and command of all the High Trinity, and with the common favour and counsel of the court of heaven, have chosen a spot in the suburb of London at Smithfield.' Rahere was to erect there a tabernacle of the Lamb. So he journeyed to the city where, in conversation with 'some barons of London', it was explained that 'the place divinely shown to him was contained within the king's market, on which it was lawful neither for the princes themselves nor for the wardens of their own authority to encroach to any extent whatever'. So Rahere sought an audience of Henry I in order to explain his divine mission to the city; the king graciously gave Rahere title to the spot which was at that time 'a very small cemetery'.

Rahere then 'made himself a fool' in order to recruit assistants in the great work of building. He 'won to himself bands of children and servants, and by their help he easily began to collect together stones'. These stones came from many parts of London, and in that sense the narrative of construction is a true representation of the fact that St Bartholomew's was a collective work and vision of the city; it became, in literal form, its microcosm.

[73] Henry II grants to the church the privilege of a fair; from *Survey of London* by John Stow.

To this priory King Henry II granted the privilege of fair, to be kept yearly at Bartholomew tide for three days, to wit, the eve, the day, and next morrow, to the which the clothiers of all England, and drapers of London, repaired, and had their booths and standings within the churchyard of this priory, closed in with walls, and gates locked every night, and watched, for safety of men's goods and wares; a court of pie powders was daily during the fair holden for debts and contracts. But now, notwithstanding all proclamations of the prince, and also the act of parliament, in place of booths within this churchyard (only let out in the fair-time, and closed up all the year after), be many large houses built, and the north wall towards Long lane taken down, a number of tenements are there erected for such as will give great rents.

[74] Archbishop Boniface makes a visitation to St Bartholomew's in 1250; from *Chronicles* by Matthew Paris.

During the same days Boniface, archbishop of Canterbury, encouraged by the bishop of Lincoln's example, who had obtained authority to visit his canons at Lincoln, tried to make a visitation of the bishops, abbots, clergy and people in his province . . .

On the fourth of the ides of May, namely the day of St

Pancratius and his companions [12 May], the aforesaid archbishop of Canterbury B. came to London to visit the bishop and chapter and the monks of that city . . .

Going to the chapter of St Paul's in London, he came to that church in great pomp in order to visit the canons. They were unwilling to admit him, resisting spiritedly, and firmly appealed to the supreme pontiff . . .

And on the following day, still swollen and inflamed with yesterday's anger, and, according to the testimony of people who saw, wearing a coat of mail under his vestments, he came to the priory of St Bartholomew to visit the canons there. As he arrived and entered the church, because the prior was away at the time, the subprior came to meet him accompanied by the convent in procession with solemnity and reverence both in the lighting of numerous candles and in the ringing of bells. They were in costly choir copes, the most precious of which was worn by the senior one of them at that time, namely the aforesaid subprior. The archbishop did not care much for the honour thus done him; he said he had come there to visit the canons. Now all the canons were in the centre of the church, that is in the choir, with the archbishop himself and the greater part of his retinue, pressed together in a disorderly manner. One of the canons replied to him on behalf of all, saying that they had an experienced and diligent bishop whose task it was to visit them when this was necessary, nor would they, or ought they to, be visited by anyone else, lest he should seem to be held in contempt. On hearing this, the archbishop, flying into a more furious rage than he ought or was proper, rushed at the subprior, forgetting his station and the holiness of his predecessors, and impiously struck that holy man, a priest and a monk, with his fist, as he stood in the middle of the church, truculently repeating the blows now on the aged breast, now on the venerable face, now on his grey-haired head and yelling 'This is how English traitors should be dealt with!' And, raving horribly with unrepeatable oaths, he vehemently demanded that his sword be brought to him.

As the tumult increased and the canons tried to rescue

their subprior from the hands of so violent an aggressor, the archbishop tore off the precious cope that the subprior was wearing and broke away the clasp, which is commonly called a morse, which was decorated with gold and silver gems, and it was smashed and lost underfoot in the crowd. That splendid cope, too, trampled on and torn, was irreparably damaged. Nor was the archiepiscopal fury averted even now, for, like a madman, pushing and forcing back that holy man with a violent onslaught, he so crushed his senile body against a pier which divided two of the stalls and was made for a podium, that he shattered his bones to the marrow and caused internal injuries. When the others saw the archbishop's lack of restraint, they managed to rescue the half-dead man from the jaws of death, after pushing the aggressor back. As he was thrown back his vestments fell aside, his coat of mail was plainly visible to many, who were horrified to see the archbishop in armour.

[75] Wat Tyler is slain in Smithfield (1381); from *Chronicles* by Froissart.

There was an usage in England, and yet is in divers countries, that the noblemen hath great franchise over the commons and keepeth them in servage, that is to say, their tenants ought by custom to labour the lords' lands, to gather and bring home their corns, and some to thresh and to fan, and by servage to make their hay and to hew their wood and bring it home. All these things they ought to do by servage, and there be more of these people in England than in any other realm. Thus the noblemen and prelates are served by them, and specially in the county of Kent, Essex, Sussex and Bedford. These unhappy people of these said countries began to stir, because they said they were kept in great servage, and in the beginning of the world, they said, there were no bondmen, wherefore they maintained that none ought to be bond, without he did treason to his lord, as Lucifer did to God; but they said they could have no such battle, for they were neither angels nor spirits, but men formed to the similitude of their lords, saying why should they then be kept so under like beasts; the which they said they would no longer suffer, for they would be all one, and if they laboured or did anything for their lords, they would have wages therefor as well as other. And of this imagination was a foolish priest in the country of Kent called John Ball, for the which foolish words he had been three times in the bishop of Canterbury's prison.

... And when this John Ball was out of prison, he returned again to his error, as he did before.

Of his words and deeds there were much people in London informed, such as had great envy at them that were rich and such as were noble; and then they began to speak among them and said how the realm of England was right evil governed, and how that gold and silver was taken from them by them that were named noblemen: so thus these unhappy men of London began to rebel and assembled them together, and sent word to the foresaid countries that they should come to London and bring their people with them, promising them how they should find London open to receive them and the commons of the city to be of the same accord, saying how they would do so much to the king that there should not be one bondman in all England.

This promise moved so them of Kent, of Essex, of Sussex, of Bedford and of the countries about, that they rose and came towards London to the number of sixty thousand. And they had a captain called Water Tyler, and with him in company was Jack Straw and John Ball: these three were chief sovereign captains, but the head of all was Water Tyler, and he was indeed a tiler of houses, an ungracious patron. When these unhappy men began thus to stir, they of London, except such as were of their band, were greatly affrayed. Then the mayor of London and the rich men of the city took counsel together, and when they saw the people thus coming on every side, they caused the gates of the city to be closed and would suffer no man to enter into the city. But when they had well imagined, they advised not so to do, for they thought they should thereby put their suburbs in great peril to be brent; and so they opened again the city, and there entered in at the gates in some place a hundred, two hundred, by twenty and by thirty, and so when they came to London, they entered and lodged: and yet of truth the third part of these people could not tell what to ask or demand, but followed each other like beasts, as the shepherds did of old time, saying how they would go conquer the Holy Land, and at last all came to nothing. In like wise these villains and poor people came to London, a hundred mile off, sixty mile, fifty mile, forty mile and twenty mile off, and from all countries about London, but the most part came from the countries before named, and as they came they demanded ever for the king. The gentlemen of the countries, knights and squires, began to doubt, when they saw the people began to rebel; and though they were in doubt, it was good reason; for a less occasion they might have been affrayed. So the gentlemen drew together as well as they might . . .

And so long they went forward till they came within a four mile of London, and there lodged on a hill called Blackheath; and as they went, they said ever they were the king's men and the noble commons of England: and when they of London knew that they were come so near to them, the mayor, as ye have heard before, closed the gates and kept straitly all the passages . . .

In the morning on Corpus Christi day King Richard heard mass in the Tower of London, and all his lords, and then he took his barge with the earl of Salisbury, the earl of Warwick, the earl of Oxford and certain knights, and so rowed down along the Thames to Rotherhithe, whereas was descended down the hill a ten thousand men to see the king and to speak with him. And when they saw the king's barge coming, they began to shout, and made such a cry, as though all the devils of hell had been among them. And they had brought with them Sir John Newton to the intent that, if the king had not come, they would have stricken him all to pieces, and so they had promised

him. And when the king and his lords saw the demeanour
of the people, the best assured of them were in dread; and
so the king was counselled by his barons not to take any
landing there, but so rowed up and down the river. And
the king demanded of them what they would, and said
how he was come thither to speak with them, and they
said all with one voice: 'We would that ye should come
aland, and then we shall shew you what we lack.' Then
the earl of Salisbury answered for the king and said: 'Sirs,
ye be not in such order nor array that the king ought to
speak with you.' And so with those words no more said:
and then the king was counselled to return again to the
Tower of London, and so he did.

And when these people saw that, they were inflamed
with ire and returned to the hill where the great band was,
and there shewed them what answer they had and how
the king was returned to the Tower of London. Then they
cried all with one voice, 'Let us go to London,' and so
they took their way thither; and in their going they beat
down abbeys and houses of advocates and of men of the
court, and so came into the suburbs of London, which
were great and fair, and there beat down divers fair
houses, and specially they brake up the king's prisons, as
the Marshalsea and other, and delivered out all the prisoners that were within: and there they did much hurt, and
at the bridge foot they threat them of London because the
gates of the bridge were closed, saying how they would
bren all the suburbs and so conquer London by force, and
to slay and bren all the commons of the city. There were
many within the city of their accord, and so they drew
together and said: 'Why do we not let these good people
enter into the city? they are our fellows, and that that they
do is for us.' So therewith the gates were opened, and then
these people entered into the city and went into houses
and sat down to eat and drink. They desired nothing but
it was incontinent brought to them, for every man was
ready to make them good cheer and to give them meat
and drink to appease them.

Then the captains, as John Ball, Jack Straw and Wat

Tyler, went throughout London and a twenty thousand with them, and so came to the Savoy in the way to Westminster, which was a goodly house and it pertained to the duke of Lancaster. And when they entered, they slew the keepers thereof and robbed and pilled the house, and when they had so done, then they set fire on it and clean destroyed and brent it. And when they had done that outrage, they left not therewith, but went straight to the fair hospital of the Rhodes called Saint John's, and there they brent house, hospital, minster and all. Then they went from street to street and slew all the Flemings that they could find in church or in any other place, there was none respited from death. And they brake up divers houses of the Lombards and robbed them and took their goods at their pleasure, for there was none that durst say them nay. And they slew in the city a rich merchant called Richard Lyon, to whom before that time Wat Tyler had done service in France; and on a time this Richard Lyon had beaten him, while he was his varlet, the which Wat Tyler then remembered, and so came to his house and strake off his head and caused it to be borne on a spear-point before him all about the city. Thus these ungracious people demeaned themselves like people enraged and wood, and so that day they did much sorrow in London . . .

The Saturday the king departed from the Wardrobe in the Royal and went to Westminster and heard mass in the church there, and all his lords with him. And beside the church there was a little chapel with an image of our Lady, which did great miracles and in whom the kings of England had ever great trust and confidence. The king made his orisons before this image and did there his offering; and then he leapt on his horse, and all his lords, and so the king rode toward London; and when he had ridden a little way, on the left hand there was a way to pass without London.

The same proper morning Wat Tyler, Jack Straw and John Ball had assembled their company to common together in a place called Smithfield, whereas every Friday there is a market of horses; and there were together all of affinity more than twenty thousand, and yet there were many still in the town, drinking and making merry in the taverns and paid nothing, for they were happy that made them best cheer. And these people in Smithfield had with them the king's banners, the which were delivered them the day before, and all these gluttons were in mind to overrun and to rob London the same day; for their captains said how they had done nothing as yet. 'These liberties that the king hath given us is to us but a small profit: therefore let us be all of one accord and let us overrun this rich and puissant city, or they of Essex, of Sussex, of Cambridge, of Bedford, of Arundel, of Warwick, of Reading, of Oxford, of Guildford, of Lynn, of Stafford, of Yarmouth, of Lincoln, of York and of Durham do come hither. For all these will come hither; Baker and Lister will bring them hither; and if we be first lords of London and have the possession of the riches that is therein, we shall not repent us; for if we leave it, they that come after will have it from us.'

To this counsel they all agreed; and therewith the king came the same way unware of them, for he had thought to have passed that way without London, and with him a forty horse. And when he came before the abbey of Saint Bartholomew and beheld all these people, then the king rested and said how he would go no farther till he knew what these people ailed, saying, if they were in any trouble, how he would rappease them again. The lords that were with him tarried also, as reason was when they saw the king tarry. And when Wat Tyler saw the king tarry, he said to his people: 'Sirs, yonder is the king: I will go and speak with him. Stir not from hence, without I make you a sign; and when I make you that sign, come on and slay all them except the king; but do the king no hurt, he is young, we shall do with him as we list and shall lead him with us all about England, and so shall we be lords of all the realm without doubt.' And there was a doublet-maker of London called John Tycle, and he had brought to these gluttons a sixty doublets, the which they ware: then he demanded of these captains who should pay him for his doublets; he demanded thirty mark. Wat Tyler answered him and said: 'Friend, appease yourself, thou shalt be well paid or this day be ended. Keep thee near me; I shall be thy creditor.' And therewith he spurred his horse and departed from his company and came to the king, so near him that his horse head touched the croup of the king's horse, and the first word that he said was this: 'Sir king, seest thou all yonder people?' 'Yea truly,' said the king, 'wherefore sayest thou?' 'Because,' said he, 'they be all at my commandment and have sworn to me faith and truth, to do all that I will have them.' 'In a good time,' said the king, 'I will well it be so.' Then Wat Tyler said, as he that nothing demanded but riot: 'What believest thou, king, that these people and as many more as be in London at my commandment, that they will depart from thee thus without having thy letters?' 'No,' said the king, 'ye shall have them: they be ordained for you and shall be delivered every one each after the other. Wherefore, good fellows, withdraw fair and easily to your people and cause them to depart out of London; for it is our intent that each of you by villages and townships shall have letters patents, as I have promised you.'

With those words Wat Tyler cast his eyen on a squire that was there with the king bearing the king's sword, and Wat Tyler hated greatly the same squire, for the same squire had displeased him before for words between them. 'What,' said Tyler, 'art thou there? Give me thy dagger.' 'Nay,' said the squire, 'that will I not do: wherefore should I give it thee?' The king beheld the squire and said: 'Give it him; let him have it.' And so the squire took it him sore against his will. And when this Wat Tyler had it, he began to play therewith and turned it in his hand, and said again to the squire: 'Give me also that sword.' 'Nay,' said the squire, 'it is the king's sword: thou art not worthy to have it, for thou art but a knave; and if there were no more here but thou and I, thou durst not speak those words for as much gold in quantity as all yonder abbey.' 'By my faith,' said Wat Tyler, 'I shall never eat meat till I have thy head': and with those words the mayor of London came to the king with a twelve horses well armed under their coats, and so he brake the press and saw and heard how Wat Tyler demeaned himself, and said to him: 'Ha, thou knave, how art thou so hardy in the king's presence to speak such words? It is too much for thee so to do.' Then the king began to chafe and said to the mayor: 'Set hands on him.' And while the king said so, Tyler said to the mayor: 'A God's name what have I said to displease thee?' 'Yes truly,' quoth the mayor, 'thou false stinking knave, shalt thou speak thus in the presence of the king my natural lord? I commit never to live, without thou shalt dearly abye it.' And with those words the mayor drew out his sword and strake Tyler so great a stroke on the head, that he fell down at the feet of his horse, and as soon as he was fallen, they environed him all about, whereby he was not seen of his company. Then a squire of the king's alighted, called John Standish, and he drew out his sword and put it into Wat Tyler's belly, and so he died.

Then the ungracious people there assembled, perceiving their captain slain, began to murmur among themselves and said: 'Ah, our captain is slain, let us go and slay them all': and therewith they arranged themselves on the place in manner of battle, and their bows before them. Thus the king began a great outrage; howbeit, all turned to the best: for as soon as Tyler was on the earth, the king departed from all his company and all alone he rode to these people, and said to his own men: 'Sirs, none of you follow me; let me alone.' And so when he came before these ungracious people, who put themselves in ordinance to revenge their captain, then the king said to them: 'Sirs, what aileth you? Ye shall have no captain but me: I am your king: be all in rest and peace.' And so the most part of the people that heard the king speak and saw him among them, were shamefast and began to wax peaceable and to depart; but some, such as were malicious and evil, would not depart, but made semblant as though they would do somewhat . . .

John Ball and Jack Straw were found in an old house

hidden, thinking to have stolen away, but they could not, for they were accused by their own men. Of the taking of them the king and his lords were glad, and then strake off their heads and Wat Tyler's also, and they were set on London bridge, and the valiant men's heads taken down that they had set on the Thursday before. These tidings anon spread abroad, so that the people of the strange countries, which were coming towards London, returned back again to their own houses and durst come no farther.

[76] A Royal Joust in Smithfield in 1467; from *Chronicles* by E. Hall.

1467: The Bastard of Burgoyne, a man of a haute corage, chalenged Anthony lord Scales, brother to the Quene, a man both egall in harte, and valyantnes with the bastard to fight with hym bothe on fote & on horsbacke, the lord Scales gladly receyved hys demaunde and promised hym on the othe of a gentleman, to aunswere hym in the felde, at the day appoynted: lyke chalenges were made by other Burgonyons, to the gentlemen of Englande, which you may surely beleve were not refused. The Kyng entendyng to see thys marciall sport and valiant chalenge performed, caused lystes royall for the champions, and costely galler-ies for Ladies to loke on, to be newly erected and edefied in West Smythfelde in London. And at the day by the Kyng assigned, the II Lordes entered within the listes, well mounted, richely trapped and curiouslye armed. On whi-che daye they ran together, certayne courses wyth sharpe speres, and so departed with egall honor. The next daye, they entered the felde, the bastarde sitting on a bay courser, beinge somewhat dymme of sight, and the lord Scales had a gray courser, on whose schaffron was a long and sharpe pyke of stele. When these II valeant persones coped together at the tornay, the lord Scales horse by chance or by custome, thrust hys pyke into the nostrelles of the horse of the bastarde, so that for very payne he mounted so hygh, that he fell on the one syde with hys

master, & the lord Scales rode round about him with his
sworde shakyeng in hys hand, tyll the Kyng commaunded
the Marshall to helpe up the bastarde, whiche openly
sayed, I can not holde by the cloudes, for though my horse
fayled me, surely I will not fayle my conter-conpaignions.
And when he was remounted, he made a countenaunce to
assayle his adversarie, but the Kyng either favoryng his
brothers honor then gotten, or mistrustyng the shame,
whiche mighte come to the bastarde, if he were agayne
foyled, caused the Heraldes to cry, *a lostel*, and every man
to departe. The morow after, the two noble men came in
to the felde on fote, with two Poleaxes, and there fought
valiantly lyke two coragious champions, but at the laste,
the point of the axe of the lord Scales happened to enter
into the sight of the healme of the bastard, & by fyne
force might have plucked hym on his knees, the Kynge
sodaynely caste doune his warder, and then the Marshalls
them severed.

[77] John Rogers, the first protestant martyr, is
burned at Smithfield (1555); from *Acts and Monuments* by J. Foxe.

And so he was brought into Smithfield by master Chester,
and master Woodroofe, then sheriffs of London, there to
be burnt; where he showed most constant patience, not
using many words, for he could not be permitted; but only
exhorting the people constantly to remain in that faith and
true doctrine which he before had taught, and they had
learned, and for the confirmation whereof he was not only
content patiently to suffer and bear all such bitterness and
cruelty as had been showed him, but also most gladly to
resign up his life, and to give his flesh to the consuming
fire, for the testimony of the same ... the fire was put
unto him; and when it had taken hold both upon his legs
and shoulders, he, as one feeling no smart, washed his
hands in the flame, as though it had been in cold water.
And, after lifting up his hands unto heaven, not removing

the same until such time as the devouring fire had consumed them – most mildly this happy martyr yielded up
his spirit into the hands of his heavenly Father. A little
before his burning at the stake, his pardon was brought, if
he would have recanted, but he utterly refused. He was
the first proto-martyr of all the blessed company that
suffered in queen Mary's time, that gave the first adventure
upon the fire. His wife and children, being eleven in
number, and ten able to go, and one sucking on her breast,
met him by the way as he went towards Smithfield. This
sorrowful sight of his own flesh and blood could nothing
move him; but that he constantly and cheerfully took his
death, with wonderful patience, in the defence and quarrel
of Christ's gospel.

[78] The Cock Lane ghost (1760); from *Extraordinary Popular Delusions* by Charles Mackay.

At the commencement of the year 1760, there resided in
Cock Lane, near West Smithfield, in the house of one
Parsons, the parish-clerk of St Sepulchre's, a stockbroker,
named Kent. The wife of this gentleman had died in child-
bed during the previous year, and his sister-in-law, Miss
Fanny, had arrived from Norfolk to keep his house for
him. They soon conceived a mutual affection, and each of
them made a will in the other's favour. They lived some
months in the house of Parsons, who, being a needy man,
borrowed money of his lodger. Some difference arose
betwixt them, and Mr Kent left the house and instituted
legal proceedings against the parish-clerk for the recovery
of his money.

While this matter was yet pending, Miss Fanny was
suddenly taken ill of the small-pox; and, notwithstanding
every care and attention, she died in a few days, and was
buried in a vault under Clerkenwell church. Parsons now
began to hint that the poor lady had come unfairly by her
death, and that Mr Kent was accessory to it, from his too
great eagerness to enter into possession of the property she

had bequeathed him. Nothing further was said for nearly two years; but it would appear that Parsons was of so revengeful a character, that he had never forgotten or forgiven his differences with Mr Kent, and the indignity of having been sued for the borrowed money. The strong passions of pride and avarice were silently at work during all that interval, hatching schemes of revenge, but dismissing them one after the other as impracticable, until, at last, a notable one suggested itself. About the beginning of the year 1762, the alarm was spread all over the neighbourhood of Cock Lane, that the house of Parsons was haunted by the ghost of poor Fanny, and that the daughter of Parsons, a girl about twelve years of age, had several times seen and conversed with the spirit, who had, moreover, informed her, that she had not died of the small-pox, as was currently reported, but of poison, administered by Mr Kent. Parsons, who originated, took good care to countenance these reports; and in answer to numerous inquiries, said his house was every night, and had been for two years, in fact, ever since the death of Fanny, troubled by a loud knocking at the doors and in the walls. Having thus prepared the ignorant and credulous neighbours to believe or exaggerate for themselves what he had told them, he sent for a gentleman of a higher class in life, to come and witness these extraordinary occurrences. The gentleman came accordingly, and found the daughter of Parsons, to whom the spirit alone appeared, and whom alone it answered, in bed, trembling violently, having just seen the ghost, and been again informed that she had died from poison. A loud knocking was also heard from every part of the chamber, which so mystified the not very clear understanding of the visitor, that he departed, afraid to doubt and ashamed to believe, but with a promise to bring the clergyman of the parish and several other gentlemen on the following day to report upon the mystery.

On the following night he returned, bringing with him three clergymen, and about twenty other persons, including two negroes, when, upon a consultation with Parsons, they resolved to sit up the whole night and await the ghost's arrival. It was then explained by Parsons, that although the ghost would never render itself visible to any body but his daughter, it had no objection to answer the questions that might be put to it by any person present, and that it expressed an affirmation by one knock, a negative by two, and its displeasure by a kind of scratching. The child was then put into bed along with her sister, and the clergymen examined the bed and bedclothes to satisfy themselves that no trick was played, by knocking upon any substance concealed among the clothes. As on the previous night, the bed was observed to shake violently.

After some hours, during which they all waited with exemplary patience, the mysterious knocking was heard in the wall, and the child declared that she saw the ghost of poor Fanny. The following questions were then gravely put by the clergyman, through the medium of one Mary Frazer, the servant of Parsons, and to whom it was said the deceased lady had been much attached. The answers were in the usual fashion, by a knock or knocks:

'Do you make this disturbance on account of the ill-usage you received from Mr Kent?' – 'Yes.'

'Were you brought to an untimely end by poison?' – 'Yes.'

'How was the poison administered, in beer or purl?' – 'In purl.'

'How long was that before your death?'– 'About three hours.'

'Can your former servant, Carrots, give any information about the poison?' – 'Yes.'

'Are you Kent's wife's sister?' – 'Yes.'

'Were you married to Kent after your sister's death?'– 'No.'

'Was any body else, besides Kent, concerned in your murder?' – 'No.'

'Can you, if you like, appear visibly to any one?' – 'Yes.'

'Will you do so?' – 'Yes.'

'Can you go out of this house?' – 'Yes.'

'Is it your intention to follow this child about everywhere?'– 'Yes.'

'Are you pleased in being asked these questions?' – 'Yes.'

'Does it ease your troubled soul?' – 'Yes.'

[Here there was heard a mysterious noise, which some wiseacre present compared to the fluttering of wings.]

'How long before your death did you tell your servant, Carrots, that you were poisoned? An hour?' – 'Yes.'

[Carrots, who was present, was appealed to; but she stated positively that such was not the fact, as the deceased was quite speechless an hour before her death. This shook the faith of some of the spectators, but the examination was allowed to continue.]

'How long did Carrots live with you?'– 'Three or four days.'

[Carrots was again appealed to, and said this was true.]

'If Mr Kent is arrested for this murder, will he confess?'– 'Yes.'

'Would your soul be at rest if he were hanged for it?'– 'Yes.'

'Will he be hanged for it?'– 'Yes.'

'How long a time first?'– 'Three years.'

'How many clergymen are there in this room?'– 'Three.'

'How many negroes?'– 'Two.'

'Is this watch (held by one of the clergymen) white?'– 'No.'

'Is it yellow?'– 'No.'

'Is it blue?'– 'No.'

'Is it black?'– 'Yes.'

[The watch was in a black shagreen case.]

'At what time this morning will you take your departure?'

The answer to this question was four knocks, very distinctly heard by every person present; and accordingly, at four o'clock precisely, the ghost took its departure to the Wheatsheaf public-house close by, where it frightened mine host and his lady almost out of their wits, by knocking in the ceiling right above their bed.

The rumour of these occurrences very soon spread over London, and every day Cock Lane was rendered impassable by the crowds of people who assembled round the house of the parish-clerk, in expectation of either seeing the ghost or of hearing the mysterious knocks. It was at last found necessary, so clamorous were they for admission within the haunted precincts, to admit those only who would pay a certain fee, an arrangement which was very convenient to the needy and money-loving Mr Parsons. Indeed, things had taken a turn greatly to his satisfaction; he not only had his revenge, but he made a profit out of it. The ghost, in consequence, played its antics every night, to the great amusement of many hundreds of people and the great perplexity of a still greater number.

Unhappily, however, for the parish-clerk, the ghost was induced to make some promises which were the means of utterly destroying its reputation. It promised, in answer to the questions of the Rev. Mr Aldritch of Clerkenwell, that it would not only follow the little Miss Parsons wherever she went, but would also attend him, or any other gentleman, into the vault under St John's Church, where the body of the murdered woman was deposited, and would there give notice of its presence by a distinct knock upon the coffin. As a preliminary, the girl was conveyed to the house of Mr Aldritch near the church, where a large party of ladies and gentlemen, eminent for their acquirements, their rank, or their wealth, had assembled. About ten o'clock on the night of the first of February, the girl having been brought from Cock Lane in a coach, was put to bed by several ladies in the house of Mr Aldritch; a strict examination having been previously made that nothing was hidden in the bed-clothes. While the gentlemen in an adjoining chamber were deliberating whether they should proceed in a body to the vault, they were summoned into the bedroom by the ladies, who affirmed, in great alarm, that the ghost was come, and that they heard the knocks and scratches. The gentlemen entered accordingly, with a determination to suffer no deception. The little girl, on being asked whether she saw the ghost, replied, 'No; but she felt it on her back like a mouse.' She was then required to put her hands out of bed, and they being held by some of the ladies, the spirit was summoned in the usual manner to answer, if it were in the room. The question was several times put with great solemnity; but the customary knock was not heard in reply in the walls, neither was there any scratching. The ghost was then asked to render itself visible, but did not choose to grant the request. It was next solicited to give some token of its presence by a sound of any sort, or by touching the hand or cheek of any lady or gentleman in the room; but even with this request the ghost would not comply.

There was now a considerable pause, and one of the clergymen went downstairs to interrogate the father of the girl, who was waiting the result of the experiment. He positively denied that there was any deception, and even went so far as to say that he himself, upon one occasion, had seen and conversed with the awful ghost. This having been communicated to the company, it was unanimously resolved to give the ghost another trial; and the clergyman called out in a loud voice to the supposed spirit, that the gentleman to whom it had promised to appear in the vault was about to repair to that place, where he claimed the fulfilment of its promise. At one hour after midnight they all proceeded to the church, and the gentleman in question, with another, entered the vault alone, and took up their position alongside of the coffin of poor Fanny. The ghost was then summoned to appear, but it appeared not; it was summoned to knock, but it knocked not; it was summoned to scratch, but it scratched not; and the two retired from the vault, with a firm belief that the whole business was a deception practised by Parsons and his daughter. There were others, however, who did not wish to jump so hastily to a conclusion, and who suggested that they were perhaps trifling with this awful and supernatural being, which, being offended with them for their presumption, would not condescend to answer them. Again, after serious consultation, it was agreed on all hands that if the ghost answered any body at all, it would answer Mr Kent, the supposed murderer; and he was accordingly requested to go down into the vault. He went with several others, and summoned the ghost to answer whether he had indeed poisoned her. There being no answer, the question was put by Mr Aldritch, who conjured it, if it were indeed a spirit, to end their doubts, make a sign of its presence, and point out the guilty person. There being still no answer for the space of half an hour, during which time all these boobies waited with the most praiseworthy perseverance, they returned to the house of Mr Aldritch, and ordered the girl to get up and dress herself. She was strictly examined, but persisted in her statement that she used no deception, and that the ghost had really appeared to her.

So many persons had, by their openly expressed belief of the reality of the visitation, identified themselves with it, that Parsons and his family were far from being the only persons interested in the continuance of the delusion. The result of the experiment convinced most people; but these were not to be convinced by any evidence, however positive, and they therefore spread abroad the rumour, that the ghost had not appeared in the vault because Mr Kent had taken care beforehand to have the coffin removed. That gentleman, whose position was a very painful one, immediately procured competent witnesses, in whose presence the vault was entered, and the coffin of poor Fanny opened. Their depositions were then published; and Mr Kent indicted Parsons and his wife, his daughter, Mary Frazer the servant, the Rev. Mr Moor, and a tradesman, two of the most prominent patrons of the deception, for a conspiracy. The trial came on in the Court of King's Bench, on 10 July, before Lord Chief-Justice Mansfield, when, after an investigation which lasted twelve hours, the whole of the conspirators were found guilty. The Rev. Mr Moor and his friend were severely reprimanded in open court, and recommended to make some pecuniary compensation to the prosecutor for the aspersions they had been instrumental in throwing upon his character. Parsons was sentenced to stand three times in the pillory, and to be imprisoned for two years;

his wife to one year's, and his servant to six months' imprisonment in the Bridewell. A printer, who had been employed by them to publish an account of the proceedings for their profit, was also fined fifty pounds, and discharged.

The precise manner in which the deception was carried on has never been explained. The knocking in the wall appears to have been the work of Parsons' wife, while the scratching part of the business was left to the little girl. That any contrivance so clumsy could have deceived any body cannot fail to excite our wonder.

[79] Wordsworth visits Bartholomew Fair (early 19th century); from *The Prelude*, Book VII.

What a shock
For eyes and ears! what anarchy and din,
Barbarian and infernal, – a phantasma,
Monstrous in colour, motion, shape, sight, sound!
Below, the open space, through every nook
Of the wide area, twinkles, is alive
With heads; the midway region, and above,
Is thronged with staring pictures and huge scrolls,
Dumb proclamations of the Prodigies;
With chattering monkeys dangling from their poles,
And children whirling in their roundabouts;
With those that stretch the neck and strain the eyes,
And crack the voice in rivalship, the crowd
Inviting; with buffoons against buffoons
Grimacing, writhing, screaming, – him who grinds
The hurdy-gurdy, at the fiddle weaves,
Rattles the salt-box, thumps the kettle-drum,
And him who at the trumpet puffs his cheeks,
The silver-collared Negro with his timbrel,
Equestrians, tumblers, women, girls, and boys,
Blue-breeched, pink-vested, with high-towering
    plumes. –
All moveables of wonder, from all parts,

Are here – Albinos, painted Indians, Dwarfs,
The Horse of knowledge, and the learned Pig,
The Stone-eater, the man that swallows fire,
Giants, Ventriloquists, the Invisible Girl,
The Bust that speaks and moves its goggling eyes,
The Wax-work, Clock-work, all the marvellous craft
Of modern Merlins, Wild Beasts, Puppet-shows,
All out-o'-the-way, far-fetched, perverted things,
All freaks of nature, all Promethean thoughts
Of man, his dulness, madness, and their feats
All jumbled up together, to compose
A Parliament of Monsters. Tents and Booths
Meanwhile, as if the whole were one vast mill,
Are vomiting, receiving on all sides,
Men, Women, three-years' Children, Babes in arms.

Oh, blank confusion! true epitome
Of what the mighty City is herself,
To thousands upon thousands of her sons,
Living amid the same perpetual whirl
Of trivial objects, melted and reduced
To one identity, by differences
That have no law, no meaning, and no end –

The Thames

[80] Fish in the Thames (16th century); from *Survey of London* by J. Stow.

What should I speak of the fat and sweet salmons daily taken in this stream, and that in such plenty (after the time of the smelt is past) as no river in Europe is able to exceed it? But what store also of barbels, trouts, chevens, perches, smelts, breams, roaches, daces, gudgeons, flounders, shrimps, eels, &c., are commonly to be had therein, I refer me to them that know by experience better than I, by reason of their daily trade of fishing in the same. And albeit it seemeth from time to time to be, as it were, defrauded in sundry wise of these, her large commodities, by the insatiable avarice of fishermen; yet this famous river complaineth commonly of no want, but the more it loseth at one time it gaineth at another.

[81] The Great Frost Fair (17th century); from *Diaries* by J. Evelyn.

1 Jan. 1683–4. The weather continuing intolerably severe, streetes of booths were set upon the Thames; the air was so very cold and thick, as of many yeares there had not ben the like.

9th. I went crosse the Thames on the ice, now become so thick as to beare not onely streetes of boothes, in which they roasted meate, and had divers shops of wares, quite acrosse as in a towne, but coaches, carts and horses, passed over. So I went from Westminster Stayres to Lambeth, and din'd with the Archbishop . . .

16th. The Thames was fill'd with people and tents, selling all sorts of wares as in the Citty.

24th. The frost continuing more and more severe, the Thames before London was still planted with boothes in formal streetes, all sortes of trades and shops furnish'd and full of commodities, even to a printing presse, where the people and ladyes tooke a fancy to have their names printed, and the day and yeare set down when printed on the Thames: this humour tooke so universally, that 'twas estimated the printer gain'd £5 a day, for printing a line onely, at sixpence a name, besides what he got by ballads, &c. Coaches plied from Westminster to the Temple, and from several other staires to and fro, as in the streetes, sleds, sliding with skeetes, a bull-baiting, horse and coach races, puppet plays and interludes, cookes, tipling, and other lewd places, so that it seem'd to be a bacchanalian triumph or carnival on the water, whilst it was a severe judgement on the land, the trees not onely splitting as if lightning-struck, but men and cattle perishing in divers places, and the very seas so lock'd up with ice, that no vessels could stir out or come in.

THE WEST END

THE OLD AND NEW HAYMARKET THEATRES

Buckingham Palace

[82] The changing of the guard; from *When We Were Very Young* (1926) by A. A. Milne.

They're changing guard at Buckingham Palace –
Christopher Robin went down with Alice.
Alice is marrying one of the guard.
'A soldier's life is terrible hard,'
    Says Alice.

They're changing guard at Buckingham Palace –
Christopher Robin went down with Alice.
We saw a guard in a sentry box.
'One of the sergeants looks after their socks,'
    Says Alice.

They're changing guard at Buckingham Palace –
Christopher Robin went down with Alice.
We looked for the King, but he never came.
'Well, God take care of him, all the same,'
    Says Alice.

They're changing guard at Buckingham Palace –
Christopher Robin went down with Alice.
They've great big parties inside the grounds.
'I wouldn't be King for a hundred pounds,'
          Says Alice.

They're changing guard at Buckingham Palace –
Christopher Robin went down with Alice.
A face looked out, but it wasn't the King's.
'He's much too busy a-signing things,'
          Says Alice.

They're changing guard at Buckingham Palace –
Christopher Robin went down with Alice.
'Do you think the King knows all about *me*?'
'Sure to, dear, but it's time for tea,'
          Says Alice.

[83] Two accounts of VE Day (1945); quoted in *The Day the War Ended, VE-Day 1945* by M. Gilbert.

'I had never been in such a vast crowd before, but there was no need to feel nervous. The people were exuberant but disciplined. I remember no incident of disorder. It seemed as if the amazing comradeship and good will that one had experienced during the war in London, in the black-out as well as the day time, in public transport, in air raid shelters – everywhere – still existed. All the way through the darkest days from 1940 onwards "brother clasped the hand of brother, stepping fearless through the night". That atmosphere was very present in the huge crowd which awaited the appearance of the leaders of the Nation, who had stood by us from beginning to end.

'When the Royal Family and the Prime Minister stepped out on to the balcony the crowd cheered and cheered with genuine warmth and affection. Some people were in tears. No one (or so it seemed) was there from curiosity. Princess Elizabeth wore WRAC uniform. Princess Margaret was still a schoolgirl. They had been based at Windsor most of the war, and the King and Queen in London, where they shared our dangers and were often with us at scenes of death and destruction. For Winston Churchill, I think that this was his finest hour. Only a few months later, when I was working in Islington at the time of the General Election of 1945, I heard him booed as he drove through the streets, standing up in a Land Rover. But on 8 May 1945 people remembered that without his leadership we might have had German troops before Buckingham Palace, and possibly Nazi leaders on the balcony.

'We stayed for an hour or more. The Royal Family appeared several times, the crowd waved little Union Jacks, sang songs, and cheered and cheered. Everyone was friendly and relaxed, though it seemed unbelievable that we could now be free of fear. I did not myself celebrate later . . . Like many others I was on my own. My husband was still on active service in the Middle East. I believe that in many parts of London there were street parties that night and festivities in hotels and restaurants. But I was in no mood for revelry. We still had a long way to go.' . . .

'Every nook and cranny of London buzzed with excitement, which manifested itself in diverse ways. The rubber-shortage interdicted the production of celebratory toy balloons: but the most enterprising breed of street-traders, then known as "spivs", were assisting patriotic celebrations by offering for sale two types of "French letters" tied to the top of thin canes; those known as "with teat", which had a little bulge at the end, sold for two-and-sixpence each, and the less sophisticated variety for a florin (two-shillings). Both found a ready market, particularly among servicemen and women, who brandished them triumphantly thereafter. Long before night threw her very incomplete mantle over Green Park couples were joyously copulating all over the grass. So natural and appropriate an expression of universal relief at the end of the War in Europe did that seem, that not even the old ladies, who normally clicked their tongues as drakes from the lake accosted more than willing ducks, expressed anything but a benign sharing of the universal happiness.'

The British Museum

[84] The famous duel behind Montague House in 1680, from *Notes and Queries* by E. F. Rimbault.

The fields behind Montagu House were, from about the year 1680, until towards the end of the last century, the scenes of robbery, murder, and every species of depravity and wickedness of which the heart can think. They appear to have been originally called the 'Long Fields', and afterwards (about Strype's time) the 'Southampton Fields'. These fields remained waste and useless, with the exception of some nursery grounds near the New Road to the north, and a piece of ground enclosed for the Toxophilite Society, towards the north-west, near the back of Gower Street. The remainder was the resort of depraved wretches, whose amusements consisted chiefly in fighting pitched battles, and other disorderly sports, especially on Sundays. Such was their state in 1800. Tradition had given to the superstitions at that period a legendary story of the period of the Duke of Monmouth's Rebellion, of two brothers, who fought in this field so ferociously as to destroy each other; since which their footsteps, formed from the venge-ful struggle, were said to remain, with the indentations produced by their advancing and receding; nor could any grass or vegetable ever be produced where these *forty footsteps* were thus displayed. This extraordinary area was said to be at the extreme termination of the north-east end of Upper Montagu Street . . . The latest account of these footsteps, previous to their being built over, with which I am acquainted, is the following, which I have extracted from one of Joseph Moser's Common-place Books: 'June 16, 1800. Went into the fields at the back of Montagu House, and there saw, for the last time, the *forty footsteps*; the building materials are there ready to cover them from the sight of man. I counted *more than forty*, but they might be the foot-prints of the workmen.'

[85] Sir Hans Sloane's 'museum' offered to Parlia-ment in 1753; from *Letters* by Horace Walpole.

Arlington Street, Feb. 14, 1753.
'. . . You will scarce guess how I employ my time; chiefly at present in the guardianship of embryos and cockle-shells. Sir Hans Sloane is dead and has made me one of the trustees to his museum, which is to be offered for twenty thousand pounds to the King, the Parliament, the Royal Academy of Petersburgh, Berlin, Paris and Madrid. He valued it at fourscore thousand; and so would anybody who loves hippopotamuses, sharks with one ear, and spiders as big as geese! It is a rent-charge to keep the foetuses in spirit! You may believe that those who think money the most valuable of all curiosities, will not be purchasers. The King has excused himself, saying he did not believe that there are twenty thousand pounds in the Treasury. We are a charming wise set, all philosophers, botanists, antiquarians, and mathematicians; and adjourned our first meeting, because Lord Macclesfield, our chairman, was engaged to a party for finding out the longitude. One of our number is a Moravian, who signs

himself Henry XXVIII, Count de Reus. The Moravian has settled a colony at Chelsea, in Sir Hans's neighbourhood, and I believe he intended to beg Count Henry XXVIIIth's skeleton for his museum.'

[86] Keats visits the Elgin Marbles (1817); from *On seeing the Elgin Marbles*.

My spirit is too weak – mortality
Weighs heavily on me like unwilling sleep,
And each imagin'd pinnacle and steep
Of godlike hardship tells me I must die
Like a sick Eagle looking at the sky.
Yet 't is a gentle luxury to weep
That I have not the cloudy winds to keep,
Fresh for the opening of the morning's eye.
Such dim-conceivèd glories of the brain
Bring round the heart an indescribable feud;
So do these wonders a most dizzy pain,
That mingles Grecian grandeur with the rude
Wasting of old Time – with a billowy main –
A sun – a shadow of a magnitude.

[87] The library of George III is given to the British Museum (1823). Letter from George IV to Lord Liverpool; from *Old and New London* by W. Thornbury.

Pavilion, Brighton, Jan. 15, 1823.
Dear Lord Liverpool

The King, my late revered and excellent father, having formed, during a long series of years, a most valuable and extensive library, consisting of about 120,000 volumes, I have resolved to present this collection to the British nation.

Whilst I have the satisfaction by this means of advancing the literature of my country, I also feel that I am paying a just tribute to the memory of a parent whose life was adorned with every public and private virtue.

I desire to add, that I have great pleasure, my lord, in making this communication through you. Believe me, with great regard, your sincere friend,

G. R.
To the Earl of Liverpool, K.G., &c.

[88] Enoch Soames visits the reading room of the British Museum (1997); an article by Thomas Wright in the *Evening Standard Magazine*.

At ten minutes past two on 3 June one of the most extraordinary of all 19th-century poets will walk through the swing doors of the Reading Room of the British Museum and lollop over to the catalogue at the centre desk. Enoch Soames's appearance will be the final act of a Faustian pact struck with the Devil himself in a Soho restaurant on the afternoon of 3 June 1897, and a group of Soames's distinguished modern-day disciples will have gathered to meet the 134-year-old versifier after his arduous journey across a century . . .

But, in spite of the zeal with which the Enoch Soames Society and its chairman, Sir Stephen Tumim, have organized this 'homecoming' party, the poet is really only an imaginary character from Max Beerbohm's short story *Enoch Soames*. In the tale, Soames, a *fin-de-siècle* man of letters literally dying for want of recognition, is overheard by the Devil in a Greek Street restaurant in 1897 uttering a wish to visit the Reading Room exactly one hundred years in the future. Once there he intends to pore over the 'endless editions, commentaries . . . biographies . . .' that are sure to venerate and memorialize the exquisite rhymes contained in his undeservedly obscure works, *Negations and Fungoids*. A bargain is struck, and so it is that the emaciated Enoch finds himself in the Reading Room in 1997. But the delicate bard discovers nothing in the catalogue under his name, and the only mention of 'Soames,

Enoch' actually occurs in a book by the 20th-century critic T. K. Nupton, who refers to him as a fictional protagonist in a short story by one 'Max Beerbohm'. So, squashed between the pages of an ironic tale, with flashing eyes and foppish hair, he returns to Soho and from there descends into Hell . . .

Nobly, the Trustees of the British Library have joined the Enoch Soames Society in refusing to accept the recognized boundaries between fact and fiction, and a series of events has been planned to commemorate what is surely the most bizarre date in the literary calendar. A corner of the Manuscript Saloon in the Library is to be devoted to an exhibition of rare Soamesiana, and among these curiosities will be several items of doubtful provenance: a portrait of Enoch, for instance, by the 19th-century illustrator William Rothenstein that has recently been 'discovered' by the artist Lawrence Mynott, and a previously unknown likeness in pen and ink by Aubrey Beardsley, which the distinguished Beardsley scholar Stephen Calloway insists is an 'original'. On 'Soamesday' itself, the Museum will be hosting a reception for the most exotic exhibits of all: the Soames Society and the many members of the Max Beerbohm Society, known as the Maximilians, who will be making the pilgrimage across the Atlantic to attend. Many of these men will be dressed to the 'Nineties' in the grey waterproof capes and soft, black, clerical hats that, according to Beerbohm, their bohemian hero affected . . . It is also known that certain members of the Enoch Soames Society have prepared a volume of their own to mark the occasion, entitled *Enoch Soames, The Critical Heritage* . . . With any luck, the volume will have been entered into the catalogue of the Reading Room before 3 June – with the happy result that when the 'shambling' Enoch arrives at ten minutes past two he will discover a real reference to the book entered beneath his name. At last, the fictitious author who has become the archetype of the failed writer will be rewarded with the eccentric immortality he surely deserves.

Covent Garden

[89] A riot at the Drury Lane Theatre (1770); from *Memoirs* by Casanova, translated by A. Machen.

We went to Drury Lane Theatre, where I had a specimen of the rough insular manners [of the English]. By some accident or other the company could not give the piece that had been announced, and the audience were in a tumult. Garrick, the celebrated actor who was buried twenty years later in Westminster Abbey, came forward and tried in vain to restore order. He was obliged to retire behind the curtain. Then the king, the queen, and all the fashionables left the theatre, and in less than an hour the theatre was gutted, till nothing but the bare walls were left.

After this destruction, which went on without any authority interposing, the mad populace rushed to the taverns to consume gin and beer. In a fortnight the theatre was refitted and the piece announced again, and when Garrick appeared before the curtain to implore the indulgence of the house, a voice from the pit shouted, 'On your knees.' A thousand voices took up the cry, 'On your knees,' and the English Roscius was obliged to kneel down and beg forgiveness. Then came a thunder of applause, and everything was over. Such are the English, and above all, the Londoners. They hoot the king and the royal family when they appear in public, and the consequence is, that they are never seen, save on great occasions, when order is kept by hundreds of constables.

[90] The Mohawks terrorize the piazza (1771); from *Memoirs of William Hickey*, edited by P. Quennell.

In the winter of 1771, a set of wild young men made their appearance, who, from the profligacy of their manners and their outrageous conduct in the theatres, taverns and coffee houses in the vicinity of Covent Garden, created general indignation and alarm, actually driving away many sedate persons from their customary amusement in an evening. They were distinguished under the title of Mohawks, and as such severely attacked by the public newspapers, which, instead of checking, seemed to stimulate their excesses. They consisted of only four in number, their Chief, Rhoan Hamilton. This gentleman, when he first came forward in the character of Mohawk, was in the prime of life, a remarkably fine figure upwards of six feet high, and perfectly well made. He, being a man of fortune, was the principal hero. The second in command was Mr Hayter, whose father was an opulent merchant and bank director; the third, a Mr Osborne, a young American who had come to England to study law; and the last, Mr Frederick, a handsome lad without a guinea, said to be a son, or grandson, of the much talked of and unfortunate Theodore, King of Corsica. He had dubbed himself with the convenient travelling title of Captain; but no one knew from what corps he derived that rank.

This quartet were in a constant state of inebriety, daily committing the most wanton outrages upon unoffending

individuals who unfortunately fell in their way. It fell to
my lot to witness much of their insolent proceedings, for
at the time they commenced them I belonged to two
different clubs, one at the Shakespeare, the other at the
Piazza coffee house; at the quitting of which I generally
fell in with those formidable fellows, and, being brim-full
of wine, I invariably attacked them, reprobating their
scandalous behaviour, and delivering my opinion thereon
in unqualified terms of disapprobation, so much so that
the bystanders have often been astonished that they did
not instantly assail me. They sometimes did violently
threaten; notwithstanding which, I persevered in reprobating their conduct and abusing them whenever we met,
becoming so determined an opponent that I was soon
distinguished by the, at least, less dishonourable title of
'The Anti-Mohawk', under which I had some high-flown
compliments paid me by the sober old dons of the coffee
houses annoyed by their enormities. These gentry did not
always act together, sometimes separating and even singly
insulting the quiet and well-disposed; but at a certain hour
of the night they always met, usually at Lovejoy's, laying
their plans of mischief for the ensuing day.

[91] The Westminster election of 1782; from *Travels
in England* by C. P. Moritz.

The cities of London and Westminster send, the one four,
and the other two members to parliament. Mr Fox is one
of the two members for Westminster; one seat was vacant;
and that vacancy was now to be filled. Sir Cecil Wray . . .
was now publicly chosen. I was told, that at these elec-
tions, when there is a strong opposition party, there is
often bloody work; but this election was, in the election-
eering phrase, a hollow thing.

   The election was held in Covent Garden, a large mar-
ket-place, in the open air. There was a scaffold erected
just before the door of a very handsome church . . . A
temporary edifice, formed only of boards and wood nailed

together, was erected on the occasion. It was called the hustings: and filled with benches; and at one end of it, where the benches ended, mats were laid; on which those who spoke to the people stood. In the area before the hustings, immense multitudes of people were assembled; of whom the greatest part seemed to be of the lowest order. To this tumultuous crowd, however, the speakers often bowed very low, and always addressed them by the title of gentlemen. Sir Cecil Wray was obliged to step forward, and promise these same *gentlemen*, with hand and heart, that he would faithfully fulfil his duties as their representative. He also made an apology, because, on account of his journey and ill-health, he had not been able to wait on them, as became him, at their respective houses. The moment that he began to speak, even this rude rabble became all as quiet as the raging sea after a storm . . . and as soon as he had done speaking, they again vociferated a loud and universal huzza, everyone at the same time waving his hat.

And now, being formally declared to have been legally chosen, he again bowed most profoundly, and returned thanks for the great honour done him: when a well-dressed man, whose name I could not learn, stepped forward, and in a well-indited speech, congratulated both the chosen and the choosers. 'Upon my word,' said a gruff carter, who stood near me, 'that man speaks well.'

Even little boys clambered up, and hung on the rails and the lamp-posts; and, as if the speeches had also been addressed to them, they too listened with the utmost attention; and they too testified their approbation of it, by joining lustily in the three cheers, and waving their hats.

. . . When the whole was over, the rampant spirit of liberty, and the wild impatience of a genuine English mob were exhibited in perfection. In a very few minutes, the whole scaffolding, benches and chairs, and everything else, were completely destroyed; and the mat, with which it had been covered, torn into ten thousand long strips, or pieces, with which they encircled multitudes of people of all ranks. These they hurried along with them, and everything else that came in their way, as trophies of joy; and thus, in the midst of exultation and triumph, they paraded through many of the most populous streets of London.

[92] The Drury Lane Theatre burns down (1809); from *Memoirs of the Life of the Right Honourable Richard Brinsley Sheridan* by Thomas Moore.

On the night of 24 February 1809, when the House of Commons was occupied with Mr Ponsonby's motion on the Conduct of the War in Spain, and Mr Sheridan was in attendance, with the intention, no doubt, of speaking, the House was suddenly illuminated by a blaze of light; and, the Debate being interrupted, it was ascertained that the Theatre of Drury Lane was on fire. A motion was made to adjourn; but Mr Sheridan said, with much calmness, that 'whatsoever might be the extent of the private calamity, he hoped it would not interfere with the public business of the country'. He then left the House; and, proceeding to Drury Lane, witnessed, with a fortitude which strongly interested all who observed him, the entire destruction of his property. It is said that, as he sat at the Piazza Coffee-house during the fire, taking some refreshment, a friend of his having remarked on the philosophic calmness with which he bore his misfortune, Sheridan answered, 'A man may surely be allowed to take a glass of wine *by his own fireside.*'

[93] O. P. Riots at the Covent Garden Theatre (1809); from *Extraordinary Popular Delusions* by C. Mackay.

On the night of 20 September 1808, the old theatre of Covent-Garden was totally destroyed by fire. Preparations were immediately made for the erection of a more splendid edifice, and the managers, Harris and the celebrated John Philip Kemble, announced that the new theatre should be without a rival in Europe. In less than three months, the rubbish of the old building was cleared away, and the foundation-stone of the new one laid with all due ceremony by the Duke of Sussex. With so much celerity were the works carried on that, in nine months more, the edifice was completed, both without and within. The opening night was announced for 18 September 1809, within two days of a twelvemonth since the destruction of the original building.

But the undertaking had proved more expensive than the Committee anticipated ... as the night of opening drew near, the Committee found that they had gone a little beyond their means; and they issued a notice, stating that, in consequence of the great expense they had been at in building the theatre, and the large salaries they had agreed to pay, to secure the services of the most eminent actors, they were under the necessity of fixing the prices of admission at seven shillings to the boxes and four shillings to the pit, instead of six shillings and three and sixpence, as heretofore.

This announcement created the greatest dissatisfaction. The boxes might have borne the oppression, but the dignity of the pit was wounded. A war-cry was raised immediately. For some weeks previous to the opening, a continual clatter was kept up in clubs and coffee-rooms, against what was considered a most unconstitutional aggression on the rights of play-going man. The newspapers assiduously kept up the excitement, and represented, day after day, to the managers the impolicy of the proposed advance. The bitter politics of the time were disregarded, and Kemble and Covent-Garden became as great sources of interest as Napoleon and France. Public attention was the more fixed upon the proceedings at Covent-Garden, since it was the only patent theatre then in existence, Drury-Lane theatre having also been destroyed by fire in the month of February previous. But great as was the indignation of the lovers of the drama at that time, no one could have anticipated the extraordinary lengths to which opposition would be carried.

First Night, September 20

The performances announced were the tragedy of *Macbeth* and the afterpiece of *The Quaker*. The house was excessively crowded (the pit especially) with persons who had gone for no other purpose than to make a disturbance. They soon discovered another grievance to add to the list. The whole of the lower, and three-fourths of the upper tier of boxes, were let out for the season; so that those who had paid at the door for a seat in the boxes, were obliged to mount to a level with the gallery. Here they were stowed into boxes which, from their size and shape, received the contemptuous, and not inappropriate designation of pigeon-holes. This was considered in the light of a new aggression upon established rights; and long before the curtain drew up, the managers might have heard in their green-room the indignant shouts of 'Down with the pigeon-holes!' – 'Old prices for ever!' Amid this din the curtain rose, and Mr Kemble stood forward to deliver a poetical address in honour of the occasion. The riot now began in earnest; not a word of the address was audible, from the stamping and groaning of the people in the pit. This continued, almost without intermission, through the five acts of the tragedy. Now and then, the sublime acting of Mrs Siddons, as 'the awful woman', hushed the noisy multitude into silence, in spite of themselves: but it was only for a moment; the recollection of their fancied wrongs made them ashamed of their admiration, and they shouted and hooted again more vigorously than before. The comedy of Munden in the afterpiece met with no better reception; not a word was listened to, and the curtain fell amid still increasing uproar and shouts of 'Old prices!' Some magistrates, who happened to be present, zealously came to the rescue, and appeared on the stage with copies of the Riot Act. This ill-judged proceeding made the matter worse. The men of the pit were exasperated by the indignity, and strained their lungs to express how deeply they felt it. Thus remained the war till long after midnight, when the belligerents withdrew from sheer exhaustion . . .

Third Night

... The placards were, also, more numerous; not only the pit, but the boxes and galleries exhibited them. Among the most conspicuous, was one inscribed, 'John Bull against John Kemble. – Who'll win?' Another bore 'King George for ever! but no King Kemble.' A third was levelled against Madame Catalani, whose large salary was supposed to be one of the causes of the increased prices, and was inscribed 'No foreigners to tax us – we're taxed enough already.' This last was a double-barrelled one, expressing both dramatic and political discontent, and was received with loud cheers by the pitites.

Sixth night

No signs of a cessation of hostilities on the one side, or of a return to the old prices on the other. The playgoers seemed to grow more united as the managers grew more obstinate. The actors had by far the best time of it; for they were spared nearly all the labour of their parts, and merely strutted on the stage to see how matters went on, and then strutted off again. Notwithstanding the remonstrance of Mr O'Reilly on the previous night, numerous placards reflecting upon Madame Catalani were exhibited. One was inscribed with the following doggerel:

> Seventeen thousand a-year goes pat,
> To Kemble, his sister, and Madame Cat.

On another was displayed, in large letters, 'No compromise, old prices, and native talent!' Some of these were stuck against the front of the boxes, and others were hoisted from the pit on long poles. The following specimens will suffice to show the spirit of them; wit they had none, or humour either, although when they were successively exhibited, they elicited roars of laughter:

> John Kemble alone is the cause of this riot;
> When he lowers his prices, John Bull will be quiet.

John Kemble be damn'd,
We will not be cramm'd.

Squire Kemble
Begins to tremble.

The curtain fell as early as nine o'clock, when there
being loud calls for Mr Kemble, he stood forward. He
announced that Madame Catalani, against whom so
unjustifiable a prejudice had been excited, had thrown up
her engagement rather than stand in the way of any
accommodation of existing differences. This announcement was received with great applause. Mr Kemble then
went on to vindicate himself and co-proprietors from the
charge of despising public opinion. No assertion, he
assured them, could be more unjust. They were sincerely
anxious to bring these unhappy differences to a close, and
he thought he had acted in the most fair and reasonable
manner in offering to submit the accounts to an impartial
committee, whose decision, and the grounds for it, should
be fully promulgated. This speech was received with cheering, but interrupted at the close by some individuals, who
objected to any committee of the manager's nomination.
This led to a renewal of the uproar, and it was some time
before silence could be obtained. When, at last, he was
able to make himself heard, he gave notice, that until the
decision of the committee had been drawn up, the theatre
should remain closed. Immediately every person in the pit
stood up, and a long shout of triumph resounded through
the house, which was heard at the extremity of Bow Street.
As if this result had been anticipated, a placard was at the
same moment hoisted, inscribed, 'Here lies the body of
NEW PRICE, an ugly brat and base born, who expired on
the 23rd of September 1809, aged six days. – *Requiescat
in pace!*'
   Mr Kemble then retired, and the pitites flung up their
hats in the air, or sprang over the benches, shouting and
hallooing in the exuberance of their joy; and thus ended
the first act of this popular farce.
   The committee . . . could do no other than recommend

the proprietors to continue the new prices . . . this report gave no satisfaction.

It would be useless to detail the scenes of confusion which followed night after night. For about three weeks the war continued with unabated fury. Its characteristics were nearly always the same. Invention was racked to discover new noises, and it was thought a happy idea when one fellow got into the gallery with a dustman's bell, and rang it furiously. Dogs were also brought into the boxes, to add their sweet voices to the general uproar. The animals seemed to join in it *con amore*, and one night a large mastiff growled and barked so loudly, as to draw upon his exertions three cheers from the gratified pitites.

So strong did the popular enthusiasm run in favour of the row, that well-dressed ladies appeared in the boxes with the letters O. P. on their bonnets. O. P. hats for the gentlemen were still more common, and some were so zealous in the cause, as to sport waistcoats with an O embroidered upon one flap and a P on the other. O. P. toothpicks were also in fashion; and gentlemen and ladies carried O. P. handkerchiefs, which they waved triumphantly whenever the row was unusually deafening. The latter suggested the idea of O. P. flags, which were occasionally unfurled from the gallery to the length of a dozen feet. Sometimes the first part of the night's performances were listened to with comparative patience, a majority of the manager's friends being in possession of the house. But as soon as the half-price commenced, the row began again in all its pristine glory. At the fall of the curtain it soon became customary to sing 'God save the King', the whole of the O. P.'s joining in loyal chorus. Sometimes this was followed by 'Rule Britannia'; and, on two or three occasions, by a parody of the national anthem, which excited great laughter. A verse may not be uninteresting as a specimen.

> O Johnny Bull, be true
> Confound the prices new,
> And make them fall!

Curse Kemble's politics,
Frustrate his knavish tricks,
On thee our hopes we fix,
T' upset them all!

This done, they scrambled over the benches, got up sham
fights in the pit, or danced the famous O. P. dance. The
latter may as well be described here: half a dozen, or a
dozen fellows formed in a ring, and stamped alternately
with the right and left foot, calling out at regular intervals,
O. P. – O. P. with a drawling and monotonous sound.
This uniformly lasted till the lights were put out, when the
rioters withdrew, generally in gangs of ten or twenty, to
defend themselves from sudden attacks on the part of the
constables . . .

All this time the disturbance proceeded at the theatre
with its usual spirit. It was now the sixty-sixth night of its
continuance, and the rioters were still untired – still determined to resist to the last. In the midst of it a gentleman
arrived from the Crown and Anchor, and announced to
the pit that Mr Kemble had attended the dinner, and had
yielded at last to the demand of the public. He stated, that
it had been agreed upon between him and the Committee
for defending the persons under prosecution, that the boxes
should remain at the advanced price; that the pit should be
reduced to three shillings and sixpence; that the private
boxes should be done away with; and that all prosecutions,
on both sides, should be immediately stayed. This
announcement was received with deafening cheers. As soon
as the first burst of enthusiasm was over, the O. P.s became
anxious for a confirmation of the intelligence, and commenced a loud call for Mr Kemble. He had not then
returned from the Crown and Anchor; but of this the pitites
were not aware, and for nearly half an hour they kept up
a most excruciating din. At length the great actor made his
appearance, in his walking dress, with his cane in hand, as
he had left the tavern. It was a long time before he could
obtain silence. He apologized in the most respectful terms
for appearing before them in such unbecoming costume,

which was caused solely by his ignorance that he should have to appear before them that night. After announcing, as well as occasional interruptions would allow, the terms that had been agreed upon, he added, 'In order that no trace or recollection of the past differences, which had unhappily prevailed so long, should remain, he was instructed by the proprietors to say, that they most sincerely lamented the course that had been pursued, and engaged that, on their parts, all legal proceedings should forthwith be put a stop to.' The cheering which greeted this speech was interrupted at the close by loud cries from the pit of 'Dismiss Brandon,' while one or two exclaimed, 'We want old prices generally – six shillings for the boxes.' After an ineffectual attempt to address them again upon this point, Mr Kemble made respectful and repeated obeisances, and withdrew. The noises still continued, until Munden stood forward, leading by the hand the humbled box-keeper, contrition in his looks, and in his hands a written apology, which he endeavoured to read. The uproar was increased threefold by his presence, and, amid cries of 'We won't hear him!' 'Where's his master?' he was obliged to retire. Mr Harris, the son of Kemble's co-manager, afterwards endeavoured to propitiate the audience in his favour; but it was of no avail; nothing less than his dismissal would satisfy the offended majesty of the pit. Amid this uproar the curtain finally fell, and the O. P. dance was danced for the last time within the walls of Covent Garden.

On the following night it was announced that Brandon had resigned his situation. This turned the tide of popular ill-will. The performances were *The Wheel of Fortune*, and an afterpiece. The house was crowded to excess; a desire to be pleased was manifest on every countenance, and when Mr Kemble, who took his favourite character of Penruddock, appeared upon the stage, he was greeted with the most vehement applause. The noises ceased entirely, and the symbols of opposition disappeared. The audience, hushed into attention, gave vent to no sounds but those of admiration for the genius of the actor. When, in the course of his part, he repeated the words, 'So! I am in London again!' the aptness of the expression to the circumstances of the night, was felt by all present, and acknowledged by a round of boisterous and thrice repeated cheering. It was a triumphant scene for Mr Kemble after his long annoyances. He had achieved a double victory. He had, not only as a manager, soothed the obstinate opposition of the playgoers, but as an actor he had forced from one of the largest audiences he had ever beheld, approbation more cordial and unanimous than he had ever enjoyed before. The popular favour not only turned towards him; it embraced everybody connected with the theatre, except the poor victim, Brandon. Most of the favourite actors were called before the curtain to make their bow, and receive the acclamations of the pit. At the close of the performances, a few individuals, implacable and stubborn, got up a feeble cry of 'Old prices for the boxes;' but they were quickly silenced by the reiterated cheers of the majority, or by cries of 'Turn them out!' A placard, the last of its race, was at the same time exhibited in the front of the pit, bearing, in large letters, the words 'We are satisfied.'

[94] The farewell speech of Joseph Grimaldi (1828); from *Memoirs of Joseph Grimaldi*, edited by Charles Dickens.

Mr GRIMALDI'S FAREWELL BENEFIT.
On Friday, June 27th, 1828,
will be performed,
JONATHAN IN ENGLAND;
after which
A MUSICAL MELANGE.
To be succeeded by
THE ADOPTED CHILD,
and concluded with
HARLEQUIN HOAX,
In which Mr Grimaldi will act clown in one scene,
sing a song,
and speak his
FAREWELL ADDRESS.

'Ladies and Gentlemen: – In putting off the clown's garment, allow me to drop also the clown's taciturnity, and address you in a few parting sentences. I entered early on this course of life, and leave it prematurely. Eight-and-forty years only have passed over my head – but I am going as fast down the hill of life as that older Joe – John Anderson. Like vaulting ambition, I have overleaped myself, and pay the penalty in an advanced old age. If I have now any aptitude for tumbling, it is through bodily infirmity, for I am worse on my feet than I used to be on my head. It is four years since I jumped my last jump – filched my last oyster – boiled my last sausage – and set in for retirement. Not quite so well provided for, I must acknowledge, as in the days of my clownship, for then, I dare say, some of you remember, I used to have a fowl in one pocket and sauce for it in the other.

'To-night has seen me assume the motley for a short time – it clung to my skin as I took it off, and the old cap and bells rang mournfully as I quitted them for ever.

'With the same respectful feelings as ever do I find myself in your presence – in the presence of my last audience – this kindly assemblage so happily contradicting the adage that a favourite has no friends. For the benevolence that brought you hither – accept, ladies and gentlemen, my warmest and most grateful thanks, and believe, that of one and all, Joseph Grimaldi takes a double leave, with a farewell on his lips, and a tear in his eyes.

'Farewell! That you and yours may ever enjoy that greatest earthly good – health, is the sincere wish of your faithful and obliged servant. God bless you all!'

It was with no trifling difficulty that Grimaldi reached the conclusion of this little speech, although the audience cheered loudly, and gave him every possible expression of encouragement and sympathy. When he had finished, he still stood in the same place, bewildered and motionless, his feelings being so greatly excited, that the little power illness had left wholly deserted him. In this condition he stood for a minute of two, when Mr Harley, who was at

the side scene, commiserating his emotion, kindly advanced
and led him off the stage, assisted by his son.

[95] Queen Victoria opens the Great Exhibition (1851); from *Gentleman's Magazine*.

The Queen left Buckingham Palace in state at twenty
minutes before twelve, accompanied by Prince Albert and
their two eldest children, the Prince and Princess of
Prussia, Prince Frederick William of Prussia, and their
respective suites. They were conveyed in nine carriages.
Some time before Her Majesty entered, the heralds in
their tabards, the officers of state, Her Majesty's ministers, the foreign ambassadors, and the officers of the
household troops, in their full costumes, with the Execu-
tive Committee and other functionaries of the Exhibition,
the architect and contractors in court dresses, and the
Lord Mayor and Aldermen in their robes, had assembled
round the platform, and the 'beef-eaters' were ranged
behind. At length a flourish of trumpets announced the
Queen's arrival at the north door of the building, and
Her Majesty and her Royal Consort, leading by the hand
the Prince of Wales and the Princess Royal, appeared
before the vast assemblage of her subjects, and 'the crystal bow' rang with enthusiastic shouts, overpowering the
sound of the cannon discharged on the other side of the
Serpentine. It was a moment of intense excitement. In the
midst of the grandest temple ever raised to the peaceful
arts, surrounded by thousands of her subjects and men of
all nations, was the ruler of this realm and its vast
dependencies, herself the centre of the great undertaking.
Her emotions, as she gracefully and repeatedly acknowledged her people's gratulations, were very evident. The
Prince Consort having conducted Her Majesty to the
throne, the National Anthem was sung by a choir of near
a thousand voices, accompanied by the organ of Messrs.
Gray and Davidson . . . the state procession was then
formed, and passed down the northern avenue of the west
nave. The spectators were arranged on either side, and as

Her Majesty passed along, the cheers were taken up in succession by the whole of the long array, and seconded with waving of hats and handkerchiefs from the galleries. Her Majesty and the Prince acknowledged these gratulations by continual bowing. The various objects of interest around were for a time almost disregarded, but the effect of the whole upon the eye, as the Sovereign and her attendants threaded their way between the living throng, and the lines of statuary and other works of art, and the rich assemblage of the products of industry, was exceedingly impressive; and the ovation of industry far outshone all the splendours of old Rome, with no fettered captives in the rear, or wailing widows and orphans at home to dim its lustre. The Duke of Wellington and the Marquis of Anglesey (who joined the procession as Commander-in-Chief and Master-General of the Ordnance), united arm-in-arm in this triumph of peace, were the objects of much attraction. When the procession reached the west end, the magnificent organ by Mr Willis, with its 4,700 pipes, commenced playing the National Anthem, which was heard to the remotest end of the building. The procession returned by the south side to the transept, round the southern part of which it passed, amidst the cheers of the people, the peals of two organs, and the voices of 700 choristers, to the eastern or foreign division of the knave, where the French organ took up the strain, and the delicate lady, whose tempered sway is owned by a hundred millions of men, pursued her course amongst the contributions of all the civilized world. As she passed the gigantic equestrian figure of Godfrey de Bouillon, by the Belgian sculptor, Simonis, which seems the very impersonation of physical strength, we could not but be struck by the contrast, and by the reflection how far the prowess of the crusader is transcended by the power of well-defined liberty and constitutional law. The brilliant train having at length made the complete circuit of the building, Her Majesty again ascended the throne, and pronounced the Exhibition opened. The announcement was repeated by the Marquis of Breadalbane as Lord

Steward, followed immediately by a burst of acclamations, the bray of trumpets, and a royal salute across the
Serpentine. The royal party then withdrew; the National
Anthem was again repeated; and the visitors dispersed
themselves through the building, to gratify their curiosity
without restraint.

[96] Henry Mayhew visits the market in 1861; from
London Labour and the London Poor.

The market itself presents a beautiful scene. In the clear
morning air of an autumn day the whole of the vast square
is distinctly seen from one end to the other. The sky is red
and golden with the newly risen sun, and the rays falling
on the fresh and vivid colours of the fruit and vegetables,
brightens up the picture as with a coat of varnish. There is
no shouting, as at other markets, but a low murmuring
hum is heard, like the sound of the sea at a distance, and
through each entrance to the market the crowd sweeps by.
Under the dark Piazza little bright dots of gas-lights are
seen burning in the shops; and in the paved square the
people pass and cross each other in all directions, hampers
clash together, and excepting the carters from the country,
every one is on the move. Sometimes a huge column of
baskets is seen in the air, and walks away in a marvellously
steady manner, or a monster railway van, laden with sieves
of fruit, and with the driver perched up on his high seat,
jolts heavily over the stones. Cabbages are piled up into
stacks as it were. Carts are heaped high with turnips, and
bunches of carrots like huge red fingers, are seen in all
directions . . .
   Inside, the market all is bustle and confusion. The
people walk along with their eyes fixed on the goods, and
frowning with thought. Men in all costumes, from the
coster in his corduroy suit to the greengrocer in his blue
apron, sweep past. A countryman, in an old straw hat and
dusty boots, occasionally draws down the anger of a
woman for walking about with his hands in the pockets

of his smock-frock, and is asked, 'if that is the way to behave on a market-day?' Even the granite pillars cannot stop the crowd, for it separates and rushes past them, like the tide by a bridge pier. At every turn there is a fresh odour to sniff at; either the bitter aromatic perfume of the herbalists' shops breaks upon you, or the scent of oranges, then of apples, and then of onions is caught for an instant as you move along. The brocoli tied up in square packets, the white heads tinged slightly red, as it were, with the sunshine, – the sieves of crimson love-apples, polished like china, – the bundles of white glossy leeks, their roots dangling like fringe, – the celery, with its pinky stalks and bright green tops, – the dark purple pickling-cabbages, – the scarlet carrots, – the white knobs of turnips, – the bright yellow balls of oranges, and the rich brown coats of the chestnuts – attract the eye on every side. Then there are the apple-merchants, with their fruit of all colours, from the pale yellow green to the bright crimson, and the baskets ranged in rows on the pavement before the little shops. Round these the customers stand examining the stock, then whispering together over their bargain, and counting their money. 'Give you four shillings for this here lot, master,' says a coster, speaking for his three companions. 'Four and six is my price,' answers the salesman. 'Say four, and it's a bargain,' continues the man. 'I said my price,' returns the dealer, 'go and look round, and see if you can get 'em cheaper; if not, come back. I only wants what's fair.' The men, taking the salesman's advice, move on. The walnut merchant, with the group of women before his shop, peeling the fruit, their fingers stained deep brown, is busy with the Irish purchasers. The onion stores too, are surrounded by Hibernians, feeling and pressing the gold-coloured roots, whose dry skins crackle as they are handled. Cases of lemons in their white paper jackets, and blue grapes, just seen above the sawdust are ranged about, and in some places the ground is slippery as ice from the refuse leaves and walnut husks scattered over the pavement.

[97] Patti sings at the Opera House (1894); from G. B. Shaw, *The World*.

I never fully appreciated Patti until one night at Covent Garden when I heard her sing, not '*Una voce*' or anything of that sort, but 'God Save the Queen'. The wonderful even soundness of the middle of her voice, its beauty and delicacy of surface, and her exquisite touch and diction, all qualify her to be great in expressive melody, and to occupy a position in the republic of art high above the pretty flummery of newspaper puffs, flowers, recalls, encores, and so forth which makes it so difficult for people who take art seriously to do justice to the talent and the artistic pains with which she condescends to bid for such high recognition.

I am so far from regretting that Time has stolen some of the five or six notes above the high B flat which she once possessed, and has made the rest hardly safe for everyday use, that I shall heartily congratulate her when the day comes when '*Bel raggio*' and '*Ah, non giunge*', in any key whatsoever, must be dropped, and replaced in her repertory by more such songs as '*Träume*'; for it is my firm belief that Patti is capable of becoming a great singer, though the world has been at such pains and expense to spoil her for the last thirty-five years.

Hyde Park

[98] Čapek visits Speakers' Corner (1935); from *Letters from England*.

It was a large open space, and anyone who likes to, can bring along a chair or a platform or nothing at all, and can start talking. After awhile he has five or twenty or three hundred people listening to him; they answer him, raise objections, nod their heads and sometimes they join the orator in singing sacred or profane hymns. Sometimes an opponent gets the people on to his side and begins to hold forth on his own; sometimes the crowd divides by a mere splitting and swelling like the lowest organisms and cell colonies. Some clusters are of a firm and steadfast consistency, others perpetually crumble and overflow, increase in size, become distended, multiply or scatter. The larger churches have perambulating pulpits, but most of the orators simply stand on the ground, suck at a moist cigarette and preach about vegetarianism, about God, about education, about reparations, or about spiritualism. Never in my life have I seen anything like it . . .

I passed over to a large crowd where an old gentleman in a top-hat was jumping about in a pulpit. I ascertained that he represented some Hyde Park Mission; he flung his hands about so much that I was afraid he would tumble over the hand-rail ... At another crowd a Catholic was preaching beneath a high crucifix; for the first time in my life I beheld the proclaiming of the faith to heretics. It was extremely nice and concluded with song, in which I attempted to sing alto; unfortunately I did not know the tune. A few crowds were devoted exclusively to song; in their midst a little man takes his stand with a baton, gives the note and the whole crowd sings, and indeed in a very decent and polyphonic manner. I wanted to listen in silence, for I don't belong to this parish, but my neighbour, a gentleman in a top-hat, urged me to sing too, so I sang aloud and glorified the Lord without words and without tune. A pair of lovers comes this way, the youth takes the cigarette from his mouth and sings, the girl also sings, an old lord sings, and a youth with a cane under his arm sings, and the shabby man in the midst of the circle gracefully conducts as in Grand Opera; nothing here has pleased me so much.

Trafalgar Square

[99] The 'Bloody Sunday' riots in 1887; from *The Life of William Morris* by J. W. Mackail.

A long-continued depression of trade had made the question of the unemployed, in London and elsewhere, more than usually serious; and the restlessness among the working classes culminated in the famous scenes of 13 November, 'Bloody Sunday', in and round Trafalgar Square. A meeting in the Square had been announced to protest against the Irish policy of the Government: it had been proclaimed by the police, and became converted into a demonstration on a huge scale. No one who saw it will ever forget the strange and indeed terrible sight of that grey winter day, the vast sombre-coloured crowd, the brief but fierce struggle at the corner of the Strand, and the river of steel and scarlet that moved slowly through the dusky swaying masses when two squadrons of the Life Guards were summoned up from Whitehall. Morris himself did not see it till all was nearly over. He had marched with one of the columns which were to converge on

Trafalgar Square from all quarters. It started in good order to the number of five or six thousand from Clerkenwell Green, but at the crossing of Shaftesbury Avenue was attacked in front and on both flanks by a strong force of police. They charged into it with great violence, striking right and left indiscriminately. In a few minutes it was helplessly broken up. Only disorganized fragments straggled into the Square, to find that the other columns had also been headed off or crushed, and that the day was practically over. Preparations had been made to repel something little short of a popular insurrection. An immense police force had been concentrated, and in the afternoon the Square was lined by a battalion of Foot Guards, with fixed bayonets and twenty rounds of ball cartridge. For an hour or two the danger was imminent of street-fighting such as had not been known in London for more than a century. But the organized force at the disposal of the civil authorities proved sufficient to check the insurgent columns and finally clear the streets without a shot being fired. For some weeks afterwards the Square was garrisoned by special drafts of police. Otherwise London next day had resumed its usual aspect.

[100] The Poll tax riots of 1990; from *Poll Tax Riot*, by Anon.

The sound of a band of drummers drew me like a moth to a light, a stick and an old discarded beer can to mark the rhythm and we were off. It was a joyful experience, dancing and shouting through the streets virtually all the way to Trafalgar Square. When we reached the Parliament end of Whitehall, a line of police had blocked the road and the crowd was diverted towards the Embankment. We could see behind the police lines rows of mounted police, ominously still and waiting. That's when I felt my first pangs of fear and anger. I remember thinking that they had some nasty plans for us, visions of being fodder for exercises in crowd control. The police in the lines looked incredibly smug.

I continued with the crowd, marching up Northumberland Avenue, the excitement and tension increasing as the band came to a standstill as we entered Trafalgar Square. The energy became warlike, the beating of the drums and the chanting seeming to get louder and louder and the crowd more and more dense as thousands more swept up Northumberland Avenue. I pushed my way through to the Whitehall junction where it became apparent that something had already started. A man was fighting his way back through the crowd, a real sense of panic hit me as I heard him shouting, 'Get any kids out of the way, they're going to charge.' Images sped through my mind of the mothers with young kids, old people, disabled people that I had seen on the march. They were all here in the Square, the bastards were going to charge us and there was no way out! Bloodbath! Severe panic.

I pushed my way towards the junction with the Strand, shouting the warning for those more vulnerable to try and get out. There was another police line across St Martins Lane and the only road free for exit was the Strand. As I looked up the length of the road, I saw a police van speeding towards us. I got out of the road and watched in horror as it sped in towards the crowd and screeched to a halt as an unsuspecting body flew through the air on impact and landed in a heap on the side of the road. This was too much! My anger exploded and I ran towards the van screaming and shouting and pulled open the door on the driver's side, screaming blue murder as the terrified officer inside wrenched the door closed. I spat, banged on the windows, thought of broken glass, didn't want to cut my hands, looking for something to throw, something to hit with.

Everything was happening at once, the man in the road with people bending over him, people crying, me shouting, spitting, furious at the police. A woman gently rocking her baby, rhythmically, protectively as she made her way across the road away from the violence. I shouted at a policewoman in the lines to let her through with her baby, realizing as I did so that it was the same policewoman I had just been screaming and spitting at when the van had hit its victim. I swallowed my fear as I walked with the woman right up to the police line, stopping just long enough to see that she got through to safety, then racing back to where the van was, thanking my fate they hadn't grabbed me.

Tyburn

[101] The execution of Perkin Warbeck (1499); from *Chronicles of London*, edited by C. L. Kingsford.

And vpon the satirday folowyng next, beyng seynt Clementes day, was drawen from the Tour vnto Tybourne Perkyn or Peter Warbek and one John a Water, some tyme Mair of Corf, as before is said; at which place of Execucion was ordeyned a small Scafold, whervpon the said Perkyn stondyng shewed to the people there in greate multitude beyng present, that he was a straunger born accordyng vnto his former confession; and took it vpon his dethe that he was neuer the persone that he was named for, that is to sey the second son of kyng Edward the iiijth. And that he was forsed to take vpon hym by the meanes of the said John a Water and other, wherof he asked god and the kyng of forgiveness; after which confession he took his dethe meekly, and was there vpon the Galowes hanged; and with hym the said John a Water; And whan they were dede, stryken downe, and their hedes striken of;

and after their bodies brought to the ffrere Augustynes, and there buryed, and their heedes set after vpon London Brigge.

[102] The execution of the Carthusian Martyrs (1535); from *The Passion and Martyrdom of the Holy English Carthusians* by Dom Maurice Chauncy (translated by A. F. Radcliffe).

They were brought from the prison and found at the door hurdles carefully provided for the occasion. On these they were flung violently, each wearing the dress of his own calling. Two and two – but the fifth had no companion – their heads thrown back and their bodies painfully strained to full length, they were tightly fastened with cruel cords.

Then came a spectacle to draw tears. Through the city of London from the Tower to Tyburn, the well-known place of public execution, they were dragged mercilessly at the horses' heels . . .

When the place of punishment was reached, the first to be approached and released from the hurdle was the venerable Father Houghton, our father and our prior worthy of every title of respect, prior of the London Charterhouse. Then the executioner kneeling before him according to custom craved pardon for the cruel death which he was going to inflict . . .

He was ordered to mount a cart placed just beneath the gallows on which he was to be hanged. Meekly he obeyed the cruel order. Then some man of note, one of the King's council present by the King's order, asked him if he would submit to the King's command and will and the public edict. 'If you will, on the King's behalf I promise you pardon and life; if not, you see what a cruel death awaits you.' The invincible soldier of Christ made answer before the people gathered in countless numbers to gaze at the tragedy: 'I call to witness heaven and earth and God the Lord of heaven and earth, and before you, my beloved, I make confession, beseeching you on the dreadful day of judgement to add your testimony to mine that my disobedience, if it deserves the name of disobedience, in refusing consent to your King and his law, arises not from malice or obstinacy or wish to rebel, but from the fear of God, King of Kings and Judge eternal, lest I may offend His glorious majesty. Our holy mother, the bride of Christ, the pillar of truth, the Catholic Church which above all we are bound to believe and obey, whose authority in all things is irrefragable, lays down and holds and teaches something far different from what those men would have us accept. Indeed, to put it more clearly and more truly, the law to which they would have us subscribe is diametrically opposed to the usage of the holy Church. Who knows not that from us obedience to God and His church is required before obedience to the King and his parliament? Therefore, my beloved, I declare before you all that I shall be ready to endure with God's help these and all other torments that they may have the wish and the power to inflict, rather than consent to fall away from right doctrine and the obedience due to God and His holy Church.'

After these words Christ's valiant soldier turned to the attendant and asked for time to read the prayer prescribed. It was taken from the thirtieth psalm, '*In te, Domine, speravi,*' down to the seventh verse, '*In manus tuas.*' Then at a signal from himself the cart was withdrawn and the holy man was hanging throttled by the noose. But before breath had quite gone from the body, the rope was cut by one of the bystanders. He fell headlong to the ground . . .

Scarcely had he begun to recover breath, a man of God fallen from a gallows, when they dragged him half alive to a spot near by. There he was stripped and laid face upwards on the cold ground like a sheep ready for slaughter. The bloodthirsty hangman cruelly cut off his privy members, ripped open his belly with an upward cut, tore his entrails apart and flung all to be burnt on a large bonfire erected there. Meanwhile he bore his sufferings like a gentle lamb. Not a murmur, not a complaint was heard. He showed no sign of resentment, but endured all with a gentleness and patience more than human. All who saw him marvelled. Praying humbly and continuously in the hour of torment – indeed, throughout his passion his prayer was unceasing – he made a rich sacrifice of sweet savour in return for an attack on truth and justice. Thus he commended his cause to God. What he offered was not the blood of goats and bulls, but himself, his own body, his own blood. When they began to tear out his heart, the gallant fighter was not far from his last breath, and his voice was sweet indeed as he exclaimed, 'Lord Jesus, lover of thy children, have mercy on me in this hour.' A strange incident is attested by those who took part in the bloody work and by many of the bystanders, men whose word may be taken. While the heart was being torn out, he still talked and tearfully asked the executioner, 'In the name of God immortal, what will you do with my heart?' No more was said. He had breathed his last. The executioner wished to display the heart to the councillors and men of note who were present, but could scarcely keep it in his hands. It was still leaping and beating. The body was dead, but the heart still lived, exulting in a sort of triumph for joy that agony and martyrdom had come to a blessed end. By its movement it signified what it had no voice to declare, that this just man's soul was in the hand of God and that the torments of death or malice could reach him no more. In the sight of the unwise he seemed to die, but he is in peace where with the just and elect he rejoices in the presence of God and is merry and joyful, because he has fought a good fight, he has kept the faith and, found faithful unto death, has received the crown of righteousness laid up for him, which the Lord God, the righteous Judge, has now given as his due.

His head was cut off, his body was quartered and the martyrdom was ended on the fourth day of May in the year of the Incarnation 1535, in about the 48th year of his age and the 5th of his office as prior. So that holy father John Houghton passing through fire and water came to a place of comfort . . .

So much for the passion and consummation of our

blessed father Houghton. A little remains to be said about the four fellow-soldiers who survived him, the holy fathers Robert Lawrence and Augustine Webster, Carthusians, and Reynolds the Brigittine and the pastor of Thistleworth. Few words are needed. On the same charge, at the same spot, on the same day, at the same hour, in the same manner, by the same mode of punishment, treated or rather butchered successively with the same cruelty as our prior Houghton, they passed from this life to the Lord. One detail must be added. Father Reynolds, that man of rare sanctity and learning, was standing on the cart waiting to be hanged. Keeping God before his eyes as he saw the gruesome murder of his companions, with a constancy and courage more than heroic he preached a godly and noble sermon to the people. He never paused for a word. His voice never faltered. Nothing in his manner suggested fear or the imminence of death. Thus those good men who loved one another in the Lord whilst they lived, in death are not divided . . .

The bodies lay lifeless, but the slayers, though their task was over, found more savage work to do. They cut off each head and mangled the bodies by quartering. All the portions – the principal object was to horrify spectators – they parboiled in cauldrons. Finally they hung them on gates or elsewhere in public places. One of the arms of our good father Houghton they hung upon the gate of our Charterhouse, to insult the dead and embitter men's contempt and hatred of us. There it hung for three years and more till the time of our expulsion. Less than a fortnight after our expulsion two of our brothers were passing that way when before their eyes – by God's will it is thought – the arm fell down. This they accepted as a happy omen. They carried off the arm and buried it in a place that seemed safe enough, but they were mistaken. It had not been hidden well enough to prevent discovery by servants of the devil, perhaps informed by the devil himself. They seized it with malicious joy and broke it into small fragments which they flung away as poisonous hatred prompted.

[103] The execution of Jonathan Wild (1725); from *Jonathan Wild* by Henry Fielding.

At length the morning came which Fortune at his birth had resolutely ordained for the consummation of our hero's GREATNESS: he had himself indeed modestly declined the public honours she intended him, and had taken a quantity of laudanum, in order to retire quietly off the stage; but we have already observed, in the course of our wonderful history, that to struggle against this lady's decrees is vain and impotent; and whether she hath determined you shall be hanged or be a prime minister, it is in either case lost labour to resist. Laudanum, therefore, being unable to stop the breath of our hero, which the fruit of hemp-seed, and not the spirit of poppy-seed, was to overcome, he was at the usual hour attended by the proper gentleman appointed for that purpose, and acquainted that the cart was ready. On this occasion he exerted that greatness of courage which hath been so much celebrated in other heroes; and, knowing it was impossible to resist, he gravely declared he would attend them. He then descended to that room where the fetters of great men are knocked off in a most solemn and ceremonious manner. Then shaking hands with his friends (to wit, those who were conducting him to the tree), and drinking their healths in a bumper of brandy, he ascended the cart, where he was no sooner seated than he received the acclamations of the multitude, who were highly ravished with his GREATNESS.

The cart now moved slowly on, being preceded by a troop of horse-guards bearing javelins in their hands, through streets lined with crowds all admiring the great behaviour of our hero, who rode on, sometimes sighing, sometimes swearing, sometimes singing or whistling, as his humour varied.

When he came to the tree of glory, he was welcomed with an universal shout of the people, who were there assembled in prodigious numbers to behold a sight much more rare in populous cities than one would reasonably imagine it should be, viz. the proper catastrophe of a great man.

But though envy was, through fear, obliged to join the general voice in applause on this occasion, there were not wanting some who maligned this completion of glory, which was now about to be fulfilled to our hero, and endeavoured to prevent it by knocking him on the head as he stood under the tree, while the ordinary was performing his last office. They therefore began to batter the cart with stones, brickbats, dirt, and all manner of mischievous weapons, some of which, erroneously playing on the robes of the ecclesiastic, made him so expeditious in his rep-etition, that with wonderful alacrity he had ended almost in an instant, and conveyed himself into a place of safety in a hackney-coach . . .

We must not, however, omit one circumstance, as it serves to shew the most admirable conservation of char-acter in our hero to his last moment, which was, that whilst the ordinary was busy in his ejaculations, Wild, in the midst of the shower of stones, etc., which played upon him, applied his hands to the parson's pocket, and emptied it of his bottle-screw, which he carried out of the world in his hand.

The ordinary being now descended from the cart, Wild had just opportunity to cast his eyes around the crowd, and to give them a hearty curse, when immediately the horses moved on, and with universal applause our hero swung out of this world.

THE EAST END

THE EAST END

The plague in Aldgate (1665); from *A Journal of the Plague Year* by Daniel Defoe.

I went all the first part of the time freely about the streets, though not so freely as to run myself into apparent danger, except when they dug the great pit in the churchyard of our parish of Aldgate. A terrible pit it was, and I could not resist my curiosity to go and see it. As near as I may judge, it was about forty feet in length, and about fifteen or sixteen feet broad, and, at the time I first looked at it, about nine feet deep; but it was said they dug it near twenty feet deep afterwards in one part of it, till they could go no deeper for the water; for they had, it seems, dug several large pits before this. For though the plague was long a-coming to our parish, yet, when it did come, there was no parish in or about London where it raged with such violence as in the two parishes of Aldgate and Whitechapel.

. . . It was about 10 September that my curiosity led, or rather drove, me to go and see this pit again, when there had been near 400 people buried in it; and I was not content to see it in the day-time, as I had done before, for then there would have been nothing to have been seen but the loose earth; for all the bodies that were thrown in were immediately covered with earth by those they called the buriers, which at other times were called bearers; but I resolved to go in the night and see some of them thrown in.

There was a strict order to prevent people coming to those pits, and that was only to prevent infection. But after some time that order was more necessary, for people that were infected and near their end, and delirious also, would run to those pits, wrapt in blankets or rugs, and throw themselves in, and, as they said, bury themselves. I cannot say that the officers suffered any willingly to lie there; but I have heard that in a great pit in Finsbury, in the parish of Cripplegate, it lying open then to the fields, for it was not then walled about, [some] came and threw themselves in, and expired there, before they threw any earth upon them; and that when they came to bury others, and found them there, they were quite dead, though not cold . . .

I got admittance into the churchyard by being acquainted with the sexton who attended, who, though he did not refuse me at all, yet earnestly persuaded me not to go, telling me very seriously, for he was a good, religious, and sensible man, that it was indeed their business and duty to venture, and to run all hazards, and that in it they might hope to be preserved; but that I had no apparent call to it but my own curiosity, which, he said, he believed I would not pretend was sufficient to justify my running that hazard. I told him I had been pressed in my mind to go, and that perhaps it might be an instructing sight, that might not be without its uses. 'Nay,' says the good man, 'if you will venture upon that score, name of God go in; for, depend upon it, 'twill be a sermon to you, it may be, the best that ever you heard in your life. 'Tis a speaking sight,' says he, 'and has a voice with it, and a loud one, to call us all to repentance;' and with that he opened the door and said, 'Go, if you will.'

His discourse had shocked my resolution a little, and I stood wavering for a good while, but just at that interval I saw two links come over from the end of the Minories, and heard the bellman, and then appeared a dead-cart, as they called it, coming over the streets; so I could no longer resist my desire of seeing it, and went in. There was nobody, as I could perceive at first, in the churchyard, or going into it, but the buriers and the fellow that drove the cart, or rather led the horse and cart; but when they came up to the pit they saw a man go to and again, muffled up in a brown cloak, and making motions with his hands under his cloak, as if he was in a great agony, and the buriers immediately gathered about him, supposing he was one of those poor delirious or desperate creatures that used to pretend, as I have said, to bury themselves. He said nothing as he walked about, but two or three times groaned very deeply and loud, and sighed as he would break his heart.

When the buriers came up to him they soon found he was neither a person infected and desperate, as I have observed above, or a person distempered in mind, but one oppressed with a dreadful weight of grief indeed, having his wife and several of his children all in the cart that was just come in with him, and he followed in an agony and excess of sorrow. He mourned heartily, as it was easy to see, but with a kind of masculine grief that could not give itself vent by tears; and calmly defying the buriers to let him alone, said he would only see the bodies thrown in and go away, so they left importuning him. But no sooner was the cart turned round and the bodies shot into the pit promiscuously, which was a surprise to him, for he at least expected they would have been decently laid in, though indeed he was afterwards convinced that was impracticable; I say, no sooner did he see the sight but he cried out aloud, unable to contain himself. I could not hear what he said, but he went backward two or three steps and fell down in a swoon. The buriers ran to him and took him up, and in a little while he came to himself, and they led him away to the Pie Tavern over against the end of Houndsditch, where, it seems, the man was known, and where they took care of him. He looked into the pit again as he went away, but the buriers had covered the bodies so immediately with throwing in earth, that though there was light enough, for there were lanterns, and candles in them, placed all night round the sides of the pit, upon heaps of earth, seven or eight, or perhaps more, yet nothing could be seen.

The cart had in it sixteen or seventeen bodies; some were wrapt up in linen sheets, some in rags, some little other than naked, or so loose that what covering they had fell from them in the shooting out of the cart, and they fell quite naked among the rest; but the matter was not much to them, or the indecency much to any one else, seeing they were all dead, and were to be huddled together into the common grave of mankind, as we may call it, for here was no difference made, but poor and rich went together; there was no other way of burials, neither was it possible there should, for coffins were not to be had for the prodigious numbers that fell in such a calamity as this.

[105] Wesley preaches at Whitechapel (1742); from *Journals* by J. Wesley.

12 Sept.1742: I was desired to preach in an open place, commonly called the Great Gardens, lying between White-chapel and Coverlet Fields, where I found a vast multitude gathered together. Taking knowledge that a great part of them were little acquainted with the things of God, I called upon them in the words of our Lord, 'Repent ye, and believe the gospel.' Many of the beasts of the people laboured much to disturb those who were of a better mind. They endeavoured to drive in a herd of cows among them; but the brutes were wiser than their masters. They then threw whole showers of stones, one of which struck me between the eyes: but I felt no pain at all; and, when I had wiped away the blood, went on testifying with a loud voice that God hath given to them that believe 'not the spirit of fear, but of power, and of love, and of a sound mind'. And, by the spirit which now appeared through the whole congregation, I plainly saw what a blessing it is when it is given us, even in the lowest degree, to suffer for His name's sake.

[106] Inspector Dew at the scene of the Ripper's last crime (1888); from *I Caught Crippen* by W. Dew.

And now I approach a phase of the Ripper story which I would give a great deal even now to have expunged from my memory.

As my thoughts go back to Miller's Court, and what happened there, the old nausea, indignation and horror overwhelm me still.

The thing of which I am about to write happened nearly fifty years ago. Yet my mental picture of it remains as shockingly clear as though it were but yesterday.

It is all before me now. Jack the Ripper at his most

devilish. No savage could have been more barbaric. No wild animal could have done anything so horrifying.

If I remember rightly it was between ten and eleven o'clock in the morning that I looked in at Commercial Street police station to get into touch with my superiors. I was chatting with Inspector Beck, who was in charge of the station, when a young fellow, his eyes bulging out of his head, came panting into the police station. The poor fellow was so frightened that for a time he was unable to utter a single intelligible word.

At last he managed to stammer out something about 'Another one. Jack the Ripper. Awful. Jack McCarthy sent me.'

Mr McCarthy was well-known to us as a common lodging-house proprietor.

'Come along, Dew,' said Inspector Beck, and gathering from the terrorized messenger that Dorset Street was the scene of whatever had happened, we made him our pilot, as we rushed in that direction, collecting as many constables as we could on the way.

The youth led us a few yards down Dorset Street from Commercial Street, until we came to a court approached by an arched passage, three feet wide and unlighted, in which there were two entrances to houses which fronted on Dorset Street. The place was known as Miller's Court.

Leaving the constables to block Dorset Street and to prevent anyone from leaving the court itself, Inspector Beck and I proceeded through the narrow archway into what might be described as a small square. It was a cul-de-sac, flanked on all four sides by a few mean houses.

The house on the left of the passage was kept by McCarthy as a chandler's shop, while one room of the houses on the right was rented by a girl named Marie Kelly.

McCarthy's messenger was by this time able to tell a more or less coherent story. He told us that some of the neighbours had become alarmed at the non-appearance that morning of Kelly. They had spoken about it to McCarthy, and he had sent the youth to find her.

The door of her room was locked, but the lad looked through a broken pane of glass in the only window in the room which faced the wider part of the court, and had seen something which froze the blood in his veins and sent him helter-skelter to the police station.

The room was pointed out to me. I tried the door. It would not yield. So I moved to the window, over which, on the inside, an old coat was hanging to act as a curtain and to block the draught from the hole in the glass.

Inspector Beck pushed the coat to one side and peered through the aperture. A moment later he staggered back with his face as white as a sheet.

'For God's sake, Dew,' he cried. 'Don't look.'

I ignored the order, and took my place at the window.

When my eyes had become accustomed to the dim light I saw a sight which I shall never forget to my dying day.

The whole horror of that room will only be known to those of us whose duty it was to enter it. The full details are unprintable.

There was a table just beneath the window. On the bed, which was drawn obliquely across the small room, was all that remained of a good-looking and buxom young woman.

There was little left of her, not much more than a skeleton. Her face was terribly scarred and mutilated.

All this was horrifying enough, but the mental picture of that sight which remains most vividly with me is the poor woman's eyes. They were wide open, and seemed to be staring straight at me with a look of terror.

Inspector Beck quickly recovered from his shock and sent messages to the chief station by quick-running constables. From there the messages were promptly relayed by telegraph to Scotland Yard.

Obviously nothing could be done for the woman, but Dr Phillips was sent for as a matter of form and was soon on the spot.

Officers were sent in all directions to make inquiries and interrogate any and every person likely to be able to give information.

No attempt was made by us to break into the room. It was deemed advisable to wait until the higher-placed officers arrived on the scene before anything was touched. This was essential if bloodhounds were to be used, although how bloodhounds could be expected to track a criminal in a place like London, I have never been able to understand.

However that may be, the Commissioner of Police and other high officers were soon on the spot, and one of the first decisions was that bloodhounds should be tried.

They never were, however, for the owner of the hounds decided that it would be utterly futile. That one can readily understand, considering that by this time thousands of people had used the adjoining thoroughfares. Moreover, it was a drizzling morning.

Again the critics of the police seized upon this to castigate the officers in charge of the case. It was said that bloodhounds should have been used and that there was unnecessary delay.

I flatly contradict the suggestion of delay. There was none, and the only reason for not using the bloodhounds was that they could not possibly have helped.

It would have been a different matter if bloodhounds had been available, and could have been put immediately on the trail. The experiment would then have been worth trying, though I doubt if it would have met with any success, as the crime was already several hours old.

There are differences of opinion as to the actual time of the Marie Kelly murder, but I have always inclined to the view that it took place somewhere between midnight and 2 a.m.

As soon as the chief officers arrived they decided to force the door which, if I remember rightly, had an automatic lock.

I followed the others into the room. The sight that confronted us was indescribable, infinitely more horrifying than what I had seen when peeping through the broken pane of glass into the room's semi-darkness.

I had seen most of the other remains. They were sickening enough in all conscience. But none of the others approached for bestial brutality the treatment of the body of poor Marie Kelly, whom I had known well by sight as a pretty, buxom girl.

The effect on me as I entered that room was as if someone had given me a tremendous blow in the stomach. Never in my life have I funked a police duty so much as I funked this one.

Whatever the state of the killer's mind when he committed the other murders, there cannot be the slightest doubt that in that room in Miller's Court he became a frenzied, raving madman.

With the state of that room in my mind, I cannot see how the murderer could have avoided being covered from head to foot with blood . . .

The girl's clothing had nearly all been cut from her body in the mad process of mutilation.

All these things I saw after I had slipped and fallen on the awfulness of that floor.

[107] The Sidney Street siege (1911); from *Thoughts and Adventures* by W. S. Churchill.

At about ten o'clock on the morning of 3 January I was in my bath, when I was surprised by an urgent knocking at the door. 'There is a message from the Home Office on the telephone absolutely immediate.'

Dripping wet and shrouded in a towel I hurried to the instrument, and received the following news: 'The anarchists who murdered the police have been surrounded in a house in the East End and are firing on the police with automatic pistols. They have shot one man and appear to have plenty of ammunition. Authority is requested to send for troops to arrest or kill them.'

I replied at once, giving the necessary permission and directing the police to use whatever force was necessary. In about twenty minutes I was at the Home Office. There I found my principal adviser, Mr Ernley Blackwell, who told me that no further information had been received, except that the anarchists had been effectually surrounded, but were still firing in all directions. No one knew how many anarchists there were or what measures were going to be taken. In these circumstances I thought it my duty to see what was going on myself, and my advisers concurred in the propriety of such a step. I must, however, admit that convictions of duty were supported by a strong sense of curiosity which perhaps it would have been well to keep in check.

We started at once in a motor-car. Down the Strand, through the City towards Houndsditch, until at length at about noon we reached the point where all traffic was stopped. We got out of the car. There was a considerable crowd of angry and alarmed people, and I noticed the unusual spectacle of Metropolitan constables armed with shot-guns hastily procured from a local gunsmith. The attitude of the crowd was not particularly friendly, and there were several cries of 'Oo let 'em in?' in allusion to the refusal of the Liberal Government to introduce drastic laws restricting the immigration of aliens. Just at this moment, however, a shot rang out perhaps a couple of hundred yards away, followed by another and another, until there was a regular fusillade.

Accompanied by an inspector we proceeded down the empty street, turned a corner, turned another corner, and reached a group of policemen, several of whom were armed, and a number of onlookers and journalists who had found themselves within the police cordon when it was originally closed and had been permitted to remain. Another street ran at right angles across our path. Up this street fifty or sixty yards to the left was the house in which the murderers had barricaded themselves. On the opposite side in front of us, police, Scots Guardsmen, and spectators were crouching behind the projecting corners of the buildings; and from both sides of the street, from the street itself, and from numerous windows, policemen and other persons were firing rifles, pistols, and shot-guns with increasing frequency at the house which harboured the desperadoes. These replied every minute or two, shooting sometimes up and down the street and sometimes at their assailants in front. The bullets struck the brickwork and ricocheted hither and thither. Nothing of the sort had ever been seen within living memory in quiet, law-abiding, comfortable England; and from this point of view at least my journey was well repaid . . .

Plans were now made to storm the building from several sides at once. One party, emerging from the next-door house, was to rush the front door and charge up the stairs; another party of police and soldiers would break into the second floor at the back through a window; a third, smashing-in the roof, would leap down on the assassins from above. There could be no doubt about the result of such an attack, but it certainly seemed that loss of life would be caused, not only by the fire of the anarchists, but also from shots fired by the attackers in the confusion. My own instincts turned at once to a direct advance up the staircase behind a steel plate or shield, and search was made in the foundries of the neighbourhood for one of a suitable size. Meanwhile, however, the problem settled itself. At about half-past one a wisp of smoke curled out of the shattered upper windows of the besieged house, and in a few minutes it was plainly on fire. The conflagration gained apace, burning downwards. To the crackling of wood succeeded the roar of flames. Still the anarchists, descending storey by storey, kept up their fire, and bullets continued to strike the brickwork of the surrounding houses and pavement.

Now occurred a curious incident, which, for the first time, made my presence on the spot useful. The ordinary functions of British life had been proceeding inflexibly to within a few feet of the danger-zone, and the postman on his rounds actually delivered his letters at the house next door. Suddenly, with a stir and a clatter, up came the fire brigade, scattering the crowds gathered on the approaches to the scene and thrusting through them until they reached the police cordon at the beginning of the danger-zone. The inspector of police forbade further progress, and the fire brigade officer declared it his duty to advance. A fire was raging, and he was bound to extinguish it. Anarchists, automatic pistols, danger-zones, nothing of this sort was mentioned in the Regulations of the London Fire Brigade. When the police officer pointed out that his men would be shot down, he replied simply that orders were orders and that he had no alternative. I now intervened to settle this dispute, at one moment quite heated. I told the fire-brigade officer on my authority as Home Secretary, that the house was to be allowed to burn down and that he was to stand by in readiness to prevent the conflagration from spreading. I then returned to my coign of vantage on the opposite side of the road.

[108] The Battle of Cable Street (1936); from Special Branch reports in *The East End Then and Now*, edited by W. G. Ramsay.

As Sir Oswald Mosley passed from Dock Street into Royal Mint Street in his Bentley car GU 2511 at 3.30 p.m., large pieces of brick were thrown toward him but none was seen to strike him or the car. He then drove past the assembled Fascists who were lined up three deep and who shouted 'M-O-S-L-E-Y Mosley!', and this was countered by anti-fascists behind the police cordons some fifty yards off singing the Internationale.' . . .

At 2 p.m., anti-fascists began to congregate in large numbers at the junction of Cable Street and Leman Street. They were later joined by a column of ex-Servicemen led by A. Harris. Anti-fascist slogans were shouted, and upon the crowd becoming unruly, police were compelled to draw batons in order to clear the streets. Brickbats were thrown through the window of a taxi-cab, and fireworks discharged. Stones were thrown at police, and marbles thrown in showers to impede police horses. A police inspector was hit in the face with a missile, and 8 persons were arrested. Later these demonstrators, numbering about 700, broke up a wooden barricade and armed themselves with the components, and, apparently under the impression that the British Union of Fascists contingent was to proceed along Cable Street, the anti-fascists over-turned a motor lorry, index number JJ. 2890. This vehicle was used as a barricade from behind which brickbats and glass were thrown at police, several of whom were injured. Numerous shop windows were broken, including those at Nos. 8, 10, 12, 14 and 16 Cable Street.

[109] The beginning of the Blitz (1944); from *Cockney Campaign* by F. Lewey.

I was watching *La Traviata* at the People's Palace in the Mile End Road when the first bombs fell in East London. At a convenient moment an announcement was made from the stage that an air raid alert had been sounded, and that anyone who wished might quietly leave the theatre.

All of us, I think, felt a faint quiver. But no one moved. The little figure of the manager discreetly withdrew. There was something apologetic about his going, as if he wished to ask his patrons pardon for stopping the show for such a slight matter.

There was time to finish the play and beat the Germans too.

The arms of the fiddlers began to saw again, and the opera unfolded gracefully as we watched. The story the players acted for us seemed more intense in meaning: the music touched depths in one's heart . . .

Somewhere a bit further along the river from us, other Cockneys were dying in smoke and noise – the first of many.

That was towards the end of August 1940 . . .

[110] The murder of George Cornell (1966); from *My Story* by Ronald Kray.

Dickson drove me and Ian Barrie to the Beggar's in one of the Firm's cars, a Ford Cortina. I can remember the date as if it was yesterday – March 6, 1966. I had already had a message that George Cornell had been involved at Mr Smith's [a reference to a fight at a south London club].

Our friend Richard Hart – a real nice feller, was shot dead. He wasn't a gangster and never deserved to get it. I had given my word that I would deal with Cornell. I'd known him since I was a kid. He was from Watney Street in the East End. We knew him but we were never what you'd call friends. Then I got a phone call. This phone call tells me that Cornell is drinking at a pub called the Blind Beggar, which is right in the middle of our manor and less than half a mile away from where we were all sat drinking. It was a depressing place; it had a flat front and two long bars which curved in a sort of U-shape and joined up the back, in the rear snug. That's all there was to it, the public bar on the right, the saloon bar on the left and the snug at the end. And the landlord's accommodation was upstairs above the bars. The place wasn't smartly done out or anything like that, and it always seemed sort of dark in there. It was a depressing pub . . .

Cornell was under six foot tall, but he was a powerful feller with a big, thick neck. He had a sort of curled lip which always made it look like he was sneering at you. He liked violence. When we arrived I told Dickson to wait outside while me and Ian Barrie went inside to see if Cornell was there. We went into the saloon bar and he was there all right, talking to two other fellers. He was sat on a stool drinking a glass of light ale. They were the only ones in the bar apart from the barmaid. There was a record on the juke box which was very popular at the time called *The Sun Ain't Gonna Shine Anymore*, by an American group called The Walker Brothers. As we walked in Cornell looked up and said, in that sneering way he had, 'Well, look who's here.' . . .

I took a 9mm Mauser pistol out of my pocket and Ian Barrie took out a .32 revolver. I was quite calm. Cornell was still sneering. I shot him. The bullet went into his forehead, just above his right eye. It went straight through his head. He fell off his stool. He just fell forward and I knew he was dead. They said in court that Ian Barrie fired a couple of shots into the ceiling. I don't know about that, I can't remember. I do remember that the needle got stuck on the record and it kept on repeating the words 'The sun ain't gonna shine anymore ... anymore ... anymore ...'

Nothing was said. Cornell's pals had disappeared, there was no sign of the barmaid. Me and Ian Barrie just walked out of the pub, got in the car and Dickson drove us back to the Lion.

[111] The building of Canary Wharf (1987); from *London Docklands* by E. Williamson, N. Pevsner and M. Tucker.

Broadgate, the City of London development begun, like the proposals for Canary Wharf, in 1985, by the developers Rosehaugh Stanhope, can be claimed as a rival in introducing to Britain the American pattern of commercial development, in which the developer provides the public realm and its works of art, often at the expense of controlling access. But the first phase of Broadgate (1985–91) was relatively intimate and sensitive. Canary Wharf introduced the British to the speed and efficiency of American fast-track construction on a huge scale, and to the size, eclecticism and luxury of North American Postmodern commercial architecture and landscape. It includes work by the famous *Skidmore Owings & Merrill*, by the Chinese-American *I.M. Pei* and by the Argentinian-American *Cesar Pelli*, who designed the single gleaming skyscraper, an inescapable reminder of Canary Wharf all over London. This tower set its own records: it was the first skyscraper in Britain and at 800 ft (244 metres) the tallest in Europe when completed in 1991. Olympia & York changed expectations not only in Docklands but also in the City of London, especially at the second phase of the Broadgate development (1990–2) and on the *Daily Telegraph* site in Fleet Street (1988–91), where *SOM* and *Kohn Pederson Fox* were also employed. Pelli's tower stimulated competition from the City of London, leading to *Sir Norman Foster's* proposal for a 1,076 ft (328 metre) rival tower in 1996. The latest post-recession, post-Olympia & York phases of Canary Wharf promise to be more global and yet more diverse in character, with so-called signature buildings commissioned from architectural stars such as *Sir Norman Foster* and the French *Philippe Starck*. The same trend is evident in every major city worldwide, including the City of London.

There is no office building on the scale of Canary Wharf in the rest of Docklands – indeed when it was conceived in 1985 Canary Wharf was the largest development in Europe. Harbour Exchange, begun in the Enterprise Zone in 1986, and Thomas More Square, Wapping, 1988–90, close to the City, both show the influence of North American office development but nothing of its lavishness. And neither are there any exciting small office developments fitted amongst the buildings in Wapping or Limehouse, except for No. 2 Pennington Street, close to Fortress Wapping, which displays layers of Postmodern clichés, some of them (like the wavy glass wall) invented by the architect *Rick Mather* himself for other buildings. Nor are there any interesting retail ventures, except for the conservation projects at Hay's Galleria and Tobacco Dock, already mentioned. The demands of the new generation of financial traders for information technology has stimulated a new building type, the telecommunications centre, a blank-faced box that houses more equipment than people. Both the *Richard Rogers Partnership*'s for Reuters and *YRM* for KDD have managed to turn this unpromising type into two of the best and most dramatic buildings in Docklands. They stand at Blackwall alongside former *Financial Times* printing works that *Nicholas Grimshaw & Partners* built in the spirit of the most famous printing works of the 20th century, the transparent boxes designed by Sir Owen Williams for the *Daily Express*. Many newspapers followed Rupert Murdoch's 1970s lead in relocating from Fleet Street: their huge printing works are without exception blots on the landscape.

WESTMINSTER
AND WHITEHALL

A View of the House of Peers, Queen Elisabeth on the Throne, the Commons attending. Taken from a Printed Print in the Cottonian Library.

Westminster Abbey & Hall

[112] The dedication of the Abbey (10th century); from *Old and New London* by W. Thornbury.

The night before the dedication, it is related that St Peter, in an unknown garb, showed himself to a fisher on the Surrey side, and bade him carry him over, with promise of reward. The fisher complied, and saw his fare enter the new-built Church of Sebert, that suddenly seemed on fire, with a glow that enkindled the firmament. Meantime, the heavenly host scattered sound and fragrance, the fisher of souls wrote upon the pavement the alphabet in Greek and Hebrew, in twelve places anointed the walls with the holy oil, lighted the tapers, sprinkled the water, and did all else needful for the dedication of a church.

These circumstances, and the signs following, were pondered on by St Edward, last but one of our Saxon kings, who earnestly desired to repair that ruined monastery, and restore it to honour and splendour. The Pope approved the plan, and one of the most magnificent fabrics in Christendom was the result.

[113] King Edward rebuilds the Abbey (10th–11th centuries); from *The Life of King Edward*, 11th century.

Outside the walls of London, upon the River Thames, stood a monastery dedicated to St Peter, but insignificant in buildings and numbers, for under the abbot only a small community of monks served Christ. Moreover, the endowments from the faithful were slender, and provided no more than their daily bread. The king, therefore, being devoted to God, gave his attention to that place, for it both lay hard by the famous and rich town and also was a delightful spot, surrounded with fertile lands and green fields and near the main channel of the river, which bore abundant merchandise of wares of every kind for sale from the whole world to the town on its banks. And, especially because of his love of the Prince of the Apostles, whom he worshipped with uncommon and special love, he decided to have his burial place there. Accordingly he ordered that out of the tithes of all his revenues should be started the building of a noble edifice, worthy of the Prince of the Apostles; so that, after the transient journey of this life, God would look kindly upon him, both for the sake of his goodness and because of the gift of lands and ornaments with which he intended to ennoble the place. And so the building, nobly begun at the king's command, was successfully made ready; and there was no weighing of the costs, past or future, so long as it proved worthy of, and acceptable to, God and St Peter. The princely house of the altar, noble with its most lofty vaulting, is surrounded by dressed stone evenly jointed. Also the passage round that temple is enclosed on both sides by a double arching of stone with the joints of the structure strongly consolidated on this side and that. Furthermore, the crossing of the church, which is to hold in its midst the choir of God's choristers, and to uphold with like support from either side the high apex of the central tower, rises simply at first with a low and sturdy vault, swells with many a stair spiralling up in artistic profusion, but then with a plain wall climbs to the wooden roof which is carefully covered with lead. Above and below are built out chapels methodically arranged, which are to be consecrated through their altars to the memory of apostles, martyrs, confessors, and virgins. Moreover, the whole complex of this enormous building was started so far to the East of the old church that the brethren dwelling there should not have to cease from Christ's service and also that a sufficiently spacious vestibule might be placed between them.

[114] The coronation of Richard I (1189); from *Itinerary of Richard I.*

Therefore in the same year, after the death of his father, Richard, Count of Poitou, having arranged his affairs in Normandy, in about two months crossed over to England, and on St Giles's Day he was received at Westminster, with a ceremonious procession; and three days afterwards, viz., on 3 September, the day of the ordination of St Gregory the Pope, which was a Sunday, he was solemnly anointed king by the imposition of hands, by Archbishop Baldwin, in virtue of his office, who performed the service, assisted by many of his suffragans. At his coronation were present his brother John, and his mother Eleanor [of Aquitaine], who, after the death of King Henry, had been, by the command of her son Richard, the new king, released from prison, where she had been ten years; and there were also present counts and barons, and an immense crowd of men and soldiers; and the kingdom was confirmed to the hands of King Richard. On 3 September, in the year of our Lord 1189, Richard was anointed king, on a Sunday, with the dominical letter A., viz., in the year after leap year. Many were the conjectures made, because the day above that was marked unlucky in the calendar; and in truth it was unlucky, and very much so to the Jews in London, who were destroyed that day, and likewise the Jews settled in other parts of England endured many hardships. Having celebrated the occasion by a festival of three days, and entertained his guests in the royal palace of Westminster, King Richard gratified all, by distributing money, without count or number, to all according to their ranks, thus manifesting his liberality and his great excellence. His generosity, and his virtuous endowments, the ruler of the world should have given to the ancient times; for in this period of the world, as it waxes old, such feelings rarely exhibit themselves, and when they do they are subjects of wonder and astonishment. He had the valour of Hector, the magnanimity of Achilles, and was equal to Alexander, and not inferior to Roland in valour; nay, he outshone many illustrious characters of our own times. The liberality of a Titus was his, and, which is so rarely found in a soldier, he was gifted with the eloquence of Nestor and the prudence of Ulysses; and he shewed himself pre-eminent in the conclusion and transaction of business, as one whose knowledge was not without active goodwill to aid it, nor his goodwill wanting in knowledge ... he was tall of stature, graceful in figure; his hair between red and auburn; his limbs were straight and flexible; his arms rather long, and not to be matched for wielding the sword or for striking with it; and his long legs suited the rest of his frame; while his appearance was commanding, and his manners and habits suitable; and he gained the greatest celebrity, not more from his high birth than from the virtues that adorned him.

[115] Christ's blood is brought to the Abbey by Henry III (1247); from *Chronicles* by Matthew Paris.

The lord king wrote to all the magnates of the kingdom ordering them all to assemble on the feast, that is the translation, of St Edward, which is a fortnight after Michaelmas [13 October], in order to hear most agreeable news of a holy benefit recently conferred by heaven on the English; secondly to honour the translation of that glorious king and martyr; and thirdly so that they could attend the initiation of the king's half-brother William of Valence, on whom he intended that day to confer the honour of knighthood, along with several other noble youths. For this multiple festivity would be more joyfully enlivened by the presence of the nobles, both prelates and others, to the honour of both king and kingdom.

When the magnates assembled in London at Westminster on the appointed day and were told about the feast of St Edward and the knighting of the said William, they enquired about the good news they were going to hear, which was said to be true and worthy of complete acceptance. [It was that] the masters of the Templars and Hospitallers with the testimony of a good many seals, namely those of the patriarch of Jerusalem and the archbishops and bishops, abbots and other prelates, and magnates of the Holy Land, had sent some of the blood of our Lord, which he shed on the cross for the salvation of the world, in a most beautiful crystal container, in the care of a certain well known brother of the Templars. The king indeed, as a most Christian prince, exalting the cross after the example of the most pious and victorious Emperor Heraclius and of the then living king of the French, Louis, who was honouring it in Paris, kept vigil on St Edward's eve devoutly and contritely, fasting on bread and water with numerous candles and devout prayers, to prepare himself suitably for the next day's solemnities . . .

The lord king ordered all London priests to assemble at St Paul's in good order and reverence early next morning, which was St Edward's day, festively dressed in hoods and surplices with their clerks suitably attired and with symbols, crosses and lighted candles. The king arrived there and, receiving the container with its treasure above-mentioned with the utmost honour, reverence and awe, he carried it publicly in front of his face, going on foot and wearing a humble dress consisting of a simple cloak without a hood. Preceded by the priests dressed as described above he went without stopping to Westminster Abbey, which is about a mile from St Paul's. It should be pointed out, too, that he carried it with both hands and even when he came to a rough or uneven section of road, he kept his eyes fixed always either on heaven or on the container itself. The pall was carried on four spears, and two assistants supported the king's arms lest his strength should fail during his exertions. The convent of Westminster together with everyone who had assembled, bishops, abbots and monks to the number of a hundred or more, tearfully singing and exulting in the holy spirit, went out to meet the king as he arrived at the gates of the bishop of Durham's palace and then returned as they had come, in procession, to Westminster Abbey, which could hardly hold them all, there were so many of them. Nor even then did the king repose, but indefatigably continued, carrying the container round the church, his palace and his own rooms. Finally he presented and offered this priceless gift, which had made all England illustrious, to God, to the church of St Peter at Westminster, to his beloved Edward, and to the holy monks who minister there to God and his saints.

[116] The King seeks the pardon of the Londoners (1250); from *Chronicles* by Matthew Paris.

On the Sunday next before the feast of Saints Perpetua and Felicitas [6 March] all the citizens of London, with their families down to twelve-year-old boys, were summoned by command of the lord king to appear before him in the large palace which is called the great hall, at Westminster; and it and the whole of its courtyard were filled with crowds of people. When they were assembled, the lord king humbly and as if with rising tears entreated each and every one of the citizens cordially in heart and voice to forgive him his anger and every sort of rancour and malevolence towards them. As he publicly confessed, he had often and his officials more often, done them all kinds of injury by injuriously confiscating, occupying or retaining their property and by frequently violating their privileges; for this he asked them to be pleased to pardon him. The citizens, realizing that anything else would be inappropriate, agreed to everything the lord king demanded, but absolutely nothing that had been taken away was restored to them.

[117] The early history of Westminster Hall; from *Survey of London* by J. Stow.

In the year 1316, Edward II did solemnize his feast of Penticost at Westminster, in the great hall; where sitting royally at the table, with his peers about him, there entered a woman adorned like a minstrel, sitting on a great horse, trapped as minstrels then used, who rode round about the tables, showing pastime, and at length came up to the king's table, and laid before him a letter, and forthwith turning her horse, saluted every one, and departed. The letter being opened, had these contents: 'Our soveraigne lord and king, hath nothing curteously respected his knights, that in his father's time, and also in his owne, have put forth their persons to divers perils, and have utterly lost, or greatly diminished their substance, for honor of the said king, and he hath inriched abundantly such as have not borne the waight as yet of the business, etc.'

This great hall was begun to be repaired in the year 1397 by Richard II, who caused the walls, windows, and roof, to be taken down, and new made, with a stately porch, and divers lodgings of a marvellous work, and with great costs; all which he levied of strangers banished or flying out of their countries, who obtained license to remain in this land, by the king's charters, which they had purchased with great sums of money; John Boterell being then clerk of the works.

This hall being finished in the year 1398, the same king kept a most royal Christmas there, with daily justings and runnings at tilt; whereunto resorted such a number of people, that there was every day spent twenty-eight or twenty-six oxen, and three hundred sheep, besides fowl without number: he caused a gown for himself to be made of gold, garnished with pearl and precious stones, to the value of three thousand marks: he was guarded by Cheshire men, and had about him commonly thirteen bishops, besides barons, knights, esquires, and other more than needed; insomuch, that to the household came every day to meat ten thousand people, as appeareth by the messes told out from the kitchen to three hundred servitors . . .

This great hall hath been the usual place of pleadings, and ministration of justice . . . it was in the year 1224, the 9th of Henry III, agreed that there should be a standing place appointed, where matters should be heard and judged, which was in the great hall at Westminster.

In this hall he ordained three judgment seats; to wit, at the entry on the right hand, the Common Pleas, where civil matters are to be pleaded, specially such as touch lands or contracts: at the upper end of the hall, on the right hand, or south-east corner, the King's Bench, where please of the crown have their hearing; and on the left hand, or south-west corner, sitteth the lord chancellor, accompanied with the master of the rolls, and other men, learned for the most part in the civil law, and called masters of the chancery, which have the king's fee. The times of pleading in these courts are four in the year, which are called terms: the first is Hillary term, which beginneth 23 January, if it be not Sunday, and endeth 12 February; the second is Easter term, and beginneth seventeen days after Easter day, and endeth four days after Ascension day; the third term beginneth six or seven days after Trinity Sunday, and endeth the Wednesday fortnight after; the fourth is Michaelmas term, which beginneth 9 October, if it be not Sunday, and endeth 28 November.

[118] The coronation of Henry IV (1399); from *Chronicles of London*, edited by C. L. Kingsford.

And the Moneday next affter in the ffest off Seint Edward, the same kyng Herry lay vpon a cloth off golde before the hyh awter in Westm'. Chirche. And there in ffoure parties off his body his clothes weren opyn, and there he was anoynted, with *Veni Creator Spiritus* y-songyn. And affter this anoyntyng his body was leffte vp into another place. And ther with grete solempnyte was corovned, and *Te Deum Laudamus* was ryally songyn. And Thomas Arundel, Erchebisshop off Caunterbury, dyd the solempnyte. And whanne alle was done alle the peple went to Westm'. halle to mete.

And ther the kyng was sette in his see, and the Erchebisshop off Caunterbury, The Bisshop off London, The Bisshop off Wynchestre, and other Bisshopes on the riht hande off the kyng setyn at the same hyh Table. And the Erchebisshop off Yorke, The Bisshop off Dirham, The Bisshop off Excetre, and other Bisshopes satyn on the tother hande off the kyng at the same Table. Herry prince off Walys, Duk off Cornevaylle, and Erle off Chestre was on the riht hande off the kyng with a newe swerde in his hande, poynteles, the which bitokenyth pees. The Conestable off England was on the tother syde with a nother swerde. And the Ceptres weren holde In yche partye off the kyng, oon ceptre on the ton syde, and a nother on that other, alder next the swerdes. And on the riht syde off the Halle at the secounde table satyn the V Portes well arrayed in Skarlett. And at that other syde table in the Halle, at the secounde table, satyn the Mair, Recordour, and Aldermen off London in oon suyt, also in Skarlett. And the Dukes of Aumarle, Surrey, Excestre, Markys, Warrewyk, and other stoden byfore the kyng at mete. And in the same tyme kome one Thomas Dymmok, knyht, wele y-armyd, rityng on the secounde beste hors off the kyngis, fforto done his servis ffor his Tenour, with two knyhtes ridyng with him. The tone beryng his spere, and the tother his shelde. And an heroude off Armes went by hym on his ffeet, and hadde the wordes ffor the same Dymmok, and seyd thus:-

'Iffe ther be eny man hyh or lowe, off what astate or condicion he be, that wole say that Herry kyng off Englond that here is, and was this day corovnyd, that he

is not rihtfull kyng ne rihtfully corovned, anoon riht or
ellys at what day oure lorde the kyng wole assigne, I wille
darrayne bataylle with my body and preve that he lieth
ffalsly.'

The which proclamation ws made thurh the Halle in
ffoure places off the Halle at this mete while, by the same
herowde off Armes bothe in Englyssh and in ffrenche. And
affter he voydyd the Halle, and the Revell endyd.

[119] The wedding banquet of Henry V (1415); from *Chronicles* by R. Holinshed.

The king himselfe, to render unto God his most humble
and hartie thanks, caused solemne processions to be
observed and kept five daies togither in everie citie and
towne. After that doone, he made great purveiance for the
coronation of his queene and spouse, the faire ladie
Katharine: which was doone the daie of S. Matthew, being
the twentie fourth of Februarie, with all such ceremonies
and princelie solemnitie as apperteined. Which because it
was full of roialtie and honour (the qualitie of the principall personages requiring no lesse) and recorded by writers
of former ages, it seemeth necessarie and convenient in
this place to report it, in such sort as it is found at large in
some, though others glansinglie passe by it, as a matter of
no great observation . . .

  After the great solemnization at the foresaid coronation
in the church of saint Peters at Westminster was ended,
the queene was conveied into the great hall of Westminster, and there set to dinner. Upon whose right hand sat at
the end of the table the archbishop of Canturburie, and
Henrie surnamed the Rich cardinall of Winchester. Upon
the left hand of the queene sat the king of Scots in his
estate, who was served with covered messe, as were the
forenamed bishops; but yet after them. Upon the same
hand and side, neere the boords end, sat the duchesse of
Yorke and the countess of Huntington. The earle of

March, holding a scepter in his hand, kneeled upon the right side: the earle marshall in like manner on the left of the queene. The countesse of Kent sat under the table at the right foot, and the countesse marshall at the left. The duke of Glocester sir Humfrie was that daie overseer, and stood before the queene bareheaded. Sir Richard Nevill was that daie carver to the queene, the earles brother of Suffolke cupbearer, sir John Steward sewar, the lord Clifford pantler in the earle of Warwikes steed, the lord Willoughbie buttler in steed of the erle of Arundell, the lord Graie Ruthin or Riffin naperer, the lord Audleie almoner in steed of the earle of Cambridge, the earle of Worcester was that daie earle marshall in the earle marshals absence; who rode about the hall upon a great courser with a multitude of tipped staves about him, to make and keepe roome in the said hall. Of the which hall the barons of the cinque ports began the table upon the right hand, toward saint Stephans chappell; and beneath them at the table sat the vowchers of the chancerie. Upon the left hand next to the cupboord sat the maior and his brethren the aldermen of London. The bishops began the table against the barons of the cinque ports; and the ladies against the maior. Of which two tables, for the bishops, began the bishop of London and the bishop of Durham; and for the ladies, the countesse of Stafford, and the countesse of March.

The feast was all of fish: for the ordering of the service whereof were diverse lords appointed head officers, as steward, controller, surveior, and other honourable officers. For the which were appointed the earles of Northumberland and Westmerland, the lord Fitz Hugh, the lord Furnevall, the lord Graie of Wilton, the lord Ferres of Grobie, the lord Poinings, the lord Harrington, the lord Darcie, the lord Dacres, and the lord de la Ware. These with others ordered the service of the feast as followeth; and thus for the first course. Brawne and mustard, eeles in burneux frument with ballen, pike in herbage, lamprie powdered, trowt, codling, plaice fried, martine fried, crabs, leech lumbard flourished, tartes; and a devise called

a pellican, sitting on hir nest with hir birds, and an image of saint Katharine holding a booke, and disputing with doctors, holding this poesie in hir right hand, written in faire and legible letters,
Madame la Royne; and the pellican answering,

> *C'est la signe et du roy, pour tenir ioy,*
> *Et a tout sa gent, elle mette sa entent.*

The second course was: gellie coloured with columbine flowers, white potage or creame of almonds, breame of the sea, coonger, soles, cheven, barbill and roch, fresh salmon, halibut, gurnard, rochet broiled, smelts fried, crevis or lobster; leech damaske, with the kings poesie flourished thereupon, *Une sans plus*; lamprie fresh baked, flampeine flourished with a scutchion roiall, and therein three crownes of gold planted with flourdeluces and floure of camomill wrought of confections: with a devise of a panther, and an image of saint Katharine with a wheele in one hand, and a scroll with a poesie in the other, to wit,

> *La royne ma file, in cesta ile,*
> *Per bon resoun, aves renoun.*

The third course was, dates in compost, creame motle, carpe deore, turbut, tench, pearch with goion, fresh sturgion with welks, porperous rosted, mennes fried, crevisse de eau doure, pranis, eeles rosted with lamprie, a leech called the white leech flourished with hawthorne leaves and red hawes; a marchpane garnished with diverse figures of angels, among which was set an image of S. Katharine, holding this posie,

> *Il est escrit, pur voir et eit,*
> *Per marriage pure, cest guerre ne dure.*

And lastlie a devise of a tiger looking in a mirror, and a man sitting on horssebacke all armed, holding in his armes a tigers whelpe with this poesie; *Per force sans resoun je ay prise ceste best*: and with his owne hand making a countenance of throwing of mirrors at the great tiger, which held this poesie; *Gile che mirrour ma feste distour.*

Thus with all honour was finished the solemne coronation, after which the queene sojourned in the palace of Westminster till Palmesundaie following; and on the morow she tooke hir journie towards Windsor; where the king and she held their Easter.

[120] William Caxton opens a shop in the Abbey and prints the first book in England (1476); from *William Caxton* by G. D. Painter.

On 30 September 1476 Caxton paid ten shillings to the sacrist and abbot John Eastney as a year's rent for a shop (*'una shopa'*) in the precincts of Westminster Abbey . . . Caxton rented these premises every year until his death in 1491 . . . in later years . . . the shop was described variously as 'adjoining the Chapter House', and 'near the south door of the Church'. This places it between the two northernmost of the Chapter House's flying buttresses, a few paces to the right as one leaves the south transept by the Poets' Corner door . . . Caxton's first datable piece of printing in England is an *Indulgence* issued by Pope Sixtus IV in aid of the war against the Turks, of which the only known copy, printed on vellum, with a manuscript entry of sale to Henry Langley and his wife Katherine on 13 December 1476 . . .

A dozen or so small undated quarto works belong to the earliest years of Caxton's Westminster press. These include two editions each of Lydgate's poems *The Horse, Sheep, and Goose*, and *The Churl and the Bird*, the first editions of which must have been among the earliest of all, in order to allow time for them to sell out and for second editions to be required. Stevenson saw that the supposed first editions have the same paper (with pregnant unicorn mark, probably from Saint-Cloud near Paris) as the first few quires of the first edition of *Canterbury Tales*, the remainder of which cannot have been completed before 1478; so he inferred that all this matter was probably printed before the end of 1476, and that *Canterbury*

Tales then had to be laid aside, so that Caxton could produce the two commissioned works for patrons, *Jason* and *Dicts*, which occupied most of the year 1477 . . .

Much of the year 1478 must have been taken up with the completion of the enormous *Canterbury Tales* which Caxton had perhaps already begun and laid aside in 1476. As a first printing of a national poem in the fifteenth century this is comparable only to the first edition of the *Divina Commedia* (1472) or Villon (1489), and for the monumental magnificence of the type page combined with the ever-new impact and wonder of the text this is perhaps Caxton's finest book (though *Morte d'Arthur*, 1485, is a good second). In the prologue to his second edition, in 1483, Caxton wrote an apology for his first: 'I find many of the said books (i.e. manuscripts of *Canterbury Tales*) which writers have abridged it and many things left out, and in some place have set certain verses that he never made nor set in his book, of which books so incorrect was one brought to me six year past, which I supposed had been very true and correct, and according to the same I did do emprint a certain number of them, which anon were sold to many and diverse gentlemen.'

[121] The coronation of Henry VIII (1509); from *Chronicles* by E. Hall.

The morrow following being sundaie, and also Midsummer daie, this noble prince with his quéene at time conuenient, vnder their canopies borne by the barons of the fiue ports, went from the said palace to Westminster abbaie vpon cloth, called vulgarlie cloth of raie; the which cloth was cut and spoiled by the rude and common people, immediatlie after their repaire into the abbaie; where, according to the sacred obseruance & ancient custome, his grace with the quéene were annointed and crowned by the archbishop of Canterburie . . . After the which solemnitie and coronation finished, the lords spirituall and temporall did to him homage, and returned to Westminster hall with the quéenes grace, euerie one vnder their canopies . . .

The kings estate on the right hand, & the queenes on the left hand, the cupboord of nine stages, their noble personages being set: first, at the bringing of the first course, the trumpets sounded. And in came the duke of Buckingham, mounted vpon a great courser, richlie trapped and imbrodered, and the lord steward in likewise on an horsse trapped in cloth of gold, riding before the seruice, which was sumptuous, with manie subtilties, strange deuices, with severall poses, and manie deintie dishes . . .

Now when the tables were voided, the wafers were brought. Then sir Stephen Genings that time maior of London, whome the king before he sat downe to dinner had dubbed knight, which began the earles table that daie, arose from the place where he sat, to serue the king with ipocras in a cup of gold: which cup, after his grace had dronken thereof, was with the couer giuen vnto the said sir Stephen, like as other his predecessors, maiors of the said citie, were woont to haue at the coronation of the king. Then after the surnap laied, and that the kings grace and the quéene had washed, euerie of them vnder their cloths of estate, the tables being auoided, went vnto their chambers. For the more honour and innobling of this triumphant coronation, there were prepared both iusts and turneis to be doone in the palace of Westminster, where, for the kings grace and the quéene, was framed a faire house, couered with tapistrie, and hanged with rich clothes of arrais, and in the said palace was made a curious founteine and ouer it a castell, on the top therof a great crowne imperiall, all the imbatelling with roses and pomegranats gilded.

Vnder and about the said castell, a curious vine, the leaues and grapes thereof gilded with fine gold, the walles of the same castell coloured white & greene losengis, and in euerie losing either a rose or a pomegranat, and a sheafe of arrowes, or else H. and K. gilded with fine gold, with certeine arches and turrets gilded, to support the same castell . . . And out at seuerall places of the same castell, aswell on the daie of the coronation, as on the said daies of the iusts & turneis, out of the mouthes of certeine beasts or gargels did run red, white, and claret wine.

[122] The fate of Oliver Cromwell's head; from *The Times* (1874).

Ireton's head was in the middle, and Cromwell's and Bradshaw's on either side [on the roof of Westminster hall]. Cromwell's head, being embalmed, remained exposed to the atmosphere for twenty-five years, and then one stormy night it was blown down, and picked up by the sentry, who, hiding it under his cloak, took it home and secreted it in the chimney corner, and, as inquiries were constantly being made about it by the Government, it was only on his death-bed that he revealed where he had hidden it. His family sold the head to one of the Cambridgeshire Russells, and, in the same box in which it still is, it descended to a certain Samuel Russell, who being a needy and careless man, exhibited it in a place near Clare Market. There it was seen by James Cox, who then owned a famous museum. He tried in vain to buy the head from Russell; for, poor as he was, nothing would at first tempt him to part with the relic, but after a time Cox assisted him with money, and eventually, to clear himself from debt, he made the head over to Cox. When Cox at last parted with his museum he sold the head of Cromwell for £230 to three men, who bought it about the time of the French Revolution to exhibit in Mead Court, Bond Street, at half-a-crown a head. Curiously enough, it happened that each of these three gentlemen died a sudden death, and the head came into the possession of the three nieces of the last man who died. These young ladies, nervous at keeping it in the house, asked Mr Wilkinson, their medical man, to take care of it for them, and they subsequently sold it to him. For the next fifteen or twenty years Mr Wilkinson was in the habit of showing it to all the distinguished men of that day, and the head, much treasured, yet remains in his family.

[123] The coronation of Queen Anne (1702); from *The Journeys of Celia Fiennes*.

[. . .] as in Case of our present Majesty Queen Ann I saw her thus; her Cannopy was Large bore by yᵉ sixteen, and she because of Lameness of yᵉ Gout had an Elbow Chaire of Crimson velvet wᵗʰ a Low back, by wᶜʰ meanes her mantle and Robe was Cast over it and bore by the Lord Master of yᵉ Robes and yᵉ first Dutchess, wᵗʰ 4 maiden Ladies, Earles Daughters on Each side Richly Dress'd in Cloth of Gold or Silver, Laced wᵗʰ Long traines, Richly Dressed in fine Linnen, and jewells in their hair, and Embroider'd on their Gowns. The Queens traine was 6 yards Long, the Mantle suitable of Crimson velvet with Earmine as yᵉ other of yᵉ nobility, only the rowes of powdering Exceeded, being six rowes of powdering. Her Robe under was of Gold tissue, very Rich Embroydery of jewellry about it, her peticoate the same of Gold tissue wᵗʰ gold and silver lace, between Rowes of Diamonds Embroyder'd, her Linnen fine. The Queen being principall of the order of yᵉ Garter had a row of Gold SS about her shoulders, yᵉ Georges[3] wᶜʰ are allwayes set with Diamonds and tyed with a blew Ribon. Her head was well dress'd wᵗʰ Diamonds mixed in yᵉ haire wᶜʰ at yᵉ Least motion Brill'd and flamed. She wore a Crimson velvet Cap with Earmine under yᵉ Circlet, wᶜʰ was set with Diamonds, and on the middle a sprig of Diamonds drops transparent hung inform of a plume of feathers, for this Cap is yᵉ Prince of Wales's Cap wᶜʰ till after yᵉ Coronation that makes them Legall king and queen – they weare. Thus to yᵉ quire doore she Came, then Leaveing yᵉ Cannopy – (yᵉ Chaire she Left at yᵉ Abby doore –) she is conducted to yᵉ Alter, which was finely deck'd wᵗʰ Gold tissue Carpet and fine Linnen, on the top all yᵉ plaite of yᵉ abby sett, yᵉ velvet Cushions to place yᵉ Crown and all yᵉ regallias on. She made her offering at yᵉ Alter, a pound weight or wedge of gold, here the Dean of Westminster and ye prebends which assists the Arch-Bishop in the Cerimonyes are arrayed in very Rich Coapes and Mitres, black velvet Embroyder'd wth gold Starrs, or Else tissue of gold and silver. Then the Littany and prayers are sung and repeated by two Bishops, wth a small organ, then the Queen being seated on a green velvet Chaire faceing the pulpit, attends ye words of ye sermon wch was by ye arch-Bishop of York, wch being ended ye Queen arose and returned thanks for ye Arch-bishops Sermon, is shewed to ye people by saying a form, Will you take this to be your Souveraigne to be over you? thus I saw the Queen turn her face to ye four sides of ye Church, then the Coronation oath is repeated to her, wch she distinctly answered each article, which oath is very Large in three articles, relateing to all priviledges of ye Church and State to which she promised to be the security and to maintaine all to us. Then she kiss'd ye Bible, then a Bible was presented to her to maintaine ye true Protestant religion. Then she being on a Little throne by the alter, Cover'd all wth Cloth of Gold, she has ye spurrs of gold brought her and they toutch her heele, then the sword of state is presented her which she offers up on the alter, wch a Lord appoynted for it redeemes ye sword for 100 shillings, and draws it out and beares it naked all ye day. After the other swords are brought and presented her wch she delivers to ye severall officers, then the ring is put on her finger to witness she is married to the Kingdom, then the orb I saw brought and presented to her and ye Scepters. Then she was anoynted in this manner: there was a Cloth of silver twilight Embroyder'd, held a Little shaddowing over her head. I saw ye Bishop bring ye oyle in a spoone, soe annoynted ye palmes of her hands, her breast and her forehead, Last of all ye top of her head, haveing taken off ye prince of Wales's Cap and ye haire being Cutt off close at ye top, ye oyle was poured on and with a fine Cloth all Dryed againe. Then Last of all ye arch Bishops held the Crown over her head, wch Crown was made on purpose for this Cerimony, vastly Rich in Diamonds, ye borders and ye Globe part very thick sett wth vast diamonds, y^e

Cross on ye top with all diamonds wch flamed at ye Least motion, this is worth a vast summe, but being made for this Cerimony and pulled to pieces againe, its only soe much for the hire of such Jewells that made it. This I saw was fix'd on ye Queen's head wth Huzza's and sounds of Drumms trumpets and gunns, and at the same tyme all ye peeres and peeresses put on their Coronets on their heads. There are divers forms of speech that belong to each Cerimony. Y^e Queen after this goes to ye alter and there I saw her receive the Sacrament, I saw the deane bring her ye bread and wine. Then she is Conducted with her Crown on, her Globe and Scepter in her hand, and seated on ye Royal throne of ye Kingdom wch is of gold finely wrought, high back and armes set on a theatre of severall steps, assent rises on four sides to it. She being thus seated is followed wth a second Huzza and sound of drums and trumpets and Gunns, then all ye Lords and Bishops pay their homage to her; the Eldest of Each ranke swears fidelity to her in his own name and in ye name of all his ranck. They all singly come and touch her Crown and some kiss her Right cheeke – they make all do soe – she kisses the Bishops. All this while anthems are sung and the Medals are Cast about by the treasurer of ye household, After wch the Queen arose and went and made her second offering, sate down on the throne on wch she was annoynted and Crown'd. After, an anthem is sung proper for the tyme, after wch the Queen retired into King Edwards Chappel to private prayer, wch being ended and her Crimson velvet mantle being taken off and one of purple velvet made just ye same put on, in ye same manner they returned Each one in his station, only the Lords ye Carryed the Regalias now tooke their places as peers with ye rest, ye Queen walked to ye doore of ye abby w obligeing Lookes and bows to all ye Saluted her and were spectatours, wch were prodigious numbers in Scaffolds built in the Abbey and all the streetes on each side reaching to Westminster hall, where the Queen againe quitted her Chaire wch was Carryed by four men, the whole procession being both going and comeing attended by ye gentlemen pensioners Clad in Scarlet Cloth w gold Lace, Holding halberds wth gold tops Like pickaxes. These make a Lane for the queen to pass and follow two and two, next them ye groomes of the bed Chamber, then the Captaine of ye guards went between ye Captaine of ye pensioner's band and the Captaine of ye yeaumen, and were attended by their officers and yeamen.

The queen being Come up to her table, wch was a great rise of stepps she was seated on her throne wch was under a fine Canopy. When King James was Crown'd he sate soe: at his Left hand sate his Queen under another Cannopy, but King William and Queen Mary being both principalls sate under one Large Cannopy on one Large throne, but our present Queen should have sate alone, as she did in ye upper End under ye Cannopy, but she sent and did invite Prince George her Consort to dine with her. So he Came and at her request tooke his seate at her Left hand without the Cannopy. The first course was served just before the Queen Came in, She being ushered in by the Earle Marshall, Lord High Steward, and Lord high Chamberlaine on horseback, their horses being finely dress'd and managed, and the Cookes Came up with their point aprons and towells about their shoulders of poynt; after wch Comes up the Lord high steward againe on horseback, with the other two Lords, and acquaints the king or queen there is their Champion without ready to Encounter or Combate with any that should pretend to dispute, after wch he is Conducted in on horseback by the Earle Marshall and ye Lord high steward, and they Come up to the stepps of the throne, and there the Champion all dress'd in armour Cap-a-pe and declares his readyness to Combate wth any that should oppose the Right of their Majestyes, and there upon throws down his gauntlet wch is giving Challenge, after wch the King or Queen drinks to him in a Gold Cup wth a Cover, ye same wch is Carryed to ye Champion and he drinks, and then he retires back and Carrys it away being his Due as is the best horse in the kings stable, ye best suite of armour in ye armory. This belongs to Sr John Dimmocks familly y^t hath a yearly salery from the Crown. My Lord Major here officiates as yᵉ kings Butler, and hath for a Reward such another Cup of gold Covered and thus the Ceremony Ends and they all retire. Westminster Hall is as full of spectatours sitting on scaffolds on Each side, under wᶜʰ are severall Long tables spread and full of all varietyes prepared for the Lords and Ladies, others for the judges, aldermen & c.

When there is a Rideing Coronation they proceed on from yᵉ abbey when a king is Crowned, all on horseback thro' yᵉ Citty in yᵉ same order as at yᵉ Entry at yᵉ peace, quite to yᵉ Tower, all richly dress'd and their horses wᵗʰ fine trappings, Led on both sides by Each Lords pages, and when its a King only, then only yᵉ Lords attend as in yᵉ Coronation of King Charles the second, but at Queen Elizabeths the Ladies alsoe attended to yᵉ Tower which is at yᵉ utmost extremity of ye Citty of London, where the Governour presents the King with yᵉ Keyes which he returns againe and after some other Cerimonyes and makeing some Knights of yᵉ Bath Either six or Eight I Cannot tell which. These are an order that prefferr such a knight above all other knights, but is not so high as a Barronet and it alsoe expires at their Death descending not to yᵉ son; they wear a scarlet Ribon round their shoulder Like a belt: then they all return back to the pallace; Usually the rideing Coronation holds two days.

[124] Addison visits the Abbey (1711); from *The Spectator*.

Nᵒ. 26. *Friday, March 30, 1711*

When I am in a serious humour, I very often walk by myself in Westminster Abbey; where the gloominess of the place, and the use to which it is applied, with the solemnity of the building, and the condition of the people who lie in it, are apt to fill the mind with a kind of melancholy, or rather thoughtfulness, that is not disagreeable. I yesterday passed a whole afternoon in the churchyard, the cloisters, and the church, amusing myself with the tombstones and inscriptions that I met with in those several regions of the dead. Most of them recorded nothing else of the buried person but that he was born upon one day and died upon another: the whole history of his life being comprehended in those two circumstances that are common to all mankind. I could not but look upon these registers of existence, whether of brass or marble, as a kind of satire upon the departed persons; who had left no other memorial of them, but that they were born and that they died. They put me in mind of several persons mentioned in the battles of heroic poems, who have sounding names given them for no other reason but that they may be killed, and are celebrated for nothing but being knocked on the head.

Γλαῦκον τε Μεδόντα τε Θερσίλοχόν τε.—ΗΟΜ.
Glaucumque, Medontaque, Thersilochumque.—VIR.

The life of these men is finely described in Holy Writ by the path of an arrow, which is immediately closed up and lost.

Upon my going into the church, I entertained myself with the digging of a grave; and saw in every shovelful of it that was thrown up, the fragment of a bone or skull intermixed with a kind of fresh mouldering earth that some time or other had a place in the composition of a human body. Upon this I began to consider with myself what innumerable multitudes of people lay confused together under the pavement of that ancient cathedral; how men and women, friends and enemies, priests and soldiers, monks and prebendaries, were crumbled amongst one another, and blended together in the same common mass; how beauty, strength, and youth, with old age, weakness and deformity, lay undistinguished in the same promiscuous heap of matter.

After having thus surveyed this great magazine of mortality, as it were in the lump, I examined it more particularly by the accounts which I found on several of the monuments which are raised in every quarter of that ancient fabric. Some of them were covered with such extravagant epitaphs that, if it were possible for the dead person to be acquainted with them, he would blush at the praises which his friends have bestowed upon him. There are others so excessively modest that they deliver the character of the person departed in Greek or Hebrew, and by that means are not understood once in a twelvemonth. In the poetical quarter, I found there were poets who had no monuments, and monuments which had no poets. I observed indeed that the present war had filled the church with many of these uninhabited monuments, which had been erected to the memory of persons whose bodies were perhaps buried in the plains of Blenheim, or in the bosom of the ocean.

I could not but be very much delighted with several modern epitaphs, which are written with great elegance of expression and justness of thought, and therefore do honour to the living as well as to the dead. As a foreigner is very apt to conceive an idea of the ignorance or politeness of a nation from the turn of their public monuments and inscriptions, they should be submitted to the perusal of men of learning and genius before they are put in execution. Sir Cloudesly Shovel's monument has very often given me great offence. Instead of the brave, rough English admiral, which was the distinguishing character of that plain, gallant man, he is represented on his tomb by the figure of a beau, dressed in a long periwig, and reposing himself upon velvet cushions under a canopy of state. The inscription is answerable to the monument; for instead of celebrating the many remarkable actions he had performed in the service of his country, it acquaints us only with the manner of his death, in which it was impossible for him to reap any honour. The Dutch, whom we are apt to despise for want of genius, show an infinitely greater taste of antiquity and politeness in their buildings and works of this nature, than what we meet with in those of our own country. The monuments of their admirals, which have been erected at the public expense, represent them like themselves, and are adorned with rostral crowns and naval ornaments, with beautiful festoons of seaweed, shells, and coral.

But to return to our subject. I have left the repository of our English kings for the contemplation of another day, when I shall find my mind disposed for so serious an amusement. I know that entertainments of this nature are apt to raise dark and dismal thoughts in timorous minds and gloomy imaginations; but for my own part, though I am always serious, I do not know what it is to be melancholy, and can therefore take a view of nature in her deep and solemn scenes, with the same pleasure as in her most gay and delightful ones. By this means, I can improve myself with those objects which others consider with terror. When I look upon the tombs of the great, every emotion of envy dies in me; when I read the epitaphs of the beautiful, every inordinate desire goes out; when I meet with the grief of parents upon a tombstone, my heart melts with compassion; when I see the tomb of the parents themselves, I consider the vanity of grieving for those whom we must quickly follow; when I see kings lying by those who deposed them, when I consider rival wits placed side by side, or the holy men that divided the world with their contests and disputes, I reflect with sorrow and astonishment on the little competitions, factions, and debates of mankind. When I read the several dates of the tombs – of some that died yesterday, and some six hundred years ago – I consider that great day when we shall all of us be contemporaries, and make our appearance together.

[125] The opening of the trial of Warren Hastings at Westminster Hall (1788); from *Diary and Letters of Madame D'Arblay*, Vol. IV).

February 13 1788 . . . The Trial, so long impending, of Mr Hastings, opened to-day . . .

The business did not begin till near twelve o'clock. The opening to the whole then took place, by the entrance of the Managers of the Prosecution . . .

I shuddered and drew involuntarily back, when, as the doors were flung open, I saw Mr Burke, as Head of the

St Paul's Church, Covent Garden Market, before the Westminster Election, from an aquatint published in 1808, by Pugin & Rowlandson

Riot at Covent Garden Theatre, in 1763, in consequence of the Managers refusing to admit half-price in the Opera of Artaxerxes.

A riot in Covent Garden theatre in 1763

The course of the Plague, 1665

John Dunstall fecit.

Parliament of Edward I

The beheading of King Charles I with portraits of his adherents

Mrs Baines addresses a mass rally of suffragettes at Trafalgar Square, London, 1908

'Buy a rabbet, a rabbet'. Street seller

Wentworth Street, Whitechapel

Tom & Jerry sporting their blunt on the Phenomenon
Monkey, Jacco Macacco, at the Westminster Pit

Music hath charms: children dancing in the street

The Drunkard's Children. *The Beer Shop*

Readers choosing books which are still intact among the charred timbers of the Holland House library, London. October 1940

Committee, make his solemn entry. He held a scroll in his hand, and walked alone, his brow knit with corroding care and deep labouring thought . . .

Then began the procession, the clerks entering first, then the Lawyers according to their rank, and the Peers, Bishops and Officers, all in their coronation robes . . . and the whole ending by the Chancellor, with his train borne. Then they all took their seats.

A Serjeant-at-Arms, arose, and commanded silence in the Court, on pain of imprisonment.

Then some other officer, in a loud voice, called out, as well as I can recollect, words to this purpose – 'Warren Hastings, Esquire, come forth! Answer to the charges brought against you; save your bail, or forfeit your recognizance!' . . .

The moment he came in sight, which was not for full ten minutes after his awful summons, he made a low bow to the Chancellor and Court facing him. I saw not his face, as he was directly under me. He moved on slowly . . . to the opening of his own Box; there, lower still, he bowed again; and then, advancing to the bar, he leant his hands upon it, and dropped on his knees; but a voice in the same moment proclaiming he had leave to rise, he stood up almost instantaneously, and a third time pro-foundly bowed to the Court.

What an awful moment this for such a man! . . . The Crier, I think it was, made, in a loud and hollow voice, a public proclamation, 'That Warren Hastings, Esquire, late Governor-General of Bengal, was now on his trial for high crimes and misdemeanours, with which he was charged by the Commons of Great Britain; and that all persons what-soever who had aught to allege against him were now to stand forth.'

[126] Wordsworth writes a sonnet on Westminster Bridge (1802); *Composed upon Westminster Bridge.*

> Earth has not anything to show more fair:
> Dull would he be of soul who could pass by

A sight so touching in its majesty:
This City now doth, like a garment, wear
The beauty of the morning; silent, bare,
Ships, towers, domes, theatres, and temples lie
Open unto the fields, and to the sky;
All bright and glittering in the smokeless air.
Never did sun more beautifully steep
In his first splendour, valley, rock, or hill;
Ne're saw I, never felt, a calm so deep!
The river glideth at his own sweet will:
Dear God! the very houses seem asleep;
And all that mighty heart is lying still!

[127] The coronation of George IV. And the bill of Fare at the feast; from *The Journals of Mrs Arbuthnot, 1820–31*, edited by F. Bamford and Duke of Wellington; and *Old and New London* by W. Thornbury.

[July] 19th . . .

The King came into the Hall at ten o'clock, the procession having been previously partly arranged. He looked at first excessively pale and tired but soon recovered and, after giving the Regalia to the different persons who were to carry it, the procession moved to the Abbey. While it proceeded by the platform to the north door of the Abbey, we went by a narrow passage erected from the door of the House of Lords to Poets' Corner and were seated in the Abbey before the procession arrived. On the King's entrance into the Abbey he was received with the loudest cheers, which were repeated with increased vehemence when the crown was placed on his head and, particularly, when the D. of York did homage and kissed him. It was a magnificent sight, that fine building full of people as it could possible hold, all magnificently dressed, peers, heroes and statesmen all joining in one unanimous hurra. The ceremony occupied till towardsthree o'clock when the

King returned to the Hall and passing through it, retired to a private room to rest till dinner.

The Duke of Wellington and Mr Arbuthnot then came to where we were and took us to Mr Bankes' in Old Palace Yard, where we had something to eat . . .

The King returned to the Hall about 5 o'clock, when the Earl Marshal, the D. of Wellington (High Constable) and Lord Anglesea (High Steward) rode up the Hall with the first course and backed out again. They came in again with the second course, and the two latter with the Champion. It was very well done; the Duke of Wellington rode a white Arabian who backed most perfectly. There were a great many services done, caps given and returned, falcons presented by the D. of Atholl. The peers drank to the King, and he in return to the peers and his good people, and the whole concluded with 'God save the King', sung by the choristers and chorused by the whole assembly. After the riding was over, the people had been allowed to crowd into the body of the Hall and only a small space was kept open at the foot of the steps, and it is not possible to describe anything finer than the scene was, the galleries all standing up waving their hats and handkerchiefs and shouting, 'God bless the King!' Altogether it was a scene I would not have missed seeing for the world, and shall never see again so fine a one.

The King behaved very indecently; he was continually nodding and winking at Lady Conyngham and sighing and making eyes at her. At one time in the Abbey he took a diamond brooch from his breast, and, looking at her, kissed it, on which she took off her glove and kissed a ring she had on!!! Any body who could have seen his disgusting figure, with a wig the curls of which hung down his back, and quite bending beneath the weight of his robes and his 60 years would have been quite sick. . . .

BILL OF FARE.

Sufficient for a siege the bill of fare;
Denuded of their tribes, earth, sea, and air
Must all contribute to the banquet's zest.

Hot Dishes

160 tureens of soup, 80 of turtle, 40 of rice, and 40 vermicelli; 160 dishes of fish, comprising 80 of turbot, 40 of trout, 40 of salmon; 160 hot joints, including 80 of venison, 40 of roast beef, with three barons, 40 of mutton and veal; 160 dishes of vegetables, including potatoes, peas, and cauliflowers; 480 sauce-boats, 240 of lobsters, 120 butter, 120 mint.

Cold Dishes

80 dishes of braized ham; 80 savory pies; 80 dishes of daubed geese, two in each; 80 dishes of savory cakes; 80 pieces of beef braized; 80 dishes of capons braized, two in each; 1,190 side-dishes of various sorts; 320 dishes of mounted pastry; 320 dishes of small pastry; 400 dishes of jellies and creams; 160 dishes of shell-fish, 80 of lobster, and 80 of crayfish; 161 dishes of cold roast fowls; 80 dishes of cold house-lamb.

Total Quantities

7,442 lbs. of beef; 7,133 lbs. of veal; 2,474 lbs. of mutton; 20 quarters of house-lamb; 20 legs of house-lamb; 5 saddles of lamb; 55 quarters of grass-lamb; 160 lambs' sweetbreads; 389 cow-heels; 400 calves' feet; 250 lbs. of suet; 160 geese; 720 pullets and capons; 1,610 chickens; 520 fowls for stock (hens); 1,730 lbs. of bacon; 550 lbs. of lard; 912 lbs. of butter; 84 hundred of eggs.

All these are independent of the eggs, butter, flour, and necessary articles in the pastry and confectionery departments – such as sugar, isinglass, fruits, &c.

WINES.
The choicest wines brought from fair Gallia's strand;
Burgundian nectar, sparkling Malvoisie,
The source of wit and gay hilarity.

The quantities ordered for the banquet were: – Champagne, 100 dozen; Burgundy, 20 dozen; claret, upwards of 200 dozen; hock, 50 dozen; Moselle, 50 dozen; Madeira, 50 dozen; sherry and port, about 350 dozen; iced punch, 100 gallons. The champagne, hock, and Moselle were iced before they went to table; and the whole of the wines were spoken of as being excellent by the thousands who had an opportunity of tasting them.

Of *ale*, 100 barrels were ordered for the use of the kitchen. The *porcelain* consisted of 6,794 dinner plates, 1,406 soup-plates, 1,499 dessert-plates, and 288 large pitchers for ale and beer. There were 240 yards of damask table-cloths for the Hall, and about 1,000 yards more laid on the tables in the other suites of rooms. The cutlery included 16,000 knives and forks, and 612 pairs of carvers.

[128] Byron's hearse on its way to the Abbey (1824); from *The Prose of John Clare*, edited by J. W. & A. Temple (London, 1951).

When I was in London the melancholy death of Lord Byron was announced in the public papers & I saw his remains borne away out of the city on its last journey to that place where fame never comes His funeral was blazed in the papers with the usual parade that accompanies the death of great men I happened to see it by chance as I was wandering up Oxford Street on my way to Mrs Emmerson's when my eye was suddenly arrested by straggling groups of the common people collected together & talking about a funeral I did as the rest did though I could not get hold of what funeral it could be but I knew it was not a common one by the curiosity that kept watch on every countenance By & by the group collected into about a hundred or more when the train of a funeral suddenly appeared on which a young girl that stood beside me gave a deep sigh & uttered 'Poor Lord Byron' I looked up at the young girl's face it was dark & beautiful & I could almost feel in love with her for the sigh she had uttered

for the poet it was worth all the newspaper puffs &
magazine mournings that ever were paraded after the
death of a poet The common people felt his merits & his
power & the common people of a country are the best
feelings of a prophecy of futurity they are the veins &
arteries that feed & quicken the heart of living fame The
breathings of eternity & the soul of time are indicated in
that prophecy They felt by a natural impulse that the
mighty was fallen & they moved in saddened silence the
streets were lined on each side as the procession passed
but they were all the commonest of the lower orders the
young girl that stood by me had counted the carriages in
her mind as they passed & she told me there were sixty
three or four in all they were of all sorts & sizes & made
up a motley show the gilt ones that led the procession
were empty the hearse looked small & rather mean & the
coach that followed carried his embers in an urn over
which a pall was thrown I believe that his liberal principles
in religion & politics did a great deal towards gaining the
notice & affections of the lower orders Be as it will it is
better to be beloved by those low & humble for undisgu-
ised honesty than flattered by the great for purchased &
pensioned hypocrisies.

[129] The coronation of Queen Victoria (1838); from *Letters and Journal*.

I was awoke at four o'clock by the guns in the Park, and
could not get much sleep afterwards on account of the
noise of the people, bands, etc., etc. Got up at seven,
feeling strong and well; the Park presented a curious
spectacle, crowds of people up to Constitution Hill,
soldiers, bands, etc. I dressed, having taken a little breakfast before I dressed, and a little after. At half past 9 I
went into the next room, dressed exactly in my House of
Lords costume . . .

At 10 I got into the State Coach with the Duchess of
Sutherland and Lord Albemarle and we began our Progress . . . It was a fine day, and the crowds of people

exceeded what I have ever seen; many as there were the day I went to the City, it was nothing to the multitudes, the millions of my loyal subjects, who were assembled *in every spot* to witness the Procession. Their good humour and excessive loyalty was beyond everything, and I really cannot say *how* proud I feel to be the Queen of *such* a Nation. I was alarmed at times for fear that the people would be crushed and squeezed on account of the tremendous rush and pressure.

I reached the Abbey amid deafening cheers at a little after half past eleven; I first went into a robing-room quite close to the entrance where I found my eight train-bearers . . .

After putting on my mantle, and the young ladies having properly got hold of it and Lord Conyngham holding the end of it, I left the robing-room and the Procession began as is described in the annexed account, and all that followed and took place. The sight was splendid; the bank of Peeresses quite beautiful all in their robes, and the Peers on the other side. My young train-bearers were always near me, and helped me whenever I wanted anything. The Bishop of Durham stood on the side near me, but he was, as Lord Melbourne told me, remarkably *maladroit*, and never could tell me what was to take place. At the beginning of the Anthem, where I've made a mark, I retired to St Edward's Chapel, a dark small place immediately behind the Altar, with my ladies and train-bearers – took off my crimson robe and kirtle, and put on the supertunica of cloth of gold, also in the shape of a kirtle, which was put over a singular sort of little gown of linen trimmed with lace; I also took off my circlet of diamonds and then proceeded bare-headed into the Abbey; I was then seated upon St Edward's chair, where the Dalmatic robe was clasped round me by the Lord Great Chamberlain. Then followed all the various things; and last (of those things) the Crown being placed on my head – which was, I must own, a most beautiful impressive moment; *all* the Peers and Peeresses put on their coronets at the same instant.

My excellent Lord Melbourne, who stood very close to me throughout the whole ceremony, was *completely* overcome at this moment, and very much affected; he gave me *such* a kind, and I may say *fatherly* look. The shouts, which were very great, the drums, the trumpets, the firing of the guns, all at the same instant, rendered the spectacle most imposing.

Whitehall

[130] Cardinal Wolsey deprived of the Great Seal (1529); from *The Life of Cardinal Wolsey* by Thomas Cavendish.

Michaelmas Term drew near, against the which my lord returned unto his house at Westminster; and when the term began, he went to the hall in such like sort and gesture as he was wont most commonly to do, and sat in the chancery, being Chancellor. After which day he never sat there more. The next day he tarried at home, expecting the coming of the two Dukes, of Suffolk and Norfolk, which came not that day; but the next day they came unto him; to whom they declared how the king's pleasure was that he should surrender and deliver up the great seal into their hands, and to depart simplily unto Esher, a house situate nigh Hampton Court, belonging to the Bishop of Winchester. My lord understanding their message, demanded of them what commission they had to give him any such commandment? Who answered him again, that they were sufficient commissioners in that behalf, having the king's commandment by his mouth so to do. 'Yet,' quoth he, 'that is not sufficient for me, without a further commandment of the king's pleasure; for the great seal of England was delivered me by the king's own person, to enjoy during my life, with the ministration of the office and high room of chancellorship of England: for my surety whereof, I have the king's letters patent to show.' Which matter was greatly debated between the dukes and him, with many stout words between them; whose words and checks he took in patience for the time: insomuch that the dukes were fain to depart again without their purpose at that present; and returned again unto Windsor to the king: and what report they made I cannot tell; howbeit, the next day they came again from the king, bringing with them the king's letters. After the receipt and reading of the same by my lord, which was done with much reverence, he delivered unto them the great seal, contented to obey the king's high commandment; and seeing that the king's pleasure was to take his house, with the contents, was well pleased simply to depart to Esher, taking nothing but only some provisions for his house.

And after long talk between the dukes and him, they departed, with the great seal of England, to Windsor, unto the king. Then went my Lord Cardinal and called all officers in every office in his house before him, to take account of all such stuff as they had in charge. And in his gallery there was set divers tables, whereupon a great number of rich stuff of silk, in whole pieces, of all colours, as velvet, satin, damask, caffa, taffeta, grograine, sarcenet, and of other not in my remembrance; also there lay a thousand pieces of fine holland cloth, whereof as I heard his say afterward, there was five hundred pieces thereof, conveyed both from the king and him.

Furthermore there was also all the walls of the gallery hanged with cloths of gold, and tissue of divers makings, and cloths of silver likewise on both the sides; and rich cloths of baudkin, of divers colours. There hung also the richest suits of copes of his own provision, which he

caused to be made for his colleges of Oxford and Ips-
wich, that ever I saw in England. Then had he two
chambers adjoining to the gallery, the one called the gilt
chamber, and the other called, most commonly, the council chamber, wherein were set in each two broad and long
tables, upon tressels, whereupon was set such a number
of plate of all sorts, as were almost incredible. In the gilt
chamber was set out upon the tables nothing but all gilt
plate; and a cupboard standing under a window, was
garnished wholly with plate of clean gold, whereof some
was set with pearl and rich stones. And in the council
chamber was set all white plate and parcel-gilt; and under
the tables, in both the chambers, were set baskets with
old plate, which was not esteemed but for broken plate
and old, not worthy to be occupied, and books counting
the value and weight of every parcel laid by them ready
to be seen; and so was also books set by all manner of
stuff, containing the contents of every thing. Thus every
thing being brought into good order and furnished, he
gave the charge of the delivery thereof unto the king, to
every officer within his office, of such stuff as they had
before in charge, by indenture of every parcel; for the
order of his house was such, as that every officer was
charged by indenture with all such parcels as belonged to
their office.

Then all things being ordered as it is before rehearsed,
my lord prepared him to depart by water. And before his
departing, he commanded Sir William Gascoigne, his
treasurer, to see these things before remembered delivered
safely to the king at his repair. That done, the said Sir
William said unto my lord, 'Sir, I am sorry for your grace,
for I understand ye shall go straightway to the Tower.' 'Is
this the good comfort and counsel,' quoth my lord, 'that
ye can give your master in adversity? It hath been always
your natural inclination to be very light of credit; and
much more lighter in reporting of false news. I would ye
should know, Sir William, and all other such blasphemers,
that it is nothing more false than that, for I never (thanks
be to God) deserved by no ways to come there under any

arrest, although it has pleased the king to take my house ready furnished for his pleasure at this time. I would all the world knew, and so I confess, to have nothing, either riches, honour, or dignity, that hath not grown of him and by him; therefore it is my very duty to surrender the same to him again as his very own, with all my heart, or else I were an unkind servant. Therefore go your ways, and give good attendance unto your charge, that nothing be embezzled.' And therewithal he made him ready to depart, with all his gentlemen and yeomen, which was no small number, and took his barge at his privy stairs, and so went by water unto Putney, where all his horses waited his coming. And at the taking of his barge there was no less than a thousand boats full of men and women of the city of London, waffeting up and down in Thames, expecting my lord's departing, supposing that he should have gone directly from thence to the Tower, whereat they rejoiced, and I dare be bold to say that the most part never received damage at his hands.

[131] Charles I 'touches' for the King's evil (later 17th century); from *MS Diary*, in *Old and New London* by W. Thornbury.

'A young gentlewoman, Elizabeth Stephens, of the age of sixteen, came to the Presence Chamber in 1640, to be "touched for the Evil", with which she was so afflicted that, by her own and her mother's testimony, she had not seen with her left eye for above a month. After prayers read by Dr Sanderson, she knelt down to be "touched", with the rest, by the King. His Majesty then touched her in the usual manner, and put a ribbon with a piece of money hanging to it about her neck. Which done, his Majesty turned to the Duke of Richmond, the Earl of Southampton, and the Earl of Lindsey, to discourse with them. And the young gentlewoman said of her own accord, openly, "Now God be praised, I can see of this sore eye," and afterwards declared that she did see more and more by it, and could by degrees endure the light of the candle.'

[132] The execution of Charles I (1648); from *Memorials of the English Affairs* by B. Whitelocke.

The King walked from St James's through the park, guarded with a regiment of foot and partisans, to Whitehall.

Divers gentlemen went bare before him, Dr Juxon followed next to him, and Colonel Thomlinson had the charge of him; they brought him to the cabinet-chamber, where he continued at his devotion.

He refused to dine, having taken the sacrament, but at about twelve o'clock at noon he drank a glass of claret wine, and eat a piece of bread; from thence he went with Dr Juxon, Colonel Thomlinson, Colonel Hacker, and the guards, through the banqueting-house, adjoining to which the scaffold was erected; it was hung with black, and the floor covered with black, and the axe and block laid in the middle of it . . .

Two men in disguises and vizors stood upon the scaffold for executioners.

Then the King called to Dr Juxon for his nightcap, and having put it on, he said to the executioner, 'Does my hair trouble you?' he desired it might all be put under the cap, which the King did accordingly, by the help of the executioner and the bishop . . .

Some other small ceremonies were passed, after which the King stooping down laid his neck upon the block, and after a very little pause, stretching forth his hands, the executioner at one blow severed his head from his body.

The King died with true magnanimity and Christian patience; his body was put in a coffin, covered with black velvet, and removed to his lodging chamber in Whitehall. At this scene were many sighs and weeping eyes, and divers strove to dip their handkerchiefs in his blood, as in the blood of a martyr.

[133] The Court of Charles II; from *The History of England* by T. B. Macaulay, edited by S. E. Winbolt.

Half the jobbing and half the flirting of the metropolis . . . went on under his roof. Whoever could make himself agreeable to the prince, or could secure the good offices of the mistress, might hope to rise in the world without rendering any service to the Government, without being even known by sight to any minister of state. This courtier got a frigate, and that a company; a third, the pardon of a rich offender; a fourth, a lease of Crown land on easy terms. If the king notified his pleasure that a briefless lawyer should be made a judge, or that a libertine baronet should be made a peer, the gravest counsellors, after a little murmuring, submitted. Interest, therefore, drew a constant press of suitors to the gates of the palace, and those gates always stood wide. The king kept open house every day, and all day long, for the good society of London, the extreme Whigs only excepted. Hardly any gentleman had any difficulty in making his way to the royal presence. The 'levee' was exactly what the word imports. Some men of quality came every morning to stand around their master, to chat with him while his wig was combed and his cravat tied, and to accompany him in his early walk through the Park. All persons who had been properly introduced might, without any special invitation, go to see him dine, sup, dance, and play at hazard, and might have the pleasure of hearing him tell stories, which indeed he told remarkably well, about his flight from Worcester, and about the misery which he had endured when he was a State prisoner in the hands of the canting meddling preachers of Scotland. Bystanders whom his Majesty recognized often came in for a courteous word. This proved a far more successful kingcraft than any that his father or grandfather had practised. It was not easy for the most austere republican of the school of Marvell to resist the fascination of so much good humour and affability; and many a veteran Cavalier in whose heart the remembrance of unrequited sacrifices and services had been festering during twenty years, was compensated in one moment for wounds and sequestrations by his sovereign's kind nod, and 'God bless you, my old friend!'

[134] William and Mary proclaimed King and Queen (1689); from *Diaries* by John Evelyn.

I saw the new Queene and King, so proclaim'd the very next day of her coming to White-hall, Wednesday 13 Feb. with wonderfull acclamation and general reception, Bonfires, bells, Gunns etc: It was believed that they both, especialy the Princesse, would have shewed some (seeming) reluctancy at least, of assuming her Fathers Crowne and made some Apologie, testifying her regret, that he should by his misgovernment necessitat the Nation to so extraordinary a proceeding, which would have shewed very handsomly to the world, (and according to the Character give[n] of her piety etc) and consonant to her husbands first Declaration, that there was no intention of Deposing the King, but of Succoring the Nation; But, nothing of all this appeared; she came into W-hall as to Wedding, riant and jolly, so as seeming to be quite Transported: rose early on the next morning of her arrival, and in her undresse (as reported) before her women were up; went about from roome to roome, to see the Convenience of White-hall: Lay in the same bed and appartment where the late Queene lay: and within a night or two, sate down to play at Basset, as the Q. her predecessor us'd to do: smiled upon and talked to every body; so as no manner of change seem'd in Court, since his Majesties last going away, save that the infinite crowds of people thronged to see her, and that she went to our prayers.

[135] Whitehall Palace burnt down (1698); from a contemporary account quoted in *The Annals of London* by J. Richardson.

A Dutch woman, who belonged to Colonel Stanley's lodgings which were near and joining to the Earl of

Portland's house in Whitehall, having a sudden occasion
to dry some linen in an upper room, for expedition sake
lighted a good quantity of charcoal and carelessly left the
linen hanging round about it, which took fire in her
absence, to such a degree that it not only consumed the
linen, but had seized the hangings, wainscots, beds, and
whatnot, and flamed and smoked in such a violent manner, that it put all the inhabitants thereabouts into conster-
nation ... in an instant (as it were) the merciless and
devouring flames got such an advantage, that, notwithstanding the great endeavours used by the water-engines,
numerous assistance, and blowing up houses to the number of about twenty, it still increased with great fury and
violence all night, till about eight of the clock next morning, at which time it was extinguished after it had burnt
down and consumed about one hundred and fifty houses,
most of which were lodgings and habitations of the chief
of the nobility.

[136] Whitehall during the Blitz (1940s); from *Their
Finest Hour* by W. Churchill.

When the bombardment first began the idea was to treat
it with disdain. In the West End everybody went about
their business and pleasure and dined and slept as they
usually did. The theatres were full, and the darkened
streets were crowded with casual traffic. All this was
perhaps a healthy reaction from the frightful squawk
which the defeatist elements in Paris had put up on the
occasion when they were first seriously raided in May. I
remember dining in a small company when very lively and
continuous raids were going on. The large windows of
Stornoway House opened upon the Green Park, which
flickered with the flashes of the guns and was occasionally
lit by the glare of an exploding bomb. I felt that we were
taking unnecessary risks. After dinner we went to the
Imperial Chemicals building overlooking the Embankment. From these high stone balconies there was a splendid view of the river. At least a dozen fires were burning

on the south side, and while we were there several heavy
bombs fell, one near enough for my friends to pull me
back behind a substantial stone pillar. This certainly confirmed my opinion that we should have to accept many
restrictions upon the ordinary amenities of life.

The group of Government buildings around Whitehall
were repeatedly hit. Downing Street consists of houses two
hundred and fifty years old, shaky and lightly built by the
profiteering contractor whose name they bear. At the time
of the Munich alarm shelters had been constructed for the
occupants of No. 10 and No. 11, and the rooms on the
garden level had had their ceilings propped up with a
wooden under-ceiling and strong timbers. It was believed
that this would support the ruins if the building was blown
or shaken down; but of course neither these rooms nor the
shelters were effective against a direct hit. During the last
fortnight of September preparations were made to transfer
my Ministerial headquarters to the more modern and solid
Government offices looking over St James's Park by
Storey's Gate. These quarters we called 'the Annexe'.
Below them were the War Room and a certain amount of
bomb-proof sleeping accommodation. The bombs at this
time were of course smaller than those of the later phases.
Still, in the interval before the new apartments were ready
life at Downing Street was exciting. One might as well
have been at a battalion headquarters in the line . . .

Another evening (October 14) stands out in my mind.
We were dining in the garden-room of No. 10 when the
usual night raid began. My companions were Archie Sin-
clair, Oliver Lyttelton, and Moore-Brabazon. The steel
shutters had been closed. Several loud explosions occurred
around us at no great distance, and presently a bomb fell,
perhaps a hundred yards away, on the Horse Guards
Parade, making a great deal of noise. Suddenly I had a
providential impulse. The kitchen at No. 10 Downing
Street is lofty and spacious, and looks out through a large
plate-glass window about twenty-five feet high. The butler
and parlourmaid continued to serve the dinner with complete detachment, but I became acutely aware of this big

window, behind which Mrs Landemare, the cook, and the kitchen-maid, never turning a hair, were at work. I got up abruptly, went into the kitchen, told the butler to put the dinner on the hot plate in the dining-room, and ordered the cook and the other servants into the shelter, such as it was. I had been seated again at table only about three minutes when a really very loud crash, close at hand, and a violent shock showed that the house had been struck. My detective came into the room and said much damage had been done. The kitchen, the pantry, and the offices on the Treasury side were shattered.

We went into the kitchen to view the scene. The devastation was complete. The bomb had fallen fifty yards away on the Treasury, and the blast had smitten the large, tidy kitchen, with all its bright saucepans and crockery, into a heap of black dust and rubble. The big plate-glass window had been hurled in fragments and splinters across the room, and would of course have cut its occupants, if there had been any, to pieces. But my fortunate inspiration, which I might so easily have neglected, had come in the nick of time. The underground Treasury shelter across the court had been blown to pieces by a direct hit, and the three civil servants who were doing Home Guard night-duty there were killed. All however were buried under tons of brick rubble, and we did not know who was missing.

As the raid continued and seemed to grow in intensity we put on our tin hats and went out to view the scene from the top of the Annexe buildings. Before doing so, however, I could not resist taking Mrs Landemare and the others from the shelter to see their kitchen. They were upset at the sight of the wreck, but principally on account of the general untidiness!

Archie and I went up to the cupola of the Annexe building. The night was clear and there was a wide view of London. It seemed that the greater part of Pall Mall was in flames. At least five fierce fires were burning there, and others in St James's Street and Piccadilly. Farther back over the river in the opposite direction there were many conflagrations. But Pall Mall was the vivid flame-picture. Gradually the attack died down, and presently the 'All Clear' sounded, leaving only the blazing fires. We went downstairs to my new apartments on the first floor of the Annexe, and there found Captain David Margesson, the Chief Whip, who was accustomed to live at the Carlton Club. He told us the club had been blown to bits, and indeed we had thought, by the situation of the fires, that it must have been hit. He was in the club with about two hundred and fifty members and staff. It had been struck by a heavy bomb. The whole of the façade and the massive coping on the Pall Mall side had fallen into the street, obliterating his motor-car, which was parked near the front door. The smoking-room had been full of members, and the whole ceiling had come down upon them. When I looked at the ruins next day it seemed incredible that most of them should not have been killed. However, by what seemed a miracle, they had all crawled out of the dust, smoke, and rubble, and though many were injured not a single life was lost. When in due course these facts came to the notice of the Cabinet our Labour colleagues facetiously remarked: 'The devil looks after his own.' Mr Quintin Hogg had carried his father, a former Lord Chancellor, on his shoulders from the wreck, as Æneas had borne Pater Anchises from the ruins of Troy. Margesson had nowhere to sleep, and we found him blankets and a bed in the basement of the Annexe. Altogether it was a lurid evening, and considering the damage to buildings it was remarkable that there were not more than five hundred people killed and about a couple of thousand injured.

The Houses of Parliament

[137] Elizabeth I opens Parliament (1584); from *A Journey through England & Scotland* by L. Von Wedel.

The Queen has reigned already twenty-six years, and during her reign Parliament has never been held. This year she enters her fifty-third year, as it is said, and she has sent orders through the whole realm to convoke Parliament. The principal cause is, I am told, that the English do not wish the King of Scotland, who is the next to the throne, to be King of England, and wish to know who after the queen's death is to wear the crown. I have forgotten the exact date, but I believe the opening of Parliament took place on 25 November. All the streets and lanes in Westminster were well cleaned and strewn with sand when the queen made her entrance into the house, for it is a custom that on the first and last day of the session the king or queen shall be present in the assembly. At the head of the procession rode, two by two, eighteen lords and gentlemen of the court, after them fifteen trumpets, two gentlemen, each with 100 soldiers uniformly clad; now came fifteen members of Parliament in long red cloth coats, lined with white rabbit and reverses of the same almost down to the girdle. Next followed two gentlemen, the first with the queen's mantle, the other with her hat, their horses were led by servants. Now came two heralds, each in a blue mantle with two wings on it of beaten gold bearing the queen's arms, then three pairs of gentlemen of the Parliament in their usual robes, two heralds like those before followed by thirteen gentlemen of the Parliament, counts and barons, like the former, two heralds, seven pairs of bishops in long red robes with broad reverses of white linen and square caps of black stuff on their heads, then came five pairs of gentlemen of the Parliament in long red coats set with four stripes of rabbit fur. Now followed the Chancellor of the realm, behind him the Treasurer and the Secretary in their usual robes, with broad golden collars hanging down in the front and back to the saddle. Followed four men with sceptres, each ornamented with a crown, followed some gentlemen of the Parliament like the others. All these, I have mentioned, had gold and silver trappings on their horses, the least valuable being velvet. Followed the huntsmen, about fifty in number, all of noble birth, with small spears. These marched on foot. Now followed a horse, led by a gentleman, the trappings, saddle and bridle all of gold covered with pearls, the latter being set with precious stones. On the forehead an ornament was fixed with one large diamond, and on the ears hung pearls. Now followed the queen in a half-covered sedan chair, which looked like a half-covered Bed. The chair and the cushions on which the queen was seated were covered with gold and silver cloth. The queen had a long red velvet parliamentary mantle, down to the waist, lined with ermine, white with little black dots, and a crown on her head. The sedan chair was carried by two cream-coloured horses with yellow manes and tails, on the heads and tails yellow and white plumes were fastened, and they had saddles and trappings of golden stuff. Behind the queen another horse was led, having trappings of red velvet fringed with gold and ornamented with plumes ... On both sides of the queen marched her guard, not in their daily suit, but clad in red cloth, covered with beaten gold. The procession took its way to Westminster Church, where all the kings are buried. Here the queen dismounted, knelt down at the entrance and said her prayers, entered the church, where prayers were offered and chants performed. Then the queen went to the house of Parliament close by, and was led into a separate chamber, on the platform of which was a splendid canopy of golden stuff and velvet, embroidered with gold, silver and pearls, and below it a throne, arranged with royal splendours, on which the queen seated herself. The benches in this chamber had their seats as well as the backs covered with red silk, in the midst four woolsacks of red cloth were laid square. The walls were entirely hung with royal tapestry. In front of the woolsacks opposite the door a low bar was fixed right across the chamber, also covered with red silk. On the woolsack nearest to the queen's throne sits the Chancellor, turning his back to the queen, on that to the right hand sit three judges, on that to the left three secretaries. Close to the bar, but outside of it, sit two [writing] clerks, on the benches around to the right side twenty bishops, two viscounts or peers, one marquis, to the left twenty counts and twenty barons. Thus the sitting of this Parliament began, they had sittings every day until Christmas, but the queen, as I said before, was present only on the first and last day. During the holy feast the sitting was suspended, but afterwards it began again and lasted until Easter, when it was again suspended, though not closed, and was to begin again.

[138] The Gunpowder Plot (1605); from *Confession of Guido Fawkes*.

I confesse, that a practise in generall was first broken unto me, against his Maiestie for reliefe of the Catholic cause, and not invented or propounded by my selfe. And this was first propounded unto mee about Easter Last was twelve moneth beyond the seas, in the Lowe Countreys of the *Archdukes* obeisance, by *Thomas Winter*, who came thereupon with mee into England, and there we imparted our purpose to three other Gentlemen more, namely, *Robert Catesby*, *Thomas Percy* and *Iohn Wright*, who all five consulting together of the means how to execute the same, and taking a vow among our selves for secrecie, *Catesby* propounded to have it performed by Gunpowder, and by making a Myne under the upper House of Parliament: which place wee made a choice of the rather because Religion having been unjustly suppressed there, it was fittest that Iustice and punishment should be executed there.

This being resolved amongst us, *Thomas Percy* hired an House at Westminster for that purpose, neere adioyning to the Parliament House, and there we begun to make our Myne about 11 December 1604.

The five that first entered into the worke were *Thomas Percy*, *Thomas Catesby*, *Thomas Winter*, *Iohn Wright* and myselfe: and soone after wee tooke another unto us, *Christopher Wright* having Sworne him also, and taken the Sacrament for secrecie.

When we came to the very foundation of the Wall of the House, which was about three yards thicke, and found it a matter of great difficultie, wee tooke unto us another Gentleman *Robert Winter*, in like maner with oath and sacrament as afore said.

It was about Christmas when we brought our myne unto the Wall, and about Candlemas we had wrought the wall halfe through: and whilst they were in working, I stood as Sentinell to descrie any man that came neere, whereof I gave them warning, and so they ceased untill I gave notice againe to proceede.

All we seven lay in the House, and had Shot and Powder, being resolved to die in that place before we should yield or be taken. As they were working upon the wall they heard a rushing in the Cellar of remooving of

Coales, whereupon we feared we had been discovered: and they sent me to go to the Cellar, who finding that the Coales were a-selling and that the Cellar was to bee let, viewing the commoditie thereof for our purpose, *Percy* went and hired the same for yeerely rent.

We had before this provided and brought into the House twentie Barrels of Powder, which we remooved into the Cellar, and covered the same with Billets and Faggots, which were provided for that purpose.

About Easter, the Parliament being prorogued till October next, we dispersed ourselves and I retired into the Low countreys by advice and direction of the rest, as well to aquaint *Owen* with the particulars of the Plot, as also lest by my longer stay I might have growen suspicious, and so have come in question.

In the meantime *Percy* having the key of the Cellar, laide in more Powder and wood into it. I returned about the beginning of September next, and then receiving the key againe of Percy, we brought in more Powder and Billets to cover the same againe, and so I went for a time into the Countrey till the 30 of October.

It was a further resolve amongst us that the same day that this act should have been performed, some other of our Confederates should have surprised the person of Lady Elizabeth the King's eldest daughter, who was kept in Warwickshire at Lo. *Harrington's* house, and presently have her proclaimed as Queen, having a project of a Proclamation ready for that purpose, wherein we made no mention of altering of Religion, nor would have avowed the deede to be ours, untill we should have had power enough to make our partie good and then we would have avowed both.

Concerning Duke Charles, the King's second sonne, wee had sundry consultations how to seise on his Person. But because we found no means how to compasse it (the Duke being kept neere London, where we had not Forces y-nough) we resolved to serve our turn with the Lady Elizabeth.

THE NAMES OF OTHER PRINCIPALL
persons, that were made privy
afterwards to this horrible
conspiracie

Everard Digby, Knight
Ambrose Rookwood
Francis Tresham
John Grant
Robert Keyes

[139] Charles I attempts to arrest five members of Parliament (1642); from *Historical Collections.*

They were no sooner in their places but the House was informed by one Captain Langrish, lately an officer in arms in France, that he came from among the officers and soldiers at Whitehall, and understanding by them that His Majesty was coming with a guard of military men, commanders and soldiers, to the House of Commons, he passed by them with some difficulty to get to the House before them, and sent in word how near the said officers and soldiers were come: whereupon a certain member of the House having also private information from the Countess of Carlisle, sister to the Earl of Northumberland, that endeavours would be used this day to apprehend the five Members, the House required the five Members to depart the House forthwith, to the end to avoid combustion in the House, if the said soldiers should use violence to pull any of them out. To which command of the House four of the said Members yielded ready obedience, but Mr Stroud was obdurate, till Sir Walter Earle (his ancient acquaintance) pulled him out by force, the King being at that time entering into the New-Palace-Yard in Westminster; and as His Majesty came through Westminster Hall, the Commanders, Reformadoes, &c that attended him made a lane on both sides the Hall, (through which His Majesty passed and came up the stairs to the House of Commons) and stood before the guard of Pensioners and

Halberdiers (who also attended the King's person), and the door of the H.o.C. being thrown open, His Majesty entered the House, and as he passed up towards the Chair, he cast his eye on the right hand near the Bar of the House, where Mr Pim used to sit; but His Majesty not seeing him there (knowing him well) went up to the Chair and said, '*By your leave, (Mr Speaker) I must borrow your chair a little*'; whereupon the Speaker came out of the Chair and His Majesty stepped up into it; after he had stood in the Chair a while, casting his eye upon the Members as they stood up uncovered, but could not discern any of the five Members to be there, nor indeed were they easy to be discerned (had they been there) among so many bare faces all standing up together.

Then His Majesty made this speech,

'Gentlemen,

I am sorry for this occasion of coming unto you. Yesterday I sent a Sergeant at Arms upon a very important occasion, to apprehend some that by my command were accused of High Treason; whereunto I did expect obedience and not a message. And I must declare unto you here, that albeit no King that ever was in England shall be more careful of your privileges, to maintain them to the uttermost of his power, than I shall be; yet you must know that in cases of treason no person hath a privilege. And therefore I am come to know if any of these persons that were accused are here. For I must tell you, gentlemen, that so long as these persons whom I have accused (for no light crime but for treason) are here, I cannot expect that this House will be in the right way that I do heartily wish for it. Therefore I am come to tell you that I must have them wheresoever I find them. Well, since I see all the birds are flown, I do expect from you that you shall send them unto me as soon as they return hither. But I assure you, on the word of a King, I never did intend any force, but shall proceed against them in a legal and fair way, for I never meant any other.

And now, since I see I cannot do what I came for, I think this no unfit occasion to repeat what I have said formerly, that whatsoever I have done in favour and to the good of my subjects, I do mean to maintain it.

I will trouble you no more, but tell you I expect as soon as they come to the House, you will send them to me; otherwise I must take my own course to find them.'

When the King was looking about the House, the Speaker standing below by the Chair, His Majesty asked him whether any of these persons were in the House, whether he saw any of them? And where were they? To which the Speaker, falling on his knee, thus answered: 'May it please your Majesty I have neither eyes to see, nor tongue to speak in this place, but as the House is pleased to direct me, whose servant I am here: and humbly beg your Majesty's pardon that I cannot give any other answer than this to what your Majesty is pleased to demand of me.'

The King having concluded his speech went out of the House again, which was in great disorder, and many members cried out aloud, so as he might hear them, Privilege! Privilege! and forthwith adjourned till the next day at one of the clock.

[140] A riot in the house (1648); from *The Clarke papers* by J. Barkstead.

May itt please your Excellency, This day was a petition presented to the Commons from the County of Surrey by neere 3000 Horse and Foote. They came to the House about 12 of the clock, and after they had staid about 3 houres they began to express much discontent that they had nott an answer, some of them saying, that they would have an answer, others that they would have such an answer as should please them. Att last they cried out with a loude acclamation, 'For God, and Kinge Charles', and soe crowding towards the doore disarm'd and knock't downe some of the sentinells, indeavouring to have surprized the whole (guard), saying, 'wee will pull them out by the eares'. Butt I having a very watchfull eye over them, and being very unwilling to give them any just occasion,

nyett seeing their outrage went thus farre, I sent downe a
partie of about 500, which came in very seasonably, for
as they came, the petitioners had begun to force the guard,
att which began a present engagement with them, in which
two of our men were kill'd, and 4 or 5 of the Enemy. The
businesse was soone over. My Lord, I am informed by
some that is amongst them this night, that they resolve to
fall on those of Col. Harrison's regiment which quarter
with them, by way of revenge. No more butt that I am
and ever shall bee, Your Excellencies most humble and
faithful servant.

[141] The Assassination of Spencer Perceval (1812); from *The Autobiography of W. Jerdan*, Vol I.

On 11 May, 1812 . . . about 5 o'clock . . . I had walked
down to the House to listen, in my turn, to the intermi-
nable debates in Committee on the Orders in Council,
which were very briefly reported in the newspapers. On
ascending the broad flight of steps which led to the folding
door of the lobby, I perceived the minister, with whom I
had the honour of a slight acquaintance, immediately
behind me, with his light and lithesome step following in
the same direction. I saluted him, and was saluted in
return, with that benevolent smile which I was so instantly
destined to see effaced for ever, and pushing open and
holding back the half door, to allow the precedence of
entering, I of course made way for him to go in.

He did enter, and there was an instant noise, but as a
physical fact it is very remarkable to state that, though I
was all but touching him, and if the ball had passed
through his body it must have lodged in mine, *I did not
hear* the report of the pistol. It is true it was fired in the
inside of the lobby, and I was just out of it; but, considering our close proximity, I have always found it difficult to
account for the phenomenon I have noticed. I saw a small
curling wreath of smoke rise above his head, as if the
breath of a cigar; I saw him reel back against the ledge on
the inside of the door; I heard him exclaim, 'Oh God!' or

'Oh my God!' and nothing more or longer (as reported by several witnesses), for even that exclamation was faint; and then making an impulsive rush, as it were, to reach the entrance to the house on the opposite side for safety, I saw him totter forward, not half way, and drop dead between the four pillars which stood there in the centre of the space, with a slight trace of blood issuing from his lips.

All this took place ere with moderate speed you could count five! Great confusion, and almost as immediately great alarm ensued. Loud cries were uttered, and rapidly conflicting orders and remarks on every hand made a perfect Babel of the scene; for there were above a score of people in the lobby, and on the instant no one seemed to know what had been done, or by whom. The corse of Mr Perceval was lifted up by Mr William Smith, the member for Norwich, assisted by Lord Francis Osborne, a Mr Phillips, and several others, and borne into the office of the Speaker's Secretary, by the small passage on the left hand, beyond and near the fire-place. – It must have been, pallid and deadly, close by the murderer; for in a moment after Mr Eastaff, one of the clerks of the Vote Office, at the last door on that side, pointed him out, and called 'That is the murderer!' Bellingham moved slowly to a bench on the hither side of the fire-place, near at hand, and sat down. I had in the first instance run forward to render assistance to Mr Perceval, but only witnessed the lifting of his body, followed the direction of Mr Eastaff's hand, and seized the assassin by the collar, but without violence on one side, or resistance on the other.

[142] The trial of Queen Caroline in the House of Lords (1820); from *The trial of Her Majesty Caroline Queen of Britain*.

The House of Peers, in pursuance of a previous order, assembled, in their legislative-judicial capacity, on Thursday, 17 August 1820, to resume their proceedings on the Bill of Pains and Penalties against her majesty the queen.

The lord high chancellor of England, as speaker of the

house, arrived, and took his seat upon the woolsack at half-past eight o'clock.

The lord bishop of Landaff, as the junior bishop, then read prayers.

As ten o'clock approached, the peers arrived in considerable numbers. The lord chief justice of the king's bench, the lord chief justice of the common pleas, the lord chief baron of the exchequer, and other of the venerable judges who had arrived in town from their circuits, took their seats on the right and left of the lord chancellor . . .

During the calling over of the names of the peers, the shouts of the people in Palace-yard announced the arrival of the queen. In a short time she entered by the passage leading from the robing-room, which is situated on the left hand of the throne. Her majesty was accompanied by lady Ann Hamilton, who, with lord Archibald Hamilton, stood close to her during the whole of the day. She was seated in an arm-chair on the left of the throne, and within the space allotted to the members of the House of Commons. On her entrance all the peers rose to receive her; she testified her feelings by a graceful obeisance, and, though evidently much affected by the novel scene to which she was introduced, took her seat with becoming grace and dignity. She was dressed in black sarsnet, very richly trimmed with lace; a large white veil partially concealed her features, and, falling in a tasteful drapery on her bosom, rendered her figure when she rose from her chair, not merely interesting, but highly commanding.

The preliminary business having been gone through, –

The Earl of LIVERPOOL moved, that the order of the day for the second reading of the Bill of Pains and Penalties be now read.

The Duke of LEINSTER, in conformity to his notice on a former day, rose to oppose the measure, and moved, 'that the said order be now rescinded.'

On division the motion was negatived, there being contents 41, and non-contents 206.

The bill, of which the subjoined is a copy, was then read a second time.

BILL to deprive Her Majesty CAROLINE AMELIA ELIZABETH of the Title, Prerogatives, Rights, Privileges, and Pretensions of Queen Consort of this Realm, and to dissolve the Marriage between His Majesty and the said Queen.

WHEREAS in the year one thousand eight hundred and fourteen, her Majesty, Caroline Amelia Elizabeth, then Princess of Wales, and now Queen Consort of this realm, being at Milan, in Italy, engaged in her service, in a menial situation, one Bartolomo Pergami, otherwise Bartolomo Bergami, a foreigner of low station, who had before served in a similar capacity:

And whereas after the said Bartolomo Pergami, otherwise Bartolomo Bergami, had so entered the service of her royal highness the said princess of Wales, a most unbecoming and degrading intimacy commenced between her royal highness and the said Bartolomo Pergami, otherwise Bartolomo Bergami:

And whereas her royal highness not only advanced the said Bartolomo Pergami, otherwise Bartolomo Bergami, to a high situation in her royal highness's household, and received into her service many of his near relations, some of them in inferior, and others in high and confidential situations about her royal highness's person, but bestowed upon him other great and extraordinary marks of favour and distinction, obtained for him orders of knighthood, and titles of honour, and conferred upon him a pretended order of knighthood, which her royal highness had taken upon herself to institute without any just and lawful authority:

And whereas her said royal highness, whilst the said Bartolomo Pergami, otherwise Bartolomo Bergami, was in her said service, further unmindful of her exalted rank and station, and of her duty to your majesty, and wholly regardless of her own honour and character, conducted herself towards the said Bartolomo Pergami, otherwise Bartolomo Bergami, and in other respects, both in public and private, in the various places and countries which her royal highness visited, with indecent and offensive familiarity and freedom, and carried on a licentious, disgraceful, and adulterous intercourse with the said Bartolomo Pergami, otherwise Bartolomo Bergami, which continued for a long period of time during her royal highness's residence abroad, by which conduct of her said royal highness, great scandal and dishonour have been brought upon your majesty's family and this kingdom ;

Therefore, to manifest our deep sense of such scandalous, disgraceful, and vicious conduct on the part of her said majesty, by which she has violated the duty she owed to your majesty, and has rendered herself unworthy of the exalted rank and station of queen consort of this realm, and to evince our just regard for the dignity of the crown, and the honour of this nation, we, your majesty's most dutiful and loyal subjects, the Lords Spiritual and Temporal and Commons in Parliament assembled, do hereby entreat your majesty, that it may be enacted;

And be it enacted, by the king's most excellent majesty, by and with the advice and consent of the Lords Spiritual and Temporal and Commons in this present Parliament assembled, and by the authority of the same, that her said majesty Caroline Amelia Elizabeth, from and after the passing of this Act, shall be and is hereby deprived of the title of queen, and of all the prerogatives, rights, privileges, and exemptions appertaining to her as queen consort of this realm; and that her said majesty shall, from and after the passing of this Act, for ever be disabled and rendered incapable of using, exercising, and enjoying the same, or any of them; and moreover, that the marriage between his majesty and the said Caroline Amelia Elizabeth be and the same is hereby from henceforth for ever wholly dissolved, annulled, and made void to all intents, constructions, and purposes whatsoever.

[143] Passing of the Reform Bill (1831); from *The Life and Letters of Lord Macaulay*.

I HAVE little news for you, except what you will learn from the papers as well as from me. It is clear that the Reform Bill must pass, either in this or in another Parliament. The majority of one does not appear to me, as it does to you, by any means inauspicious. We should perhaps have had a better plea for a dissolution if the majority had been the other way. But surely a dissolution under such circumstances would have been a most alarming thing. If there should be a dissolution now, there will not be that ferocity in the public mind which there would have been if the House of Commons had refused to entertain the Bill at all. I confess that, till we had a majority, I was half inclined to tremble at the storm which we had raised. At present I think that we are absolutely certain of victory, and of victory without commotion.

Such a scene as the division of last Tuesday I never saw, and never expect to see again. If I should live fifty years, the impression of it will be as fresh and sharp in my mind as if it had just taken place. It was like seeing Caesar stabbed in the Senate House, or seeing Oliver taking the mace from the table; a sight to be seen only once, and never to be forgotten. The crowd overflowed the House in every part. When the strangers were cleared out, and the doors locked, we had six hundred and eight members present, – more by fifty-five than ever were in a division before. The Ayes and Noes were like two volleys of cannon from the opposite sides of a field of battle. When the Opposition went out into the lobby, an operation which took up twenty minutes or more, we spread ourselves over the benches on both sides of the House: for there were many of us who had not been able to find a seat during the evening. When the doors were shut we began to speculate on our numbers. Everybody was desponding. 'We have lost it. We are only two hundred and eighty at most. I do not think we are two hundred and fifty. They are three hundred. Alderman Thompson has counted them. He says they are two hundred and ninety-nine.' This was the talk on our benches. I wonder that men who have been long in Parliament do not acquire a better coup d'oeil for numbers. The House, when only the ayes were in it, looked to me a very fair House, – much fuller than it generally is even on debates of considerable interest. I had no hope, however, of three hundred. As the tellers passed along our lowest row on the left hand side the interest was insupportable, – two hundred and ninety-one, – two hundred and ninety-two, – we were all standing up and stretching forward, telling with the tellers. At three hundred there was a short cry of joy, – at three hundred and two another, – suppressed however in a moment: for we did not yet know what the hostile force might be. We knew, however, that we could not be severely beaten. The doors were thrown open, and in they came. Each of them, as he entered, brought some different report of their numbers. It must have been impossible, as you may conceive, in the lobby, crowded as they were, to form any exact estimate. First we heard that they were three hundred and three; then that number rose to three hundred and ten; then went down to three hundred and seven. Alexander Barry told me that he had counted, and that they were three hundred and four. We were all breathless with anxiety, when Charles Wood, who stood nearest the door, jumped up on a bench and cried out, 'They are only three hundred and one.' We set up a shout that you might have heard to Charing Cross, waving our hats, stamping against the floor, and clapping our hands. The tellers scarcely got through the crowd: for the House was thronged up to the table, and all the floor was fluctuating with heads like the pit of a theatre. But you might have heard a pin drop as Duncannon read the numbers. Then again the shouts broke out, and many of us shed tears. I could scarcely refrain. And the jaw of Peel fell; and the face of Twiss was as the face of a damned soul; and Herries looked like Judas taking his necktie off for the last operation. We shook hands, and clapped each other on the back, and went out laughing, crying, and huzzaing into the lobby.

[144] The burning of Parliament (1834); from *Letters and Memorials* by T. Carlyle, edited by J. A. Froude.

I SAW the fire of the two Parliament Houses; and, what was curious enough, Matthew Allan found me out in the crowd there, whom I had not seen for years. The crowd was quiet, rather pleased than otherwise; *whew'd* and whistled when the breeze came as if to encourage it: 'there's a *flare-up* (what we call *shine*) for the House o' Lords.' – 'A judgment for the Poor Law Bill!' – 'There go their *hacts*' (acts)! Such exclamations seemed to be the prevailing ones. A man *sorry* I did not anywhere see.

[145] The suffragettes in Parliament Square (1908); from *The Suffragette* by E. S. Pankhurst.

Meanwhile, the W. S. P. U. again and again urged Mr Asquith to receive a deputation, but he still refused, and at last he was informed that the deputation would start from the Women's Parliament on 30 June, and would wait upon him at the House of Commons at half past four that afternoon. Once more he returned a refusal to see the women, but Mrs Pankhurst herself replied, as their leader, that the deputation would arrive at the appointed hour. Next day Mrs Pankhurst, Mrs Pethick Lawrence and eleven other women set out from the Caxton Hall. At the main entrance of the building Superintendent Wells was waiting with a body of some twenty constables and, at his orders, as soon as the thirteen women had emerged, the doors were locked and even the Pressmen begged in vain to be released. Then the Superintendent constituted himself the leader and protector of the deputation and led them quickly through the cheering crowds who pressed forward pushing and struggling to catch a glimpse of the little band of women. Straight up Victoria Street he led them and right to the door of the Stranger's Entrance where they were met by the burly and familiar form of Inspector Scantlebury surrounded by his minions. He stepped forward and addressed Mrs Pankhurst gravely, 'Are you Mrs Pankhurst, and is this your deputation?' he asked. She answered, 'Yes,' and he said, 'I have orders to exclude you from the House of Commons.' 'Has Mr Asquith received my letter?' she questioned him in turn, and, replying, 'Yes,' the Inspector drew the document from his pocket, adding in response to a further inquiry, that Mr Asquith had sent no message of any kind by way of reply. Then Inspector Scantlebury turned away and walked into the House, leaving behind him a strong force of police to guard the door. For an instant or two the women stood there baffled, but they had to remember the resolve that this effort to interview the Prime Minister should be entirely peaceful. Moreover, there was the Mass Meeting of the evening. They therefore merely turned and made their way back to the Caxton Hall. Meanwhile larger and larger crowds were flocking towards Parliament from every direction, and long before eight o'clock, the time at which they had been asked to assemble, it was estimated by the newspapers that more than 100,000 people had collected in Parliament Square. The police had made most extensive preparations to prevent any meeting being held and it was said that more than 5,000 ordinary constables and upwards of fifty mounted men had been requisitioned for this purpose.

When, at eight o'clock, the women sallied forth in groups from the Caxton Hall to speak to the great multitude that had assembled in response to their appeal, the scene was already becoming turbulent. There were no platforms to speak from, and it would have been useless to provide them, for the police would instantly have dragged them from the ground. But it is possible to hold a meeting without official sanction and to make speeches without platforms and the women bravely essayed the task. Some of them clung to the railings of Palace Yard to raise themselves above the crowd, others mounted the steps of the offices in Broad Sanctuary, others the steps of the Government buildings at the top of Parliament Street opposite the Abbey, whilst others again merely spoke from the pavement wherever and whenever the police would cease for an instant from driving them along. Every woman who attempted to speak was torn by the harrying constables from the spot where she had found a foothold and was either hurled aside and flung into the dense masses that were being kept constantly on the move or placed under arrest. Meanwhile, the crowd was always surging and swaying forward shouting out mingled cheers and jeers.

Some groups of the men stood with linked arms around the women who were striving to make speeches, bodies of others pushed little band of Suffragettes forward against the rows of constables with cries of 'Votes of Women,' 'we'll get you to the House of Commons,' and 'back up the women and push them through!' Again and again the police lines were broken and again and again the mounted men charged and beat the people back. Mr Lloyd George, Mr Winston Churchill, Mr Herbert Gladstone, Lord Rosebery and other members of both Houses stood in Palace Yard, and near the Strangers' entrance watching the scene. As it became dark the disorder grew, and gangs of roughs who supported neither the government nor the women kept making concerted rushes, sweeping the rest of the people on before them, absolutely heedless of trampling others under foot. In some cases isolated women were surrounded by them and with difficulty rescued from their ill treatment by the soberer and more respectable members of the gathering. But, undaunted either by violence from the roughs or from the police, the Suffragettes, though their slight frames were bruised and almost worn out by the constant battering of those who were so much heavier, stronger and more numerous than themselves, still continued to address the throng. Every woman who was arrested was followed to the police station by a stream of cheering people and was saluted with raised hats and waving handkerchiefs.

As Mr Asquith passed from the House of Commons to Downing Street in his motor-car he was hooted by the crowd. He arrived home to find his windows broken, for

Mrs Leigh and Mrs New had driven swiftly past the guardian policemen at the entrance to the street in a taxicab and had each thrown two small stones through two of the lower windows of Number 10 before an arm of the Law had been stretched out to drag them away to Canon Row. Meanwhile Miss Mary Phillips had endeavoured to dash into the House of Commons by way of Palace Yard in the midst of a little company of Parliamentary waitresses but half way across the Yard had been seized and dragged back. Miss Lena Lambert had chartered a little rowing boat and had set off in the darkness to reach the House from the river side. Crowds of Members were lounging on the lighted terrace that hot summer's night when she and her little craft appeared out of the darkness, to urge them to determine that the simple measure of justice, which was being so hardly fought for, should be carried into law. But not many words had she spoken, when the police boats swooped down on her and she was towed away, lest she should irritate and annoy the people's representatives by telling them of the battle whose dull roar nothing could shut out.

So the night wore on and that weary fight continued. Not until twelve o'clock did the police at last succeed in clearing the streets, and it was then found that twenty-nine women had been arrested.

LONDON LIFE,
CUSTOMS,
MORALS

London Characters

[146] Dick Whittington c.16th; from *Chronicles* by R. Holinshed.

In this kings time, and in the eighth yeare of his reigne . . . a worthie citizen of London named Richard Whitington, mercer and alderman, was elected maior of the said citie, and bare that office three times. This man so bestowed his goods and substance, that he hath well deserved to be registred in chronicles. First he erected one house or church in London to be a house of praier, and named the same after his owne name, Whitington college, remaining at this daie. In the said church, besides certeine preests and clearks, he placed a number of poore aged men and women, builded for them houses and lodgings, and allowed them wood, coles, cloth, and weekelie monie to their great releefe and comfort. This man also at his owne cost builded the gate of London called Newgate in the yeere of our Lord 1422, which before was a most ouglie and lothsome prison. He also builded more than the halfe of S. Bartholomews hospitall in west Smithfield. He builded likewise the beautifull librarie in the graie friers in London now called Christs hospitall, standing in the north part of the cloister thereof, where in the wall his armes be graven in stone. He also builded for the ease of the maior of London, his brethren, and the worshipfull citizens, on the solemne daies of their assemblie, a chapell adjoining to the Guildhall; to the intent that before they entered into anie of their worldlie affaires, they should begin with praier and invocation to God for his assistance.

[147] Samuel Pepys, The last diary entry (1669); from *Diaries*.

[Up] very betimes, and so continued all the morning, with W. Hewer, upon examining and stating my accounts, in order to the fitting myself[a] to go abroad beyond sea, which the ill condition of my eyes, and my neglect[b] for a year or two, hath kept me behindhand in, and so as to render it very difficult now, and troublesome to my mind to do it; but I this day made a satisfactory entrance therein. Dined at home, and in the afternoon by water to White-hall, calling[c] by the way at Michell's, where I have not been many a day till just the other day; and now I met her mother there and knew her husband to be out of town. And here yo did besar ella, but have not opportunity para[d] hazer mas with her[e] as I would have offered if yo had had[e] it. And thence had another meeting with the Duke of York at White-hall with the Duke of York on yesterday's work, and made a good advance; and so being called by my wife, we to the park, Mary Batelier, a Duch gentleman, a friend of hers, being[f] with us. Thence to the World's-end, a drinking-house by the park, and there merry; and so home late.

And thus ends all that I doubt I shall ever be able to do with my own eyes in the keeping of my journall, I being not able to do it any longer, having done now so long as to undo my eyes almost every time that I take a pen in my hand; and therefore, whatever comes of it, I must forbear;

and therefore resolve from this time forward to have it
kept by my people in long-hand, and must therefore be
contented to set down no more then is fit for them and all
the world to know; or if there be anything (which cannot
be much, now my amours to Deb^g are past, and my eyes
hindering me in almost all other pleasures), I must endeavour to keep a margin in my book open, to add here and
there a note in short-hand with my own hand. And so I
betake myself to that course which [is] almost as much as
to see myself go into my grave – for which, and all the
discomforts that will accompany my being blind, the good
God prepare me.

May. 31. 1669.   S.P.

[148] Charles Lamb, Letter to Wordsworth (1801); from *The Letters of Charles Lamb*.

I dont much care if I never see a mountain in my life. I
have passed all my days in London, until I have formed as
many and intense local attachments, as any of your moun-
taineers can have done with dead nature. The Lighted
shops of the Strand and Fleet Street, the innumerable
trades, tradesmen and customers, coaches, waggons, playhouses, all the bustle and wickedness round about Covent
Garden, the very women of the Town, the watchmen,
drunken scenes, rattles, – life awake, if you awake, at all
hours of the night, the impossibility of being dull in Fleet
Street, the crowds, the very dirt and mud, the Sun shining
upon houses and pavements, the print shops, the old book
stalls, parsons cheap'ning books, coffee houses, steams of
soup from kitchens, the pantomimes, London itself a
pantomime and a masquerade, – all these things work
themselves into my mind and feed me without a power of
satiating me. The wonder of these sights impells me into
nightwalks about the crowded streets, and I often shed
tears in the motley Strand from fulness of joy at so much
Life. – All these emotions must be strange to you. So are

your rural emotions to me. But consider, what must I have been doing all my life, not to have lent great portions of my heart with usury to such scenes? –

My attachments are local, purely local. I have no passion (or have had none since I was in love, and then it was the spurious engendering of poetry and books) to groves and vallies. The rooms where I was born, the furniture which has been before my eyes all my life, a book case which has followed me about (like a faithful dog, only exceeding him in knowledge) wherever I have moved, old tables, streets, squares, where I have sunned myself, my old school, – these are my mistresses. Have I not enough, without your mountains? I do not envy you. I should pity you, did I not know, that the Mind will make friends of any thing. Your sun and moon and skies and hills and lakes affect me no more, or scarcely come to me in more venerable characters, than as a gilded room with tapestry and tapers, where I live with handsome visible objects. I consider the clouds above me but as a roof, beautifully painted, but unable to satisfy the mind, and at last, like the pictures of the apartment of a connoisseur, unable to afford him any longer a pleasure. So fading upon me, from disuse, have been the Beauties of Nature, as they have been constantly called; so ever fresh and green and warm are all the inventions of men in this great city.

[149] Ann 1822; from *The Confessions of an English Opium Eater* by Thomas De Quincey.

This person was a young woman, and one of that unhappy class who belong to the outcasts and pariahs of our female population. I feel no shame, nor have any reason to feel it, in avowing that I was then on familiar and friendly terms with many women in that unfortunate condition . . . being myself, at that time, of necessity a peripatetic, or a walker of the streets, I naturally fell in more frequently with those peripatetics who are technically called street-walkers.

Some of these women had occasionally taken my part against watchmen who wished to drive me off the steps of houses where I was sitting; others had protected me against more serious aggressions. But one amongst them – the one on whose account I have at all introduced this subject – yet no! let me not class thee, O noble-minded Ann – with that order of women; let me find, if it be possible, some gentler name to designate the condition of her to whose bounty and compassion – ministering to my necessities when all the world stood aloof from me – I owe it that I am at this time alive. For many weeks I had walked, at nights, with this poor friendless girl up and down Oxford Street, or had rested with her on steps and under the shelter of porticos. She could not be so old as myself: she told me, indeed, that she had not completed her sixteenth year.

. . . That which she rendered to me, and which was greater than I could ever have repaid her, was this. One night, when we were pacing slowly along Oxford Street, and after a day when I had felt unusually ill and faint, I requested her to turn off with me into Soho Square. Thither we went; and we sat down on the steps of a house, which to this hour I never pass without a pang of grief, and an inner act of homage to the spirit of that unhappy girl, in memory of the noble act which she there performed. Suddenly, as we sat, I grew much worse. I had been leaning my head against her bosom, and all at once I sank from her arms, and fell backwards on the steps. From the sensations I then had, I felt an inner conviction of the liveliest kind, that, without some powerful and reviving stimulus, I should either have died on the spot, or should, at least, have sunk to a point of exhaustion from which all re-ascent, under my friendless circumstances, would soon have become hopeless. Then it was, at this crisis of my fate, that my poor orphan companion, who had herself met with little but injuries in this world, stretched out a saving hand to me. Uttering a cry of terror, but without a moment's delay, she ran off into Oxford Street, and, in less time than could be imagined, returned to me with a glass of port-wine and spices, that acted upon my empty stomach (which at that time would have rejected all solid food) with an instantaneous power of restoration; and for this glass the generous girl, without a murmur, paid out of her own humble purse, at a time, be it remembered when she had scarcely wherewithal to purchase the bare necessaries of life, and when she could have no reason to expect that I should ever be able to reimburse her. O youthful benefactress! how often in succeeding years, standing in solitary places, and thinking of thee with grief of heart and perfect love – how often have I wished that, as in ancient times the curse of a father was believed to have a supernatural power, and to pursue its object with a fatal necessity of self-fulfilment, even so the benediction of a heart oppressed with gratitude might have a like prerogative; might have power given it from above to chase, to haunt, to waylay, to pursue thee into the central darkness of a London brothel, or (if it were possible) even into the darkness of the grave, there to awaken thee with an authentic message of peace and forgiveness, and of final reconciliation!

Some feelings, though not deeper or more passionate, are more tender than others; and often when I walk, at this time, in Oxford Street by dreamy lamp-light, and hear those airs played on a common street-organ which years ago solaced me and my dear youthful companion, I shed tears, and muse with myself at the mysterious dispensation which so suddenly and so critically separated us for ever.

[150] Nollekens (1829); from *Nollekens and his Times* by J. T. Smith.

His singular and parsimonious habits were most observable in his domestic life. Coals were articles of great consideration with Mr Nollekens, and these he so rigidly economized, that they were always sent early, before his men came to work, in order that he might have leisure time for counting the sacks, and disposing of the large coals in what was originally designed by the builder of his house for a wine-cellar, so that he might lock them up for parlour use. Candles were never lighted at the commencement of the evening, and whenever they heard a knock at the door, they would wait until they heard a second rap, lest the first should have been a runaway, and their candle wasted. Mr and Mrs Nollekens used a flat candle-stick when there was any thing to be done; and I have been assured that a pair of moulds, by being well nursed, and put out when company went away, once lasted them a whole year! . . . a candle with Nollekens . . . was a serious article of consumption: indeed so much so, that he would frequently put it out, and, merely to save an inch or two, sit entirely in the dark, at times too when he was not in the least inclined to sleep. So keen was he in watching the use of that commodity, that whenever Bronze ventured into the yard with a light, he always scolded her for so shamefully flaring the candle. One evening, his man Dodimy, who then slept in the house, came home rather late, but quite sober enough to attempt to go up-stairs unheard without his shoes; but, as he was passing Nollekens's door, the immensely-increased shape of the key-hole shone upon the side of the room so brilliantly, that he cried out, 'Who's there?' 'It's only me, Sir,' answered Dodimy, 'I am going to bed.' – 'Going to bed, you extravagant rascal! why don't you go to bed in the dark, you scoundrel?' – 'It's my own candle,' replied Dodimy. 'Your own candle! Well, then, mind you don't set fire to yourself. Well, how did you come on at Lord George Cavendish's? You have been cleaning bustos there these six days; I told you, Dodimy, things could not be done so soon; – no, things are not to be done in a hurry, Master Dodimy.' – 'Lord bless you, Sir, I had some turtle-soup there to-day, and such ale!' 'Well, well, take care of yourself; I say things must not be done in a hurry.'

At the commencement of the French Revolution, when such immense numbers of Priests threw themselves upon the hospitality of this country, Nollekens was highly indignant at the great quantity of bread they consumed. 'Why, do you know, now,' said he, 'there's one of 'em living next door but one to me, that eats two whole quartern loaves a-day to his own share! and I am sure the fellow's body could not be bigger, if he was to eat up his blanket.'

Whenever Nollekens crossed the water, he always carried the money the waterman was to have for his fare, in his mouth: he kept it between his teeth, not in imitation of Egyptian mummies, whose mouths held a piece of gold to pay old Charon his fare, but in order that he might not, in getting out of the boat, lose his money by taking more out than he wanted . . .

One day, when Mr Nollekens was walking in Cavendish-square, attended by his man Dodimy, he desired him to take up some sop which a boy had just thrown out of a beer-pot, observing that it would make a nice dinner for his dog Cerberus. 'Lord, Sir! I take it up!' exclaimed Dodimy, 'what! in the sight of your friends, Lord Besborough and Lord Brownlow? See Sir, there's Mr Shee looking down at you. No, Sir, I would not do it, if you were even to *scratch me*!'

[151] Street Urchin; from *London Labour and the London Poor* by H. Mayhew (London, 1861).

Another boy, . . . gave me his notions of men and things. He was a thick-limbed, red-cheeked fellow; answered very freely, and sometimes, when I could not help laughing at his replies, laughed loudly himself, as if he entered into the joke.

Yes, he had heer'd of God who made the world. Couldn't exactly recollec' when he'd heer'd on him, but he had, most sarten-ly. Didn't know when the world was made, or how anybody could do it. It must have taken a long time. It was afore his time, 'or yourn either, sir.' Knew there was a book called the Bible; didn't know what it was about; didn't mind to know; knew of such a book to a sartinty, because a young 'oman took one to pop (pawn) for an old 'oman what was on the spree – a bran new 'un – but the cove wouldn't have it, and the old 'oman said he might be d—d. Never heer'd tell on the deluge; of the world having been drownded; it couldn't, for there wasn't water enough to do it. He weren't a going to fret hisself for such things as that. Didn't know what happened to people after death, only that they was buried. Had seen a dead body laid out; was a little afeared at first; poor Dick looked so different, and when you touched his face, he was so cold! oh, so cold! Had heer'd on another world; wouldn't mind if he was there hisself, if he could do better, for things was often queer here. Had heered on it from a tailor – such a clever cove, a stunner – as went to 'Straliar (Australia), and heer'd him say he was going into another world. Had never heer'd of France, but had heer'd of Frenchmen; there wasn't half a quarter so many on 'em as of Italians, with their earrings like flash gals. Didn't dislike foreigners, for he never saw none. What was they? Had heer'd of Ireland. Didn't know where it was, but it couldn't be very far, or such lots wouldn't come from there to London. Should say they walked it, aye, every bit of the way, for he'd seen them come in, all covered with dust. Had heer'd of people going to sea, and had seen the ships in the river, but didn't know nothing about it, for he was very seldom that way. The sun was made of fire, or it wouldn't make you feel so warm. The stars was fire, too, or they wouldn't shine. They didn't make it warm, they was too small. Didn't know any use they was of. Didn't know how far they was off; a jolly lot higher than the gas lights some on 'em was. Was never in a church; had heer'd they worshipped God there; didn't know how it was done; had heer'd singing and playing inside when he'd passed; never was there, for he hadn't no togs to go in, and wouldn't be let in among such swells as he had seen coming out. Was a ignorant chap, for he'd never been to school, but was up to many a move, and didn't do bad. Mother said he would make his fortin yet.

Had heer'd of the Duke of Wellington; he was Old Nosey; didn't think he ever seed him, but had seed his statty. Hadn't heer'd of the battle of Waterloo, nor who it was atween; once lived in Webber-row, Waterloo-road. Thought he had heerd speak of Buonaparte; didn't know what he was; though he had heer'd of Shakespeare, but didn't know whether he was alive or dead, and didn't care. A man with something like that name kept a dolly and did stunning; but he was sich a hard cove that if *he* was dead it wouldn't matter. Had seen the Queen, but didn't recollec' her name just at the minute; oh! yes, Wictoria and Albert. Had no notion what the Queen had to do. Should think she hadn't such power [he had first to ask what 'power' was] as the Lord Mayor, or as Mr Norton as was the Lambeth beak, and perhaps is still. Was never once before a beak and didn't want to. Hated the crushers; what business had they to interfere with him if he was only resting his basket in a street? Had been once to the Wick, and once to the Bower: liked tumbling better; he meant to have a little pleasure when the peas came in.

[152] Wakefield; from 'Wakefield' (mid 19th century) by N. Hawthorne.

In some old magazine or newspaper, I recollect a story, told as truth, of a man – let us call him Wakefield – who absented himself for a long time from his wife. The fact, thus abstractedly stated, is not very uncommon, nor – without a proper distinction of circumstances – to be condemned either as naughty or nonsensical. Howbeit, this, though far from the most aggravated, is perhaps the strangest instance on record of marital delinquency; and, moreover, as remarkable a freak as may be found in the whole list of human oddities. The wedded couple lived in London. The man, under pretence of going a journey, took lodgings in the next street to his own house, and there, unheard of by his wife or friends, and without the shadow of a reason for such self-banishment, dwelt upwards of twenty years. During that period he beheld his home every day, and frequently the forlorn Mrs Wake-

field. And after so great a gap in his matrimonial felicity –
when his death was reckoned certain, his estate settled, his
name dismissed from memory, and his wife, long, long
ago, resigned to her autumnal widowhood – he entered
the door one evening, quietly, as from a day's absence,
and became a loving spouse till death.

[153] Sherlock Holmes and Dr Watson; from *The
Sign of Four* by Arthur Conan Doyle (London, 1890).

Sherlock Holmes took his bottle from the corner of the
mantelpiece, and his hypodermic syringe from its neat
morocco case. With his long, white, nervous fingers he
adjusted the delicate needle and rolled back his left shirt-
cuff. For some little time his eyes rested thoughtfully upon
the sinewy forearm and wrist, all dotted and scarred with
innumerable puncture-marks. Finally, he thrust the sharp
point home, pressed down the tiny piston, and sank back
into the velvet-lined armchair with a long sigh of
satisfaction.

Three times a day for many months I had witnessed this
performance, but custom had not reconciled my mind to
it. On the contrary, from day to day I had become more
irritable at the sight, and my conscience swelled nightly
within me at the thought that I had lacked the courage to
protest. Again and again I had registered a vow that I
should deliver my soul upon the subject; but there was
that in the cool, nonchalant air of my companion which
made him the last man with whom one would care to take
anything approaching to a liberty. His great powers, his
masterly manner, and the experience which I had had of
his many extraordinary qualities, all made me diffident
and backward in crossing him.

Yet upon that afternoon, whether it was the Beaune
which I had taken with my lunch or the additional exas-
peration produced by the extreme deliberation of his
manner, I suddenly felt that I could hold out no longer.

'Which is it to-day,' I asked, 'morphine or cocaine?'

He raised his eyes languidly from the old black-letter volume which he had opened.

'It is cocaine,' he said, 'a seven per cent solution. Would you care to try it?'

'No, indeed,' I answered brusquely. 'My constitution has not got over the Afghan campaign yet. I cannot afford to throw any extra strain upon it.'

He smiled at my vehemence. 'Perhaps you are right, Watson,' he said. 'I suppose that its influence is physically a bad one. I find it, however, so transcendently stimulating and clarifying to the mind that its secondary action is a matter of small moment.'

'But consider!' I said earnestly. 'Count the cost! Your brain may, as you say, be roused and excited, but it is a pathological and morbid process which involves increased tissue-change and may at least leave a permanent weakness. You know, too, what a black reaction comes upon you. Surely the game is hardly worth the candle. Why should you, for a mere passing pleasure, risk the loss of those great powers with which you have been endowed? Remember that I speak not only as one comrade to another but as a medical man to one for whose constitution he is to some extent answerable.'

He did not seem offended. On the contrary, he put his finger-tips together, and leaned his elbows on the arms of his chair, like one who has a relish for conversation.

'My mind,' he said, 'rebels at stagnation. Give me problems, give me work, give me the most abstruse cryptogram, or the most intricate analysis, and I am in my own proper atmosphere. I can dispense then with artificial stimulants. But I abhor the dull routine of existence. I crave for mental exaltation. That is why I have chosen my own particular profession, or rather created it, for I am the only one in the world.'

'The only unofficial detective?' I said, raising my eyebrows.

'The only unofficial consulting detective,' he answered. 'I am the last and highest court of appeal in detection. When Gregson, or Lestrade, or Athelney Jones are out of their depths – which, by the way, is their normal state – the matter is laid before me. I examine the data, as an expert, and pronounce a specialist's opinion. I claim no credit in such cases. My name figures in no newspaper. The work itself, the pleasure of finding a field for my peculiar powers, is my highest reward. But you have yourself had some experience of my methods of work in the Jefferson Hope case.'

'Yes, indeed,' said I cordially. 'I was never so struck by anything in my life. I even embodied it in a small brochure, with the somewhat fantastic title of "A Study in Scarlet."'

He shook his head sadly.

'I glanced over it,' said he. 'Honestly, I cannot congratulate you upon it. Detection is, or ought to be, an exact science and should be treated in the same cold and unemotional manner. You have attempted to tinge it with romanticism, which produces much the same effect as if you worked a love-story or an elopement into the fifth proposition of Euclid.'

'But the romance was there,' I remonstrated. 'I could not tamper with the facts.'

'Some facts should be suppressed, or, at least, a just sense of proportion should be observed in treating them. The only point in the case which deserved mention was the curious analytical reasoning from effects to causes, by which I succeeded in unravelling it.'

I was annoyed at this criticism of a work which had been specially designed to please him. I confess, too, that I was irritated by the egotism which seemed to demand that every line of my pamphlet should be devoted to his own special doings. More than once during the years that I had lived with him in Baker Street I had observed that a small vanity underlay my companion's quiet and didactic manner. I made no remark, however, but sat nursing my wounded leg. I had had a Jezail bullet through it some time before, and though it did not prevent me from walking it ached wearily at every change of the weather.

[154] Charles Pooter (London, 1892); from *The Diary of a Nobody* by G. & W. Grossmith.

My dear wife Carrie and I have just been a week in our new house, 'The Laurels', Brickfield Terrace, Holloway – a nice six-roomed residence, not counting basement, with a front breakfast-parlour. We have a little front garden; and there is a flight of ten steps up to the front door, which, by-the-by, we keep locked with the chain up. Cummings, Gowing, and our other intimate friends always come to the little side entrance, which saves the servant the trouble of going up to the front door, thereby taking her from her work. We have a nice little back garden which runs down to the railway. We were rather afraid of the noise of the trains at first, but the landlord said we should not notice them after a bit, and took £2 off the rent. He was certainly right; and beyond the cracking of the garden wall at the bottom, we have suffered no inconvenience.

After my work in the City, I like to be at home. What's the good of a home, if you are never in it? 'Home, Sweet Home,' that's my motto. I am always in of an evening. Our old friend Gowing may drop in without ceremony; so may Cummings, who lives opposite. My dear wife Caroline and I are pleased to see them, if they like to drop in on us. But Carrie and I can manage to pass our evenings together without friends. There is always something to be done: a tin-tack here, a Venetian blind to put straight, a fan to nail up, or part of a carpet to nail down – all of which I can do with my pipe in my mouth; while Carrie is not above putting a button on a shirt, mending a pillow-case, or practising the 'Sylvia Gavotte' on our new cottage piano (on the three years' system), manufactured by W. Bilkson (in small letters), from Collard and Collard (in very large letters). It is also a great comfort to us to know that our boy Willie is getting on so well in the Bank at Oldham. We should like to see more of him.

[155] Dan Leno; from *Around Theatres* by Max Beerbohm.

So little and frail a lantern could not long harbour so big a flame. Dan Leno was more a spirit than a man. It was inevitable that he, cast into a life so urgent as is the life of a music-hall artist, should die untimely. Before his memory fades into legend, let us try to evaluate his genius. For mourners there is ever a solace in determining what, precisely, they have lost ... Well, where lay the secret of that genius? How came we to be spell-bound?

Partly, without doubt, our delight was in the quality of the things actually said by Dan Leno. No other music-hall artist threw off so many droll sayings – droll in idea as in verbal expression. Partly, again, our delight was in the way that these things were uttered – in the gestures and grimaces and antics that accompanied them; in fact, in Dan Leno's technique. But, above all, our delight was in Dan Leno himself. In every art personality is the paramount thing, and without it artistry goes for little. Especially is this so in the art of acting, where the appeal of personality is so direct. And most especially is it so in the art of acting in a music-hall, where the performer is all by himself upon the stage, with nothing to divert our attention. The moment Dan Leno skipped upon the stage, we were aware that here was a man utterly unlike any one else we had seen. Despite the rusty top hat and broken umbrella and red nose of tradition, here was a creature apart, radiating an ethereal essence all his own. He compelled us not to take our eyes off him, not to miss a word that he said. Not that we needed any compulsion. Dan Leno's was not one of those personalities which dominate us by awe, subjugating us against our will. He was of that other, finer kind: the lovable kind. He had, in a higher degree than any other actor that I have ever seen, the indefinable quality of being sympathetic. I defy any one not to have loved Dan Leno at first sight. The moment he capered on, with that air of wild determination, squirming in every limb with some deep grievance, that must be outpoured, all hearts were his. That face puckered with cares, whether they were the cares of the small shopkeeper, or of the landlady, or of the lodger; that face so tragic, with all the tragedy that is writ on the face of a baby-monkey, yet ever liable to relax its mouth into a sudden wide grin and to screw up its eyes to vanishing point over some little triumph wrested from Fate, the tyrant; that poor little battered personage, so 'put upon', yet so plucky with his squeaking voice and his sweeping gestures; bent but not broken; faint but pursuing; incarnate of the will to live in a world not at all worth living in – surely all hearts went always out to Dan Leno, with warm corners in them reserved to him for ever and ever.

To the last, long after illness had sapped his powers of actual expression and invention, the power of his personality was unchanged, and irresistible. Even had he not been in his heyday a brilliant actor, and a brilliant wag, he would have thrown all his rivals into the shade. Often, even in his heyday, his acting and his waggishness did not carry him very far. Only mediocrity can be trusted to be always at its best. Genius must always have lapses proportionate to its triumphs. A new performance by Dan Leno was almost always a dull thing in itself. He was unable to do himself justice until he had, as it were, collaborated for many nights with the public. He selected and rejected according to how his jokes, and his expression of them 'went'; and his best things came to him always in the course of an actual performance, to be incorporated in all the subsequent performances. When, at last, the whole thing had been built up, how perfect a whole it was! Not a gesture, not a grimace, not an inflection of the voice, not a wriggle of the body, but had its significance, and drove its significance sharply, grotesquely, home to us all. Never was a more perfect technique in acting. The technique for acting in a music-hall is of a harder, perhaps finer, kind than is needed for acting in a theatre; inasmuch as the artist must make his effects so much more quickly, and without the aid of any but the slightest 'properties' and scenery, and without the aid of any one else on the stage.

It seemed miraculous how Dan Leno contrived to make you see before you the imaginary persons with whom he conversed. He never stepped outside himself, never imitated the voices of his interlocutors. He merely repeated, before making his reply, a few words of what they were supposed to have said to him. Yet there they were, as large as life, before us.

Fairs, Sports, Games, Spectacles

[156] Sports and recreation in medieval London (12th century); from 'Description of London' by William Fitzstephen.

London, instead of theatrical shows and scenic entertainments, has dramatic performances of a more sacred kind, either representations of the miracles which holy confessors have wrought, or of the passions and sufferings in which the constancy of martyrs was signally displayed. Moreover, to begin with the sports of the boys (for we have all been boys), annually on the day which is called Shrovetide, the boys of the respective schools bring each a fighting cock to their master, and the whole of that forenoon is spent by the boys in seeing their cocks fight in the school-room. After dinner, all the young men of the city go out into the fields to play at the well-known game of foot-ball. The scholars belonging to the several schools have each their ball; and the city tradesmen, according to their respective crafts, have theirs. The more aged men, the fathers of the players, and the wealthy citizens, come on horseback to see the contests of the young men, with whom, after their manner, they participate, their natural heat seeming to be aroused by the sight of so much agility, and by their participation in the amusements of unrestrained youth. Every Sunday in Lent, after dinner, a company of young men enter the fields, mounted on warlike horses –

'On coursers always foremost in the race;'

of which

'Each steed's well-train'd to gallop in a ring.'

The lay-sons of the citizens rush out of the gates in crowds, equipped with lances and shields, the younger sort with pikes from which the iron head has been taken off, and there they get up sham fights, and exercise themselves in military combat. When the king happens to be near the city, most of the courtiers attend, and the young men who form the households of the earls and barons, and have not yet attained the honour of knighthood, resort thither for the purpose of trying their skill. The hope of victory animates every one. The spirited horses neigh, their limbs tremble, they champ their bits, and, impatient of delay, cannot endure standing still. When at length

'The charger's hoof seizes upon the course,'

the young riders having been divided into companies, some pursue those that go before without being able to overtake them, whilst others throw their companions out of their course, and gallop beyond them. In the Easter holidays they play at a game resembling a naval engagement. A target is firmly fastened to the trunk of a tree which is fixed in the middle of the river, and in the prow of a boat driven along by oars and the current stands a young man who is to strike the target with his lance; if, in hitting it, he break his lance, and keep his position unmoved, he

gains his point, and attains his desire: but if his lance be
not shivered by the blow, he is tumbled into the river, and
his boat passes by, driven along by its own motion. Two
boats, however, are placed there, one on each side of the
target, and in them a number of young men to take up the
striker, when he first emerges from the stream, or when

'A second time he rises from the wave.'

On the bridge, and in balconies on the banks of the river,
stand the spectators,

'well disposed to laugh.'

During the holydays in summer the young men exercise
themselves in the sports of leaping, archery, wrestling,
stone-throwing, slinging javelins beyond a mark, and also
fighting with bucklers. Cytherea leads the dances of the
maidens, who merrily trip along the ground beneath the
uprisen moon. Almost on every holyday in winter, before
dinner, foaming boars, and huge-tusked hogs, intended for
bacon, fight for their lives, or fat bulls or immense boars
are baited with dogs. When that great marsh which washes
the walls of the city on the north side is frozen over, the
young men go out in crowds to divert themselves upon
the ice. Some, having increased their velocity by a run,
placing their feet apart, and turning their bodies sideways,
slide a great way: others make a seat of large pieces of ice
like mill-stones, and a great number of them running
before, and holding each other by the hand, draw one of
their companions who is seated on the ice: if at any time
they slip in moving so swiftly, all fall down headlong
together. Others are more expert in their sports upon the
ice; for fitting to, and binding under their feet the shin-
bones of some animal, and taking in their hands poles
shod with iron, which at times they strike against the ice,
they are carried along with as great rapidity as a bird
flying or a bolt discharged from a cross-bow. Sometimes
two of the skaters having placed themselves a great dis-

tance apart by mutual agreement, come together from opposite sides; they meet, raise their poles, and strike each other; either one or both of them fall, not without some bodily hurt: even after their fall they are carried along to a great distance from each other by the velocity of the motion; and whatever part of their heads comes in contact with the ice is laid bare to the very skull. Very frequently the leg or arm of the falling party, if he chance to light upon either of them, is broken. But youth is an age eager for glory and desirous of victory, and so young men engage in counterfeit battles, that they may conduct themselves more valiantly in real ones. Most of the citizens amuse themselves in sporting with merlins, hawks, and other birds of a like kind, and also with dogs that hunt in the woods. The citizens have the right of hunting in Middlesex, Hertfordshire, all the Chilterns, and Kent, as far as the river Cray.

[157] Medieval May Day celebrations; from *Survey of London* by John Stow.

[The church is] called St Andrew Undershaft, because that of old time, every year on May-day in the morning, it was used, that an high or long shaft or May-pole, was set up there, in the midst of the street, before the south side of the said church; which shaft when it was set on end and fixed in the ground, was higher than the church steeple. Geoffrey Chaucer, writing of a vain boaster, hath these words, meaning of the said shaft:

> 'Right well aloft, and high ye beare your heade,
> The weather cocke, with flying, as ye would kill,
> When ye be stuffed, bet of wine, then brede,
> Then looke ye, when your wombe doth fill,
> As ye would beare the great shaft of Cornehill,
> Lord, so merrily crowdeth then your croke,
> That all the streete may heare your body cloke.'

This shaft was not raised at any time since evil May-day (so called of an insurrection made by apprentices and other young persons against aliens in the year 1517); but the said shaft was laid along over the doors, and under the pentises of one row of houses and alley gate, called of the shaft Shaft alley (being of the possessions of Rochester bridge), in the ward of Lime street. It was there, I say, hung on iron hooks many years, till the third of King Edward VI, that one Sir Stephen, curate of St Katherine Christ's church, preaching at Paules cross, said there that this shaft was made an idol, by naming the church of St Andrew with the addition of 'under that shaft': he persuaded therefore that the names of churches might be altered; also that the names of days in the week might be changed; the fish days to be kept any days except Friday and Saturday, and the Lent any time, save only betwixt Shrovetide and Easter. I have oft times seen this man, forsaking the pulpit of his said parish church, preach out of a high elm-tree in the midst of the churchyard, and then entering the church, forsaking the altar, to have sung his high mass in English upon a tomb of the dead towards the north. I heard his sermon at Paules cross, and I saw the effect that followed; for in the afternoon of that present Sunday, the neighbours and tenants to the said bridge, over whose doors the said shaft had lain, after they had well dined, to make themselves strong, gathered more help, and with great labour raising the shaft from the hooks, whereon it had rested two-and-thirty years, they sawed it in pieces, every man taking for his share so much as had lain over his door and stall, the length of his house; and they of the alley divided among them so much as had lain over their alley gate. Thus was this idol (as he termed it) mangled, and after burned.

[158] An Elizabethan playhouse; from *Travels in London* by T. Platter.

On another occasion not far from our inn, in the suburb at Bishopsgate, if I remember, also after lunch, I beheld a play in which they presented diverse nations and an Eng-

lishman struggling together for a maiden; he overcame
them all except the German who won the girl in a tussle,
and then sat down by her side, when he and his servant
drank themselves tipsy, so that they were both fuddled
and the servant proceeded to hurl his shoe at his master's
head, whereupon they both fell asleep; meanwhile the
Englishman stole into the tent and absconded with the
German's prize, thus in his turn outwitting the German; in
conclusion they danced very charmingly in English and
Irish fashion. Thus daily at two in the afternoon, London
has two, sometimes three plays running in different places,
competing with each other, and those which play best
obtain most spectators. The playhouses are so constructed
that they play on a raised platform, so that everyone has a
good view. There are different galleries and places, however, where the seating is better and more comfortable and
therefore more expensive. For whoever cares to stand
below only pays one English penny, but if he wishes to sit
he enters by another door, and pays another penny, while
if he desires to sit in the most comfortable seats which are
cushioned, where he not only sees everything well, but can
also be seen, then he pays yet another English penny at
another door. And during the performance food and drink
are carried round the audience, so that for what one cares
to pay one may also have refreshment. The actors are
most expensively and elaborately costumed; for it is the
English usage for eminent lords or Knights at their decease
to bequeath and leave almost the best of their clothes to
their serving men, which it is unseemly for the latter to
wear, so that they offer them then for sale for a small sum
to the actors.

[159] The Punch & Judy Man (London, 1861); from
London Labour and the London Poor by H.
Mayhew.

The performer of Punch that I saw was a short, dark,
pleasant-looking man, dressed in a very greasy and very

shiny shooting-jacket. This was fastened together by one
button in front, all the other button-holes having been
burst through. Protruding from his bosom, a corner of the
pandean pipes was just visible, and as he told me the story
of his adventures, he kept playing with the band of his
very limp and very rusty old beaver hat . . .

'Ah, it's a great annoyance being a public kerrackter,
I can assure you, sir; go where you will, it's "Punchy,
Punchy!" As for the boys, they'll never leave me alone
till I die, I know; and I suppose in my old age I shall
have to take to the parish broom. All our forefathers died
in the workhouse. I don't know a Punch's showman that
hasn't. One of my pardners was buried by the workhouse; and even old Pike, the most noted showman as
ever was, died in the workhouse – Pike and Porsini. Porsini was the first original street Punch, and Pike was his
apprentice; their names is handed down to posterity
among the noblemen and footmen of the land. They both
died in the workhouse, and, in course, I shall do the
same. Something else *might* turn up, to be sure. We can't
say what the luck of this world is. I'm obliged to strive
very hard – very hard indeed, sir, now, to get a living;
and then not to get it after all – at times, compelled to
go short, often.

'Punch, you know, sir, is a dramatic performance in
two hacts. It's a play, you may say. I don't think it can be
called a tragedy hexactly; a drama is what we names it.
There is tragic parts, and comic and sentimental parts too.
Some families where I performs will have it most sentimental – in the original style; them families is generally sentimental theirselves. Others is all for the comic, and then I
has to kick up all the games I can. To the sentimental folk
I'm obliged to perform werry steady and werry slow, and
leave out all comic words and business. They won't have
no ghost, no coffin, and no devil; and that's what I call
spiling the performance entirely. It's the march of hintel-
lect wot's a doing all this – it is, sir . . .

'We've got more upon the comic business now, and
tries to do more with Toby than with the prison scene.

The prison is what we calls the sentimental style. Formerly Toby was only a stuffed figure. It was Pike who first hit upon hintroducing a live dog, and a great hit it were – it made a grand alteration in the hexibition, for now the performance is called Punch and Toby *as well*. There is one Punch about the streets at present that tries it on with three dogs, but that ain't much of a go – too much of a good thing I calls it . . .

'We start on our rounds at nine in the morning, and remain out till dark at night. We gets a snack at the publics on our road. The best hours for Punch are in the morning from nine till ten, because then the children are at home. Arter that, you know, they goes out with the maids for a walk. From twelve till three is good again, and then from six till nine; that's because the children are mostly at home at them hours. We make much more by horders for performance houtside the gennelmen's houses, than we do by performing in public in the hopen streets. Monday is the best day for street business; Friday is no day at all, because then the poor people has spent all their money. If we was to pitch on a Friday, we shouldn't take a halfpenny in the street, so we in general on that day goes round for horders. Wednesday, Thursday, and Friday is the best days for us with horders at gennelmen's houses. We do much better in the spring than at any other time in the year, excepting holiday time, at Midsummer and Christmas. That's what we call Punch's season. We do most at hevening parties in the holiday time, and if there's a pin to choose between them, I should say Christmas holidays was the best. For attending hevening parties now we generally get one pound and our refreshments – as much more as they like to give us. But the business gets slacker and slacker every season. Where I went to ten parties twenty years ago, I don't go to two now. People isn't getting tired of our performances, but stingier – that's it. Everybody looks at their money now afore they parts with it, and gennelfolks haggles and cheapens us down to shillings and sixpences, as if they was guineas in the holden time.

'Our business is werry much like hackney-coach work; we do best in vet veather. It looks like rain this evening, and I'm uncommon glad on it, to be sure. You see, the vet keeps the children in-doors all day, and then they wants something to quiet 'em a bit; and the mothers and fathers, to pacify the dears, gives us a horder to perform. It mustn't rain cats and dogs – that's as bad as no rain at all. What we likes is a regular good, steady Scotch mist, for then we takes double what we takes on other days. In summer we does little or nothing; the children are out all day enjoying themselves in the parks . . .

'We generally walks from twelve to twenty mile every day, and carries the show, which weighs a good half-hundred, at the least. Arter great exertion, our voice werry often fails us; for speaking all day through the "call" is werry trying, 'specially when we are chirruping up so as to bring the children to the vinders. The boys is the greatest nuisances we has to contend with. Wherever we goes we are sure of plenty of boys for a hindrance; but they've got no money, bother 'em! and they'll follow us for miles, so that we're often compelled to go miles to awoid 'em. Many parts is swarming with boys, such as Vitechapel. Spitalfields, that's the worst place for boys I ever come a-near; they're like flies in summer there, only much more thicker. I never shows my face within miles of them parts. Chelsea, again, has an uncommon lot of boys; and wherever we know the children swarm, there's the spots we makes a point of awoiding. Why, the boys is such a hobstruction to our performance, that often we are obliged to drop the curtain for 'em.'

[160] Tiddy Doll at the Great Frost Fair on the Thames (late 17th century); from *Trivia* by John Gay.

O roving Muse, recal that wond'rous Year,
When Winter reign'd in bleak *Britannia's* Air;
When hoary *Thames*, with frosted Oziers crown'd,
Was three long Moons in icy Fetters bound.

The Waterman, forlorn along the Shore,
Pensive reclines upon his useless Oar,
Sees harness'd Steeds desert the stony Town;
And wander Roads unstable, not their own:
Wheels o'er the harden'd Waters smoothly glide,
And rase with whiten'd Tracks the slipp'ry Tide.
Here the fat Cook piles high the blazing Fire,
And scarce the Spit can turn the Steer entire.
Booths sudden hide the *Thames*, long Streets appear,
And num'rous Games proclaim the crouded Fair.
So when a Gen'ral bids the martial Train
Spread their Encampment o'er the spatious Plain;
Thick-rising Tents a Canvas City build,
And the loud Dice resound thro' all the Field.
'Twas here the Matron found a doleful Fate:
Let Elegiac Lay the Woe relate,
Soft, as the Breath of distant Flutes, at Hours,
When silent Ev'ning closes up the Flow'rs;
Lulling, as falling Water's hollow noise;
Indulging Grief, like *Philomela's* Voice.

Doll ev'ry Day had walk'd these treach'rous Roads;
Her Neck grew warpt beneath autumnal Loads
Of various Fruit; she now a Basket bore,
That Head, alas! shall Basket bear no more.
Each Booth she frequent past, in quest of Gain,
And Boys with pleasure heard her shrilling Strain.
Ah *Doll!* all Mortals must resign their Breath,
And Industry it self submit to Death!
The cracking Crystal yields, she sinks, she dyes,
Her Head, chopt off, from her lost Shoulders flies:
Pippins she cry'd, but Death her Voice confounds,
And Pip-Pip-Pip along the Ice resounds.
So when the *Thracian* Furies *Orpheus* tore,
And left his bleeding Trunk deform'd with Gore,
His sever'd Head floats down the silver Tide,
His yet warm Tongue for his lost Consort cry'd;
Eurydice, with quiv'ring Voice, he mourn'd,
And *Heber's* Banks *Eurydice* return'd.

[161] Handel's Water Music on the Thames (1717); from *Daily Courant*.

On Wednesday evening at about eight the King took water at Whitehall in an open barge . . . and went up the river towards Chelsea. Many other barges with persons of quality attended, and so great a number of boats, that the whole river in a manner was covered. A City Company's barge was employed for the music, wherein were fifty instruments of all sorts, who played all the way from Lambeth, while the barges drove with the tide without rowing as far as Chelsea, the finest symphonies, composed express for this occasion by Mr Handel, which His Majesty liked so well that he caused it to be played over three times in going and returning. At eleven His Majesty went ashore at Chelsea, where a supper was prepared, and then there was another very fine consort of music, which lasted till two, after which His Majesty came again into his barge and returned the same way, the music continuing to play until he landed.

[162] Bull Baiting; from *London in 1710* by Von Uffenbach.

23 June 1710: Towards evening we drove to see the bull-baiting, which is held here nearly every Monday in two places. On the morning of the day the bull, or any other creature that is to be baited, is led round. It takes place in a large open space or courtyard, on two sides of which high benches have been made for the spectators. First a young ox or bull was led in and fastened by a long rope to an iron ring in the middle of the yard; then about thirty dogs, two or three at a time, were let loose on him, but he made short work of them, goring and tossing them high in the air above the height of the first storey. Then amid shouts and yells the butchers to whom the dogs belonged sprang forward and caught their beasts right side up to break their fall. They had to keep fast hold of the dogs to hinder them from returning to the attack without barking.

Several had such a grip of the bull's throat or ear that their mouths had to be forced open with poles. When the bull had stood it tolerably long, they brought out a small bear and tied him up in the same fashion. As soon as the dogs had at him, he stood up on his hind legs and gave some terrific buffets; but if one of them got at his skin, he rolled about in such a fashion that the dogs thought themselves lucky if they came out safe from beneath him. But the most diverting and worst of all was a common little ass, who was brought out saddled with an ape on his back. As soon as a couple of dogs had been let loose on him, he broke into a prodigious gallop – for he was free, not having been tied up like the other beasts – and he stamped and bit all round himself. The ape began to scream most terribly for fear of falling off. If the dogs came too near him, he seized them with his mouth and twirled them round, shaking them so much that they howled prodigiously. Finally another bull appeared, on whom several crackers had been hung: when these were lit and several dogs let loose on him on a sudden, there was a monstrous hurly-burly. And thus was concluded this truly English sport, which vastly delights this nation but to me seemed nothing very special.

[163] Ranelagh Gardens (1749); from *Letters* by H. Walpole.

3 May 1749

We have at last celebrated the Peace, and that as much in extremes as we generally do everything, whether we have reason to be glad or sorry, pleased or angry. Last Tuesday it was proclaimed: the King did not go to St Paul's, but at night the whole town was illuminated. The next day was what was called 'a jubilee-masquerade in the Venetian manner' at Ranelagh: it had nothing Venetian in it, but was by far the best understood and the prettiest spectacle I ever saw: nothing in a fairy tale ever surpassed it. One of the proprietors, who was a German, and belongs to

Court, had got my Lady Yarmouth to persuade the King to order it. It began at three o'clock, and, about five, people of fashion began to go. When you entered, you found the whole garden filled with masks and spread with tents, which remained all night *very commodely*. In one quarter, was a May-pole dressed with garlands, and people dancing round it to a tabor and pipe and rustic music, all masqued, as were all the various bands of music that were disposed in different parts of the garden; some like huntsmen with French horns, some like peasants, and a troop of harlequins and scaramouches in the little open temple on the mount. On the canal was a sort of gondola, adorned with flags and streamers, and filled with music, rowing about. All round the outside of the amphitheatre were shops, filled with Dresden china, japan, &c., and all the shop-keepers in mask. The amphitheatre was illuminated; and in the middle was a circular bower, composed of all kinds of firs in tubs, from twenty to thirty feet high: under them orange-trees, with small lamps in each orange, and below them all sorts of the finest auriculas in pots; and festoons of natural flowers hanging from tree to tree. Between the arches too were firs, and smaller ones in the balconies above. There were booths for tea and wine, gaming-tables and dancing, and about two thousands persons. In short, it pleased me more than anything I ever saw . . . The next day were the fire-works, which by no means answered the expense, the length of preparation, and the expectation that had been raised; indeed, for a week before, the town was like a country fair, the streets filled from morning to night, scaffolds building wherever you could or could not see, and coaches arriving from every corner of the kingdom. This hurry and lively scene, with the sight of the immense crowd in the Park and on every house, the guards, and the machine itself, which was very beautiful, was all that was worth seeing. The rockets, and whatever was thrown up into the air, succeeded mighty well; but the wheels, and all that was to compose the principal part, was pitiful and ill-conducted, with no changes of coloured fires and shapes: the illumination was mean, and lighted so slowly that scarce anybody had patience to wait the finishing; and then, what contributed to the awkwardness of the whole, was the right pavilion catching fire, and being burnt down in the middle of the show.

[164] Early days at Lords (19th century); contemporary account quoted in *London Revisited* by E. V. Lucas.

'In the then Pavilion, a small one-roomed building, surrounded with a few laurels and shrubs, and capable of holding forty or fifty members, I can see Mr Aislabie, the Secretary of the Club, a big fat man over twenty stone in weight, fussing about with a red book in which he was entering subscriptions for some desired match of which the funds of the Club could not afford the expense. And here sat Lord Frederick Beauclerk, then the Autocrat of the Club and of Cricket in general, laying down the law and organizing the games. On these he always had a bet of a sovereign, and he himself managed them while sitting alongside the scorers at the top of the ground, whence he issued his orders to the players. He himself had then given up playing.

'Round the ground there were more of these small benches without backs, and a pot-boy walked round with a supply of Beer and Porter for the public, who had no other means of refreshing themselves. Excepting these benches there were no seats for spectators. At the south-west corner of the ground there were large stacks of willow-blocks to be seasoned and made into bats in the workshop adjoining. On the upper north-east corner was a large sheep-pen. In the centre of the ground, opposite the Pavilion, was a square patch of grass which was kept constantly rolled and taken care of. No scythe was allowed to touch it, and mowing machines were not then invented. The rest of the ground was ridge and furrow – not very easy for fielding on, nor made any easier by the number of old pitches which abounded, for on non-match days the public could have a pitch for a shilling, a sum which included the use of stumps, bat and ball, the last-named selected from half a dozen or so from the capacious breeches pockets of "Steevie" Slatter, Mr Dark's factotum, which never seemed to be empty.

'The grass, as I have said, was never mowed. It was usually kept down by a flock of sheep, which was penned up on match days, and on Saturdays four or five hundred sheep were driven on to the ground on their way to the Monday Smithfield Market. It was marvellous to see how they cleared the herbage. From the pitch itself, selected by Mr Dark, half a dozen boys picked out the rough stalks of the grass. The wickets were sometimes difficult – in a dry north-east wind, for instance; but when they were in good order it was a joy to play on them, they were so full of life and spirit. The creases were cut with a knife, and, though more destructive to the ground, were more accurate than those marked subsequently with white paint!'

[165] Twentieth-century street games; from *London Street Games* by N. Douglas.

I say: hoops be blowed. With all respect to Aunt Eliza, I might have swallowed marbles, but I can't swallow hoops; not on this side of the year after next. I know this, at least, that if a big lad were seen playing, or ever had been seen playing with a hoop, down our way, except, perhaps, an iron one – why, his own parents wouldn't know him again, when he got home, if he ever did, which I rather doubt. But that's neither here nor there, except in so far as it shows what Aunt Eliza's explanations are worth. Mr Perkins, of Framlingham Brothers (a good old firm – and a nice place he's got, too) – he's an understandable kind of gentleman and he gets talking about things after his second pint of Burton and he says, speaking of marbles, that he's noticed the same thing as I have. And when I asked him *why* marbles are going out of fashion, he says:

'Marbles are going out of fashion,' he says, 'because they're getting unpopular. That's why.'

[166] The F.A. Cup final at Wembley (12 May 1979); from *Fever Pitch* by N. Hornby.

Arsenal scored twice in the first half, the opening goal after twelve minutes (the first time in four games I had seen Arsenal take the lead at Wembley), the second goal right before half-time; the interval was a blissfully relaxed fifteen minutes of raucous celebration. Most of the second half passed by in the same way, until with five minutes to go Manchester United scored . . . and with two minutes to go, in traumatizing and muddled slow motion, they scored again. We had thrown the game away, players and fans all knew that, and as I watched the United players cavort on the touchline at the far end I was left with the terrible feeling that I'd had as a child – that I hated Arsenal, that the club was a burden I could no longer carry but one that I would never, ever be able to throw off.

I was high up on the terraces with the other Arsenal fans, right behind the goal that Manchester United were defending; I sat down, too dizzy with pain and anger and frustration and self-pity to remain on my feet any longer. There were others who did the same, and behind me a pair of teenage girls were weeping silently, not in the hammy fashion of teenage girls at Bay City Rollers concerts, but in a way that suggested a deep and personal grief.

I was looking after a young American lad for the afternoon, a friend of the family, and his mild sympathy but obvious bafflement threw my distress into embarrassing relief: I *knew* that it was only a game, that worse things happened at sea, that people were starving in Africa, that there might be a nuclear holocaust within the next few months; I knew that the score was still 2– 2, for heaven's sake, and that there was a chance that Arsenal could somehow find a way out of the mire (although I also knew that the tide had turned, and that the players were too demoralized to be able to win the game in extra time). But none of this knowledge could help me. I had been but five minutes away from fulfilling the only fully formed ambition I had ever consciously held since the age of eleven; and if people are allowed to grieve when they are passed over for promotion, or when they fail to win an Oscar, or when their novel is rejected by every publisher in London – and our culture allows them to do so, even though these people may only have dreamed these dreams for a couple of years, rather than the decade, the *half-lifetime*, that I had been dreaming mine – then I was bloody well entitled to sit down on a lump of concrete for two minutes and try to blink back tears.

And it really was for only two minutes. When the game restarted, Liam Brady took the ball deep into the United half (afterwards he said that he was knackered, and was only trying to prevent the loss of a third goal) and pushed it out wide to Rix. I was watching this, but not *seeing* it; even when Rix's cross came over and United's goalkeeper Gary Bailey missed it I wasn't paying much attention. But then Alan Sunderland got his foot to the ball, poked it in, right into the goal in front of us, and I was shouting not 'Yes' or 'Goal' or any of the other noises that customarily come to my throat at these times but just a noise, 'AAAARRRRGGGGHHHH', a noise born of utter joy and stunned disbelief, and suddenly there were people on the concrete terraces again, but they were rolling around on top of each other, bug-eyed and berserk. Brian, the American kid, looked at me, smiled politely and tried to find his hands amidst the mayhem below him so that he could raise them and clap with an enthusiasm I suspected he did not feel.

Eating, Drinking and Clubbing

[167] Coffee-houses (late 18th century); from *Travels* by C. P. Moritz.

I would always advise those who wish to drink coffee in England, to mention before hand how many cups are to be made with half an ounce; or else the people will probably bring them a prodigious quantity of brown water; which (notwithstanding all my admonitions) I have not yet been able wholly to avoid. The fine wheaten bread which I find here, besides excellent butter and cheshire-cheese, makes up for my scanty dinners. For an English dinner, to such lodgers as I am, generally consists of a piece of half-boiled, or half-roasted meat; and a few cabbage leaves boiled in plain water; on which they pour a sauce made of flour and butter. This, I assure you, is the usual method of dressing vegetables in England.

The slices of bread and butter, which they give you with your tea, are as thin as poppy leaves. But there is another kind of bread and butter usually eaten with tea, which is toasted by the fire, and is incomparably good. You take

one slice after the other and hold it to the fire on a fork
till the butter is melted, so that it penetrates a number of
slices all at once. This is called Toast . . .

In these coffee-houses, however, there generally prevails
a very decorous stillness and silence. Every one speaks
softly to those only who sit next him. The greater part
read the newspapers, and no one ever disturbs another.
The room is commonly on the ground floor, and you enter
it immediately from the street, the seats are divided by
wooden wainscot partitions. Many letters and projects are
here written and planned, and many of those that you find
in the papers are dated from some of these coffee-houses.
There is, therefore, nothing incredible, nor very extraordinary, in a person's composing a sermon here, excepting
that one would imagine it might have been done better at
home, and certainly should not have thus been put off to
the last minute.

[168] Drunk after an annual club dinner (18th century); from *Memoirs of William Hickey*, edited by P.
Quennell.

Our club consisted of twenty, and was always well
attended; any member who absented himself, no matter
from what cause, on a club day forfeited half a crown,
which was put through a hole made in the lid of a box,
kept under lock and key, and opened only once a year,
when the amount of forfeits was laid out in an extra
dinner at the Red House, generally about 20 December,
and consisting of venison and of all sorts of dainties, the
liquors being claret and madeira, purchased for the
occasion . . .

The annual dinner I have above alluded to, took place
this year (1767) on 19 December, on which day I rowed
myself up to the Red House, got abominably drunk, as
did most of the party, and in spite of the remonstrances of
Burt and his wife, backed by Sally too, I, at two o'clock in
the morning, staggered to my boat, which I literally tum-

bled into, and, without recollecting one word of the matter, obstinately refused to let anyone accompany me, and pushed off. Whether, intoxicated as I was, it came into my head everybody would be in bed at Roberts's at Lambeth, where my boat was kept, or not, I cannot tell, or what guided my proceedings; but it seems I ran her ashore at Milbank, there got out, and endeavoured to walk home. Unfortunately for me they were then paving anew the lower parts of Westminster, and I in consequence encountered various holes, and various heaps of stone and rubbish, into and over which I tumbled and scrambled, God only knows how, or how I contrived to get so far on my way as Parliament Street; but a little after seven in the morning, a party who had supped, and afterwards played whist all night, at a Mr James's, were just sallying forth to get into a hackney coach, waiting to convey them to their respective homes. Mr Smith, one of the company, who was a riding master of His Majesty's, stepping to the rear of the coach to make water, descried a human figure laying in the kennel, whereupon he called to his companions, who, upon examination, found it was poor pilgarlic in woeful plight.

Being thus recognized, though I was utterly incapable of giving any account of myself, or of even articulating, they lifted me into their coach, Mr Smith and another attending to support me; and thus I was conveyed to my father's and there put to bed, having no more recollection of a single circumstance that had occurred for the preceding twelve hours, than if I had been dead. My boat, which was known to all the watermen above bridge, was found at daylight laying aground at Milbank, having only one scull in her. Upon enquiry, a watchman said he had observed a young gentleman, who appeared very tipsy, land from her, and seeing how incapable he was of walking, and that he fell every yard, offered to assist him, which was violently rejected; and he therefore went to his watch-house, it being near break of day.

I awoke the following day in my own bed, as from a horrible dream, unable to move hand or foot, being most

miserably bruised, cut and maimed in every part of my
body. The three first days, my old friend Dr Nugent, and
Mr Samuel Hayes, an eminent surgeon, were much
alarmed, telling my father I was in imminent danger, a
strong fever having come on, and from some symptoms
they apprehended serious internal injury. Youth, however,
and a naturally good constitution, befriended me. I got
better in a week, and on the tenth day was allowed to rise
for an hour; but more than three weeks elapsed ere I left
my chamber.

[169] The betting book at Brooks's (late 18th century); from *Brooks's 1764–1964* by H. S. Eeles &
Earl Spencer.

'22 June 1771. Mr William Hanger bets Mr Lee Twenty
Guineas to 25 that Mlle Heinel does not dance in England
at the Opera House next winter.'

'2 March 1774. Lord Northington betts Mr Plumer 300
Guineas to 50 either the Duke of Devonshire, Lord Chol-
mondley, Mr Wm. Hanger or Mr Plumer is married before
his Lordship.'

'21 March 1774. Lord Clermont has given Mr Craufurd
ten guineas upon the condition of receiving £500 from
him, whenever Mr Charles Fox shall be worth £100,000
clear of debts.'

'4 June 1774. Lord Northington betts Mr C. Fox that he
(Mr Fox) is not called to the barr before this day 4 years.'

'Mr Fitzpatrick bets Lord Cholmondely 500 Gs to 10 that
no Minister is beheaded before 6 Feb 1778.'

'D. Leinster betts Mr Codrington Ten Guineas neither of
the Perreaus are hanged publicly.'

'Mr Fitzpatrick and Mr Hanger have agreed that whenever

either of them shall go to a Bawdy house in King's Court he shall pay ten guineas to the other toties quoties.'

witnesses

The D. of Devonshire

Ld. E. Bentinck

Mr Charles Fox

'Lord Ilchester betts Mr Hanger 20 Gs that he does not miss two out of the first ten pheasants he shoots at after 30 Sept 1777.'

'1777. Mr K. Stewart betts Mr Coke 10 Gs that the average weight of sheep sold at Smithfield is not 120 p each sheep.'

[170] Attempt to beat up William Pitt outside Brooks's, 28 February 1784, as described by Pitt's brother Chatham; from *The Younger Pitt Vol I* by John Ehrman.

He was attended by a great concourse of people, many of the better sort, all the way down the Strand, as well as by a considerable Mob – the Populace insisted on taking off the Horses and drawing the Coach – A Mob is never very discreet, and unfortunately they stopped outside Carlton House and began hissing, and it was with some difficulty we forced them to go on. As we proceeded up St James's Street, there was a great Cry, and an attempt made to turn the Carriage up St James's Place to Mr Fox's house (he then lived at Ld Northingtons) in order to break his windows and force him to light [them], but which we at last succeeded in preventing their doing. I have often thought this was a trap laid for us, for had we got up, there, into a Cul de Sac, Mr Pitt's situation, would have been critical indeed. – This attempt brought us rather nearer in contact with Brooks, and the moment we got opposite . . . a sudden and desparate attack was made upon the Carriage . . . by a body of Chairmen armed with bludgeons, broken Chair Poles – (many of the waiters, and

several of the Gentlemen among them) – They succeeded
in making their way to the Carriage, and forced open the
door. Several desperate blows were aimed at Mr Pitt, and
I recollect endeavouring to cover him, as well as I cou'd,
in his getting out of the Carriage. Fortunately however, by
the exertions of those who remained with us, and by ye
timely assistance of a Party of Chairmen, and many Gentlemen from Whites, who saw his danger, we were extri-
cated from a most unpleasant situation, and with
considerable difficulty, got into some adjacent houses, . . .
and from thence to White's. The Coachmen, and the
Servants were much bruised, and the Carriage nearly
demolished . . . I never went to Brooks any more, and I
was never able to ascertain further what passed or what
first led to the Outrage that night . . .

[171] The 'immortal dinner' at Hampstead (1817);
from *The Autobiography and Memoirs of B. R.
Haydon*, edited by T. Taylor.

In December Wordsworth was in town, and as Keats
wished to know him I made up a party to dinner of
Charles Lamb, Wordsworth, Keats, and Monkhouse, his
friend; and a very pleasant party we had . . .

On 28 December the immortal dinner came off in my
painting-room, with Jerusalem towering up behind us as a
background. Wordsworth was in fine cue, and we had a
glorious set-to – on Homer, Shakespeare, Milton, and
Virgil. Lamb got exceedingly merry and exquisitely witty;
and his fun in the midst of Wordsworth's solemn inton-
ations of oratory was like the sarcasm and wit of the fool
in the intervals of Lear's passion. He made a speech and
voted me absent, and made them drink my health. 'Now,'
said Lamb, 'you old Lake poet, you rascally poet, why do
you call Voltaire dull?' We all defended Wordsworth, and
affirmed there was a state of mind when Voltaire would
be dull. 'Well,' said Lamb, 'here's Voltaire – the Messiah
of the French nation, and a very proper one too.'

He then, in a strain of humour beyond description, abused me for putting Newton's head into my picture; 'a fellow', said he, 'who believed nothing unless it was as clear as the three sides of a triangle.' And then he and Keats agreed he had destroyed all the poetry of the rainbow by reducing it to the prismatic colours. It was impossible to resist him, and we all drank 'Newton's health and confusion to mathematics'. It was delightful to see the good humour of Wordsworth in giving in to all our frolics without affectation and laughing as heartily as the best of us.

By this time other friends joined, among them poor Ritchie, who was going to penetrate by Fezzan to Timbuctoo. I introduced him to all as 'a gentleman going to Africa'. Lamb seemed to take not notice; but all of a sudden he roared out: 'Which is the gentleman we are going to lose?' We then drank the victim's health, in which Ritchie joined.

In the morning of this delightful day, a gentleman, a perfect stranger, had called on me. He said he knew my friends, had an enthusiasm for Wordsworth, and begged I would procure him the happiness of an introduction. He told me he was a comptroller of stamps, and often had correspondence with the poet. I thought it a liberty; but still, as he seemed a gentleman, I told him he might come.

When we retired to tea we found the comptroller. In introducing him to Wordsworth I forgot to say who he was. After a little time the comptroller looked down, looked up, and said to Wordsworth: Don't you think, sir, Milton was a great genius?' Keats looked at me, Wordsworth looked at the comptroller. Lamb who was dozing by the fire turned round and said: 'Pray, sir, did you say Milton was a great genius?' 'No, sir: I asked Mr Wordsworth if he were not.' 'Oh,' said Lamb, 'then you are a silly fellow.' 'Charles! my dear Charles!' said Wordsworth; but Lamb, perfectly innocent of the confusion he had created, was off again by the fire.

After an awful pause the comptroller said: 'Don't you think Newton a great genius?' I could not stand it any

longer. Keats put his head into my books. Ritchie squeezed
in a laugh. Wordsworth seemed asking himself: 'Who is
this?' Lamb got up, and taking a candle said: 'Sir, will you
allow me to look at your phrenological development?' He
then turned his back on the poor man, and at every
question of the comptroller he chaunted:

> Diddle, diddle dumpling, my son John
> Went to bed with his breeches on.

The man in office, finding Wordsworth did not know
who he was, said in a spasmodic and half-chuckling
anticipation of assured victory: 'I have had the honour of
some correspondence with you, Mr Wordsworth.' 'With
me, sir?' said Wordsworth, 'not that I remember.' 'Don't
you, sir? I am a comptroller of stamps.' There was a dead
silence, the comptroller evidently thinking that was
enough. While we were waiting for Wordsworth's reply,
Lamb sung out:

> Hey diddle diddle,
> The cat and the fiddle.

'My dear Charles!' said Wordsworth.

> Diddle diddle dumpling, my son John,

chaunted Lamb, and then rising, exclaimed: 'Do let me
have another look at that gentleman's organs.' Keats and
I hurried Lamb into the painting-room, shut the door, and
gave way to inextinguishable laughter. Monkhouse followed and tried to get Lamb away. We went back, but the
comptroller was irreconcilable. We soothed and smiled,
and asked him to supper. He stayed, though his dignity
was sorely affected. However, being a good-natured man,
we parted all in good humour, and no ill effects followed.

All the while, until Monkhouse succeeded, we could
hear Lamb struggling in the painting-room, and calling at
intervals: 'Who is that fellow? Allow me to see his organs
once more.'

It was indeed an immortal evening. Wordsworth's fine
intonation as he quoted Milton and Virgil, Keats' eager

inspired look, Lamb's quaint sparkle of lambent humour, so speeded the stream of conversation, that in my life I never passed a more delightful time.

[172] George Sala describes 'The Old Cheshire Cheese' pub (19th century), Fleet Street. 'Brain Street'.

It is a little lop-sided, wedged-up house, that always reminds you, structurally, of a high-shouldered man with his hands in his pockets. It is full of holes and corners and cupboards and sharp turnings; and in ascending the stairs to the tiny smoking-room you must tread cautiously, if you would not wish to be tripped up by plates and dishes momentarily deposited there by furious waiters. The waiters at the 'Cheese' are always furious. Old customers abound in the comfortable old tavern, in whose sanded-floored eating-rooms a new face is a rarity; and the guests and the waiter are the oldest of familiars. Yet the waiter seldom fails to bite your nose off as a preliminary measure when you proceed to pay him. How should it be otherwise when on that waiter's soul there lies heavy a perpetual sense of injury caused by the savoury odour of steaks and 'muts' to follow; of cheese bubbling in tiny tins – the original 'speciality' of the house; of floury potatoes and fragrant green peas; of cool salads, and cooler tankards of bitter beer; of extra-creaming stout and 'goes' of Cork and 'rack', by which is meant gin; and, in the winter-time, of Irish stew and rumpsteak pudding, glorious and grateful to every sense? To be compelled to run to and fro with these succulent viands from noon to late at night, without being able to spare time to consume them in comfort – where do waiters dine, and when, and how? – to be continually taking other people's money only for the purpose of handing it to other people – are not these grievances sufficient to cross-grain the temper of the mildest-mannered waiter? Somebody is always in a passion at the 'Cheese': either a customer because there is not fat enough on his 'point' steak, or because there is too much bone in his mutton-chop; or else the waiter is wroth with the cook; or the landlord with the waiter, or the barmaid with all. Yes, there is a barmaid at the 'Cheese', mewed up in a box not much bigger than a birdcage, surrounded by groves of lemons, 'ones' of cheese, punch-bowls, and cruets of mushroom-catsup. I should not care to dispute with her, lest she should quoit me over the head with a punch-ladle, having a William-the-Third guinea soldered in the bowl.

[173] Dickens and Thackeray argue at the Garrick (19th century). Dickens letter quoted in *The Garrick Club 1831–1947*.

The Garrick is in convulsions. The attack is consequent on Thackeray's having complained to the Committee (with an amazing want of discretion, as I think) of an article about him by Edmund Yates in a thing called *Town Talk*. The article is in bad taste, no doubt, and would have been infinitely better left alone. But I conceive that the Committee have nothing earthly, celestial, or infernal to do with it. Committee thinks otherwise, and calls on E. Y. to apologize or retire. E. Y. can't apologize (Thackeray having written him a letter which renders it impossible) and won't retire. Committee therefore call a General Meeting, yet pending. Thackeray *thereupon*, by way of showing what an ill thing it is for writers to attack one another in print, denounces E. Y. (in *Virginians* as 'Young Grub Street'). Frightful mess, muddle, complication, and botheration ensue – which witch's broth is now in full boil.

Sex in the City

[174] Medieval Punishment of Whoremongers and Bawds; from *Liber Albus* by J. Carpenter (1419), edited and translated by H. T. Riley.

Of a man who is found to be a Whoremonger or Bawd, and of his Punishment.

In the first place, if any man shall be found to be a common whoremonger or bawd, and shall of the same be attainted, first, let all his head and beard be shaved, except a fringe on the head, two inches in breadth; and let him be taken unto the pillory, with minstrels, and set thereon for a certain time, at the discretion of the Mayor and Aldermen. And if he shall be a second time attainted thereof, let him have the same punishment, and in the same manner for a certain time, at the discretion of the Mayor and Aldermen; and besides this, let him have ten days' imprisonment, without ransom. And the third time, let him have the same punishment, and in the same manner for a certain time, at the discretion of the Mayor and

Aldermen; and afterwards let him be taken to one of the City Gates, and there let him forswear the City for ever.

Item, if any woman shall be found to be a common receiver of courtesans or bawd, and of the same shall be attainted, first, let her be openly brought, with minstrels, from prison unto the thew, and set thereon for a certain time, at the discretion of the Mayor and Aldermen, and there let her hair be cut round about her head. And if she shall be a second time attainted thereof, let her have the same punishment, and in the same manner for a certain time, at the discretion of the Mayor and Aldermen; and besides this, let her have ten days' imprisonment, without ransom. And the third time, let her have the same punishment, and in the same manner for a certain time, at the discretion of the Mayor and Aldermen; and after this, let her be taken to one of the Gates of the said city, [and let her there forswear the City] for ever.

Item, if any woman shall be found to be a common courtesan, and of the same shall be attainted, let her be taken from the prison unto Algate, with a hood of ray, and a white wand in her hand; and from thence, with minstrels, unto the thew, and there let the cause be proclaimed; and from thence, through Chepe and Newgate to Cokkeslane, there to take up her abode. And if she shall be a second time attainted thereof, let her be openly brought, with minstrels, from prison unto the thew, with a hood of ray, and set thereon for a certain time, at the discretion of the Mayor and Aldermen. And the third time, let her have the same punishment, at the discretion of the Mayor and Aldermen, and let her hair be cut round about her head while upon the thew, and, after that, let her be taken to one of the City Gates, and let her [there] forswear the City for ever.

[175] 'A Ramble in St James's Park' (1680); Lord Rochester.

> Much wine had passed, with grave discourse
> Of who fucks who, and who does worse

(Such as you usually do hear
From those that diet at the Bear),
When I, who still take care to see
Drunkenness relieved by lechery,
Went out into St James's Park
To cool my head and fire my heart.
But though St James has th' honor on 't,
'Tis consecrate to prick and cunt.
There, by a most incestuous birth,
Strange woods spring from the teeming earth;
For they relate how heretofore,
When ancient Pict began to whore,
Deluded of his assignation
(Jilting, it seems, was then in fashion),
Poor pensive lover, in this place
Would frig upon his mother's face;
Whence rows of mandrakes tall did rise
Whose lewd tops fucked the very skies.
Each imitative branch does twine
In some loved fold of Aretine,
And nightly now beneath their shade
Are buggeries, rapes, and incests made.
Unto this all-sin-sheltering grove
Whores of the bulk and the alcove,
Great ladies, chambermaids, and drudges,
The ragpicker, and heiress trudges.
Carmen, divines, great lords, and tailors,
Prentices, poets, pimps, and jailers,
Footmen, fine fops do here arrive,
And here promiscuously they swive.

[176] Police report of a raid at Mother Clap's Molly
House (1725); quoted in *Mother Clap's Molly House*
by R. Norton.

I found between 40 and 50 Men making Love to one
another, as they call'd it. Sometimes they would sit on one
another's Laps, kissing in a lewd Manner, and using their

Hands indecently. Then they would get up, Dance and make Curtsies, and mimick the voices of Women. *O, Fie, Sir! – Pray, sir. – Dear Sir. Lord, how can you serve me so? – I swear I'll cry out. – You're a wicked Devil. – And you're a bold Face. – Eh ye little dear Toad! Come, buss!* – Then they'd hug, and play, and toy, and go out by Couples into another Room on the same Floor, to be marry'd, as they call'd it.

[177] Fanny Hill becomes a whore (1749); from *Memoirs of a woman of pleasure* by J. Cleland.

Presently, assuming more courage and seeking some diversion from my uneasy thoughts, I ventured to lift up my head a little and sent my eyes on a course round the room where they met full tilt with those of a lady (for such my extreme innocence pronounced her) sitting in a corner of the room, dressed in a velvet manteel (*nota bene*, in the midst of summer) with her bonnet off; squob-fat, red-faced, and at least fifty.

She looked as if she would devour me with her eyes, staring at me from head to foot, without the least regard to the confusion and blushes her eyeing me so fixedly put me to and which were to her, no doubt, the strongest recommendation and marks of my being fit for her purpose. After a little time, in which my air, person, and whole figure had undergone her strict examination, which I had, on my part, tried to render favourable to me by primming, drawing up my neck, and setting my best looks, she advanced and spoke to me with the greatest demureness:

'Sweet heart, do you want a place?'

'Yes! and please you' (with a curtsy down to the ground) . . .

Madam was . . . so well pleased with her bargain, that fearing, I presume, lest better advice or some accident might occasion my slipping through her fingers, she would officiously take me in a coach to my inn where, calling herself for my box, it was, I being present, delivered without the least scruple or explanation as to where I was going.

This being over, she bid the coachman drive to a shop in St Paul's Churchyard, where she bought a pair of gloves, which she gave me and thence renewed her directions to the coachman to drive to her house in—street, who accordingly landed us at her door, after I had been cheered up and entertained by the way with the most plausible flams, without one syllable from which I could conclude anything but that I was by the greatest good luck fallen into the hands of the kindest mistress, not to say friend, that the varsal world could afford; and accordingly I entered her doors with most complete confidence and exultation . . .

My mistress first began her part with telling me that I must have good spirits and learn to be free with her; that she had not taken me to be a common servant, to do domestic drudgery, but to be a kind of companion to her; and that, if I would be a good girl, she would do more than twenty mothers for me; to all which I answered only by the profoundest and the awkwardest curtsies and a few monosyllables, such as 'yes! no! to be sure'.

Presently my mistress touched the bell, and in came a strapping maidservant who had let us in: 'Here, Martha,' said Mrs Brown, 'I have just hired this young woman to look after my linnen, so step up and show her her chamber; and I charge you to use her with as much respect as you would myself, for I have taken a prodigious liking to her, and I do not know what I shall do for her.'

Martha, who was an arch jade, and being used to this decoy, had her cue perfect, made me a kind of half-curtsy and asked me to walk up with her and accordingly showed me a neat room, two pair of stairs backwards, in which there was a handsome bed where Martha told me I was to lie with a young gentlewoman, a cousin of my mistress's, who she was sure would be vastly good to me. Then she ran out into such affected encomiums on her good mistress! her sweet mistress! and how happy I was to light upon her, that I could not have bespoke a better, with

other the like gross stuff, such as would itself have started
suspicions in any but such an unpractised simpleton who
was perfectly new to life and who took every word she
said in the very sense she laid out for me to take it; but
she readily saw what a penetration she had to deal with
and measured me very rightly in her manner of whistling
to me, so as to make me pleased with my cage and blind
to its wires . . .

To slip over minutes of no importance to the main of
my story, I pass the interval to bedtime in which I was
more and more pleased with the views that opened to me
of an easy service under these good people; and after
supper, being showed up to bed, Miss Phoebe, who
observed a kind of modest reluctance in me to strip and
go to bed in my shift before her now the maid was
withdrawn, came up to me, and beginning with unpinning
my handkerchief and gown, soon encouraged me to go on
with undressing myself, and, still blushing at now seeing
myself naked to my shift, I hurried to get under the
bedclothes out of sight. Phoebe laughed and was not long
before she placed herself by my side. She was about five
and twenty, by her own most suspicious account, in
which, according to all appearances, she must have sunk
at least ten good years, allowance too being made for the
havoc which a long course of hackneyship and hot waters
must have made of her constitution and which had already
brought on, upon the spur, that stale stage in which those
of her profession are reduced to think of *showing* company instead of *seeing* it.

No sooner then was this precious substitute of my
mistress's lain down, but she, who was never out of her
way when any occasion of lewdness presented itself,
turned to me, embraced and kissed me with great eagerness. This was new, this was odd; but imputing it to
nothing but pure kindness, which, for aught I knew, it
might be the London way to express in that manner, I was
determined not to be behind-hand with her and returned
her the kiss and embrace with all the fervour that perfect
innocence knew.

Encouraged by this, her hands became extremely free and wandered over my whole body, with touches, squeezes, pressures that rather warmed and surprised me with their novelty than they either shocked or alarmed me . . .

In the morning I awoke about ten, perfectly gay and refreshed; Phoebe was up before me and asked me in the kindest manner how I did, how I had rested, and if I was ready for breakfast, carefully at the same time avoiding to increase the confusion she saw I was in, at looking her in the face, by any hint of the night's bed scene. – I told her if she pleased I would get up and begin any work she would be pleased to set me about. She smiled; presently the maid brought in the tea equipage, and I just huddled my clothes on, when in waddled my mistress. I expected no less than to be told off, if not chid for, my late rising, when I was agreeably disappointed by her compliments on my pure and fresh looks. I was 'a bud of beauty' (this was her style) and how vastly all the fine men would admire me! to all which my answers did not, I can assure you, wrong my breeding: they were as simple and silly as they could wish, and, no doubt, flattered them infinitely more than they had proved me enlightened by education and knowledge of the world.

We breakfasted; and the tea things were scarce removed, when in were brought two bundles of linen and wearing apparel; in short, all the necessaries for *rigging me out*, as they termed it, completely.

Imagine to yourself, Madam, how my little coquette-heart fluttered with joy at the sight of a white lutestring, flowered with silver, scoured indeed, but passed on me for spick and span new, a Brussels lace cap, braided shoes, and the rest in proportion, all second-hand finery, and procured instantly for the occasion by the diligence and industry of the good Mrs Brown, who had already a chapman for me in the house before whom my charms were to pass in review; for he had not only in course insisted on a previous sight of the premises, but also on immediate surrender to him, in case of his agreeing for me; concluding very wisely that such a place as I was in was of the hottest to trust the keeping of such a perishable commodity in as a maidenhead.

The care of dressing and tricking me out for the market was then left to Phoebe, who acquitted herself, if not well, at least perfectly to the satisfaction of everything but my impatience of seeing myself dressed . . .

Well then, dressed I was, and little did it then enter into my head that all this gay attire was no more than decking the victim out for sacrifice, whilst I innocently attributed all to sheer friendship and kindness in the sweet good Mrs Brown, who, I was forgetting to mention, had, under the pretence of keeping my money safe, got from me, without the least hesitation, the driblet (so I now call it) which remained to me after the expenses of my journey.

After some little time, most agreeably spent before the glass in scarce self-admiration, since my new dress had by much the greatest share in it, I was sent for down to the parlour where the old lady saluted me, and wished me joy of my new clothes, which, she was not ashamed to say, fitted me as if I had worn nothing but the finest all my lifetime; but what was it she could not see me silly enough to swallow? At the same time she presented me to another cousin of her own creation, an elderly gentleman, who got up at my entry into the room, and on my dropping a curtsy to him, saluted me and seemed a little affronted that I had only presented my cheek to him, a mistake which, if one, he immediately corrected by glueing his lips to mine with an ardour which his figure had not at all disposed me to thank him for: his figure, I say, than which nothing could be more shocking or detestable; for ugly and disagreeable were terms too gentle to convey a just idea of it.

Imagine to yourself a man rather past threescore, short and ill made, with a yellow cadaverous hue, great goggling eyes that stared as if he was strangled; an out-mouth from two more properly tushes than teeth, livid lips, and a breath like a jakes. Then he had a peculiar ghastliness in his grin that made him perfectly frightful, if not dangerous to women with child; yet, made as he was thus in mock of man, he was so blind to his own staring deformities as to think himself born for pleasing, and that no woman could see him with impunity; in consequence of which idea he had lavished great sums on such wretches as could gain upon themselves to pretend love to his person, whilst to those who had not art or patience to dissemble the horror it inspired he behaved even brutally. Impotence, more than necessity, made him seek in variety the provocative that was wanting to raise him to the pitch of enjoyment, which too he often saw himself balked of by the failure of his powers: and this always threw him into a fit of rage, which he wreaked, as far as he durst, on the innocent objects of his fit of momentary desire.

This then was the monster to which my conscientious benefactress, who had long been his purveyor in this way, had doomed me, and sent for me down purposely for this examination.

[178] Harris's List of Covent Garden Ladies (1764); from *Harris's List of Covent Garden Ladies*.

Polly Gold. Spring Gardens. Short pretty and very agreeable as to her Person and sings a good song. Has been on the Town about ten years . . . she is like a *Kite*, sometimes high and sometimes low. She and Miss Metham are constant customers at *The Yellow Cat* near Exeter Exchange.

Poll Talbot. Bow Street, Covent Garden. A fair comely Dame who by long intercourse . . . has learnt that the profession of a Purveyor is more profitable than that of a Private Trader, and for that reason has opened a House for the amusement of genteel Company where Gentlemen and Ladies will meet with a Civil Reception. She loves the smack of the Whip sometimes . . .

Poll Davis. Manchester Square. A delicate genteel Lady of the First Fashion and Price . . . seldom to be seen in the street unless in a Sedan-chair . . . her connections are mostly with Gentlemen of Rank and Fortune . . . never less than Ten Guineas and half-a crown for her servant.

Poll Johnson. Russell St, Covent Garden. A delicate plump girl who has various prices from ten shillings to Five Guineas according to the pocket of the *Cull*. Her principal Trade is with Petty Officers, some of whom have paid handsomely for their frolics.

Miss Bird *alias* Johnson. Brydges St, Covent Garden. A tall thin genteel girl agreeable in her manners . . . seen every night at the *Ben Jonsons Head*. She has a northern brogue and is too often in a state of intoxication.

[179] Gay Soho; from *The Naked Civil Servant* by Q. Crisp.

When I left King's College, London (needless to say without a Diploma in Journalism), I could at first find no better occupation than sitting at home getting on my parents' nerves. I became so listless that my mother thought it only polite to regard me as ill. She sent me to her doctor. Without making even the most cursory examination of me he declared that all I needed was a lesson in life. My father was very annoyed. He realized that he would have to pay a consultation fee for these few glib words. He was lucky that psychology had not yet reached the middle classes. He might have had to pay much more for less. At the time, my own reaction to the doctor's remark was blank incomprehension. Later when, to vary the monotony of my existence, I took to wandering about the streets of the West End, I stumbled on the very truth that was just what the doctor had ordered. I learned that I was not alone.

As I wandered along Piccadilly or Shaftesbury Avenue, I passed young men standing at the street corners who said, 'Isn't it terrible tonight, dear? No men about. The Dilly's not what it used to be.' Though the Indian boy at school had once amazed us all with the information that in Birmingham there were male prostitutes, I had never believed that I would actually see one. Here they were for all the world to recognize – or almost all the world. A passer-by would have to be very innocent indeed not to catch the meaning of the mannequin walk and the stance in which the hip was only prevented from total dislocation by the hand placed upon it . . .

We sat huddled together in a café called the Black Cat. (We were not putting up with any such nonsense as 'Au Chat Noir' which was written over the window.) This was in Old Compton Street. It looked like a dozen other cafés in Soho. It had a horseshoe bar of occasionally scrubbed wood, black and white check linoleum floor and mirrors everywhere. The deafening glass boxes in which nowadays customers sit and eat with their ankles on view to the public had not then been built. In that happier time all was squalor and a silence spangled only with the swish of knives and the tinkle of glass as the windows of the Black Cat got pushed in.

Day after uneventful day, night after loveless night, we sat in this café buying each other cups of tea, combing each other's hair and trying on each other's lipsticks. We were waited on with indulgent contempt by an elderly gentleman, who later achieved a fame that we would have then thought quite beyond him, by being involved in a murder case. Had the denizens of the Black Cat known he was such a desperate character, they would doubtless have done much more to provoke him. As it was we only bored him by making, with ladylike sips, each cup of tea last as long as a four-course meal. From time to time he threw us out. When this happened we waltzed round the neighbouring streets in search of love or money or both. If we didn't find either, we returned to the café and put on more lipstick. It never occurred to any of us to try to be more loveable. Even if it had, I do not think we would have adopted a measure so extreme. Occasionally, while we chattered on the street corner one of our friends would go whizzing past crying, 'They're coming.' At this we would scatter. It meant that, while being questioned, one of the boys had bolted and his inquisitors were after him. At such times, if a detective saw his quarry escaping, he would seize upon the nearest prey, however innocently that person might be behaving. We treated the police as it is said you should treat wild animals. As we passed them, we never ran but, if they were already running, we spread out so that only one of our number would die. Policemen in uniform were not classed as man-eaters. I had no idea what the rules were but they never seemed to give chase; they only moved us on . . .

I have known female whores who spoke very bitterly of their calling. 'If they don't like my face, they can put a cushion over it. I know it's not *that* they're interested in.' But to the boys this profession never seemed shameful. It was their daytime occupations for which they felt they needed to apologize. In some instances, these were lower class or humdrum or, worst of all, unfeminine. At least whoring was never that . . .

I disliked the coarseness of the situations in which I found myself. Courtship consisted of walking along the street with a man who had my elbow in a merciless grip until we came to a dark doorway. Then he said, 'This'll do.' These are the only words of tenderness that were ever uttered to me.

London and Londoners

[180] 'London Lickpenny' (15th century); by J. Lydgate.

LONDON LICKPENNY

To London once my steps I bent,
   Where truth in no wise should be faint;
To Westminster-ward I forthwith went
   To a man of law to make complaint.
   I said: 'For Mary's love, that holy saint,
     Pity the poor that would proceed!'
     But for lack of money I could not speed.

And as I thrust the press among,
   By froward chance my hood was gone;
Yet for all that I stayed not long
   Till at the King's Bench I was come.
   Before the judge I kneeled anon
     And prayed him for God's sake to take heed;
     But for lack of money I might not speed . . .

Unto the Common Place I yode tho
   Where sat one with a silken hood;

I did him reverence – for I ought to do so –
    And told my case as well as I could,
    How my goods were defrauded me by falsehood.
        I gat not a mum of his mouth for my meed,
        And for lack of money I might not speed . . .

In Westminster Hall I found out one
    Which went in a long gown of ray;
I crouched and kneeled before him anon,
    For Mary's love of help I him pray.
    'I wot not what thou meanst,' gan he say;
        To get me thence he did me beed:
        For lack of money I could not speed.

Within this hall neither rich nor yet poor
    Would do for me aught, although I should die;
Which seeing, I gat me out of the door,
    Where Flemings began on me for to cry:
    'Master, what will you copen or buy?
        Fine felt hats, or spectacles to read?
        Lay down your silver, and here you may speed.' . . .

Then unto London I did me hie –
    Of all the land it beareth the prise!
'Hot peascods!' one began to cry,
    'Strawberry ripe!' and 'cherries in the rise!'
    One bad me come near and buy some spice;
        Pepper and saffron they gan me beede;
        But for lack of money I might not speed.

Then to the Cheap I gan me drawn,
    Where much people I saw for to stand:
One offered me velvet, silk, and lawn;
    Another he taketh me by the hand,
        'Here is Paris thread, the finest in the land'.
        I never was used to such things in deed,
        And, wanting money, I might not speed.

Then went I forth by London Stone,
    Throughout all Canwike Street:
Drapers much cloth me offered anon;

Then comes me one, cried 'Hot sheep's feet!'
One cried 'Mackerel!'; 'Rishes green!' another gan greet.
  One bad me buy a hood to cover my head;
  But for want of money I might not speed.

Then I hied me into East Cheap.
  One cries 'Ribs of beef and many a pie!'
Pewter pots they clattered on a heap;
  There was harp, pipe, and minstrelsie.
  'Yea, by cock!' 'Nay, by cock!' some began to cry.
    Some sung of Jenken and Julian for their meed.
    But for lack of money I might not speed.

Then into Cornhill anon I yode,
  Where was much stolen gear among;
I saw where hong mine own hode
  That I had lost among the throng.
  To buy my own hood I thought it wrong –
    I knew it well as I did my Creed:
    But for lack of money I could not speed.

The taverner took me by the sleeve:
  'Sir,' saith he, 'will you our wine assay?'
I answered: 'That can not much me grieve;
  A penny can do no more than it may.'
  I drank a pint and for it did pay;
    Yet sore a-hungered from thence I yede,
    And, wanting money, I could not speed.

Then hied I me to Billingsgate,
  And one cried: 'Hoo! go we hence!'
I prayed a barge-man for God's sake
  That he would spare me my expense.
  'Thou 'scapst not here', quod he, 'under two pence;
    I list not yet bestow my alms-deed.'
    Thus, lacking money, I could not speed.

Then I conveyed me into Kent,
  For of the law would meddle no more;
Because no man to me took entent
  I dight me to do as I did before.

Now Jesus that in Bethlem was bore,
   Save London, and send true lawyers their meed!
   For whoso wants money with them shall not speed.

[181] Aggressive London (1719); from *Mr Misson's Memoirs and Observations* by Misson de Valbourg.

If two little boys quarrel in the street, the passengers stop, make a ring round them in a moment, and set them against one another, that they may come to fisticuffs ... During the fight the ring of bystanders encourages the combatants with great delight of heart, and never parts them while they fight according to the rules. And these bystanders are not only other boys, porters, and rabble, but all sorts of men of fashion, some thrusting by the mob that they may see plainly, others getting upon stalls, and all would hire places, if scaffolds could be built in a moment. The fathers and mothers of the boys let them fight on as well as the rest, and hearten him that gives the ground, or has the worst. These combats are less frequent among grown men than children, but they are not rare. If a coachman has a dispute about his fare with a gentleman that has hired him, and the gentleman offers to fight him to decide the quarrel, the coachman consents with all his heart. The gentleman pulls off his sword, lays it in some shop with his cane, gloves and cravat, and boxes in the same manner as I have described above. If the coachmen gets soundly drubbed, which happens almost always, that goes for payment, but if he is the beater, the beatee must pay the money about which they quarrelled. I once saw the late Duke of Grafton at fisticuffs in the open street, with such a fellow, whom he lambed most horribly.

[182] The silent Londoners (1747); from *Letters on the English and French nations* by J. B. le Blanc.

The English do not live and converse as much with one another as the French; wherefore, to fill up the vacuity of their lives, they are obliged to read or do nothing ... They are naturally inclined to silence, as we are to exhaust ourselves in discourse; and silence inspires a taste for reading, as much as talkativeness is averse to it. Perhaps even a great many persons, who in this country write books, would never have attempted any such employment if they had had spirit enough to do anything else.

[183] The insolence and racism of the mob (1772); from *A Tour of London* by J. P. Grosley.

The day after my arrival, my servant discovered, by sad experience, what liberties the mob are accustomed to take with the French, and all who have the appearance of being such. He had followed the crowd to Tyburn, where three rogues were hanged, two of whom were father and son. The execution being over, as he was returning home through Oxford-road, with the remains of the numerous multitude which had been present at the execution, he was attacked by two or three blackguards; and the crowd having soon surrounded him, he made a sight for the rabble. Jack Ketch, the executioner, joined in the sport, and, entering the circle, struck the poor sufferer upon the shoulder. They began to drag him about by the skirts of his coat, and by his shoulder-knot; when, luckily for him, he was perceived by three grenadiers belonging to the French guards, who, having deserted, and crossed the seas, were then drinking at an ale-house hard by the scene of action. Armed with such weapons as chance presented them, they suddenly attacked the mob, laid on soundly upon such as came within their reach, and brought their countryman off safe to the ale-house, and from thence to my lodgings. Seven or eight campaigns, which he had served with an officer in the gens-d'armes, and a year which he afterwards passed in Italy, had not sufficiently inured him to bear this rough treatment: it had a most surprising effect upon him. He shut himself up in the house a fortnight, where he vented his indignation in continual imprecations against England and the English.

Strong and robust as he was, if he had any knowledge of the language and the country, he might have come off nobly, by proposing a boxing-bout to the man whom he thought weakest amongst the crowd of assailants: if victorious, he would have been honourably brought home, and had his triumph celebrated even by those who now joined against him. This is the first law of this species of combat; a law, which the English punctually observe in the heat of battle, where the vanquished always find a generous conqueror in that nation. This should seem to prove, in contradiction to Hobbes, that, in a state of nature, a state with which the street-scufflers of London are closely connected, man, who is by fits wicked and cruel, is, at the bottom, good-natured and generous.

I have already observed, that the English themselves are not secure from the insolence of the London mob. I had a proof of this from the young surgeon, who accompanied me from Paris to Boulogne.

At the first visit which he paid me in London, he informed me, that, a few days after his arrival, happening to take a walk through the fields on the Surrey side of the Thames, dressed in a little green frock, which he had brought from Paris, he was attacked by three of those gentlemen of the mobility [sic], who, taking him for a Frenchman, not only abused him with the foulest language, but gave him two or three slaps on the face: 'Luckily, added he in French, I did not return their ill language; for, if I had, they would certainly have thrown me into the Thames, as they assured me they would, as soon as they perceived I was an Englishman, if I ever happened to come in their way again, in my Paris dress.'

A Portuguese of my acquaintance, taking a walk in the same fields, with three of his countrymen, their conversation in Portuguese was interrupted by two watermen, who, doubling their fists at them, cried, 'French dogs, speak your damned French, if you dare.'

I say nothing of the throwing of stones one day about noon, in the midst of Holborn, into a coach, where I happened to be, with three Frenchmen, one of whom was struck on the shoulder: those stones might, perhaps, have been aimed elsewhere, and have hit us only by accident.

Happening to go one evening from the part of town where I lived, to the Museum, I passed by the Seven Dials. The place was crowded with people, waiting to see a poor wretch stand in the pillory, whose punishment was deferred to another day. The mob, provoked at this disappointment, vented their rage upon all that passed that way, whether a-foot or in coaches; and threw at them dirt, rotten eggs, dead dogs, and all sorts of trash and ordure, which they had provided to pelt the unhappy wretch, according to custom. Their fury fell chiefly upon the hackney coaches, the drivers of which they forced to salute them with their whips and their hats, and to cry 'huzza': which word is the signal for rallying in all public frays. The disturbance, upon this occasion, was so much the greater, as the person who was to have acted the principal part in the scene, which, by being postponed, had put the rabble into such an ill humour, belonged to the nation which that rabble thinks it has most right to insult.

In England, no rank or dignity is secure from their insults. The young queen herself was exposed to them upon her first arrival at London: the rabble was affronted at her majesty's keeping one window of her sedan-chair drawn up.

This insolence is considered by many only as the humour and pleasantry of porters and watermen; but this humour and pleasantry was, in the hands of the long parliament, one of their chief weapons against Charles the First.

The politeness, the civility, and the officiousness of people of good breeding, whom we meet in the streets, as well as the obliging readiness of the citizens and shopkeepers, even of the inferior sort, sufficiently indemnify and console us for the insolence of the mob; as I have often experienced . . .

It should, notwithstanding, be remarked by the way, that many particulars, connected with the English manners and customs, and which necessarily result from thence, might be mistaken for . . . animosity, though they are quite foreign to it, however observers may be imposed upon by first appearances.

Of this nature was the abrupt manner, in which people rose, and quitted me, to seek for a person that spoke French: this was the heighth of politeness; but before I became used to it, I considered it only as an instance of surliness and ill-humour, arising from the antipathy between the two nations.

The French are likewise apt to imagine, that it is on account of their country, they are pushed and shoved in the most frequented streets, and often driven into the kennel [gutter]; but they are mistaken. The English walk very fast: their thoughts being entirely engrossed by business, they are very punctual to their appointments, and those, who happen to be in their way, are sure to be sufferers by it: constantly darting forward, they justle them with a force proportioned to their bulk and velocity of their motion. I have seen foreigners, not used to this exercise, let themselves be tossed and whirled about a long time, in the midst of a crowd of passengers, who had nothing else in view, but to get forward. Having soon adopted the English custom, I made the best of my way through crowded streets, exerting my utmost efforts to shun persons, who were equally careful to avoid me.

[184] 'The Garden' (1785) by W. Cowper.

The Garden
      Ambition, avarice, penury incurr'd
By endless riot, vanity, the lust
Of pleasure and variety, dispatch,
As duly as the swallows disappear,
The world of wandering knights and squires to town.
London ingulfs them all! The shark is there,
And the shark's prey; the spendthrift, and the leech
That sucks him; there the sycophant, and he
Who, with bare-headed and obsequious bows,
Begs a warm office, doom'd to a cold jail,

And groat per diem, if his patron frown.
The levee swarms, as if in golden pomp
Were character'd on every statesman's door,
'BATTER'D AND BANKRUPT FORTUNES
   MENDED HERE.'
These are the charms that sully and eclipse
The charms of nature. 'Tis the cruel gripe
That lean hard-handed Poverty inflicts,
The hope of better things, the chance to win,
The wish to shine, the thirst to be amused,
That at the sound of Winter's hoary wing
Unpeople all our counties of such herds
Of fluttering, loitering, cringing, begging, loose,
And wanton vagrants, as make London, vast
And boundless as it is, a crowded heap.
O thou, resort and mart of all the earth,
Chequer'd with all complexions of mankind,
And spotted with all crimes; in whom I see
Much that I love, and more that I admire,
And all that I abhor; thou freckled fair
That pleases and yet shock'st me, I can laugh,
And I can weep, can hope, and can despond,
Feel wrath and pity, when I think on thee!
Ten righteous would have saved a city once,
And thou hast many righteous. – Well for thee –
That salt preserves thee; more corrupted else,
And therefore more obnoxious, at this hour,
Than Sodom in her day had power to be,
For whom God heard his Abraham plead in vain.

[185] Doctor Johnson on London; from various sources (late 18th century), James Boswell.

Talking of London, he observed, 'Sir if you wish to have a just notion of the magnitude of this city, you must not be satisfied with seeing its great streets and squares, but must survey the innumerable little lanes and courts. It is not in the showy evolutions of buildings, but in the multiplicity of human habitations which are crowded together, that the wonderful immensity of London consists.' . . .

We walked in the evening in Greenwich Park. He asked me, I suppose, by way of trying my disposition, 'Is not this very fine?' Having no exquisite relish of the beauties of Nature, and being more delighted with 'the busy hum of men', I answered, 'Yes, Sir; but not equal to Fleet-Street'. JOHNSON. 'You are right, Sir.'

[. . .] Johnson was much attached to London: he observed, that a man stored his mind better there, than any where else; and that in remote situations a man's body might be feasted, but his mind was starved, and his faculties apt to degenerate, from want of exercise and competition. No place, (he said,) cured a man's vanity or arrogance so well as London; for as no man was either great or good 'per se', but as compared with others not so good or great, he was sure to find in the metropolis many his equal and some his superiours. He observed, that a man in London was in less danger of falling in love indiscreetly, than any where else; for there the difficulty of deciding between the conflicting pretensions of a vast variety of objects, kept him safe. He told me, that he had frequently been offered country preferment, if he would consent to take orders; but he could not leave the improved society of the capital, or consent to exchange the exhilarating joys and splendid decorations of public life, for the obscurity, insipidity, and uniformity of remote situations.

[. . .] I suggested a doubt, that if I were to reside in London, the exquisite zest with which I relished it in occasional visits might go off, and I might grow tired of it. JOHNSON. 'Why Sir! you find no man, at all an intellectual, who is willing to leave London. No, Sir, when a man is tired of London, he is tired of life; for there is in London all that life can afford.' [. . .]

And such was his love of London, so high a relish had he of its magnificent extent, and variety of intellectual entertainment, that he languished when absent from it, his mind having become quite luxurious from the long habit of enjoying the metropolis; and, therefore, although at Lichfield, surrounded with friends, who loved and revered him, and for whom he had a very sincere affection, he still found that such conversation as London affords, could be found no where else. These feelings, joined, probably, to some flattering hopes of aid from the eminent physicians and surgeons in London, who kindly and generously attended him without accepting of fees, made him resolve to return to the capital . . .

[186] A city of extremes (1820); from *Life in London* by P. Egan.

The EXTREMES, in every point of view, are daily to be met with in the Metropolis; from the most rigid, persevering, never-tiring industry, down to laziness, which, in its consequences, frequently operates far worse than idleness. The greatest love of and contempt for money are equally conspicuous; and in no place are pleasure and business so much united as in London. The highest veneration for and practice of religion distinguishes the Metropolis, contrasted with the most horrid commission of crimes: and the *experience* of the oldest inhabitant scarcely renders him safe against the specious plans and artifices continually laid to entrap the most vigilant. The next-door neighbour of a man in London is generally as great a stranger to him, as if he lived at the distance of York. And it is in the Metropolis that *prostitution* is so profitable a business, and conducted so openly, that hundreds of persons keep houses of ill-fame, for the reception of girls not more than *twelve* and *thirteen* years of age, without a blush upon their cheeks, and mix with society heedless of stigma or reproach; yet honour, integrity, and independence of soul, that nothing can remove from its basis, are to be found in every street in London. Hundreds of persons are always going to bed in the morning, besotted with dissipation and gaming, while thousands of his Majesty's liege subjects are quitting their pillows to pursue their useful occupations. The most bare-faced villains, swindlers, and thieves, walk about the streets in the day-time, committing their various depredations, with as much confidence as men of unblemished reputation and honesty. In short, the most vicious and abandoned wretches, who are lost to every friendly tie that binds man to man, are to be found in swarms in the Metropolis; and so depraved are they in principle, as to be considered, from their uncalled-for outrages upon the inhabitants, a *waste of wickedness*, operating as a complete terror, in spite of the *activity* of the police. Yet, notwithstanding this dark and melancholy part of the picture, there are some of the worthiest, most tender-hearted, liberal minds, and charitable dispositions, which ornament London, and render it the delight and happiness of society.

Indeed, the Metropolis is a complete CYCLOPÆDIA, where every man of the most religious or moral habits, attached to any sect, may find something to please his palate, regulate his taste, suit his pocket, enlarge his mind, and make him happy and comfortable. If places of worship give any sort of character to the *goodness* of the Metropolis, between four and five hundred are opened for religious purposes on Sundays. In fact, every SQUARE in the Metropolis is a sort of *map* well worthy of exploring, if riches and titles operate as a source of curiosity to the visitor. There is not a *street* also in London, but what may be compared to a large or small volume of intelligence, abounding with anecdote, incident, and peculiarities. A *court* or *alley* must be obscure indeed, if it does not afford some remarks; and even the *poorest* cellar contains some *trait* or other, in unison with the manners and feelings of this great city, that may be put down in the note-book, and reviewed, at an after period, with much pleasure and satisfaction.

[187] Byron on London (1824); from *Don Juan* Cantos 10 & 11.

> The sun went down, the smoke rose up,
>   as from
> A half-unquench'd volcano, o'er a
>   space

Which well beseem'd the 'Devil's drawing-
    room,'
  As some have qualified that wondrous
    place:
But Juan felt, though not approaching
    home,
  As one who, though he were not of the
    race,
Revered the soil, of those true sons the
    mother,
Who butcher'd half the earth, and bullied
    t'other.

A mighty mass of brick, and smoke, and
    shipping,
  Dirty and dusky, but as wide as eye
Could reach, with here and there a sail
    just skipping
  In sight, then lost amidst the forestry
Of masts; a wilderness of steeples peeping
  On tiptoe through their sea-coal canopy;
A huge, dun cupola, like a foolscap crown
On a fool's head – and there is London
    Town . . .

I say, Don Juan, wrapt in contemplation,
  Walk'd on behind his carriage, o'er the
    summit,
And lost in wonder of so great a nation,
  Gave way to't, since he could not over-
    come it.
'And here,' he cried, 'is Freedom's
    chosen station;
  Here peals the people's voice, nor can
    entomb it
Racks, prisons, inquisitions; resurrection
Awaits it, each new meeting or election.

'Here are chaste wives, pure lives; here
    people pay

But what they please; and if that things
　　be dear,
'Tis only that they love to throw away
　　Their cash, to show how much they
　　　have a year.
Here laws are all inviolate; none lay
　　Traps for the traveller; every highway's
　　　clear;
Here' – he was interrupted by a knife,
With – 'Damn your eyes! your money or
　　　your life!' – . . .

Through Groves, so call'd as being void of
　　　trees,
　　(Like *lucus* from *no* light); through
　　　prospects named
Mount Pleasant, as containing nought to
　　please,
　　Nor much to climb; through little boxes
　　　framed
Of bricks, to let the dust in at your ease,
　　With 'To be let,' upon their doors pro-
　　　claim'd;
Through 'Rows' most modestly call'd
　　　'Paradise,'
Which Eve might quit without much
　　　sacrifice; –

Through coaches, drays, choked turn-
　　　pikes, and a whirl
　　Of wheels, and roar of voices, and con-
　　　fusion;
Here taverns wooing to a pint of 'purl',
　　There mails fast flying off like a
　　　delusion;
There barbers' blocks with periwigs in
　　　curl
　　In windows; here the lamplighter's
　　　infusion

Slowly distill'd into the glimmering glass
(For in those days we had not got to
    gas –);

Through this, and much, and more, is the
    approach
  Of travellers to mighty Babylon:
Whether they come by horse, or chaise,
    or coach,
  With slight exceptions, all the ways seem
    one.
I could say more, but do not choose to
  encroach
  Upon the Guide-book's privilege. The
    sun
Had set some time, and night was on the
    ridge
Of twilight, as the party cross'd the bridge.

That's rather fine, the gentle sound of
    Thamis –
  Who vindicates a moment, too, his
    stream –
Though hardly heard through multi-
    farious 'damme's.'
  The lamps of Westminster's more
    regular gleam,
The breadth of pavement, and yon shrine
    where fame is
  A spectral resident – whose pallid beam
In shape of moonshine hovers o'er the
    pile –
Make this a sacred part of Albion's isle.

The Druid's groves are gone – so much
    the better:
  Stonehenge is not –but what the devil
    is it? –
But Bedlam still exists with its sage fetter,

That madmen may not bite you on a
    visit;
The Bench too seats or suits full many a
        debtor;
    The Mansion-House, too (though some
        people quiz it),
To me appears a stiff yet grand erection;
But then the Abbey's worth the whole
    collection.

The line of lights, too, up to Charing
        Cross,
    Pall Mall, and so forth, have a corus-
        cation
Like gold as in comparison to dross,
    Match'd with the Continent's illumin-
        ation,
Whose cities Night by no means deigns to
    gloss.
    The French were not yet a lamp-
        lighting nation,
And when they grew so – on their new-
    found lantern,
Instead of wicks, they made a wicked man
    turn . . .

Over the stones still rattling, up Pall Mall,
    Through crowds and carriages, but
        waxing thinner
As thunder'd knockers broke the long-
        seal'd spell
    Of doors 'gainst duns, and to an early
        dinner
Admitted a small party as night fell, –
    Don Juan, our young diplomatic
        sinner,
Pursued his path, and drove past some
    hotels,
St James's Palace and St James's 'Hells'.

[188] A city for the philosopher (early 19th century); from *English Fragments* by H. Heine.

I have seen the most marvellous thing that the world can show to the astonished soul. I have seen it and am still amazed – my thoughts are bewildered in this labyrinth of masonry, through the midst of which the surging stream of living men's faces is rushing to and fro, with all their tumultuous passions, with all their insatiable haste of love, of hunger, and of hate – I speak of London.

You may send a philosopher to London, but for heaven's sake, do not send a poet! Send your philosopher, and set him at a corner of Cheapside. He will learn more there than out of all the books at the Leipsic Fair; and, as the waves of humanity roar around him, so also shall a sea of new thoughts rise up before him. The Eternal Spirit hovering overhead, will breathe upon him and the most hidden secrets of the social order will suddenly be disclosed to him. He will distinctly hear and clearly see the pulsation of the world – for, if London be the right hand of the world, the active, powerful, dexter hand, so must this street, leading to Downing Street from the Exchange, be considered as a main artery.

But send no poet to London! That stern earnestness in all things, that colossal uniformity, that mechanical motion, that irksomeness of joy itself, that inexorable London stifles phantasy and rends the heart. And did you wish to send a German poet there, a dreamer, who would remain standing at every strange sight, before a ragged beggar-woman or a shining goldsmith's shop – oh, then it would go hard with him, and he would be pressed along from every side or be told mildly to 'move on!' just as he was jostled over. Oh, that confounded pushing! I soon observed this people has much to do. They live in great style, and although food and clothing in their land are dearer than in ours, yet they still make a point of being better fed and better clad than we. As is usual with superiority of rank, they have also their heavy debts; but notwithstanding, out of mere ostentation, they will throw

their guineas out at the window, and pay other nations to
purvey their pleasures, yet at the same time they give a
generous regal maintenance to the Crown. For all these
reasons John Bull has to work day and night to replenish
his exchequer in order to balance accounts with his extrav-
agance. Day and night must he tax his brains for the
invention of new machines; now he sits and calculates in
the sweat of his brow, anon he runs and races through the
streets, without looking much about him, from the
wharves to the Exchange, from the Exchange to the
Strand. And it is very pardonable that he somewhat
roughly brushes against, with a hasty expletive, a poor
German poet at the corner of Cheapside, who is staring
open-mouthed into a picture shop.

But the picture at which I was staring open-mouthed
represented the passage of the French army over the river
Beresina.

From the contemplation of this picture I was thus
roused again to look upon the multitudinous streets, where
a motley group of men, women, and children, horses,
coaches, amongst them also a funeral, rolled on in a
seething, surging, crying, groaning chaos. These it seemed
to me as if the whole of London were just such another
Beresina bridge, where every one in frantic eagerness, in
order to prolong his little bit of life, were forcing a passage
for himself through the crowd; where the poor foot-
passenger is trampled underfoot by the reckless rider;
where he who falls to the ground is lost for ever; where
the closest comrades, devoid of feeling, hurry over the
prostrate forms of their fellow-conscripts: and thousands,
faint and bleeding, vainly striving to clamber on the planks
of the bridge, fall down in the icy pool of death.

How much more serene and blissful is it, on the other
hand in our dear Germany! How dreamily soft, how
sabbatically peaceful do things adjust themselves there!
How quietly the guard is mounted, placid sunshine glances
on the uniforms and athwart the houses, the swallows
flutter on the pavements, the lusty wives of the councillors
laugh merrily from the windows, there is room enough in

the echoing streets. The dogs here, quite undisturbed, can graciously exchange compliments through the nose. The people can with comfort remain standing while they discuss the theatre, and pay an old courtly homage to my highborn little black-guard or his little henchman as they pass decked with many-coloured ribbons on their scurvy coats, or as a powdered, gilded rogue of a chamberlain, consequently returning the greeting, prances along!

I had made up my mind not to be overpowered by the magnificence of London, about which I had heard so much. But it fared with me as with the poor schoolboy who had determined not to feel the whipping he was about to get. The state of the case was this, that he expected the usual lashes with the usual cane, instead of which he got a severe drubbing. I expected grand palaces, and saw nothing but small houses. It was, however, just this monotonous uniformity at which I felt so awestricken.

[189] Selfish London (1844); from 'Physiology of London Life' by J. Fisher Murray.

In many points of view, London is not a desirable place to dwell; in many more it is positively objectionable; to the young and inexperienced, it is in almost every sense highly dangerous. Let the young man, excited by what he may have heard or read of London, and who finds in this, as in every other case, how greatly

Distance lends enchantment to the view,

pause before he swells the full tide of existence struggling in London, and hear what one old and experienced in its ways has to say.

Let him recollect, in the first place, that the London labour-market is always overstocked. We do not refer only to mere mechanic toil; professional skill is supplied in much greater abundance than is required by the demand. [. . .]

For, in truth, the warfare of London life is a contest in

which the raw recruit has all disadvantages to contend with, save youth, activity, and the desire of doing; he has to force a place among thousands, whose places are already settled and made fast; he has before him the difficult *premier pas qui coute*.

In the next place, everything in London is done by CONNEXION. Connexion necessarily implies introduction; not the ordinary letter of introduction which, when young and inexperienced, we carried with us to town by pocketsful, and found to introduce us to just nothing at all; but the introduction of knowledge, experience, skill applicable in a high degree to some useful, practical purpose of life, for which men are wanted, and for which, when they *are* wanted, they are accustomed to be paid. Of course, if you go to London for the gratification of your vanity, or as an author, or other poor devil of that sort, or because you think yourself a clever fellow, or your parents think so for you, that is another affair. I only recommend you to take plenty of money in your pocket. I am now writing for the information of people who mean to do well, *in a well-doing way*, and not for clever fellows or madmen. [. . .]

Another word in your ear; if, unhappily, you may be a bit of scamp, which is not at all unlikely, don't be fool enough to imagine that you can go on with your pranks in London without paying the customary penalty. London is a wide place and a long, but rumour has wider scope and a longer tongue; nor is there any place I have seen (and this I tell you in good time) where *character*, in the most comprehensive sense of the word, is so vital, or where the want of it is so fatal to a man's success as London.

Never imagine that London wraps a man's vices or follies all over like a cloak. It does no such thing. When we told you that there is freedom here from observation and neighbourly gossip, we told the truth; but the truth holds only of those who choose to live alone, and who, perchance, may have reasons for living alone. If you choose to be a recluse, or to lead the life of an outlaw, London is the greatest desert you can find, and a more secluded hermitage than mountains can bestow. So long as you pay your way, annoy nobody, and be not found out, you can go on as you please, and pursue, without interference or observation, your especial vice or dissipation.

If you are a man of any note, or striving to make a name for yourself, you will, of course, have enemies. Nowhere will you have more than in London, because nowhere is competition, not only for fortune, but for that bombastic bladder of wind, *fame*, more active and unremitting. Of course your enemies will have a fling at you; and your friends, if you have any, you may rest assured will be very little behind your enemies, in damning with faint praise, assenting with civil leer, and good-naturedly bringing on the *tapis*, which they are sure to do, whatever defects in your life or conversation their intimacy may have given them an opportunity of becoming acquainted with.

This observation may seem harsh, and derogatory to the dignity of friendship; but every reader has it in his power to test its truth; and if he comes forward and says, that in any conversation about an absent friend among friends, he has not heard the predominant vice, folly, or eccentricity of that friend incidentally touched upon, at least *once* in the course of the evening, then I beg pardon for the calumny, and desire the pleasure of his better acquaintance.

In London, especially among the enterprising and ambitious, we have often sighed over the hollowness and selfishness that exist even among friends. The field being unlimited, and the horizons boundless, each man's desires, each man's ambition, are perpetually extending from the centre of the self. Nowhere is commendation less warm, nowhere encouragement less hearty, nowhere does failure or misfortune find less compassion, pity, or relief.

This all-absorbing selfishness is one of the greatest evils attending a London life; it reacts upon yourself, hardens your heart in your own defence, and renders you incapable of those tender promptings of pity, and those delicate sensibilities of affection without which, in our estimation, a man is no more than a two-legged rhinoceros.

[190] Wicked London (1848); from *Chronicles* by Richard of Devizes, translated by J. A. G. Giles.

You will come to London. Behold, I warn you, whatever of evil or of perversity there is in any whatever in all parts of the world, you will find in that city alone. Go not to the dances of panders, nor mix yourself up with the herds of the stews; avoid the talus and the dice, the theatre and the tavern. You will find more braggadocios there than in all France, while the number of flatterers is infinite. Stage players, buffoons, those that have no hair on their bodies, Garamantes, pickthanks, catamites, effeminate sodomites, lewd musical girls, druggists, lustful persons, fortune-tellers, extortioners, nightly strollers, magicians, mimics, common beggars, tatterdemalions – this whole crew has filled every house. So if you do not wish to live with the shameful, you will not dwell in London.

[191] Henry James on London (late 19th century); from various sources.

London is on the whole the most possible form of life. I take it as an artist and as a bachelor; as one who has the passion of observation and whose business is the study of human life. It is the biggest aggregation of human life – the most complete compendium of the world. The human race is better represented here than anywhere else, and if you learn to know your London you learn a great many things . . .

Have now been in London some ten days and actually feel very much at home here – feel domesticated and naturalized in fact, to quite a disgusting extent. I feel that in proportion as I cease to be perpetually thrilled surprised and delighted, I am being cheated out of my fun. I really feel as I had lived – I don't say a lifetime – but a year in this murky metropolis . . . up to this time I have been crushed under a sense of the mere magnitude of London – its inconceivable immensity – in such a way as to paralyse my mind for any appreciation of details. This is gradually subsiding; but what does it leave behind it? An extraordinary intellectual depression, as I may say, and an indefineable flatness of mind. The place sits on you, broods on you, stamps on you with the feet of its myriad bipeds and quadrupeds. In fine, it is anything but a cheerful or a charming city. Yet it is a very splendid one. It gives you, here at the West End and in the city proper, a vast impression of opulence and prosperity.

[192] Dostoyevsky on London (late 19th century); from *Winter Impressions of Summer Notes* by F. Dostoyevsky.

Only spent eight days altogether in London and the impression it left upon my mind – superficially at least – was of something on a grand scale, of vivid planning, original and not forced into a common mould. Everything there is so vast and so harsh in its originality. This originality is even a bit deceptive. Every harshness and every inconsistency is able to live in harmony with its antithesis and persist in walking hand-in-hand with it, continuing to be inconsistent, but apparently by no means excluding its antithesis. Each part stoutly upholds its own way and apparently does not interfere with the other parts of the whole. And yet there too the same stubborn, silent and by now chronic struggle is carried on, the struggle to the death of the typically Western principle of individual isolation with the necessity to live in some sort of harmony with each other, to create some sort of community and to settle down in the same ant-hill; even turning into an ant-hill seems desirable – anything to be able to settle down without having to devour each other – the alternative is to turn into cannibals . . .

Even superficially, how different it is from Paris! The immense town, forever bustling by night and by day, as vast as an ocean, the screech and howl of machinery, the railways built above the houses (and soon to be built under them) the daring of enterprise, the apparent disorder which in actual fact is the highest form of bourgeois order, the polluted Thames, the coal-saturated air, the magnificent squares and parks, the town's terrifying districts such as Whitechapel with its half-naked, savage and hungry population, the City with its millions and its world-wide trade, the Crystal Palace, the World Exhibition . . .

The Exhibition is indeed amazing. You feel the terrible force which has brought these innumerable people, who have come from the ends of the earth, all together into one fold; you realize the grandeur of the idea; you feel that something has been achieved here, that here is victory and triumph. And you feel nervous. However great your independence of mind, a feeling of fear somehow creeps over you. Can this, you think, in fact be the final accomplishment of an ideal state of things? Is this the end, by any chance? Perhaps this really is the 'one fold'? Perhaps we shall really have to accept this as the whole truth and cease from all movement thereafter? It is all so solemn, triumphant and proud that you are left breathless. You look at those hundreds of thousands, at those millions of people obediently trooping into this place from all parts of the earth – people who have come with only one thought in mind, quietly, stubbornly and silently milling round in this colossal palace, and you feel that something final has been accomplished here – accomplished and completed. It is a Biblical sight, something to do with Babylon, some prophecy out of the Apocalypse being fulfilled before your very eyes. You feel that a rich and ancient tradition of denial and protest is needed in order not to yield, not to succumb to impression, not to bow down in worship of fact, and not to idolize Baal, that is, not to take the actual for the ideal.

[193] Londoners (1905); from *The Soul of London* by F. Madox Ford.

With the coming of the Modern Newspaper, the Book has been deposed from its intimate position in the hearts of men. You cannot in London read a book from day to day, because you must know the news, in order to be a fit companion for your fellow Londoner. Connected thinking has become nearly impossible, because it *is* nearly impossible to find any general idea that will connect into one train of thought: 'Home Rule for Egypt,' 'A Batch of Stabbing Cases,' and 'Infant Motorists.' It is hardly worth while to trace the evolution of this process. In the 70s–80s the Londoner was still said to get his General Ideas from the leader writers of his favourite paper. Nowadays even the leader is dying out.

So that, in general, the Londoner has lost all power of connected conversation, and nearly all power of connected thought . . .

In London society you may be – it is considered commendable to be – devout in private, but it is a shuddering offence to mention the Deity in company. Similarly all metaphysical topics, all political matters going below the surface or likely to cause heat, the consideration of sexual questions, the mention of the poor or the suffering, are avoided. This is, in origin, because your neighbour at dinner has his or her private views, and has a right to them. You do not enquire into them, you do not know them, and you cannot air your own views because they will probably give offence.

The net result is to make London conversations singularly colourless; but they become singularly unexhausting. No call is made upon your brain or your individuality; it is precisely not 'good form' to make any kind of display. You may be yourself as much as you please, but it must be yourself in a state of quiescence. No strain at all is put upon you, because it is the height of good manners to have no manners at all.

This of course is most noticeable abroad, where the Londoner is celebrated for his atrociously bad manners. He does not bow over his hat on entering a room; he sits down on any chair, he has no gesticulations of pleasure, he stops short at being well groomed and undemonstrative. There is not, in fact, any etiquette in London, there is only a general rule against obtruding your personality – a general rule against animation in society.

[194] Lonely London (1925); from *Letters from England* by K. Čapek.

It is perhaps through sheer taciturnity that the English swallow half of every word, and then the second half they somehow squash; so it is difficult to understand them . . . But if you get to know them closer, they are very kind and gentle; they never speak much because they never speak about themselves. They enjoy themselves like children, but with the most solemn, leathery expression; they have lots of ingrained etiquette, but at the same time they are as free-and-easy as young whelps. They are hard as flint, incapable of adapting themselves, conservative, loyal, rather shallow and always uncommunicative; they cannot get out of their skin, but it is a solid, and in every respect, excellent skin. You cannot speak to them without being invited to lunch or dinner; they are as hospitable as St Julian, but they can never overstep the distance between man and man. Sometimes you have a sense of uneasiness at feeling so solitary in the midst of these kind and courteous people; but if you were a little boy, you would know that you can trust them more than yourself, and you would be free and respected here more than anywhere else in the world; the policeman would puff out his cheeks to make you laugh, an old gentleman would play at ball with you, and a white-haired lady would lay aside her four-hundred-page novel to gaze at you winsomely with her grey and still youthful eyes.

[195] London Language (1931); from *Englishmen, Frenchmen, Spaniards* by S. de Madariaga.

There is deep satisfaction in the thought that English – the language of the man of action – is a monosyllabic language. For the man of action, as we know, lives in the present, and the present is an instant with room for no more than one syllable. Words of more than one syllable are sometimes called in English 'dictionary' words, that is, words for the intellectual, for the bookworm, for the crank, almost for the un-English. They are marvellous, those English monosyllables, particularly, of course, those which represent acts. Their fidelity to the act which they represent is so perfect that one is tempted to think English words are the right and proper names which those acts were meant to have, and all other words but pitiable failures. How could one improve on *splash, smash, ooze, shriek, slush, glide, squeak, coo?* Who could find anything better than *hum*, or *buzz*, or *howl*, or *whir?* Who could think of anything more sloppy than *slop?* Is not the word *sweet* a kiss in itself, and what could suggest a more peremptory obstacle than *stop?*

Such persistence in success cannot be explained away as a mere whim of nature. It is in fact one of the ways in which there is shown at work that infallible sense of matter which we have observed as one of the features of the English character. But in the monosyllabic tendency of the language, other English features co-operate, as for instance, the utilitarian sense which disregards all considerations but results, quick and efficient service. Utilitarian and empirical, the Englishman sees no difficulty in cutting down *perambulator* to *pram, omnibus* to *bus, bicycle* to *bike.*

[196] The London poor; from *The Conditions of the Working Class in England* by F. Engels (London, 1844). (English translation by W. O. Henderson and W. H. Chaloner.)

London is unique, because it is a city in which one can roam for hours without leaving the built-up area and without seeing the slightest sign of the approach of open country. This enormous agglomeration of population on a single spot has multiplied a hundred-fold the economic strength of the two and a half million inhabitants concentrated there. This great population has made London the commercial capital of the world and has created the gigantic docks in which are assembled the thousands of ships which always cover the River Thames . . .

It is only later that the traveller appreciates the human suffering which has made all this possible. He can only realize the price that has been paid for all this magnificence after he has tramped the pavements of the main streets of London for some days and has tired himself out by jostling his way through the crowds and by dodging the endless stream of coaches and carts which fills the streets. It is only when he has visited the slums of this great city that it dawns upon him that the inhabitants of modern London have had to sacrifice so much that is best in human nature in order to create those wonders of civilization with which their city teems. The vast majority of Londoners have had to let so many of their potential creative faculties lie dormant, stunted and unused in order that a small, closely knit group of their fellow citizens could develop to the full the qualities with which nature has endowed them. The restless and noisy activity of the crowded streets is highly distasteful, and it is surely abhorrent to human nature itself. Hundreds of thousands of men and women drawn from all classes and ranks of society pack the streets of London. Are they not all human beings with the same innate characteristics and potentialities? Are they not all equally interested in the pursuit of happiness? And do they not all aim at happiness by following similar methods? Yet they rush past each other as if they had nothing in common. They are tacitly agreed on one thing only – that everyone should keep to the right of the pavement so as not to collide with the stream of people moving in the opposite direction. No one even thinks of sparing a glance for his neighbour in the streets. The more that Londoners are packed into a tiny space, the more repulsive and disgraceful becomes the brutal indifference with which they ignore their neighbours and selfishly concentrate upon their private affairs. We know well enough that this isolation of the individual – this narrow-minded egotism – is everywhere the fundamental principle of modern society. But nowhere is this selfish egotism so blatantly evident as in the frantic bustle of the great city. The disintegration of society into individuals, each guided by his private principles and each pursuing his own aims has been pushed to its furthest limits in London. Here indeed human society has been split into its component atoms.

[197] Stoical London (1940s); from *Their Finest Hour* by W. Churchill (London, 1949).

These were the times when the English, and particularly the Londoners, who had the place of honour, were seen at their best. Grim and gay, dogged and serviceable, with the confidence of an unconquered people in their bones, they adapted themselves to this strange new life, with all its terrors, with all its jolts and jars . . .

I was glad that, if any of our cities were to be attacked, the brunt should fall on London. London was like some huge prehistoric animal, capable of enduring terrible injuries, mangled and bleeding from many wounds, and yet preserving its life and movement. The Anderson shelters were widespread in the working-class districts of two-storey houses, and everything was done to make them habitable and to drain them in wet weather. Later the Morrison shelter was developed, which was no more than a heavy kitchen table made of steel with strong wire sides, capable of holding up the ruins of a small house and thus giving a measure of protection. Many owed their lives to it. For the rest, 'London could take it'. They took all they got, and could have taken more. Indeed, at this time we saw no end but the demolition of the whole Metropolis. Still, as I pointed out to the House of Commons at the time, the law of diminishing returns operates in the case of the demolition of large cities. Soon many of the bombs would only fall upon houses already ruined and only make the rubble jump. Over large areas there would be nothing more to burn or destroy, and yet human beings might make their homes here and there, and carry on their work with infinite resource and fortitude. At this time anyone would have been proud to be a Londoner. The admiration of the whole country was given to London, and all the other great cities in the land braced themselves to take their bit as and when it came and not to be outdone. Indeed, many persons seemed envious of London's distinction, and quite a number came up from the country in order to spend a night or two in town, share the risk, and 'see the fun'. We had to check this tendency for administrative reasons.

Bibliography

ACKROYD, PETER, *London: The Biography*, London, 2000.

ADDISON, JOSEPH AND STEELE, RICHARD, *Selections from* The Tatler *and* The Spectator ed. A. Ross, London, 1982.

ANON, *Memoirs of the Life and Times of Daniel Defoe*, London, 1830.

—, *Poll Tax Riot*, London, 1990.

—, *The Trial of Her Majesty Caroline Queen of Britain*, London, 1820.

—, *Itinerary of Richard I*, London, 1865.

—, *England's Joy*, London, 1660.

—, *Harris's List of Covent Garden Ladies*, London, 1764.

—, *Reliquiae Wottoniae*, London, 1685.

ARBUTHNOT, HARRIET, *The Journals of Mrs Arbuthnot*, *1820–31*, edited by Frances Bamford and the Duke of Wellington, London, 1950.

BARRON, XAVIER, *London 1066–1914. Literary Sources and Documents. 3 Vols.*, Robertsbridge, 1997.

BEDE, *The Ecclesiastical History of the English people* trans. J. A. Giles, London, 1903.

BEERBOHM, MAX, *Around Theatres*, London, 1953.

BELL, WALTER, *Fleet Street in Seven Centuries*, London, 1912.

BOAS, GUY, *The Garrick Club 1831–1947*, London, 1948.

BOSWELL, JAMES, *The Life of Samuel Johnson*, London, 1791.

BUXTON, THOMAS FOWELL, *An Inquiry whether Crime and Misery are produced or prevented by our present system of Prison Discipline*, London, 1818.

BYRON, LORD GEORGE GORDON, *Don Juan*, Cantos 10 & 11, London, 1824.

CAMPBELL, LADY COLIN, *Diana in Private*, London, 1992.

ČAPEK, KAREL, *Letters from England*, trans Paul Selver, London, 1925.

CARLYLE, THOMAS, *Letters and Memorials of Thomas Carlyle*, edited by James A., Froude, London, 1883.

CARPENTER, JOHN, *Liber Albus* (1419), edited and translated by H. T. Riley, London, 1861.

CASANOVA, GIACAMO, *Memoirs*, translated by Arthur Machen, London, 1922.

CAVENDISH, THOMAS, *The Life of Cardinal Wolsey*, London, 1885.

CHAUCER, GEOFFREY, *The Canterbury Tales*, London, 1889.

CHAUNCY, DOM MAURICE, *The Passion and Martyrdom of the Holy English Carthusians*, translated by A.F. Radcliffe, London, 1935.

CHURCHILL, WINSTON, *Thoughts and Adventures*, London, 1932.

—, *Their Finest Hour*, London, 1949.

CLARE, JOHN, *The Prose of John Clare*, edited by J. W. & A. Tibble, London, 1970.

CLARENDON, E., *The History of The Rebellion and Civil Wars in England*, London, 1702–4.

CLELAND, JOHN, *Memoirs of a Woman of Pleasure*, London, 1749.

CONAN DOYLE, ARTHUR, *The Sign of Four*, London, 1890.

COWPER, WILLIAM, *The Complete Poetical Works*, London, 1905.

CRISP, QUENTIN, *The Naked Civil Servant*, London 1968.

CROSSMAN, RICHARD, H.S., *The Crossman Diaries 1964–1970*, edited by Anthony Howard, London, 1979.

D'ARBLAY, FRANCES, *Diary and Letters of Madame D'Arblay*, 7 vols, London, 1842–6.

DEFOE, DANIEL, *A Journal of the Plague Year*, London, 1722.

DE QUINCEY, THOMAS, *The Confessions of an English Opium Eater*, London, 1922.

DEVIZES, RICHARD OF, *The Chronicles of Richard of Devizes*, trans, Giles, J.A.G., London, 1848.

DEW, WALTER, *I Caught Crippen*, London & Glasgow, 1938.

DICKENS, CHARLES, *Barnaby Rudge*, London, 1899.

—, *Memoirs of Joseph Grimaldi*, ed. Charles Dickens, London 1838.

DOSTOYEVSKY, FYODOR, *Winter Impressions of Summer Notes*, London, 1955.

DOUGLAS, NORMAN, *London Street Games*, London, 1931.

EARLE, JOHN, *Micro-cosmographie*, London, 1732.

EDWARDS, ROBERT, *Goodbye Fleet Street*, London, 1988.

EELES, HENRY, S. & EARL SPENCER, *Brooks's 1764–1964*, London, 1964.

EGAN, PIERCE, *London*, 1820.

ENGELS, FREDERICK, *The Conditions of the Working Class in England*, English translation by W.O. Henderson and W.H. Chaloner, Oxford, 1958.

EVELYN, JOHN, *Diaries*, London, 1879.

FAWKES, GUIDO, *Confession of Guido Fawkes*, London, 1605.

FIELDING, HENRY, *Jonathan Wild*, London, 1743.

FIENNES, CELIA, *The Journeys of Celia Fiennes*, London, 1888.

FITZSTEPHEN, WILLIAM, 'Description of London' (c.12th) in Stow, John, *Survey of London*, London, 1598.

FORSTER, JOHN, *The Life of Charles Dickens*, London, 1872.

FOXE, JOHN, *The Acts and Monuments of John Foxe*, London, 1870.

FROISSART, JEAN, *Chronicles*, London, 1906.

GAY, JOHN, *Trivia*, London, 1716.

GILBERT, MARTIN, *The Day the War Ended, VE-Day in Europe and around the World*, London, 1995.

GERARD, JOHN, *The Autobiography of an Elizabethan*, trans P. Carman, London, 1951.

GOWER, RONALD, S., *The Tower of London*, London 1902.

GREGORY, GEORGE, *The Life of Thomas Chatterton*, London, 1803.

GROSLEY, JEAN P., *A Tour of London*, London, 1772.

GROSSMITH, G & W, *The Diary of a Nobody*, London, 1892.

HAINING, PETER, *Sweeny Todd*, London, 1993.

HALL, EDWARD, *Chronicles*, London, 1906.

HAWTHORNE, NATHANIEL, *The Complete Short Stories of Nathaniel Hawthorne*, Garden City, 1959.

HAYDON, BENJAMIN, *The Autobiography and Memoirs of B. R. Haydon*, edited by Tom Taylor, London, 1926.

HEINE, HEINRICH, *English Fragments*, trans Sarah Norris, Edinburgh, 1880.

HICKEY, WILLIAM, *Memoirs of William Hickey*, edited by P. Quennell, London, 1960.

HOLINSHEAD, RALPH, *Chronicles*, London, 1905.

HOME, GORDON, *Roman London*, London, 1926.

HOPE ST J., WILLIAM, *The History of the London Charterhouse*, London, 1925.

HORNBY, NICK, *Fever Pitch*, London, 1992.

JAMES, HENRY, *Selected Letters*, ed. L. Edel, London, 1987.

JERDAN, WILLIAM, *The Autobiography of W. Jerdan*, London, 1852.

KEATS, JOHN, *Poems*, ed. Bullett, Gerald, London, 1906.

KINGSFORD, CHARLES L., ed. *Chronicles of London*, London, 1977.

KNAPP, ANDREW, & BALDWIN, WILLIAM, ed., *The Newgate Calendar*, London 1826.

KRAY, RONALD, *My Story*, London, 1993.

LAMB, CHARLES, *The Letters of Charles Lamb*, Boston, 1905.

LE BLANC, J.B., *Letters on the English and French nations*, London, 1747.

LEWEY, FRANK, *Cockney Campaign*, London, 1944.

LUCAS, EDWARD, V., *London Revisited*, London, 1916.

LYDGATE, JOHN, *Poems*, Oxford, 1960.

MACAULAY, THOMAS, B., *The History of England*, ed. S. E. Winbolt, London, 1919.

—, *The Life and Letters of Lord Macaulay* ed. G. O. Trevelyan, London, 1876.

MADARIAGA DE, SALVADOR, *Englishmen, Frenchmen, Spaniards*, Oxford, 1931.

MADOX FORD, FORD, *The Soul of London*, London, 1905.

MACKAIL, JOHN, W., *The Life of William Morris*, London, 1899.

MACKAY, CHARLES, *Extraordinary Popular Delusions*, London, 1841.

MATTHEWS, W.R., ATKINS W.M., *A History of Saint Paul's*, London, 1957.

MAYHEW, HENRY, *London Labour and the London Poor*, London, 1861.

MILMAN, HENRY, H., *Annals of Saint Paul's Cathedral*, London, 1868.

MILNE, ALAN, *When We Were Very Young*, London, 1926.

MONMOUTH, GEOFFREY OF, *The History of the Kings of Britain*, (trans S. Evans, London, 1904).

MONTGOMERY HYDE, H., *The Trials of Oscar Wilde*, London, 1962.

MOORE, THOMAS, *Memoirs of the Life of the Right Honourable Richard Brinsley Sheridan*, London, 1825.

MORE, THOMAS, *The History of King Richard III* ed. P. Kendall, London, 1965.

MORITZ, POSSELT, C., *Travels in England*, London, 1782.

NICHOLS, J.G. (ed.), *The Chronicle of Queen Jane and of two years of Queen Mary*, London, 1850.

NORTON, RICTOR, *Mother Clap's Molly House*, London, 1992.

OPIE, IONA & PETER, *The Oxford Dictionary of Nursery Rhymes*, Oxford, 1951.

PAINTER, GEORGE, D., *William Caxton*, London, 1976.

PANKHURST, ESTELLE. S., *The Suffragette*, London, 1912.

PARIS, MATTHEW, *Chronicles*, London, 1903.

PEPYS, SAMUEL, *Diaries*, London, 1906.

PEVSNER, NIKOLAUS, WILLIAMSON, ELIZABETH WITH
TUCKER, MALCOLM, *London Docklands*, London, 1998.

PLATTER, THOMAS, *Travels in London*, London, 1599.

RAMSAY, WINSTON, G., (ed.), *The East End Then and Now*,
London, 1994.

RICHARDSON, JOHN, *The Annals of London*, London, 2000.

RICKETT, COMPTON, ARTHUR, *The London Life of Yesterday* by Arthur Compton, London, 1909.

ROCHESTER, *Poems*, London, 1907.

ROPER, WILLIAM, *The Life of Thomas More*, London,
1896.

SMITH, JOHN, T. *Nollekens & His Times*, London, 1829.

SOAMES, ENOCH, *Fungoids*, London, 1891.

STOW, JOHN, *Survey of London*, London, 1598.

SNORRI STURLUSON, *The Olaf Sagas* with poems by Ottar
Svarte, trans by S. Laing, New York, 1915.

TACITUS, *The Life of Agricola*, trans, Thomas Gordon, London, 1890.

TAYLOR, F. & ROSKELL, J.S. (ed.), *Gesta Henri Quinti* (The
Deeds of Henry V), Oxford, 1975.

TAYLOR, WILLIAM, F., *The Charterhouse of London*, New
York, 1912.

THORNBURY, WALTER & WALFORD, EDWARD, *Old & New
London*, 6 Vols, London, 1873–8.

VICTORIA, QUEEN, *The Letters of Queen Victoria* (ed.)
George Buckle, London, 1929.

VON UFFENBACH, ZACHARIAS, *London in 1710* trans & ed.
W.H. Quarrel & M. More, London, 1934.

VALBOURG, MISSON DE, *Mr Misson's Memoirs and Observations*, London, 1719.

WALPOLE, HORACE, *Letters*, London, 1840.

WALTON, ISAAC, *Life of John Donne*, London, 1640.

WARD, NED, *The London Spy*, London 1703.

WESLEY, JOHN, *Journals*, Boston, 1819.

WHATLEY, GORDON, E., edited and trans, *The Saint of
London, The Life and Miracles of Saint Erkenwald*, London, 1989.

WHITELOCKE, BULSTRODE, *The History of England, Memorials of the English Affairs*, London, 1713.

WILKES, JOHN, *The Correspondence of the late John Wilkes,* London, 1805.

WORDSWORTH, WILLIAM, *The Prelude,* London, 1850.

WREN, CHRISTOPHER, *The Life and work of Sir Christopher Wren from Parentalia or Memoirs of his Son Christopher Wren,* London, 1903.

WRIOTHESLEY, CHARLES, *A Chronicle of England by Charles Wriothesley,* ed. W.D. Hamilton, London 1875–7.

Index

The *Traveller's Companions*

The *Traveller's Companion* series was born out of the need to provide information for tourists whose imaginations and interest needed to be stimulated and amused by quality material that went beyond the standard travel guide.

The guiding principles for selecting material were (a) a master list of places to visit; (b) the most exciting historical events that happened in each place; and (c) the most colourful and vivid descriptions of these events.

A lot of research is required in the production of each title but the result, I hope, is a series of timeless companions to exhilarating cities.

Laurence Kelly, *Series Editor*

Praise for the series

'Nothing less than a masterpiece ... the perfect companion for the intending traveller, bringing the city's every aspect vividly alive.'

Sunday Times (*A Traveller's Companion to St Petersburg*)

'A brilliant historical anthology ... which I read from cover to cover, relishing the author's witty selection of writings.'

Spectator (*A Traveller's Companion to Venice*)

'The best conceivable companion guide to the city.'

Country Life (*A Traveller's Companion to Florence*)

To order further *Traveller's Companions*

No. of copies	Title	Price (incl. p & p)	Total
	Dublin	£9.99	
	Edinburgh	£9.99	
	Florence	£9.99	
	London	£12.99	
	St Petersburg	£9.99	
	Venice	£9.99	
	Grand Total		£

Name: _____

Address: _____

_____ Postcode: _____

Daytime Tel. No. / Email _____
(in case of query)

Three ways to pay:

1. For express service telephone the TBS order line on 01206 255 800 and quote 'CRBK'. Order lines are open Monday–Friday 8:30am–5:30pm

2. I enclose a cheque made payable to TBS Ltd for £ _____

3. Please charge my ☐ Visa ☐ Mastercard ☐ Amex ☐ Switch (switch issue no. . . . .) £ _____

   Card number: _____

   Expiry date: _____ Signature _____

   (your signature is essential when paying by credit card)

Please return forms (*no stamp required*) to Constable & Robinson Ltd, FREEPOST NAT6619, 3 The Lanchesters, 162 Fulham Palace Road, London W6 9ER.

Enquiries to readers@constablerobinson.com
www.constablerobinson.com